"An Arch Rebel Like Myself"

ALSO BY GENE C. ARMISTEAD
AND FROM MCFARLAND

*Horses and Mules in the Civil War:
A Complete History with a Roster of More
Than 700 War Horses* (2013)

"An Arch Rebel Like Myself"

Dan Showalter and the Civil War in California and Texas

GENE C. ARMISTEAD *and*
ROBERT D. ARCONTI

McFarland & Company, Inc., Publishers
Jefferson, North Carolina

ISBN (print) 978-1-4766-7461-2
ISBN (ebook) 978-1-4766-3338-1

LIBRARY OF CONGRESS CATALOGUING-IN-PUBLICATION DATA

BRITISH LIBRARY CATALOGUING DATA ARE AVAILABLE

© 2018 Gene C. Armistead and Robert D. Arconti. All rights reserved

No part of this book may be reproduced or transmitted in any form or by any means, electronic or mechanical, including photocopying or recording, or by any information storage and retrieval system, without permission in writing from the publisher.

Front cover: *inset* This formal portrait of Dan Showalter by an unknown photographer was probably taken during his 1861 term in the California Assembly (courtesy Robert L. Showalter); *foreground* artist's depiction of the capture of *Harriet Lane*, January 1, 1863 (U.S. Department of the Navy–Naval Historical Center)

Printed in the United States of America

*McFarland & Company, Inc., Publishers
Box 611, Jefferson, North Carolina 28640
www.mcfarlandpub.com*

To our wives,
Darlene Armistead and Carol Arconti,
who may well have felt themselves to be "war widows"
of the Civil War during much of the course of researching
and writing this book, but nevertheless persevered
in their understanding and support.

Table of Contents

Acknowledgments	ix
Introduction: The Love Letter	1
ONE • Before California	5
TWO • Mariposa Life and Political Beginnings	15
THREE • The California Assembly of 1861	36
FOUR • The Duel and Its Aftermath	71
FIVE • The Showalter Party	86
SIX • Texas and the Indian Territory, 1863	110
SEVEN • On the Rio Grande, 1864	128
EIGHT • Arch Rebel to the End	157
NINE • The Man Dan Showalter	176
Appendix A: Regina Seeley's Letter	183
Appendix B: Showalter in Fiction	188
Appendix C: Prevalent Misinformation Refuted	190
Appendix D: Memorialization of Showalter	193
Chapter Notes	197
Bibliography	215
Index	227

Acknowledgments

This study could not have been accomplished without the assistance of many individuals. If there are errors, misinterpretations or omissions in this work, they are those of ourselves, the authors, and certainly not of the many who helped us with information or research.

Our sincere and grateful appreciation is due the officials and staffs of many institutions which graciously provided us with assistance in our research, searching out and making available valuable information or images: Ms. Pamalla Anderson (Head of Public Services), DeGolyer Library at Southern Methodist University, Dallas, TX; Mr. Matthew Bellah (Superintendent), Capitol Museum, Sacramento, CA; Ms. Vicki Betts (Librarian), University of Texas at Tyler, Tyler, TX; Mr. Travis Bible (Museum Collections Coordinator), Galveston & Texas History Center at Rosenberg Library, Galveston, TX; Mr. Donaly E. Brice (Senior Research Assistant), Texas State Library & Archives Commission, Austin, TX; Ms. Jennifer Coleman (Archivist), Pearce Civil War & Western Art Museum at Navarro College, Corsicana, TX; Ms. Kathleen A. Correia (Supervising Librarian), California State Library, Sacramento, CA; Mrs. Donna Crippen (Curator), El Monte Historical Museum, El Monte, CA; Ms. Sally DeBauche (Reference Intern), Dolph Briscoe Center for American History at University of Texas Libraries, Austin, TX; Mr. David Frazee at the Escondido Public Library, Escondido, CA, was always very helpful with interlibrary loans for research materials; Mr. David Kessler (Staff), Bancroft Library at University of California–Berkeley, Berkeley, CA; Ms. Carolyn Krumanocker (Research Library), Oklahoma Historical Society, Oklahoma City, OK; Ms. Jean H. Lythgoe, Rockland Public Library, Rockland, IL; Ms. Doreen Mileto, Timothy Hughes Rare & Early Newspapers, Williamsport, PA; Ms. Susan Ogle (Director), Drum Barracks Civil War Museum, Wilmington, CA; Ms. Marisue Potts, West Texas Historical Association, Lubbock, TX; Mr. Andrew Rhodes (Special Collections Specialist), McCain Library at the University of Southern Mississippi, Hattiesburg, MS; Mr. William Sagar (Secretary), Fairfax Historical Society, Fairfax, CA; Ms. Mary Ann Schneider (Assistant Curator), Texas Heritage Museum at Hill College, Hillsboro, TX; Ms. Natalia Sciarnine (Stacks Management Lead), Beinecke Library at Yale University, New

Haven, CT; Mr. Shannon Simpson (Director), Ellis County Museum, Waxahachie, TX; Ms. Cathy Smith (Volunteer), Haley Memorial Library & History Center, Midland, TX; Ms. Erika Van Vranken (Reference Specialist), State Historical Society of Missouri, Columbia, MO; and Ms. Erin Renee Wahl (Archivist-Librarian), Arizona Historical Society, Tucson, AZ.

Others as individuals shared information with us, conducted research for us, or provided guidance and encouragement. To them we also express our gratitude and appreciation: Ms. Sheri Fenley, El Toyon Chapter NSDAR, Sytockton, CA; Dr. Mary Lamonica, Associate Professor at New Mexico State University, Las Cruces, NM, was a wonderful resource on early Texas newspaper commentators; Mr. Ron J. Pastore, Butler County, KS; Mr. Michael E. Patterson, Colleyville, TX, carefully checked the Texas Confederate Pension Applications of members of Showalter's regiment; Dr. Walter Earl Pittman, Roswell, NM, kindly shared information on sources; Mr. J. H. "Hank" Segars, Madison, GA; Mrs. Sally A. Stanley, Coker, AL, tediously located a rare copy of an old magazine and extracted information; and Mr. Richard Winger (Editor, *Ballot Access News*), San Francisco, CA, whose expertise on ballot access in the United States was helpful in understanding the 1860 election in California.

Especial thanks are due to Dr. Jerry D. Thompson, Regents Professor of History at Texas A&M International University, Laredo, TX, who was most generous with information and guidance about historical personages of the Rio Grande Valley and provided invaluable encouragement.

Relatives of persons associated with Dan Showalter kindly provided information relating to those associates: Mr. Don E. Baird, Palmdale, CA—great-great-grandson of Spruce McCoy Baird; Mr. Bruce Pawlak, Tonawanda, NY—a relative of Anna Forman; Ms. Fannie Kavanaugh Smith, Shawnee, KS—a relative of F. E. Kavanaugh; Ms. Shirley Anne Wellman South, Oberlin, OH—a relative of Chancey Wellman; and Mr. Larry Vermeulen, Napa, CA—a descendant of Anna Forman.

It was particularly gratifying to receive the help—and encouragement—of so many wonderful members of the Showalter family who generously shared family records, photographs and information with us: Dr. John Kudlik, Pittsburgh, PA; Col. Clyde E. Noble, Athens, GA; Mr. Edward D. Showalter, Latrobe, PA; Mr. Kenton D. Showalter, Sarasota, FL; Mr. Robert L. Showalter, Chalfont, PA: and Dr. Susan M. Showalter, Pittsburgh, PA.

Thank you, all.

Introduction: The Love Letter

Captain Henry Skillman had freighted and carried the mails between San Antonio, Texas, and El Paso since 1849. When the Confederate Army of New Mexico retreated from that territory in 1862, he became the Confederacy's agent in charge of trade through Presidio del Norte (now Ojinaga), Chihuahua, Mexico, and ran its espionage effort in the area between San Antonio and El Paso, which included delivery of correspondence to secessionists in Arizona (the southern part of New Mexico Territory) and even California. As such, he was a thorn in the side of the California Federal volunteers occupying lower New Mexico. He endeavored to prevent further Union movement east into Texas by spreading rumors of Confederate strength and activity in the area. Union commanders were soon weary of his activities. Union Brigadier General Joseph R. West, commanding the District of Arizona, on May 26, 1863, wrote to Reuben W. Creel, United States agent at Chihuahua, that the Skillman-sowed fears were a myth and that "Skillman [was] a crafty disseminator of reports to perplex us."[1]

Union authorities resolved to eliminate Skillman's activities and influence in the trans-Pecos area of Texas. Colonel George W. Bowie of the 1st California Cavalry, who was then the Union commander at Fort Bliss, detailed Captain Albert H. French to track down and intercept Skillman. French set out from San Elizario, Texas (then county seat of El Paso County; now submerged within the City of El Paso), on April 3, 1864, with a scout, two guides, and twenty-five men of his Company A, 1st California Cavalry. French and his men traveled the military road to the Chihuahua trail and then down that trail to nine miles beyond Cottonwood Spring, where they dismounted to wait while the guides were sent ahead. Just after midnight on April 14, the guides returned with news that Skillman was camped at the ranch of John Spencer (now part of Presidio, Texas). Leaving their horses at a deserted ranch house, French led his men to the Confederate encampment. The Confederates was soon surrounded. At 1:30 a.m., French shouted out the order for the Confederates to surrender. Rather than comply, some of the Confederates went for their pistols and gunshots erupted. The Confederates' horses stampeded. Return fire from the Union cavalrymen quickly ended the firefight after only a few moments. Captain Skillman and one other were killed, two more were mortally wounded, four were taken prisoner, and two other Confederates managed to escape across the Rio Grande into Mexico. French and his detachment captured five horses, four mules, the arms and provisions of Skillman and his men, and a packet of mail and dispatches.[2]

The dispatches and correspondence taken from Skillman eventually reached Department headquarters. Months later, on January 22, 1865, Brigadier General James H. Carleton, commanding the Union Department of New Mexico, referred to Major General Irwin McDowell, newly-appointed commander over his own and the Department of the Pacific, a November 1864 report of a Confederate plan for David S. Terry of California to raise a brigade in Houston and advance through El Paso to California, where he would raise a larger force. For some reason, General Carleton included as an endorsement one of the pieces of correspondence found on the person of Captain Skillman. Carleton wrote, "It is from a man named Dan Showalter, who killed a man in a duel in California. The man's name was Percy [sic]. They were members of the California Legislature. I caused Showalter to be arrested and confined at Fort Yuma. He was released on taking the oath, and afterward made his way to Texas. The lady addressed is the daughter of Col. Ferris Forman. This Showalter is the one referred to herein."[3]

When the United States War Department went through its records of the Civil War, selecting and compiling them, between 1880 and 1901, into 128 volumes of 138,579 pages, this 870-word letter was included. One could even construe this document a "love letter"—the only intimately personal document of the thousands published in the *Official Records of the Union and Confederate Armies in the War of the Rebellion*.

San Antonio, February 8, 1864
Miss Anna Forman:

My Dear Friend Anna: I arrived here yesterday from Arkansas and the Indian Department, where I have been with my command for the past nine months, and you can scarcely imagine my delight and surprise on learning that a party of my old friends had arrived the day before, among the number Mrs. Judge Terry, bearing to me your most welcome message.

I had abandoned the hope, so long fondly cherished, of hearing from you during the present war. I would have written to you long since, but feared it might bring you or your parents into serious trouble if it were known that you corresponded with an arch rebel like myself. Silent as I have been, I have often thought of you while walking my lonely beat at night, and on the battlefield, when comrades were fast falling around me, and the firm belief that your heart and sympathies were with us, gave me additional courage and cheered me on the path of duty and honor. Anna, I have not yet had cause to regret the course I marked out at the commencement of this long, bloody, and desolating war. I am proud to fight, and, if necessary, die, with a people who have contended so gallantly for their liberties against such fearful odds. If you could see them as I have, the old and the young, marching on apparently to certain death, and the noble women of the land, unaccustomed to labor, working day and night, knitting, spinning, and weaving to clothe our gallant soldiers, taking their carpets from their parlors to make blankets and their surplus wearing apparel to make shirts—were I to tell you all that these people have suffered without a murmur, you would say with me (as I am sure you do), having purchased liberty at such a frightful sacrifice, they are deserving of it, and never can be conquered. Our army is now in a better condition than at any time since the war commenced, while our people all over the country are more firmly united than ever. It is true we have lost a great many gallant men; indeed, almost every house in the land is in mourning over some fallen relation. Still, we have enough left to continue the war for years, and we feel that it would be much better that the last man should perish in defense of his rights rather than live the despised serfs of a Northern despot. The enemy have landed at several points along the coast, and are evidently preparing to make one last desperate effort to crush and subjugate us. All is as yet quiet, but it is the calm which precedes the storm, and we may soon expect to have the clash of arms all along the coast from the Rio Grande to New Orleans. Come as they may, we are prepared to meet them, and if forced to fall back before superior numbers, we have determined to lay waste every field, burn every dwelling, and leave the invaders no mark of civilization save the ruins of our once happy homes, the deserted fields, and the mangled bodies of the slain. I am truly gratified to hear of your father's resignation. You know we were always firm friends, and it pained me to

think that we should be arrayed against each other. When I arrived in Texas I found myself a stranger in a strange land. Those whom I expected to meet were either dead or in our army east of the Mississippi. I, however, soon met with Capt. George L. Patrick, of Tuolumne. You doubtless remember meeting his sister Annie at Sacramento, during the session of 1861. I at once joined his company as a private, and soon after had the honor of participating in the battle of Galveston, and soon after in the naval engagement off Sabine Pass, when we captured the enemy's blockading fleet. My name was favorably mentioned in the reports of both those fights, and soon after the latter I was promoted to a lieutenant-colonelcy. I have since organized a fine cavalry regiment and been in several engagements in Arkansas and the Indian Nation. My command will in all probability remain in Texas during the next campaign. I would like very much to have you write to Miss Patrick; tell her George is well and in Texas. I would also like to have you write to my sister Kate; she will be delighted to hear that I am living and well. I have not heard a word from my people since I left California. I fear my brothers in Pennsylvania may have gone into the Northern Army; if so, I can only pity; I have no desire to see them again. I would be delighted to see you. Indeed, if I had only twenty years to live, I would give up ten years of that time to see you and talk with you one hour. I may survive this war. If so, we may meet again; but should I fall, you will have the last kind thought, the last fervent prayer of
Your devoted friend,
Dan Showalter
Write often; do not wait to hear from me, but write whenever an opportunity presents itself.
Dan[4]

From its sheer eloquence, one can gauge that its author was certainly an educated and accomplished man. The names Terry, Patrick, and even Forman mentioned in the letter were prominent names in California politics of the time, and reference to "the session of 1861" refers to the California legislative session of that year and implies that both he and his "Dear Friend Anna" would both have been present there. Yet when the author writes in early 1864, he is in San Antonio, Texas, and a lieutenant-colonel of the Confederate Army. He indicates affection for Anna's father, his own sister Kate, and the Patrick family. Avowing himself an "arch rebel," the correspondent displays a very strong allegiance to the cause of the Confederate States of America. He imagines that brothers in Pennsylvania are serving in the Union Army and no longer desires any communication with them—and delights that Anna's father has resigned from that same army.

Who was this Dan Showalter? This proved to be a somewhat difficult question to answer. He had no descendants to carry forward his memory. He died young, leaving behind only a very few letters. For only two years of his life is there a relative wealth of information—the two terms he spent in the California legislature, a duel, and his 1861 capture in Southern California by Union forces were well reported in the press of the day. The records of his service in the Confederate Army are sparse, and his military career can hardly be reconstructed from that of his regiment since only eight regimental returns (and no muster rolls) survive from its two and a half years of service. Additionally, the unit with which Showalter served came to be confused with three other Texas units. The few accounts about him during his day were highly colored by political opinion. More recent published accounts of his life or activities, based on partial or biased information, are confusing and often completely unfounded.

Yet in his day, Dan Showalter was a name well known in California and even across the United States. His was the name that became most associated in California with treason after the outbreak of the American Civil War. As a result, to quote Samuel Johnson, "Many things which are false are transmitted from book to book, and gain credit in the world." The result is that the real Dan Showalter has become minimally remembered and virtually unknown. The fragmentary, sketchy, and conflicting information that remains does little to reveal his true identity, the complexities of his—as with anyone's—nature. Answering that question, who Dan Showalter really was, required a concerted effort to find, collate, and analyze everything available, published and unpublished, that even mentioned him. The authors have striven to report everything said about him in order to present a complete story and as real an evaluation as possible. A man of his frontier times, Dan Showalter was nothing if not an interesting man.

One

Before California

Today the name Showalter can be found in almost every part of the United States. Originally from the foothills of the Swiss Alps in the canton of St. Gall, these Schauwalder immigrants had moved to the Pflatz area of Germany around 1712 following the religious wars between Catholics and Protestants in northern and western Europe. Today's American Showalters seemingly all trace their descent back to Mennonite immigrants who, in the mid eighteenth century, responded to William Penn's promise of religious tolerance in Pennsylvania. These Showalters in the United States are believed to be descended from two of three Showalter brothers who came to Pennsylvania between 1744 and 1750.[1]

John Showalter, a Mennonite missionary, landed at Philadelphia in 1744 from the ship *Mascliff Galley*. Christian Showalter arrived in Pennsylvania in 1749. Jacob Showalter arrived at Philadelphia on November 3, 1750, aboard the ship *Brotherhood*. All three settled in Pennsylvania. John died without any known descendants. Christian had numerous descendants, as did Jacob. In fact, five male children over sixteen years of age arrived in America with Jacob aboard the *Brotherhood*. Jacob had signed the ship's manifest as Schauwalder, but his sons signed with an already Americanized Showalter.

Jacob and his family settled on the west bank of the Lehigh River on a 450-acre parcel now part of the town of Cementon, Pennsylvania. He had eight sons and three daughters who reached adulthood. While at the time this area had been settled and was being farmed by a mixture of German, Swiss, English and Irish families, Indians still surrounded the area and hostilities occasionally broke out. Youngest son Ulrich, born in 1743 and seven years old when the family came to America, at age thirteen was responsible for rescuing the four-year-old daughter of a Watterson family during an Indian attack in 1756. Both of the girl's parents and a sibling were killed. This daughter, Susannah, was taken in by the Showalter family. In 1768, when Ulrich was twenty-five and Susannah sixteen, they were married.[2]

Ulrich Showalter seems to have broken with family tradition in two significant ways. The first was to marry Susannah Watterson, who, although cared for by his family following her rescue and presumably then raised as a Mennonite, was not of German or Swiss ancestry. The second is that, contrary to Mennonite pacifist tradition, Ulrich joined the Northampton County Militia under Colonel John Siegfried (also the son of Mennonites, who lived on the opposite bank of the Lehigh River from the Showalters and was Ulrich's junior by two years), with which he fought for American independence throughout the duration of the Revolutionary War.

In 1790, Ulrich moved his family, which would eventually include nine children, to

Rockingham County, Virginia, where other Showalters had already settled, and purchased farmland from his brother Daniel. In 1806, Ulrich and Susannah moved again, this time to Fayette County, Pennsylvania, where some of their grown children were then living. The couple died there, Susannah passing in 1815, and Ulrich either that same year or in 1816.[3]

Joseph Showalter, the second son and child of Ulrich and Susannah, born in 1773, had married Anne Burkholder. Their first son and child, John Watterson Showalter, was most probably born October 7, 1798, while still in Rockingham County, Virginia.[4] Whether Joseph and his family had moved to Fayette County, Pennsylvania, prior to or at the same time as Ulrich and Susannah is not known, but both households were located there by the enumerator of the Federal Census of 1810.[5]

In 1821, John Watterson Showalter married Irish immigrant Mary Ann Donley. Her family surname has alternatively been given as "Donnelly" or "O'Donnell" in family genealogies and records, and sometimes with the given name of Anna Marie. She may have been born in 1796. They had the first of their eleven children, Elihu Thomas, in 1822. A daughter, Elizabeth, followed in 1824. By the time the third child, William Aloysius, was born on December 4, 1826, the family had moved to the Whiteley Township of Greene County, Pennsylvania. William was followed by brother John A. on November 2, 1827. Their fifth child was Daniel,[6] who referred to himself and signed his name as Dan throughout his life.

The exact date of Dan Showalter's birth is unknown. Some genealogical materials that have been published over time have given his birth as occurring in 1829.[7] Records maintained by present-day members of the Showalter family do not contain any reference to his birth date other than those from extraneous published sources. The information found for the family in the 1840 Federal Census for Greene County names only the male head of household and provides only age ranges for males under twenty years of age. Calculating from the known dates of birth of some of his siblings, Dan and brother Jacob would be the two noted as between ages five and ten. This would give him a birth year of 1830 or later. In the 1850 census, the household was enumerated on July 29, 1850, with Daniel listed by name with his age as nineteen. This would argue a birth date of late 1830 or 1831. The Federal Census of 1860 for Mariposa County, California, dated July 9 of that year, recorded his age as thirty, implying birth in late 1829 or early 1830.[8] Unfortunately, baptismal records for St. James Parish in West Alexandria, Pennsylvania—the parish which would have been closest to Greene County but was merged with Sacred Heart Parish in Claysville, Pennsylvania, in 1857—have been lost or destroyed.[9] In a statement given on November 30, 1861, to Major Edwin A. Rigg of the Union volunteer army, Showalter stated that he was thirty years of age,[10] indicating birth in late 1830 or in 1831. Clarence Clendenen, in the only scholarly article devoted to Dan Showalter, quoted this statement,[11] implying the 1830–1831 period. A cenotaph at the Jefferson Davis Home, Beauvoir, Mississippi (placed at some time probably during the 1970s or 1980s by a distant relative[12]), cites a birth date of 1831.[13] The preponderance of evidence would seem to argue for a year of birth of 1831 or, at the earliest, late 1830.

Family records for the children following Dan are even more sketchy, those known being Jacob, Nancy, Ulrich, Christian, Fannie—not necessarily in this order, though it does appear that Jacob immediately followed Dan—and finally Katherine, who is usually referred to as Kate. The 1850 census gave her age as seven, so she would have been born around 1843. In Whiteley Township, Greene County, Dan's father John worked as a bricklayer and burner, both manufacturing and laying brick. When not engaged in this trade, John worked the farmland he owned and on which his family grew. The bricklaying trade was passed on to sons Elihu, William and John, Jr. Each of them practiced this trade for at least some part of their lives, but there are no indications that this was even a part of young Dan's life.[14] Family tradition holds that this Showalter family possessed the first cuckoo clock brought to America from Switzerland.[15]

At some time between 1842 and 1845, the family moved to Unity Township in Westmoreland County, Pennsylvania, where patriarch John became a tenant farmer at a place called Sportsman's Hall.[16] Sportsman's Hall, the name given to a log house that had been built in the late 1700s, had become the common reference for a growing Catholic community that was formally known as the parish of St. Vincent. While it might be presumed that John would have adopted Catholicism in order to marry Irish immigrant Mary Ann, it seems that such was not, in fact, the case. It was not until sometime after the move to Westmoreland County that John did indeed break the Showalter Mennonite tradition. Family records note that he was received into the Catholic Church by Father Michael Gallagher, who was ordained in 1837 and served at St. Vincent parish until 1847. John and his eldest son Elihu (the only son to have then reached majority) both signed, with fifty-one others, an 1846 letter to the Rev. Boniface Wimmer, O.S.B., supporting establishment of a monastery in the community.[17] While John may not have converted to Catholicism until as late as this date, it is presumed that, according to Catholic practice regarding mixed marriages in that day and in the absence of any comment to the contrary in family records, the children—including Dan—would have been baptized as Catholics in infancy. As a result of that letter and under the guidance of Father Wimmer, the foundation of today's St. Vincent Archabbey, the first Roman Catholic monastery in the United States, was laid in October of that year in what was in time to become the city of Latrobe, Pennsylvania.[18]

Family records note that, in November of 1846, John sold his fall harvest to Father Wimmer and his fellow monks, who were badly in need of provisions. He also gave up the Sportsman's Hall house to become the monks' residence.[19] It was perhaps at this time that the family took up residence in a "dog-trot house,"[20] a common type of frontier house which consisted of two cabins with a continuous roof joining them to provide a breezeway or central room. The Sportsman's Hall building had been a large, solid, two-story log structure. The eventual convent building itself was built with bricks manufactured by the Showalter family.[21]

At some time prior to 1850, Dan accompanied his brother John westward, as so many others did, to hunt for gold. The precise location of this early adventure was remembered as Montana by a later family member,[22] but it is more likely that the trip was to California inasmuch as this was the heyday of the great California Gold Rush and that gold was not discovered in the Montana area until 1860. Since Dan's brother John is known to have successfully mined gold in Montana in the early 1860s—even being cited as a gold mining expert[23]—it seems probable that the later naming of Montana as the location of the early trip was an accidental conflation of these two episodes. In any event, the brothers were successful in making a "small fortune," which they brought back with them to Latrobe. Some of this money was used to build a butcher shop and a brick works with which the Showalters were subsequently associated.[24]

Most likely it was during the period from 1850 until about the time of attaining his majority that Dan attended Madison College in Uniontown, Pennsylvania.[25] Originally incorporated in Uniontown in 1808, the college was even then the successor of earlier schools extending back to 1791. Madison College had achieved significant standing as an educational institution by the 1840s, being one of the few schools of the time that provided agricultural training as well as a classical education in both preparatory and collegiate divisions. At the time Dan would have attended, the institution was operated by the Methodist Protestant Church.[26] The college was later merged into what is now Waynesburg College in Waynesburg, Greene County, Pennsylvania.

Throughout his life, Dan Showalter appears to have been very likeable and a tremendous conversationalist. It can be inferred that this would have been the case through his adolescent and early adult period. His extant letters and speeches demonstrate a natural eloquence. Clendenen commented on his fiery red hair and piercing eyes and that he was over six feet tall.[27] That he had a short temper will be demonstrated by events to come. It would also appear that early on he took advantage of his effect on young ladies. Showalter descendant Regina Seeley remembered in 1978:

> My mother, later on, as I grew older said that Uncle Dan was quite fickle and had a way of jilting women. Mama said he was like old Jeb Stuart—both men were described as having "petticoat fever." There was sort of a hushed story that one of his "loves" asked for his picture and a lock of his red hair—before he went to California and Uncle Dan obliged her about the picture—only instead of a lock of his auburn curls he is said to have a small amount of "pubic hair" tied with some baby blue ribbon. It seems that the Showalter women didn't approve of Uncle Dan's amorous affairs. The other Showalter men presumably married and led circumspect lives.[28]

Mary Ann Showalter died in 1851, an event which apparently had great effect upon the family. In November of 1852, after approximately a year of seemingly secret planning and on rather sudden notice (perhaps upon attaining his majority and leaving Madison College), Dan Showalter took passage on the Pennsylvania Railroad line, newly built just the year before, from its western terminal at Latrobe (which came into existence that same year) and left Pennsylvania. For Dan, the Showalter home, without the presence of his mother, was no longer a home and, to make matters worse, his father seemed determined to marry again. Perhaps together with a desire to return to the adventure of the gold fields, this change in home environment was sufficient for him to leave family and friends for California.

From Lovejoy's Hotel in New York, while awaiting ship passage for California, Dan wrote the following letter to Sam O'Connor, husband of his sister Elizabeth, on November 13, 1852:

Mr. Sam O'Connor
  Dear brother, here I am in the great city of New York and it is hardly necessary to say that I am this far on my road to that land of promise called California. I left Pittsburgh Nov. the 2nd and came to Latrobe on the same day. I went to see all my old chums in old Westmoreland and on Thursday took my farewell of all my dear friends. I would faire have paid you a visit but, believe me, I could not possibly do it as you know my friends are limited and I have a very long trip before me but should I be so fortunate to ever return to my native home, you can rest assured I will take a trip through old Green. As you know I have had this trip in contemplation for the last year you will not then be surprised at me leaving so unceremoniously. The friends were all well at home but things are not going to please me as I find the old man is determined to have a wife, let the consequences be what they may. The place no longer appears like a home to me, it does not bear the faintest resemblance of what it once was. For this reason, in a great measure I have determined to leave that place where once I could boast of a happy home and try my fortune in a distant land among strangers. How this may do time will tell. As I told you before on Thursday at 2 o'clock

P.M. I took leave of my friends and in a short time we arrived at Johnstown and commenced crossing the Allegheny Mountains. We took supper at the Mountain House and breakfast next morning at Lancaster. We arrived in Philadelphia at eleven o'clock A.M. and at 2 P.M. crossed the Delaware into New Jersey where we took the cars of the Camden and Amboy Railroad for Sandy Hook, a distance of sixty five miles. This is one of the best roads I have ever seen and the country is as level as a floor all the way but the soil is very red and sandy and more than one half of the country is covered with thick underbrush not over ten feet high. If we are to judge from the appearance of the soil I do not think it would produce a crop of buckwheat. From Sandy Hook we took the steamboat for this place and arrived here last night at 6 o'clock, a distance of 35 miles. All safe and sound forked end down. I will write you from the isthmus of Darien when I arrive there I will not leave before Wednesday. Tell Bob I would like to have him along as I am all alone. Give my love to all my old schoolmates and friends.

Adieu dear brother and sister.

Dan Showalter[29]

Dan accompanied his brother John Showalter on an early mining trip to California (courtesy Robert L. Showalter).

Dan's forebodings proved to be well-founded as, twelve days later, on November 25, 1852, his father, John Showalter, Sr., married his second wife, Sarah Kelley. Seven more Showalter children would result of this marriage.[30] It is not known whether Dan ever had any contact with his new siblings.

There remains no personal record of Dan Showalter's journey to California other than his letter from New York to his brother-in-law. Much can, however, be inferred about his journey from the contemporaneous writings of others who followed that same route in 1852 or 1853 and from ship passenger lists of the period. When Showalter set out for California in late 1852, there were three established routes. A "gold rusher" could take a sailing vessel around Cape Horn, a passage requiring four to five months, or longer if the weather was rough. He could travel across the settled states to Missouri and then travel across the plains and mountains. This route was feasible only during the summer and took that entire season. The third—and fastest—route was via the Isthmus of Panama. This involved traveling by steamer from New York, with a stop at Kingston, Jamaica, to Aspinwall (just a few miles below the mouth of the Chagres River); then up the Chagres River, followed by mule ride or travel by foot to Panama City on the Pacific Coast, where another steamship journey—this time to San Francisco—would follow.[31] Dan chose the quicker route.

Showalter had written Sam O'Connor that he would be leaving New York "before Wednesday," which would have been November 17, 1852. In fact, the next ship leaving New York for Panama after his letter was the SS *Illinois*, departing on November 20 for

Aspinwall.³² This 2,500-ton, 268-foot long sidewheel passenger steamer had been built the year before in New York for service from that point to Central America. It had returned to New York from Aspinwall on November 12 bearing, in addition to news, mail and a long list of passengers, gold dust valued at $1,995,881. She would continue on the Central American run until 1859, then running for a year in the immigrant trade between Le Havre, France, and New York. When the Civil War began, the *Illinois* was chartered as a troop transport and, after the war, as a hospital ship. Postwar it was sold, in 1866, to the New York Quarantine Department. There is no record of what eventually happened to the ship and it disappeared from records about 1870.³³

Those who chose the Panama route could purchase tickets for both the ship to Panama and the ship from Panama to California as a package, with choice of first cabin (or class), second cabin, or steerage. Steerage accommodations were an assigned bunk among hundreds stacked one above the other in berths. Daniel Cooledge Fletcher, who made the trip in steerage with his brother at the beginning of 1852, described steerage bunks being covered with white sheets and with other amenities provided while in port under inspection. But once the ship left port, the white sheets and amenities disappeared. He described the fare upon which they lived as "wormy bread, poor beef, fish, stale bread and poor coffee." He believed that steerage accommodations were purposely poor so that, once confined aboard, passengers would balk and purchase a higher-priced cabin passage. He said that once warmer tropical weather was reached, most steerage passengers resorted to sleeping on deck.³⁴

When lists were printed of the passengers arriving into a port, cabin passengers were listed by name, but those in steerage were lumped together as "unidentified passengers in steerage." On this basis, with his name not appearing on any passenger list between November 1852 and January 6, 1853, it must be presumed that Dan Showalter—like Fletcher and his brother—toughed it out in steerage. Having likely made the trip once before with his brother John,³⁵ he knew what was coming and perhaps figured that he'd made it once before and could do it again. Steerage passengers tended to be miners and engineers, who were, like Showalter, headed directly for the mines. He may have preferred that company to the more genteel of the cabin classes. With what must have been a fair amount of the earlier gold field earnings used to establish the family brickyard and butchery in Latrobe, steerage may have been the only realistic option. With mining experience behind him, Dan would also have known that an allotment of funds needed to be retained for prospecting equipment and supplies for his new venture in California. As shall be seen later, he consistently demonstrated being what today might be referred to as "fiscally conservative." It could also be that, given Dan's hasty departure likely brought on by his father's announcement of remarriage, he and his father were not on good terms with each other and funds for cabin class could not or would not be spared.

No date for the arrival of the *Illinois* and Dan Showalter at Aspinwall on this particular run is known. It would have taken eight to twelve days.³⁶ Aspinwall—today known as Colon—had been established in 1850 as the Atlantic terminus of the then under construction Panama Railroad by William Henry Aspinwall, founder of the Pacific Mail Steamship Company and a promoter of the railroad. This "Americanized" port replaced the older Spanish town of Chagres across the river. In 1852 alone, more than 20,000 people passed through on the way to California—an annual number that would continue to pass through until the transcontinental railroad in the United Sates was completed in 1869.³⁷

Physically getting to the town of Aspinwall from the steamer was a difficult process. Due to the depth over the sandbar at the mouth of the Chagres River, or lack of it to be precise (it was only thirteen feet[38]), incoming steamers had to anchor about two miles offshore. Passengers were then loaded into rowboats and taken to shore by natives, which was no mean feat due to wave action. In Fletcher's words:

> The sea was rough, and we found it difficult to get into the boats.
>
> Sometimes the boat was ten feet below us; then a big wave would float it up to where we were, and in we jumped. Thinking it very dangerous, I hesitated to go at first, but there was no other way to land. Finally when a big wave brought up the boat, I jumped in, and landed all right, but I was wet through before we reached the shore. We expected that the boat would be overturned, so rough was the sea.[39]

This portion of the journey to California took about eight days.[40]

Arrival in Aspinwall was neither a welcome relief after a long sea journey nor a highly anticipated stop. Guidebooks of the day all agreed that the climate of the town was hot and humid with no relieving wind—perfect conditions for waterborne diseases in those days before refrigerated food storage and efficient sanitation. One resident wrote of the place, "I do not know of any one you can get to come here who will not be sick part of the time." Guidebooks urged travelers to get out of town as soon as possible.[41] Malaria (the often-mentioned "Panama fever" was probably some form of this) was endemic to the area and common. Cholera epidemics were frequent.[42] Heavy showers were almost constant during the wet season. The dry season lasted from December to June.[43] Nevertheless, Fletcher, who crossed in January of 1852, said, "Very likely the traveling was much better in the dry season."[44] Ulysses S. Grant, in his memoirs, described crossing during the summer of that same year with the 4th Infantry Regiment as being during the wet season.[45] He recalled that of those that had left New York with the regiment, about one-seventh (approximately 100) were buried on the isthmus or on an island in Panama Bay after a cholera outbreak.[46] Upon arrival at either New York or San Francisco, every ship's report contained lists of passengers who had died from illness en route.

The first part of the journey across the isthmus was to the town of Gorgona, which could be reached either by river or by rail. By river, the town was thirty-nine miles from its mouth, and the journey usually took three days by canoe or ship's boat, sometimes pulled by small steamers. During the rainy season, this route could be difficult and sometimes dangerous due to a swollen river. It was also uncomfortable. Travelers using this method were advised to remain in their boats overnight rather than seek accommodations ashore. They could, at the expense of an additional day due to an increased swift current of the river, continue on upriver four miles to the town of Cruces.[47] The trip by train, which reached a point two miles short of Gorgona at the time, was quicker and, by the time of Showalter's crossing, had been cleared of robbers who had plagued it.[48] It can be imagined that, eager to reach the California gold fields, Showalter chose the rails over the river.

Leaving Gorgona (or Cruces), the remaining distance to Panama City and the Pacific coast, approximately twenty-five miles, had to be traversed by mule or afoot. The road from Gorgona was unpaved and impassible in wet weather, but easier to travel during the dry season. The Cruces road was better. It followed what was the old colonial Spanish treasure trail, which had been paved with cobblestones. Though the paving was in great disrepair, it was usable in all seasons even though neglect and erosion had created thirty-foot deep gullies at places which were wide enough for only one mule at a time.[49] The

Gorgona road overlaid the cobblestoned Spanish road for the last several miles into Panama City.[50] Mark A. Evans, who had crossed the isthmus in August of 1850, wrote to his brother about the road: "It is not worth my while to try to describe it [.] [Y]ou can take the worst road you have ever seen and put it over the most hilly part of the country you have ever seen and it can not be half so bad."[51]

This portion of the crossing took one day by mule or two days if walking.[52] The difficulty of this leg of the journey is perhaps illustrated by the observation of a young miner who made the trip in September of 1863. Horace Snow of Bridgewater, Massachusetts, said that the side of the road was so littered that one could trace their path by the empty liquor bottles.[53] In good weather and absent any other difficulties, the isthmus could be crossed by travelers like Showalter in as little as four days.

Overnight accommodations for travelers across the isthmus were generally described as minimal and undesirable. Guidebooks urged them to provide themselves with their own bedding.[54] A correspondent of the *Sydney Morning Herald* who crossed the isthmus in mid 1853 en route to Australia from England commented upon them: "These places on the Isthmus of Panama generally consist of a bar below, and a loft above, containing from 100 to 150 beds. However, the great fatigue of the day, coupled with the intense heat, made outward show quite indifferent, and, notwithstanding the noise of the birds above, the fighting of the rats below, leaving alone the creatures of a more diminutive size, we soon fell asleep."[55] For the budget-conscious traveler, another option was available. Horace Snow wrote that one could sleep "on the soft side of a pine board" for a dollar.[56] A year earlier, Daniel Fletcher had also paid a dollar in Gorgona—to sleep on the ground in a shed.[57]

Upon arrival in Panama City, the major obstacle was potential delay in boarding an outgoing steamer. The ocean passage in the Pacific was longer and weather conditions were generally rougher at sea, so delay in leaving Central America was reasonably likely, although by that time much improved from the very early days of the California Gold Rush. In those days there were fewer and smaller ships in the Pacific service and passengers could potentially be delayed in Panama City for months.[58] Panama City was unlike any of the previous stops on the isthmus route. It was a stately old Spanish colonial city, and any delay was not so onerous as earlier, and accounts are given of such delightful sights as old cobblestone streets and cathedrals, colorful parrots, and bountiful vultures, which were legally protected as their scavenging helped keep the city clean—and presumably healthier than other Panama locales. Fletcher reported Sunday in Panama City as being "a regular holiday."[59]

Boarding ship at Panama City was at first a slow and not always welcome process (especially by female travelers) of passenger and trunk having to be carried one by one on the shoulders of natives to waiting boats, which took them out to the steamship. By the time of Dan Showalter's trip, steam tenders belonging to the Pacific Mail eased embarkation.[60] Once aboard the outgoing steamer, the prospects of rough weather, mishaps, and even unforeseen encounters were before them. The regular mail and supply stop at Acapulco, Mexico, afforded the opportunity of a good meal and amusement from watching eager boys swimming off the side of the ship and diving for ten-cent pieces thrown by the passengers. According to Fletcher: "Very often the money would go down fifteen or twenty feet in the water, but they always got it, and held it up for us to see, grinning from ear to ear. It was great sport for the passengers." He also told of his ship being stopped in transit and boarded by whalers who had been at sea for eighteen months.

In return for a gift of a large sea turtle, the steamship captain gave the whalers several bottles of wine, the New York newspapers, and an hour of conversation—interspersed with continued requests of the captain for them to leave so that his ship could resume its voyage.[61] There was one further mail stop at San Diego before reaching San Francisco. Most of the voyage was made within sight of land.[62]

In his November 1861 statement, Dan Showalter said that he arrived in California in 1852.[63] Based upon the records of ships entering San Francisco around the 30-day period expected for a trip starting on November 20, it seems likely that he completed his journey and set foot on California soil on the very last day of 1852—December 31—when the SS *Winfield Scott* docked. It was fourteen days out of Panama City with stops at Acapulco (where it was detained twenty-three hours) and San Diego. It had faced 72 hours of "strong gales" from the northwest and thereafter "gales from the southeast with thick, heavy weather." It had to wait three days off the coast of San Francisco before entering the bay due to "dense fog."[64] While San Francisco fogs are well-known, they were a dangerous hazard along the entire California coast. Barely a year after this probable landing date for Dan Showalter in San Francisco, the *Winfield Scott* crashed into Middle Anacapa Island off the coast of Southern California during a heavy fog. Its submerged remains can be studied today within the Channel Islands National Marine Sanctuary/Channel Islands National Park.[65]

The journey from New York to San Francisco was also costly. Chastina Walbridge Rix of Vermont travelled with her small child to join her husband in California just after Dan Showalter had made the trip. Mrs. Rix kept an account of all of her expenses from her Vermont home by train to New York and then by ship to Panama, through the isthmus, and than again by ship until she was finally able to bathe and rest at the Orange Grove Hotel in San Francisco, where she arrived on February 16, 1853. Most of Dan's expenses would not have been much different. Her train from Vermont to New York—about the same distance as Dan's from Latrobe—cost her $7.25. The first cabin through fare (both steamers) purchased in New York was $305. She paid $8.00 for the Panama Railroad and then $3.50 to reach Cruces by boat. An exorbitant $45.80 was expended for two mules to carry herself and her trunk from there to Panama City. The total, including accommodations, baggage handling, meals, ticket recording charges, boarding expenses, a book for the trip (Dickens' *David Copperfield*), and that bath at journey's end was $408.64.[66]

Given that he, unlike Mrs. Rix, traveled in steerage, the major difference in the expenses incurred by Dan Showalter would have been the cost of the steamship voyages from New York to Panama and then from Panama to San Francisco. This price was variable depending upon the time of purchase of the ticket. Day-to-day variations of the price were caused by fluctuation in the demands for space.[67] Daniel Fletcher paid $180 for his ticket, whereas his brother, who had bought his a month earlier, paid only $150.[68] The *Alexandria Gazette & Virginia Advertiser* of April 3, 1853, reported the price for a steerage ticket to San Francisco as $85 (as opposed to $200 for first cabin and $150 for second cabin).[69] An estimated $100 for steerage and a reasonable allowance for other expenses would indicate that Dan's cost for the trip would have been somewhere around $200.

These expenses for the New York to San Francisco journey were considerable for the day. Mrs. Rix's expense of $408.64 in 1853 would, using a purchasing power calculator, have been the equivalent of $12,500 in 2013. Dan Showalter's estimated $200 cost would have been $6,130 in 2013 dollars.[70] These costs would have been wall above the average yearly income of Americans in 1850. At that time, average annual wages were between $200 and $300. A farmhand earned only $13 per year.[71] It was no inconsiderable sum that Dan had to pay just to reach California, giving credence to the family story that he had made a successful pre–1850 mining trip. Dan arrived in San Francisco, doubtlessly weary from a long, expensive, tedious and often dangerous trip, to face the new year of 1853 with probably some excitement. He had made it, in his words, "safe and sound forked side down."[72]

Two

Mariposa Life and Political Beginnings

As with his early life and his 1852 journey to California, there is little information regarding Dan Showalter personally during his first eight years in California. When he arrived at San Francisco on the last day of 1852, steamers left there daily for the mining regions. They carried these latter day "forty-niners" to Sacramento, from where they could travel overland to the so-called Northern mines—established centers such as Grass Valley and Nevada City. Other steamers carried them to Stockton on the San Joaquin River. From there they could travel to the southern mining region. It is not known exactly where Dan Showalter went upon leaving San Francisco, but, if not immediately, he is known to have ultimately ended up in Mariposa County, at the southern end of the "Mother Lode Country." He lived and worked at a place called Horseshoe Bend on the Merced River.[1] An early date in this area is probable since, just four years after his arrival in California, he was elected to represent that area in the state legislature.

The Mariposa County of today, nestled in the foothills of the Sierra Nevada, is but a shadow of its former size. It had been the largest of the original counties created in 1850. Over the next decade, twelve other counties would be carved from it, giving it the title Mother of Counties.[2] Today Mariposa is a small county among other small counties. But when Showalter arrived there in 1853, even though Tulare and Los Angeles Counties had already incorporated its most southern reaches, it still stretched from the western side of the coastal range east to the Utah Territory (now Nevada) and south to what is now Fresno County. Still overwhelmingly rural and containing parts of what are now the Sierra and Stanislaus National Forests and Yosemite National Park, it has a population of only 18,251 per the 2010 Federal Census and no incorporated cities. This might seem to be somewhat of a regression from the Gold Rush period in that Hornitos, the largest community near Horseshoe Bend, had been incorporated in 1850.[3]

Hornitos (Spanish for "little ovens"), named after small Mexican graves resembling bake-ovens in the area, was founded by Mexican miners expelled from the town of Quartzburgh by a "Law and Order Committee," but was then itself nearly overrun by American whites when placer mining gave out in their own settlements. Upon their arrival, they incorporated Hornitos as a city and passed municipal ordinances consistent with their concept of "law and order." Their first ordinance required the licensing of dogs—to reduce the great number of dogs owned by the Mexican citizenry. The second ordinance ordered the bodies of the Mexican dead removed from their above-ground vaults near the town's main street.[4] In addition to the plaza—the center of all celebrations—there were Mexican dance halls that ran all night, lodges of the Odd Fellows and the Masons, five stores, four hotels, three livery stables and six saloons,[5] all of which did a lively business. Hornitos had early become an important stop on the route between Stockton and Los Angeles.[6] Despite its continuing Americanization, Hornitos was noted for maintaining its Mexican customs perhaps longer than any other mining town in California. It oldest pioneer Mexican resident, Dona Candelaria de Saphien, died in 1903.[7]

A frequent visitor to Hornitos, and one whose notoriety goes far to suggest just how rough and tumble the city actually was, was the famed bandit Joaquin Murietta. How frequently he visited is evident in that he had a secret tunnel under the main street running from one of the saloons to the stable where he kept his horse in the event a quick exit was necessary. Shortly after Dan Showalter arrived in California and was presumably in the area, in May 1853, a company of twenty-five men was authorized by the State of California to capture and kill Murietta. This company was organized at a ranch four miles west of Hornitos. When Murietta was killed—reportedly by a bullet fired by Bill Burns of Hornitos—he was decapitated and the head transported to San Francisco via Hornitos and Quartzburgh for identification.[8]

Mining brought a burgeoning populace to Hornitos. Upon arriving there in 1851, Belgian Jean-Nicolas Perlot commented that "all around Hornitos, in the creeks, in the gulches, we saw nothing but people occupied in seeking the precious metal."[9] In 1851, out of only fifty-seven post offices in the entire state, three—Mariposa, Agua Fria, and Quartzburgh—were within a twenty-five-mile radius of Hornitos. By the time Showalter arrived in 1853, two more post offices had been established, at Maxwell's Creek and Mt. Ophir.[10] The area's growth was impelled by both placer mining and the discovery of gold-bearing quartz deposits. At least two quartz mills had been established in the immediate area by early 1851.[11] In time, the Hornitos mining district was to become the most productive area of the western Sierra Nevada, with a belt of lode-gold several miles in width extending from what was then the area of the mining camp of Horseshoe Bend (now beneath the waters of Lake McClure following construction of the Exchequer Dam in 1926) and another camp at Indian Gulch. Like so many other old mining centers, Indian Gulch is now a ghost town.[12] When the placer mining ethic of one man's profit from one man's work—initially embedded in the California Constitution's prohibition against corporations[13]—early on gave way, the state's second corporation was formed precisely to reap the profits of this area: the Mariposa Mining Company.[14]

It is not known exactly when Dan Showalter settled at Horseshoe Bend, a mining camp north of Hornitos

Horseshoe Bend of the Merced River, Showalter's Mariposa County, California, home community, as sketched by naturalist John Muir in 1869 is now beneath the waters of Lake McClure (John Muir, *My First Summer in the Sierra* [Boston: Houghton Mifflin, 1911], p. 17).

on the southern bank of the Merced River. It had previously been the site of the Miwok (or Mewan) Indian village of Se-saw-che.[15] The famed naturalist John Muir gave a vivid description of Horseshoe Bend's natural beauty even though his first sight of the area was not until June 5, 1869, twenty years after miners had inundated the region and almost a decade after Showalter had left the area:

> The hopes excited concerning the outlook to be obtained, a magnificent section of the Merced Valley at what is called Horseshoe Bend came full in sight—a glorious wilderness that seemed to be calling with a thousand songful voices. Bold, down-sweeping slopes, feathered with pines and clumps of Manzanita with sunny, open spaces between them, make up most of the foreground; the middle and background present fold beyond fold of finely modeled hills and ridges rising into mountain-like masses in the distance, all covered with a shaggy growth of chaparral, mostly adenostoma, planted so marvelously close and even that it looks like soft, rich plush without a single tree or bare spot. As far as the eye can reach it extends, a heaving, swelling sea of green as regular and continuous as that produced by the heaths of Scotland. The sculpture of the landscape is as striking in its main lines as in its lavish richness of detail; a grand congregation of massive heights with the river shining between, each carved into smooth, graceful folds without leaving a single rocky angle exposed, as if the delicate fluting and ridging fashioned out of metamorphic slates had been carefully sandpapered. The whole landscape showed design, like man's noblest sculptures. How wonderful the power of its beauty! Gazing awe-stricken, I might have left everything for it.[16]

This spectacular scenery was no doubt enjoyed by Dan Showalter, but not the reason he settled there. The attraction was the gold mining, which was particularly rewarding. While many sources claim that the greatest gold production in California was in the first few years of the Gold Rush, the Hornitos district, which included Horseshoe Bend, was the most productive area in all the Sierra Nevada western gold belt and did not reach the height of its mining activity until the 1860s through the 1890s, and continued sporadically until the 1930s.[17] The Merced River is noted to have had many profitable operations in general during the mid–1850s, with the section between Horseshoe Bend and Washington Flat producing heavily in 1856,[18] by which time Showalter would certainly have been well established in the area. Unfortunately, there are no surviving records that provide information regarding any mining claims he may have registered.

There exists no information about Dan Showalter's life (other than political) in Mariposa County, but a record of life in Mariposa County during 1854—which would have been similar to situations faced or seen by Showalter—has been left behind by Horace Snow, a young Massachusetts native who resided that year, with his brother, in Agua Fria, about nineteen miles east of Showalter's location.[19] News to and from relatives in the eastern states was slow. Snow wrote a friend that he'd received a letter on April 1, 1854, that had taken two months and seven days to reach

Showalter (right) as a young miner with an unknown Native American or Hispanic helper was photographed probably in the mid-1850s by an unknown person (Peter Palmquist Cased Photographs Collection, Yale Collection of Western Americana, Beinecke Rare Book and Manuscript Library, Yale University, New Haven, Connecticut).

him.[20] Sundays were apparently, for most miners, a day of rest, but churches were few. Snow wrote that there was "more intoxication, more fighting, and more disturbances on the Sabbath than any other day in the week." According to Snow, there was a "perfect mania" for reading novels and every man had one in his pocket.[21] Travel was by mule on roads cheaply constructed. Perhaps, like Snow, Dan Showalter lived in a log cabin made of large logs, mossed over, with mud floor, one door and one window. The roof would have been oak shingles with cotton drilling over them to keep water out.[22] Supplies were costly. Some September 1854 prices reported by Snow included: butter or candles, 40 cents per pound ($11.40 in 2013 purchasing power); sugar or lard, 20 cents per pound ($5.72); chocolate, 36 cents per pound ($10.30); beans, 10 cents per pound ($2.86); and flour, $18 per barrel ($515).[23] Fortunately for those who could collect it, gold was valued at $17 per ounce.[24] With a developing interest in political affairs, Dan Showalter perhaps did not share the aversion of many of his fellow miners to jury duty. Snow commented on this in two of his letters, in one stating that when the sheriff reached a store where some eligible citizens were gathered, they ran, and in another that "you would laugh to see the miners take to the bushes when the Sheriff makes his appearance on the creek." Snow observed that "the miners are determined not to go if they can possibly help it, as they get nothing for pay."[25]

Though their precise relationship to Dan is unknown, there were other Showalters in California mining regions during the same period that he was in Mariposa County. The names of an Isaac Showalter, a Jacob Showalter, and a John Showalter (not Dan's older brother) are all found in lists of unclaimed letters published in Sacramento newspapers in 1851 and 1852.[26] Isaac appeared only once and is otherwise unknown. Jacob and John are found subsequently in reporting from San Andreas, in Calaveras County, just north of Mariposa County. Jacob partnered with German immigrant Arnold Friedberger in a business, Friedberger & Showalter, that was among numerous concerns suffering significant losses in a great fire in San Andreas on June 2, 1858.[27] Jacob is presumably the same as a J. Showalter listed in association with Friedberger as proprietor of the Union Tunnel Company, which successfully completed a 720-foot-long mining tunnel in the San Andreas area on September 9, 1858.[28]

John Showalter was elected treasurer of the Odd Fellows lodge in San Andreas in July 1856.[29] He was apparently a successful miner, as the *Mining & Scientific Press* reported a "find" on January 19, 1867: "From the San Andreas Register of Jan. 12th: We saw a nugget taken from Messrs. Marshall & Showalter's claim, a day or two since, on Douglass' Hill, of pure gold, weighing a small fraction less than ten ounces. These gentlemen inform us that lumps of from half an ounce to two ounces are quite common. They are down 134 feet, on what evidently has been an old river bottom, and are drifting along the ledge. About two feet on the bedrock is 'pay dirt.' They inform us that Messrs. Gilchrist & Co., their next door neighbors, are doing first rate."[30] Presumably this is the John Showalter, born in 1828 in Pennsylvania, who died in San Andreas on January 5, 1887, and was buried in San Andreas' Protestant Cemetery.[31]

Two more cryptic references to Showalters in California mining regions are found. On March 21, 1881, a land patent for 160 acres in Mariposa County was issued to a John Showalter.[32] Although not in the San Andreas vicinity, this perhaps might be the same John as in the preceding paragraph. Then, there was one Chris Showalter listed as the owner of "Showalter's Mine" in Mariposa County as of 1865.[33] While there is nothing to substantiate it, it is tempting to think that perhaps this "Chris" may have been Dan's younger half-brother Christian, left to run his mine after Dan left California for Texas in late 1861.

Though obviously busy with his mining activities, Dan Showalter had also taken an interest in the governance of the state and the nation. After passage of the Compromise of 1850, the Whig Party had begun to break down and, following the introduction of the Kansas-Nebraska Act in 1854, the Democratic Party was increasingly split into Lecompton and Anti-Lecompton wings (a reference to proposed pro- and anti-slavery constitutions for the Kansas territory). In that same year, many anti-slavery parties that would two years later coalesce into the Republican Party were formed in the Northern states. This reorganization of national political groupings was reflected in California politics. During the 1850s, all of California's constitutional officers (governor, etc.) and state senators were elected for two-year terms, and members of the State Assembly (the lower house of the legislature) were elected annually for one-year terms. Half of the State Senate was elected each year.

The California general election in September 1855 was contested by two parties, the Democrats and the Know-Nothings. Surprisingly, members of the Know-Nothing Party were elected to serve as Governor, Lieutenant Governor, Controller, Treasurer, Attorney General, and Surveyor General. The general election of November 6, 1856, coincided with the national presidential election. Democrat James Buchanan won California's electoral votes with 48.4 percent of the vote. He was followed by former President Millard Fillmore of the Know-Nothing Party with 32.7 percent of the vote. Trailing was Californian John C. Frémont of the new Republican Party with just 18.9 percent of the vote. By similar margins, the Democrats won the offices of Clerk of the Supreme Court and Superintendent of Public Instruction. Races for the State Senate and Assembly saw Republicans winning some seats for the first time, some Know-Nothings being returned, and the Democrats predominating.

The 6th Senate District was entitled to three assemblymen. One of these was allotted to the district's southern county, Tulare. Two seats were the apportionment for Mariposa County. A convention of the Democrats of Mariposa County nominated William James Howard and Dan Showalter. Howard was well-known and wealthy, and seems to have been the senior candidate on the ticket. He was one of the California Rangers who had pursued and slain the notorious bandit Joaquin Murrieta. He also maintained a large stable of racehorses. During the campaign, he and Showalter canvassed the county together. They mixed with voters of all classes, occupations, and nationalities.[34] When the votes were counted, they both won. Showalter led with 1,269 votes followed by Howard with 1,099. Their opponents, Know-Nothing candidate Kelly and an apparent independent, Lamon, received 870 and 824 votes, respectively.[35] The Tulare county seat was won by Know-Nothing Orson K. Smith.

The Assembly convened on January 5, 1857, with fifty-two Democrats, eleven Republicans, and eight Know-Nothings.[36] The major issue that they would face would be the financial condition of the state's government. There was little money in the treasury, and there were disputes over both interest payments from it and warrants issued in relation to the state prison. Contention over the election of two United States Senators was expected. There were also assumptions that the matter of the 1856 Vigilance Committees in San Francisco would require attention.[37] The newspapers of the state all hoped for a short session. The *Sacramento Daily Union* expressed this hope with the words, "If the members desire to do the State a real service, they will meet and adjourn at the end of the first month." It felt that the essential measures could be taken care of in that time.[38]

James M. Anderson, clerk of the previous session of the Assembly, called to order the Eighth Session of the California House of Assembly at noon on Monday, January 5, 1857. Most of the members, including Dan Showalter, were present and were sworn into office by Judge A.C. Monson. No further action was taken by the Assembly that day, and Showalter thus began his first term of service in the California legislature.[39] Four additional members arrived on Tuesday and were sworn in. Los Angeles Democratic Party "boss" Joseph Lancaster Brent was chosen Speaker *pro tem* for the day and proceeded to receive nominations for Speaker of the Assembly. The nominees (in the order nominated) were Calaveras County Democrat Elwood T. Beatty, San Francisco Republican William W. Shepherd, and Solano County Know-Nothing Andrew M. Stevenson. In the ballot that immediately followed, Beatty was elected by the overwhelming vote of the Democrats (including Showalter). After being sworn in, Beatty addressed the Assembly, advising them of the important work to be done. He highlighted the need to elect two United States Senators and the fact that the state's indebtedness exceeded the amount prescribed by the organic law of California.[40]

The Assembly then quickly proceeded to elect a Clerk, Assistant Clerk, Sergeant-at-Arms, Enrolling Clerk, Engrossing Clerk, and Doorkeeper. All of these employees were Democrats and elected by the large and united Democratic majority. The rules of the last session were adopted for temporary use and a committee of five appointed to develop rules for the current session. Assemblyman Gavin D. Hall then moved a resolution that the Rev. Dr. William Anderson Scott of San Francisco's Calvary Presbyterian Church be invited to serve as Chaplain of the Assembly. Stephen Whipple then offered a substitute resolution that the Assembly defer election of a chaplain until the next day. This substitute motion passed 40–36, with Dan Showalter voting with the minority,[41] evidently preferring to elect a chaplain right away. The election of a chaplain was surprisingly controversial, with some thinking the reason was the recent stand of the Reverend Doctor against vigilantism in San Francisco. This would not be Dr. Scott's only brush with prominent controversy. In 1861 he would be deposed by his church and run out of San Francisco after refusing to preach loyalty to the Union government and offering prayer equally for Jefferson Davis and Abraham Lincoln.[42]

When the assemblymen reconvened on Wednesday the 7th, they authorized the Speaker to appoint four pages and two porters for the Assembly. Then the matter of the chaplain came up. Assemblyman Harrison moved that Dr. Scott be invited to hold a divine service in the Assembly chamber the following Sunday. Assemblyman Shepherd moved an amendment that two other ministers be invited for the following two Sundays. A motion by Safford followed to indefinitely postpone the whole thing. Both Safford's motion and Shepherd's amendment lost. Showalter was among the majority that defeated the amendment, 18–59, and then passed the motion inviting Dr. Scott, 65–13.[43] Dr. Scott declined the invitation since it conflicted with a scheduled communion service at his church. The Assembly never elected a chaplain for itself that term.[44]

The Assembly then turned to more strictly legislative matters. They received a message from the State Senate to meet in joint convention on Saturday the 10th to elect two United States Senators. This was followed by the reading of a message from Governor J. Neely Johnson (elected in 1855 as a Know-Nothing). His lengthy message stressed the need for the legislature to address such matters as the May 1856 vigilantism in San Francisco, difficulties with Indians in northern counties, the need for a "refuge" for juvenile offenders and an additional prison, the lack of a Death Registry, and other topics, but the major portion of his message centered upon the condition of the state's finances.[45] The following day, Thursday, January 8, the Assembly concurred with the Senate to meet together in convention on the 9th to open and publish returns of an election that had been held on amendments to the state constitution. After this, they adjourned in honor of General Andrew Jackson's 1815 victory at the Battle of New Orleans.[46] Friday was also a light day of work in the Assembly. They adopted "Standing Rules and Orders" for themselves, met with the Senate and reported a majority of 29,705 for constitutional amendments, and voted for some additional employees. Showalter was among the 23–46 majority that defeated a motion for two additional porters and among another majority disapproving three additional clerks.[47] On Saturday, January 10, Speaker Beatty announced the standing committees of the Assembly. Dan Showalter was assigned to two of them: the Internal Improvements Committee and, appropriately, to the important Mines and Mining Interests Committee.[48] A motion to allow each assemblyman four daily newspapers (at state expense) passed, with Showalter voting in opposition.[49]

The Senate then joined them in the Assembly chamber for the joint convention to elect United States Senators. The need to elect two senators had arisen out of the Know-Nothing Party's capture of the legislature in 1855 and factionalism within the Democratic Party between William McKindry Gwin and David C. Broderick—mostly over control of federal patronage within California. The Know-Nothing legislatures of 1855 and 1856 had adjourned without having elected a successor to Gwin, whose term had expired on March 4, 1855. John B. Weller had been California's only United States Senator for those two years and his term would expire on March 4, 1857. Broderick and Gwin had been political enemies, but there were indications that they had made up their differences for the 1857 election. The other major candidates were sitting Senator Weller and Milton S. Latham, Collector of the Port of San Francisco and former congressman. Broderick had the upper hand and was determined that he be elected first and to the long term. He could then dictate the winner of the short term and control the patronage.[50]

Numerous caucuses had occurred since the legislative session had begun. There was reportedly agreement for Broderick to get his friends to vote for Latham, making Latham the short-term senator. Then, on the Friday evening before the joint convention, Thomas L. Smiley, who had been on the executive committee of the San Francisco Vigilance Committee, released a statement that, while Collector of the Port of San Francisco, Latham had agreed to not permit the U.S. revenue cutter in San Francisco Bay to interfere with the committee's "deportations" of opponents. Smiley also avowed that Latham had provided government jobs for Vigilance Committee supporters and that his brother was a member of that organization. This put Latham, an officer of the United States, in the position of having conspired with an illegal group to break the law. The Vigilance Committee and its activities had become extremely unpopular and, when Smiley's statement was broadcast by Gwin supporters on Saturday morning, it produced dismay in the ranks of Latham's supporters. Sentiment and support for him began to quickly melt away. Some became involved in fights and duels over the matter. One of Latham's most determined supporters, Dan Showalter, was enraged and sought to overcome the effect of Smiley's revelations with threats and curses. His imprudent and violent language had exactly the reverse effect. Broderick reneged on his agreement to support Latham for the second senate seat.[51]

When the joint convention met at 1:00 pm on Saturday, Broderick was quickly elected, and the Convention adjourned until Monday.[52] Two Democratic caucus ballots that night failed to settle on a nominee for the second seat.[53] Arguments and negotiations continued. Assembly business on Monday, January 12, was limited due to the scheduled joint convention to elect the other senator. Dan Showalter did give notice that he intended to introduce a bill to reduce the salary of the Mariposa County Judge.[54] Then, when the joint convention met, it voted 79–32 to adjourn until the next day. Showalter voted with the majority for postponement.[55] The Democratic caucus met that evening and balloted thrice without selecting a nominee. Finally, after a total of 14 ballots, Gwin received the nomination on Sunday. Though, according to one early historian, Latham "had supporters of the most steadfast and uncompromising unyielding stamp," they then joined the rest on a motion to make Gwin's nomination unanimous.[56] With the Democrats now finally united, Monday's joint convention reelected him, after two years, by a substantial majority.[57]

There was little significant activity in the Assembly during the next three days. The Committee on Mileage did present its report on Friday, and Showalter was allowed $60 for 300 miles travel.[58] On Saturday, January 17, long-time Assemblyman Jose Maria Covarrubias of Santa Barbara County moved an unusual resolution:

> Whereas, The Senators and members of the Assembly have been invited to partake the hospitality of Hon. Messrs. Broderick and Gwin, United States Senators, in the city of San Francisco, therefore,
> Resolved, That when this House adjourn, it do adjourn till Tuesday next at 11 o'Clock A.M.

Assemblyman Catlin immediately moved that the preamble (first paragraph) be stricken.

Catlin's amendment failed 32–35, with Dan Showalter opposed. A vote on Covarrubias' motion then followed. It failed by a vote of 27–35. Again, Showalter had voted in opposition.[59] A similar motion in the State Senate also failed.[60] A majority of both houses of the legislature, Showalter included, obviously did not feel it would be politik to adjourn their sessions for such a purpose.

When the Assembly was called to order on Monday, January 19, the Speaker was absent. When Assemblyman Richard Irwin took the chair, it was found that there was no quorum present, and those few present adjourned until 10:00 on Tuesday morning.[61] The situation was likewise in the Senate.[62] Despite have voted against recessing on Monday so that they could attend the Broderick-Gwin function in San Francisco, a large majority of both houses had taken the day off to do so. The correspondent of San Francisco's *Daily Alta California* wrote that evening that "of course there was no quorum present in either House of the Legislature to-day, and the whole of [the] state are blocked for the next twenty-four hours in consequence thereof."[63]

The *Marysville Daily Herald* pulled no punches in writing about it: "On Monday, the cold victuals of the Senators elect, proved more attractive to the members of the Legislature than their official duties, and the consequence was that both Houses were left without a quorum. They did not manfully adjourn to attend the lunch, but sneaked off as though they were doing something which they knew was discreditable." The paper went on to publish the names of those legislators who had remained behind in Sacramento prepared to perform their duties.[64] The *Sacramento Daily Union* also disapproved and published the names of those who had voted for and against the adjournment motions and the names of those present and absent on the legislative floor on Monday. It pointed out that if all those who had voted against adjournment had stayed, then quorums would have been present to conduct state business.[65] The next day, on the 22nd, it editorialized further, pointing to "malfeasance in office and a total abrogation, by a majority of men elected to responsible positions, of all moral obligations and all idea of personal honor." It suggested that a few impeachments were in order.[66] Like all too many others, Dan Showalter (who was also absent on Tuesday[67]) had voted right—but acted wrongly and deserved the censure of the press.

Over the next two weeks, the Assembly principally devoted its attention to legislation. On Friday, January 23, the Committee on Internal Improvements (of which Showalter was a member) recommended indefinite postponement of a bill granting the right to build a tool bridge over the Tuolumne River. The committee felt that the county's board of supervisors could do so under provisions of general law and that it would be a bad precedent for the legislature to do so.[68] On Wednesday, January 28, Showalter was part of a bare 34–33 majority voting for an act to guard against the loss of property on the Sacramento River by sparks from the chimneys of steamboats.[69] On February 3, the Internal Improvements Committee recommended against an act to encourage construction of a railroad and telegraph line from San Francisco Bay to the eastern border of the state. They said passage would be "exceedingly unwise" since the route from the east to California was not known and the inducements for construction to be granted by the state were too great.[70] Showalter was appointed by the Speaker, on February 6, to a select committee of five to examine a bill to prohibit weirs (dams) and other obstructions to salmon runs.[71] The election of Assemblyman Estevan Castro had been challenged by an opponent, who claimed that Castro was not a United States citizen. Dan Showalter was one of a 62–7 majority voting, on the 6th, that Castro was a citizen and entitled to the seat.[72]

The Assembly turned its attention to serious matters on February 9 and 10. On Monday the 9th, on recommendation of a Select Committee on the State Controller, they adopted a resolution that a committee be appointed to draw up charges for impeachment of Controller George W. Whitman.[73] The next day, a similar recommendation by a Select Committee on the State Treasury targeted against Treasurer Henry Bates was brought up. Showalter was among the sixty-one assemblymen who voted for both of these resolutions—none opposed.[74] He had not been a member of either select committee nor was he appointed to the committees to draw up impeachment charges. On Friday the 13th, the Assembly concurred with a Senate resolution to cancel all warrants issued by the controller. Then, by a vote of 55–15, it approved impeachment of Whitman. Two members were named to try the impeachment case before the Senate.[75] Upon hearing of the Assembly's action on the 9th and also facing court action from the State Attorney General, Treasurer Bates immediately resigned.[76] Despite his resignation, he was found guilty on March 13, 1857, and barred from holding office in California.[77] Controller Whitman was suspended from office and his trial consumed much time in the Senate until April 22, 1857, when he was acquitted on all charges and restored to office.[78]

Once the articles of impeachment against the two Know-Nothing officials were passed, the Assembly's attentions were devoted to regular legislative activities, many of them related to the financial condition of the state. On Saturday, February 14, the Committee on Mines and Mining Interests, on which Showalter sat, reported on two bills, AB102 and SB44, both of which were to protect property owners who were growing crops in mining districts. They recommended passage of the Assembly bill.[79] The following Tuesday, February 17, the Assembly adopted a concurrent resolution from the Senate under which the chairman of the Senate Ways and Means Committee and the chairman of the Assembly Finance Committee took possession of the keys of the vaults and safe of the State Treasurer until a successor was appointed.[80] The Committee on Mines and Mining Interests, on Wednesday the 18th, recommended against Assembly Bill 94 on "Mining Partnerships." Showalter and his fellows on the committee were "of the opinion that it is injudicious and inexpedient at any time for the Legislature to interfere by special enactment in the regulation of mining affairs." They praised the policy of previous legislatures to refuse such a bill and stated that it might be in conflict with the state constitution.[81]

On Friday, February 20, Dan Showalter moved that Assembly Bill 147, an "Act to Re-incorporate the City of San Jose," be taken up. The Assembly did so, amended it, and passed the bill.[82] Governor Johnson vetoed this bill, and Showalter voted with forty-nine others not to override the veto on March 9.[83] On the same day, Showalter voted with the majority to increase the salary of judges of three judicial districts from $4,000 to $5,000.[84] The next day, Saturday, he was part of a minority (about 25 percent) of members who voted against adjournment until Tuesday the 24th in commemoration of the birthday of George Washington.[85] A resolution moved by Showalter on February 24 was adopted: "Resolved, That the Governor, State Treasurer, State Controller and Secretary of State, furnish this House with the number of Clerks employed in each office, and the amount of their compensation."[86] When this information was received, the Assembly used it to seek reductions in the expenses of the State.

Speaker Beatty appointed Showalter and eighteen others to a Select Committee on a proposed "Act to Divide the State into Congressional Districts" (the state's congressmen were elected at large, on a state-wide basis) on Thursday, February 26.[87] When this committee reported back on March 5 recommending passage of the act, for some unknown reason, Showalter's name was not signed to the report.[88] (California continued to elect its Representatives in Congress on a state-wide basis until the election of 1872.) The Committee on Mines and Mining Interests, on Monday, March 5, reported a substitute for an act concerning logs and other timber floating in the streams of the state. Senate Bill 37, "An Act Exempting Mining Claims and Mining Instruments from Forced Sale in Certain Cases," was referred to the committee on the same date.[89] The 4th found Showalter part of a 38–24 majority voting to indefinitely postpone the bill for protection of growing crops and buildings in mining districts.[90] He gave notice on March 6 that he intended to offer an amendment, on the next day, to the 3rd Standing Rule of the Assembly.[91] He moved the amendment on March 11, to change the Assembly's meeting time from eleven o'clock to ten o'clock in the morning. It was adopted.[92]

On Friday, March 13, the Assembly and Senate met in joint convention to elect two doctors and three trustees for the State Insane Asylum. Of the four nominees for Resident Physician, Showalter's favorite, Dr. W.D. Aylett, won with eighty-three of the total ninety-two votes cast. For Visiting (or Assistant) Physician, Showalter was again part of the considerable majority, voting for Dr. Thomas Kendall. Seven men were nominated for the three Trustee positions. The three for whom Showalter voted all won.[93] On March 14, the Assembly decided to elect a permanent Speaker *pro tem*. James D. O'Neill was elected by a small majority that included Showalter.[94]

Dan Showalter voted with the majority in passing, on Tuesday, March 17, a bill to impose stamp duties[95] and, the next day, in defeating a senate bill for a bridge over the Sacramento River.[96] On the 19th, a report signed by himself and all other members of the Committee on Mines and Mining Interests recommended a substitute for the senate bill exempting mining claims and instruments from forced sales.[97] The next day he was part of a 58–13 majority to recommend Senate Bill 1, which called for the electors of the state to vote on whether or not to hold a convention to revise the state constitution.[98] The 30th of March found Showalter voting for construction of canals to drain and reclaim swamp lands and against creation of Eureka County. Both measures passed.[99] However, when amendments to the bill creating Eureka County came up on April 3, his vote was against the amendments and to print the bill.[100] A final vote on Eureka County was taken, on April 4, to reconsider. He voted with the majority to table creation of the county.[101] Again, on April 8, he voted against creation of the county, after which the subject was indefinitely postponed upon his motion.[102]

On April 9, Showalter voted against a bill to create an Office of State Librarian, but it was passed.[103] He also made a motion (which was defeated) to indefinitely postpone a bill permitting the testimony of children and "other than White Persons."[104] He then moved a resolution that the Speaker appoint a Select Committee of five members to prepare and report a bill paying off James M. Estell, leaseholder of the state prison, and cancel the existing state prison contract. Upon its passage, Speaker Beatty appointed Dan chairman of the select committee.[105] The very next day, Showalter reported for the committee and introduced just such a bill, but it was tabled after two readings.

Democratic Assemblyman John Moore then moved reconsideration of the motion ordering engrossment of the bill creating the Office of State Librarian. He complained that the bill was an "onerous tax upon the lawyers." Fellow Democrat Irwin alleged that the acting librarian had been "log-rolling for the past two sessions in order to secure the passage of a bill similar to this." William Graves (another Democrat) stated it was identical to a bill he had introduced two years past. A lengthy discourse by Assemblyman Robert C. Clark, a Know-Nothing, avowed that the bill was a play by the Democratic Party to secure all of the state offices. He said there had been no complaints of the performance on the job by the clerk of the Secretary of State, who was acting in the post. He urged Democrats to defer until after the next election, when they would control all offices, and to leave the Know-Nothing clerk in office until January. He agreed with Irwin that the bill would tax the lawyers. One of the Democratic leaders, Joseph S. Watkins, then also protested $15 per year to support the new office. Dan Showalter then spoke about the bill—his first address reported at length in the press:

> It seems to me that we propose by this bill to legislate a man out of office. Now it seems to me that this is a very small transaction for a great, victorious party. If the object is simply to effect retrenchment, why not introduce a bill reducing the salary of the clerk who is now acting Librarian? That is easily done. I repeat, I think it is a very small thing for the representatives of the great Democratic party, acting in the capacity of grave and reverent legislators, to legislate—to permanently legislate the last remains of Know Nothingism out of office. I think it is a shame for the great Democracy to come on the quarter-deck of the Ship of State, and throw this little fellow over the taffrail rail. Your own constituency from one end of the State to the other will despise you for such mean tricks. I do hope that this vote will be reconsidered, and that we will exhibit that magnanimity which is well known we possess, by leaving this office entirely alone until we come into full and entire supremacy.

Reconsideration failed 37–39, but the bill was recommitted to a special committee.[106]

Once this was completed, Showalter moved that his State Prison Bill be taken up from the table. This was done, and the bill referred to the Assembly as a committee of the whole.[107] Know-Nothing Assemblyman Clark criticized the bill as a matter that had wasted much time already in fruitless discussion and concluded, "I am sick and tired and worn out with it, and I therefore move to lay this matter on the table until the 4th of next July." (The legislature would by then have been adjourned.) Assemblyman John M. McKune wished to return the bill to the table. Showalter responded that he couldn't see the reason for this and hoped that the Assembly would vote on the bill. McKune, who was ruled out of order by the Speaker, then stated that the special committee (which was headed by Showalter) was composed of members who were in accordance with the state prison lessee (fellow Assemblyman James M. Estell of Marin County). Estell questioned what McKune had said. McKune responded that the committee membership was just what he would have wanted if he were in Estell's place since the bill was for the benefit of the lessee. Showalter denied that Estell had any part in appointment of the committee. He said he favored the portion of the bill making a payment to Lessee Estell because Estell had complied with his portion of the contract and that he (Showalter) had never favored Estell.

Dan then launched into McKune:

> If the gentleman from Sacramento [McKune] would be as straightforward in all his actions as I have been, he might, with better grace, cast imputations upon other members of this House. But it is perfectly evident in the whole course of the gentleman's conduct on the State Prison matter that his object has been to gratify the little petty hatred and spleen which he has against the State Prison Lessee. His whole endeavor has been to legislate this man out of office.
>
> I do not believe that he has desired to save the State anything. No, but he would like to plunge the State into unending litigation, and so shape matters that the Lessee would be knocking at the bar of the House, asking for the passage of relief bills for the next twenty years. The gentleman from Sacramento, I am convinced, would do anything to please his petty feeling of hatred towards the Lessee. I have watched the frequent disputes between that gentleman and the present State Prison Lessee, which have been distasteful in the extreme and disgraceful to this body. And yet this gentleman presumes to get up here and impugne [sic] the motives of the committee. Why would he not permit this committee measure to come up and be passed upon its merits? I detest such a course of action as the gentleman has adopted. If the gentleman, with all his eloquence and trickery and intrigue can defeat this bill, well and good but let him, at least, in some degree, exhibit some other disposition besides that of injuring Gen. Estell.

McKune, of course, responded to Showalter's strong attack with feeling: "I have listened to the lengthy tirade of the gentleman from Mariposa, and such language I never heard from any other gentleman in any deliberative body. And the aspersions which he has cast upon me are as devoid of truth as they are uncalled for. Take the word 'intrigue' for instance. What does the gentleman mean by this word? Have I ever spoken to a member upon this floor in any intriguing way? Most assuredly I have not. What then is meant by the term 'intrigue?'"

Showalter answered that he believed McKune's whole purpose was to injure Estell. McKune sarcastically retorted that "the gentleman from Mariposa seems to have set himself up as the special guardian of Gen. Estell." He then accused Showalter of imputing dishonorable motives and charging a member of the Assembly (McKune) with disreputable actions. At this point the *Sacramento Daily Union* ceased its report of the debate with a promise to conclude it in the issue of the next Monday, April 13.[108] The opinion of the paper, in a separate article, was that if a satisfactory agreement with Estell were made, it would have "accomplished something for the good of the State."[109]

As promised, the *Union* continued its report—using three full columns—on the

Showalter-McKune debate in its Monday the 13th edition. Dan rose on a question of privilege to comment on the "What Does It Mean?" article in the *Union*'s April 11 issue. That article had said that Estell had approached Showalter to add a clause pledging a lien on monies recovered from the state treasurer or his bondsmen, and that Showalter had refused to do so. Showalter stated that the report was incorrect, that it was Assemblyman John Hume who had made the proposal, and that he (Showalter) had rejected the clause as uncalled for and unnecessary and because he thought it wrong to pledge the faith of the state for any appropriation. Estell also denied making the proposal and stated that he had no affiliation with the editor of the *Union*. Assemblyman Gabriel Swezy said that he did not favor the *Union* reporting debates, but that, if it did do so, its reporter should report them accurately. McKune spoke at length. He averred that Estell was trying to connect him with people with whom such connection would injure him and that this was the reason why Estell had attacked the report in the *Union*. Committee member John Hume stated that it had been he who had proposed the clause to Showalter and that fellow committee members Isaac Hare and Richard Irwin had no objections to it. According to Hume, the account of the matter given by Showalter was accurate and there was no effort on Estell's part to force the clause upon the committee. He said that McKune was impugning the committee and that the reporter had been inaccurate. Assemblyman W.W. Shepherd of San Francisco then spoke about the difficulty of reporting debates extensively. Robert C. Clark then rose to defend the reporter, saying that a change in the print format of the paper over the weekend was the reason for any inaccuracy. Isaac Hare of the committee spoke last. He denied that there had been even the slightest degree of impropriety by himself or the committee. He opined that the Assembly should either decide (that is, vote on) the issue or "let the whole matter alone."[110]

Dan Showalter's State Prison Bill—Assembly Bill 432—was eventually passed and reported to the Senate on April 25, where it was referred to the Senate Judiciary Committee.[111] It was never reported back to the Senate for a vote,[112] probably because it was by then too late in the legislative session for further action. In the matter of the State Prison Bill, Showalter had become prominent in a legislative controversy. Curiously, other newspapers barely mentioned the debate. San Francisco's *Daily Alta California* gave it only two sentences.[113] The *Marysville Daily Herald* called the debate "a good method of advertising the merits of that paper [the *Union*]. But altogether too expensive a proceeding to suit the interests of the people."[114]

On Friday, April 10, Showalter again had voted for canals to drain swamp lands, and the measure passed on this final vote. A bill to fund the "legal and equitable debt of the City of San Francisco," which Showalter had opposed, also passed on that date.[115] A potentially controversial resolution was introduced on that day by his Mariposa colleague, William J. Howard. The resolution called for an act to protect the state against "great numbers of free negroes and mulattoes" that were increasingly arriving in the state. This resolution was referred to the Assembly Judiciary Committee with instructions to report a bill for "mild and wholesome laws as will prevent such persons from coming within the limits of this State."[116] This bill, AB411, was reported back on Wednesday, April 22. Assemblyman Isaac Hare moved that it be amended to add "Chinese" after "mulattoes." This amendment failed, with Showalter among those opposing it. A motion to engross the bill (that is, print in final form) then passed 33–31, with Showalter voting for it. This was, on the part of Showalter, a legislative tactic. Only members who had voted in a majority were able to move reconsideration of a bill. The purpose was to call for a new vote when the member's real preference in regard to a bill might gain a majority. Following the vote passing the bill, Showalter therefore moved reconsideration. Assemblyman John C. Burch then moved that reconsideration be indefinitely postponed (another legislative tactic, meaning a matter would not again come up for consideration). Surprisingly, Showalter himself voted in favor of the postponement, which passed 34–33.[117] One newspaper editor criticized defeat of the bill, writing, "We trust that none of the majority, in the Assembly, will need the testimony of Chinese, or other than white persons, to save them from hanging, but would dislike to warrant their necks against such an immunity."[118] The bill was reconsidered on Saturday, April 25, and failed 30–32, with Showalter in the minority.[119] Despite the efforts of Dan Showalter for the bill, California was thus spared the racial restrictions on residence that some eastern states had.

Showalter and the Committee on Mines and Mining Interests had one last bill to discuss and recommend upon before the end of the session. This was Senate Bill 4, "An Act for Better Protection of Mining Interests," which had been referred to them on Thursday, April 23. This act was in the form of a concurrent resolution asking Congress to survey mineral lands. The committee reported back to the Assembly on Friday, April 24, recommending its indefinite postponement, saying that they were unable to comprehend its object and saw no advantage to the state in it. They opined that only a very small portion of lands in mining districts was susceptible to cultivation, that the present policy on the matter was long established, and that the policy recommended by the bill had already been once defeated in the U.S. Congress.[120] The resolution never was passed by the Assembly.

Other legislative activity by Dan Showalter during the 1857 session's last week included a successful vote defeating creation of the Office of State Librarian.[121] He voted with the majority in a 6–55 vote against an "Act to Prohibit Gaming"[122] and was part of a 27–33 minority to indefinitely postpone Senate Bill 142, that would "prohibit noisy and barbarous amusements on Sunday." (This bill was aimed at the California/Mexican minority of the state, who enjoyed cock fights, bull baiting, and horse racing at their fiestas.) This bill was, however, tabled and never enacted.[123] The last vote taken in the Assembly was whether to override Governor Johnson's veto of an act to authorize introduction of water (a waterworks) in San Francisco city. Only nine members voted to override. Showalter was among the 57 voting against.[124]

Dan Showalter's experience during the legislative session of 1857 was not all work. He had, of course, attended January's Broderick-Gwin luncheon in San Francisco. He had also availed himself of attendance at the theater while in Sacramento—not a diversion available to him back in small, rough Horseshoe Bend. On the 28th of February, he was one of seventy-four notables (mostly state legislators, but including the state's Adjutant General William C. Kibbe and Supreme Court Justice David S. Terry) who requested George Ryer, a stock actor and manager of a touring company performing at the Edwin Forrest Theatre in Sacramento,[125] to extend his stay in the city. Their petition complimented his "consummate ability" and requested that he remain one night longer so that they, his "numerous friends and admirers may have an opportunity to give you a testimonial of their esteem." Ryer, of course, agreed to hold over his company for the "benefit occasion" and promised that the then noted actress Julia Dent Hayne would perform.[126] On the final day of the session, April 30, 1857, the houses had to await a final message from the governor. This provided the assemblymen with an hour which they devoted to frivolous bills and facetious debate. Dan took a minor part in the "debate" on "An Act to

Restrain and Prevent the Immigration Into, and Residence in this State of Dogs ... and to Provide for the Registration of the Births, Deaths, and Marriages of Members of the Species and to Levy a Tax Upon the Same." He called for a division (recording the vote of each member) on the "bill" after the acting Speaker had ruled in favor of the "Noes" when such had received but a few voice votes. At the very end, Showalter moved to table the "Dog Bill" until the next session.[127]

The governor's message still not having been received, at noon Speaker Beatty gave a brief valedictory address, and the Assembly then adjourned on April 29.[128] The legislature had not completed its business in a month-long session, as some had hoped, but taken a full four months. It had passed 290 bills, of which, according to the *Daily Alta California*, two-thirds were of a local or special character. They had, without undue delay, elected two United States Senators. They had addressed the financial condition of the state by impeaching the State Treasurer and State Controller and passing specific legislation reducing expenses. They had failed to solve the state prison contract, with the result that the lessee would continue to draw $10,000 per month.[129] During the session, members had risen to speak on "a question of privilege" so often that one paper characterized it as "the Legislature of a Thousand Privileges."[130] The editor of the *Marysville Daily Herald* called it similarly the "Personal Explanation Legislature."[131] The *Los Angeles Star*, reprinting an article from the San Francisco *Bulletin*, believed that the impeachment proceedings had been a heavy expense for the state, but would have a beneficial effect for the future. Overall, it stated that the Legislature had turned out to have been much better than had been anticipated and that "they may be considered the least hurtful of any legislative body which has held its sessions in our state for several years."[132]

Dan's performance as a member of the Assembly in 1857 had mixed results and was indicative of his then personal leanings politically. He had generally followed what today would be called a "fiscally conservative" line, voting against expenditures for bridges and dams, inducements for construction of a railroad, the state's paying the debt of San Francisco, the cost of creating an Office of State Librarian, and increasing the number of daily newspapers provided at state cost to assemblymen. He had likewise voted in favor of studying the number of clerks in executive departments as a means of reducing expenses. As a miner, in committee and on the floor, he had supported the status quo, opposing changes in the laws on mining partnerships and the surveying of mineral lands. He also opposed exemption of mining claims from forced sales to pay off indebtedness. Showalter had supported the positions of the state's California/Mexican minority in voting for the seating of Assemblyman Castro and against prohibition of gaming and "noisy and barbarous entertainments." His support of the bill to protect against immigration of "negroes and mulattoes" was definitely in line with the majority of his day. Although certainly racist by today's standards, it was in line with the general notion of racial superiority held by all whites in the nineteenth century. As recently as 1854, the California Supreme Court, in *People v. Hall*, had equated Chinese with blacks, mulattoes and Indians as being inferior.[133] His opposition to including Chinese in the bill was likely due to the fact that many Chinese were hired as laborers in the mines. In the case of the State Prison Bill, he exhibited a strong stance when he felt his honor was being challenged. Dan consistently supported his party and faction within it. His excessive ardor in support of Latham for the Senate exhibited his strong loyalty to friends. Though Dan Showalter was far from a "star" of the 1857 Assembly, he was a creditable member of it.

As the session was drawing to a close, on April 26, Showalter had been designated, along with colleague Howard and Senator S.A. Mettitt (also of Mariposa County), one of fifteen delegates from Mariposa County to a Wagon Road Convention, to be held on May 4 at Mokelumne Hill, then the seat of Calaveras County.[134] There was, that spring, considerable interest in the construction and improvement of wagon roads to cross the Sierra Nevada to the mining districts of western Utah Territory (now western Nevada). The existing old emigrant trails were little more than tracks. For the purpose of freighting, only pack trains could navigate them. At the end of April, residents of Genoa (located in the Carson Valley, forty-two miles south of present-day Reno) also elected delegates to the Mokelumne Hill Wagon Road Convention.[135] The convention was well attended, according to *The Union Democrat* published in Sonora, California. A.C. Baine of Stockton was elected president and a committee was appointed to take steps to put the road immediately under contract.[136] The convention voted to raise $30,000 ($814,000 in 2013 purchasing power[137]) to jointly improve the "Big Trees route" across the mountains, with feeder roads at the lower elevations left to local communities.[138] It is not known exactly what role Dan Showalter played during the convention. Eventually routes across the Sierras were completed, but not so soon as had been hoped by the various wagon road conventions (the more northern communities of California favored a more northern route).

Showalter evidently was quite active in Democratic Party affairs and had enjoyed his experience in the 1857 Assembly and in the Wagon Road Convention. On July 1, 1857, the Democratic Central Committee of Mariposa County, of which he was a member, meeting in Mariposa, announced that its nominating convention would be held in Mariposa on August 1 and invited, for the purpose of nominating candidates for the Assembly, the Democrats of Merced County to join them.[139] On July 15, he was one of seven Mariposa County citizens among the delegates to the Democratic State Convention held in Sacramento.[140] The editor of the *Sacramento Daily Union* believed that the delegates were "the ablest of any ever elected by the Democratic party in the State," with "much less of the rowdy element present."[141] Little is known about Showalter's participation in this convention other than his vote on some of the nominees. He and the other Mariposa County delegates all voted to nominate John B. Weller for Governor, Thomas Finlay for State Treasurer, H.C. Patrick for State Printer, and Horace A. Higley for Surveyor General. For the other state offices, the county's votes were divided, with no indication which candidates had Showalter's support. The votes of the Mariposans were likewise divided on a substitute platform plank proclaiming support for the constitutions and laws of the United States and California, the Bill of Rights, and *habeas corpus*.[142] When the Democrats of Mariposa and Merced counties met together, they nominated J.W. Ward and Showalter as candidates for the two seats of Assembly District 06. The American (formerly Know-Nothing) Party nominated John H. Tatman. The only detail of Showalter's reelection campaign is that his 1857 colleague, Howard, allowed Dan the use of a horse. On September 10, the *Mariposa Democrat* reported that "Mr. W. J. Howard's famous riding horse Waterloo, having been ridden to Horseshoe Bend by Mr. Daniel Showalter, was turned loose with a letter tied around his neck, for his owner, Mr. Howard, and in two hours and a half was at his master's door on Burn's creek—a distance of twenty-five miles—neighing a call for the postmaster. Swift and sure ought to be the motto of his rider."[143]

The results of the election held on September 2 were:

Candidate (Party)	Mariposa Co.	Merced Co.	Total
Showalter (D)	720	218	938
Tatman (A)	941	82	1,023
Ward (D)	261	1,256	1,517[144]

No doubt, Dan was disappointed to finish last—and not reelected.

Upon his return to Mariposa County, Showalter resumed mining—with an added sideline. More entrepreneurs during the Gold Rush years prospered "mining the miners," that is, selling equipment and supplies to miners, than by mining. It was apparently during his legislative service in Sacramento that Dan became acquainted with Arthur St. Clair Denver, an El Dorado County lawyer (and brother of James W. Denver, who was later Colorado Territorial Governor and for whom the city of Denver was named). Sometime during the 1850s, Denver had organized the Denver Quicksilver Mining Company, which owned and operated three quicksilver mines in Sonoma County. Placer miners strained their washings through a sheet of perforated iron and then washed it through a box having riffle cleats. Quicksilver (mercury) was important to this process, being placed against the cleats to make the gold adhere.[145] Dan invested in this company, owning fifteen shares. Each quarter, investors paid a capital assessment used to operate the company.[146] The company was apparently successful, with its annual meetings being reported as late as December 1875.[147] Unfortunately, nothing is known regarding Showalter's return on investment in the company.

Great social changes were under way in the California mining districts by the middle 1850s. Throughout the early half of the decade, the egalitarian ethic of the early Gold Rush held sway and, as late as 1854, generally a miner held one claim for himself and one for each hired man.[148] But by the later 1850s, the majority of miners were working for corporations as wage laborers.[149] The mystique of the rugged adventurer obtaining fabulous wealth through his own industry was quickly giving way to the hard realization that those still working in the mines—only 38 percent of Californians in 1860 contrasted to 75 percent in 1850[150]—had become an increasingly desperate underclass. A miner's average daily earnings had declined over that decade from $20 ($629 in 2013 purchasing power) per day before 1850 to $3.00 ($86.70) per day in 1860.[151] These changes only further contributed to growing tension in the state.

In 1859, California's Democrats held two state conventions in Sacramento, with the Anti-Lecompton Democrats meeting the third week of June and the Lecompton Democrats meeting a week later. The Lecompton Democrats met under the permanent chairmanship of James W. Denver, head of the Denver Quicksilver Mining Company in which Dan Showalter held stock. Showalter was one of seven delegates from Mariposa County to the convention. With Los Angeles County having sent two delegations, the work of the Credentials Committee, on which Showalter served, was important. After the convention adjourned the first day's session that evening, the committee met. They first took up the matter of Los Angeles County having sent one delegation headed by Joseph Lancaster Brent and another headed by John G. Downey. The committee, with Showalter voting with the majority, voted to seat the Downey delegation 23–12.[152] The full convention, on June 22, the second day of its sessions, supported the recommendation of the Credentials Committee 163–94. The other six Mariposa County delegates voted with Showalter for the Downey delegation. The principal activity of the conventioneers on this day was to nominate candidates for governor and lieutenant governor. It took two ballots to choose Milton S. Latham over John B. Weller as the nominee for governor.

Showalter and the other six Mariposans all supported and voted for Latham. John G. Downey of Los Angeles was nominated by acclamation for the second spot.[153]

About one-half of the delegates had left for their homes and did not attend the sessions of the convention's third day. Dan Showalter and his six fellow Mariposans were in attendance, though, to vote on nominees for Congress and the other state offices. They all voted for John C. Burch for the northern congressional district nomination and Samuel A. Merritt of Mariposa County for the southern congressional district nomination. Burch won nomination, but Merritt came in second to Charles L. Scott of Tulare County. The Mariposa County delegation split its vote for nominees for most of the state offices, and no report remains of how Showalter voted. However, the Mariposans were united in voting to nominate Charles S. Fairfax of Sacramento County for Clerk of the Supreme Court. Dan Showalter himself had nominated H.C. Patrick of San Joaquin County for the position of State Printer. Patrick finished a poor third with only one other vote from Mariposa County besides Showalter's. There was some mention of Showalter to serve on the State Central Committee, but S.A. Merritt was chosen to represent the Lecompton Democrats of the county on that committee. Showalter voted in favor of a resolution to print "tickets" calling for a state constitutional election, one of the last actions of the convention.[154]

The question of slavery had long been a divisive issue in the nation. Expansion of United States territory after the Mexican War and partition with Great Britain of the Oregon country intensified sentiments and division over slavery, with the long-present issue of states' rights becoming interrelated with it. A compromise negotiated in Congress in 1850 served only to forestall disruption. As noted earlier, in 1856, a northern, anti-slavery party, the Republican Party, had arisen. The Know-Nothing (or American) Party, with an anti-immigrant focus, had been formed at the same time, and the old Whig Party had begun to dissolve. Though left as the only nationally-based party, the Democratic Party itself had competing factions centered about the concept of "popular sovereignty," which held that the people of territories would decide, when applying for statehood, whether their areas would become "free" or "slave." Some southern Democrats opposed this as a restriction on slavery, whereas some of those in the north opposed it as leaving territories open to slavery. The organization of government in the Kansas Territory accentuated the division among Democrats. Those supportive of a proposed constitution drafted at Lecompton, Kansas, permitting slavery became known as Lecompton Democrats and those opposed as Anti-Lecompton Democrats. This de facto split in the Democratic Party was evident in California. In June of 1859, a Lecompton County Convention in Mariposa selected seven delegates to the Democratic state convention. Among them was Dan Showalter.[155]

Insight into the ethnic and racial makeup of the Hornitos/Horseshoe Bend area is provided by the 1860 Federal Census. Of the just over 2,000 population of Mariposa's Township No. 1 (Hornitos), thirty-two were identified as "colored" and two as Indians. There were very large numbers of Mexicans noted and Chinese were possibly one-half of the total. The white population listed people from almost any state or European country. There were approximately eight females to every eight males. The overwhelming majority of the ladies were Mexican or Chinese, with the few white females nearly all being the wives and daughters of a few of the more prosperous (generally shop owners) white males.[156] Dan Showalter was enumerated on July 9, 1860, as residing in Township No. 1, with his post office as Hornitos. He was listed as age thirty in dwelling number 529 along with one Giles Gifford, a Massachusetts-born thirty-five-year-old. Dwelling number 528 was occupied by two Cantonese, Ah Fong (age thirty) and Ah Yong (age twenty-five). The only occupant of dwelling number 530 was an E.J. Smith, aged fifty-one, who told the enumerator that he was born in Spain. Of the forty persons listed on page forty-eight of the census for the township, twenty-two were Chinese. There was only one woman and four children (one of them female).[157]

The political party divisions would only harden and, in 1860, lead to a four-way contest for the presidency. The Republicans nominated Abraham Lincoln of Illinois as their candidate. Remnants of the old Whig and the newer American parties coalesced together into a Constitutional Union Party advocating solely national union. They chose former Senator John Bell of Tennessee as their candidate. The Democratic Party, the only nationally organized party, would have seemed to have been the favorite to win. But, at its national convention held at Charleston, South Carolina, it was unable to achieve the super-majority necessary to nominate its preeminent candidate, Senator Stephen A. Douglas of Illinois. Almost all of the delegates from the Deep South walked out. The convention reassembled at Baltimore with the "fire-eaters" of the Deep South and nominated Senator Douglas. The other faction, meeting in Richmond, Virginia, nominated Vice President John C. Breckinridge of Kentucky.

In those days, election ballots were neither printed nor regulated by the state governments—government-printed ballots did not begin until the 1890s. Parties or factions printed their own "tickets" and distributed them to supporters and others for deposit in ballot boxes. In fact, any voter could modify a party ticket or write up their own ticket and deposit it in the ballot box.[158] Much is made nowadays that Lincoln "wasn't on the ballot" in most of the Southern states. The fact is that there were no official ballots in any state for either he or anyone else to be on. In the Southern states, it was simply a matter of there being no persons in those states willing (or given the times, perhaps foolish enough) to present themselves on an elector slate for Lincoln or visibly cast a ticket for him. In fact, none of the four candidates had a ticket in all of the states. The "Union" amalgamation for Bell did not present a ticket in Minnesota, New Jersey, New York or Rhode Island. The Breckinridge Democrats lacked a ticket in New Jersey, New York and Rhode Island. The Douglas Democrats lacked a ticket in Texas and, in the three states of New Jersey, New York and Rhode Island, was only the principal candidate of a "fusion" ticket. No candidate had a ticket in South Carolina—the last remaining state to retain for its legislature the sole right to select presidential electors. California was one of eighteen states in which voters had the choice of tickets of all four candidates.[159]

The national division into four political groupings in 1860 was reflected in California. With respect to the presidential race, votes were tallied for all four candidates except in three counties—San Luis Obispo, Santa Barbara and Sutter, where no votes were recorded for Bell.[160] In the case of local and district (State Senate and Assembly) elections, the number of tickets presented to or prepared by voters seemed to vary dependent upon local conditions. In larger areas like San Francisco, there were four "slates," and in others (like San Bernardino County) only two "slates" competing. Much attention has been given to the presidential race, but very little to the local races, and details regarding down-ticket candidates and their votes is missing in most cases. The Mariposa County Democratic Convention had, in September, nominated Dan Showalter, along with incumbent Assemblyman Andrew J. Gregory, for the 6th Assembly District.[161] In the election held on November 6, Republican Lincoln received statewide a narrow plurality of 32.3 percent and won California's four electoral votes. Douglas received 31.7 percent, Breckinridge got 28.4 percent, and Bell but 7.6 percent. There were even fifteen write-in votes for a now unknown candidate(s).[162] A total of 1,885 votes were cast for the presidency in Mariposa County. Its vote was quite different from the statewide result. Breckinridge received 815 votes (43.2 percent), Douglas garnered 489 (25.9 percent), Bell got 319 (16.9 percent), and Lincoln was last, with 262 votes (13.9 percent).[163] Breckinridge faction Assembly candidates Showalter and Gregory both won—and it can be surmised from the county's presidential vote that they won handily.

When all of the results were in, it was obvious that there would be a three-way division in the 1861 legislature. Californians had elected eight Douglas Democrats, five Breckinridge Democrats, and four Republicans to the State Senate. With half of the senate seats being held over from the 1859 election, the senate's composition would be nineteen affiliated with the Douglas faction of Democrats, eleven affiliated with the Breckinridge faction, and five Republicans—a solid majority for the "national" wing of the Democrats. The result for the Assembly was quite different. With thirty-eight members, the Douglas Democracy were the largest group by far, but two short of a majority. The Breckinridge Democrats (or "the Chivalry," as they were beginning to be called due to their association with the South) were the second largest faction. There would be twelve Republicans. Orson K. Smith, representing Fresno and Tulare Counties, would be the lone member of the "Union" faction.[164]

Among those elected were several who would play significant roles when the Assembly convened in January. Frank F. Fargo, from the Republican stronghold of San Francisco, was the leader of that party's representation. John Conness of El Dorado County was the leader of the Douglas Democrats. He would figure prominently in all of the deliberations of the Assembly. The leader of the "Chivalry" was Zachariah Montgomery from Sutter County. George W. Patrick of Tuolumne County and Thomas Laspeyre of San Joaquin County, both Breckinridge Democrats, would become close associates and friends of Dan Showalter. Though he was never to take any leadership role in the Assembly, Charles W. Piercy (his name often was spelled "Percy," including in the *Journal* of the Assembly, presumably reflecting his pronunciation of it) of San Bernardino County would become significant in the life of Dan Showalter. His election to the Assembly had been somewhat "under a cloud."

Piercy had been associated with and leader of a group of "roughs" who disrupted and disgusted the townspeople of San Bernardino. His cohorts were noted for their almost violent opposition to the "Mormon element," which had dominated the town until 1859. Nevertheless, he had been elected sheriff of San Bernardino County in November of 1859. By the spring of 1860, his supporters were already mentioning him as a candidate for the Assembly at the next election. Incumbent Assemblyman William A. Conn had been prominent in the advancement of San Bernardino and had served the county well. He had the support of the principal citizens. Piercy resigned as sheriff on October 31, 1861 (after less than a year in office), to campaign for the Assembly.[165] Conn and Piercy were the only candidates. It would be a particularly hard-fought campaign. Piercy's supporters, according to leading merchant Morris Katz, were "sharp shrewd political tricksters." Though the editor of the county's only newspaper was a Conn supporter, he was usually drunk. Piercy's supporters got control of the type from him to print their posters and tickets, and then left the type scattered about the newspaper's floor so that it could not be used by their opponents. Fortunately, the Conn supporters had anticipated such a problem and had their tickets printed in Los Angeles. There was frequent intimidation of Conn supporters on election day—one was even shot at for betting on Conn.[166]

When the votes were counted, Conn had 396, but Piercy had 400—a four-vote victory margin.[167] The "principal citizens," however, believed that Conn had been duly elected.[168] Prior to the election, it had been anticipated that it would be decided by voters in the Bear Valley area, which was then more populous than the rest of the county.[169] As it turned out, the election was decided by the Temescal Valley precinct at the southern edge of the county. The manager of this precinct was a Piercy supporter. It was believed that he kept the polls there open for two weeks—and as votes for Piercy were needed, they were furnished here.[170] Piercy's win was challenged in court at San Bernardino. During arguments over depositions in the case, the two attorneys got into an altercation and the attorney for Conn's supporters was stabbed. That night, according to the *Los Angeles Star*, a "rowdy gang took possession of the town. They smashed Jacob's bar and demolished signs of nearly every Jew store in town and broke into two stores. No arrests."[171] Ex-sheriff Piercy had matters well in hand and was declared elected. It was later reported that he had been elected by a combination of Douglas men and Republicans.[172] There may well have been some truth to this allegation since the county was the only one in the southern part of the state that delivered a plurality (37.4 percent) for Lincoln in the presidential race.[173]

Dan Showalter left his home at Horseshoe Bend for Sacramento about Christmas of 1860. He left with the good wishes of his home-county newspaper. The editor of the *Mariposa Gazette* opined that the county would be "never so well represented in the Legislature," regretting only that Showalter and Gregory were not members of "the party in the ascendant." Still, the editor felt that they would show themselves "in the advantage of the county as well as to their own benefit."[174]

Three

The California Assembly of 1861

Throughout this chapter, in order to facilitate identification of the faction to which an assemblyman belonged, upon first appearance their name will be followed parenthetically with a letter identifying their faction following the name(s) of the county or counties which they represented. Factions are identified with a "B" for a Breckinridge Democrat (variantly referred to as "Brecks" and "Chivalry"), a "D" for a Douglas Democrat (variantly referred to as "Douglasite"), an "R" for a Republican, and a "U" for Constitutional Union. Assemblymen having the same surname will be distinguished by adding "of County" after their name.

The Twelfth Session of the House of Assembly of the State of California was called to order at noon on Monday, January 7, 1861, by J.M. Anderson, who had been the Clerk of the Assembly (an elected employee) for the prior year's session. An attempt by the Douglas Democrats to elect one of their number as temporary Speaker quickly failed. A motion by Frank Fargo (R–San Francisco) that Anderson act as temporary Speaker was carried, with neither Anderson nor anyone else present realizing that he would preside over the Assembly for the better part of two weeks. An Assistant Sergeant-at-Arms was appointed to assist Anderson, and the call of the roll of counties was conducted with members present responding. After conclusion of the call, those members present—including Dan Showalter—were sworn in by a Judge Baldwin and took their seats. Of the three members absent, two arrived the next day and the third two weeks later. The rules of the Eleventh Session were adopted until such time as the new Assembly could adopt its own.[1] Then the difficulties that would characterize the Assembly of 1861 began.

Assemblyman William Ross (B–Sonoma) then moved to proceed with the organization of the Assembly. Immediately, two Douglas Democrats, including their leading member, John Conness (D–El Dorado), moved that Ross' motion be postponed until the next day. Their motion was supported by a minority, consisting solely of the twenty-eight Douglasites, and failed. John White (D–Shasta) then moved that Ross' motion be tabled. It was apparent that the Douglas men were stalling on organization. Later, Conness would admit that this tactic was to provide them with an opportunity to converse in caucus on their candidates for Assembly offices. Ross, W.C. Wood (B–Yolo) and Dan Showalter (B–Mariposa) all demanded that the decision to table be decided by a roll call vote. The motion to table failed 28–48, again with only the Douglasites in favor. Showalter then made his first motion in the Assembly of 1861—he moved "the previous question" (for a vote on Ross' motion to organize). His motion passed 47–29, with only the Douglas men opposed. The first order of business to organize would be election of a Speaker of the House.²

The first nominee for Speaker was Zachariah Montgomery (B–Sutter). The next was N. Greene Curtis (D–Sacramento), followed by Conness. This revealed that there was some division among the Douglas Democrats (Curtis was among the Lecompton Democrats who had supported Douglas). The final nominee was Frank F. Fargo. When balloting commenced, none of the nominees would vote. Later, nominees would cast their own votes for some other member. This was in accordance with the custom of the time, that it was unseemly to appear to want an office. The result of the first ballot was Conness—24, Montgomery—21, Fargo—18, and Curtis—10. The sole member not part of any of the factions, Orson K. Smith (U–Fresno and Tulare), voted with the Lecompton Douglasites for Curtis. A majority was necessary to elect. The *Journal of the House of Assembly of the Twelfth Session* recorded for the first time what would become repetitive:

"There being no choice, the House proceeded to vote [another] time." Three more ballots were taken that first day of the session without any change in the results. Finally, they adjourned at 1:45 in the morning, until 11:00 a.m. the next day.³

Balloting for Speaker on the second day was briefly delayed by a failed motion to immediately adjourn in commemoration of General Andrew Jackson's 1815 victory at the Battle of New Orleans. When the voting began, it was evident that the Douglas faction had settled their differences. The nomination of Curtis was withdrawn and, for the future, Curtis and his previous supporters would vote for Conness. Conness would continue to not cast a vote, but both Montgomery and Fargo would cast "scattered" ballots. This tactic of casting isolated votes for non-candidates served to make it more difficult for a candidate (specifically Conness) to receive a majority. The fifth ballot's result was Conness—30, Montgomery—21, Fargo—18 and "scattered"—2. Fargo had voted for John W. Cherry (R–San Francisco) and Montgomery for Dan Showalter. Montgomery was joined on the tenth ballot in voting for Showalter by O.K. Smith. Tuesday's balloting set the pattern for future days: numerous ballots with "no choice" interspersed with failed motions to adjourn. Later there would occur addresses by members seeking compromise and/or attacking other factions for preventing election of a Speaker. Roll call counts on adjournment motions—except the final one each day—would always be taken upon demand by one or more members. On one occasion on January 8, Showalter made such a demand. After fifteen fruitless ballots, the Assembly adjourned at thirty minutes past midnight, until 11:00 a.m. the next day.⁴

On Wednesday the 9th, an Assistant Sergeant-at-Arms was appointed to assist Anderson, the Clerk/acting Speaker, and then balloting resumed. There was virtually no change on the nineteenth ballot except for Fargo altering his "scattered" vote to a different Republican. Then Montgomery rose to withdraw his name as a candidate. He suggested that the Douglas Democrats nominate a Breckinridge man whom they could support or allow the Breckinridge Democrats to nominate a Douglas man that they could support. This proposal went nowhere with the Douglasites, so Lloyd Magruder (B–Yuba) nominated Dan Showalter as the new candidate of the Brecks. The twentieth ballot revealed Showalter receiving a few more votes than Montgomery had received, with the result of Conness—32, Showalter—23, Fargo—18, scattered—2. Following the custom, Showalter's own vote was one of those scattered—for George W. Patrick (B–Tuolumne). After the twenty-fifth ballot, the legislators must have been getting hungry. Charles W. Piercy (D–San Bernardino) moved an adjournment until 7:30 p.m. Two motions were made to amend the time until into the next day. Both of the amendments and Piercy's original motion failed. From this point onward, legislators, in ones and twos, began to absent themselves for one or two ballots as they attended to "comfort needs." Scattered ballots also increased very slightly as various assemblymen perhaps "tested" names of possible compromise candidates. Following the thirty-fifth ballot, adjournment until the next day finally was approved, at forty-five minutes after midnight.[5]

Before reconvening on Thursday, January 10, the Assembly members were greeted by disgusted comments in the *Sacramento Daily Union*: "The Assembly has been three days in the contest for Speaker without accomplishing an election, and if the three parties stand by their nominations they may consume three weeks in the senseless squabble. Every day thus spent costs the people of the State about fifteen hundred dollars; voting from day to day unsuccessfully for Speaker, is therefore a very unprofitable business for taxpayers. Members owe it to themselves and to the people to put an end to the contest, by electing a Speaker and proceeding with the legitimate business before the Legislature."[6]

This editorial did not have any effect. The results of the thirty-sixth through fiftieth ballots were virtually unchanged and there was still no Speaker elected. Adjournment

The California legislature convened on the second floor of the Second Capitol Building at Sacramento between 1855 and 1869. None of the workers or other persons in the photograph are identifiable. The date of the photograph is unknown but obviously at some point near the end of its construction (courtesy California History Room, California State Library, Sacramento, California).

again was at forty-five minutes past midnight. Friday the 11th was the fifth day of balloting. The fifty-first ballot was unchanged from the established pattern. At this point, Ross tried to break the deadlock. He moved that all the candidates be requested to withdraw their names. He felt that all factions had made "good and sufficient effort" to elect their candidate, but that it was time for all factions to make some sacrifices to prevent deadlock. Showalter's friend, Thomas Laspeyre (B–San Joaquin), with Ross' consent, modified the resolution, adding that the withdrawals were necessary "for the purpose of harmonizing conflicting elements, and effecting speedy organization." This effort failed when it was tabled on a 40–35 vote. After one more ballot without result, Ames Adams (D–Sacramento) moved that, instead of a majority, the candidate with the most votes (his man, Conness, of course) be declared elected. This also was tabled and two more fruitless ballots conducted until adjournment, at 12:20, until later Saturday morning.[7]

In what the *Sacramento Daily Union* facetiously referred to as continuation by the Assembly of a "pleasant but not very profitable exercise," the assemblymen gathered late Saturday morning. The deliberations and the sixty-sixth through seventy-second ballots proved as inconclusive as were those on the preceding days. Assemblyman P. Munday (D–Placer) protested that he was unfamiliar with politics and, agreeing with articles in the *Daily Union* that extended balloting was a waste of state funds, suggested that his faction take down their candidate in favor of another. Magruder moved that they stay in session until midnight unless a Speaker should be elected. Brief remarks by Assemblyman Thomas O'Brein (D–Calaveras) followed. The punning originality of his remarks merit quotation:

> Whereas, It is apparent to this body that we are in a "sea of Trouble" Relative to the selection of a commander to steer us clear of *shoal-water* and cannot *far go* in our present *Helpless* condition: therefore,
> *Resolved*, that in order to avoid successfully the *breakers* and Black Clouds ahead, John Conness is hereby unanimously called to take the helm.[8]

All three motions failed, Laspeyre again proposed that all three candidates withdraw. At this point, Showalter offered remarks for the first time in the Assembly of 1861. He agreed that no organization could be effected as things stood, but that the minority faction of the Democrats had some right to consideration. He stated that he had proposed several times to his supporters that he withdraw, and he stood ready to do so if the opposition offered a candidate he could consistently support. N.C. Miller (D–Nevada) responded, deploring the failure of the Breckinridgers to unite with his faction. Debate was continued by Montgomery, who accused the Douglas faction of prolonging the process and cited one of their members, J. Dougherty (D–Sierra), as commenting, "We will keep you sitting here until the end of the year, unless you elect our man as Speaker." Samuel Hill (D–El Dorado) argued that his faction had a large plurality and that no other could represent a majority. Laspeyre again called for all candidates to withdraw. Dougherty said that both Showalter and Montgomery were wrong and that their "party" would go out of existence. Republican Fargo said he could not withdraw without the consent of his friends, although he recognized that the Republicans were not a majority and could not claim organization of the Assembly. Argument continued with Joseph Powell (D–Sacramento) stating that he would not be found pandering to "this secessionist element." The resolution of Laspeyre was tabled 45–30. H.W. Briggs (R–Santa Clara) presented a resolution that all of the members should "attend religious worship to-morrow, to be earnest in their devotions, to repent of the sins of the present week, and come up to the House on Monday with an honest determination to do right." After much laughter, the Clerk ruled the resolution out of order. Anderson would not read another resolution from Munday saying it was out of order, but Charles Crocker (D–Sacramento) insisted and it was read "for information." Munday's resolution called for the unanimous election of the Rev. John H. Watson of Santa Cruz as Chaplain of the Assembly and that a committee of Showalter, Conness and Fargo be sent to inform the reverend of his election. Even greater laughter resulted.[9]

Proposals and efforts to break the deadlock continued. Assemblyman S.S. Tilton (R–San Francisco) offered a resolution that was ingenuous. He proposed that all three candidates be elected Speaker and serve for a week at a time in rotation (Fargo then Conness then Showalter). Montgomery objected that a Speaker could not be elected that way. Anderson responded that it was not up to the Clerk to decide which way a Speaker could be elected. Montgomery said that even if the method were lawful, he would oppose it because (curiously paraphrasing Abraham Lincoln) "a House divided against itself certainly could not stand." Crocker said that he'd vote for it "notwithstanding its novelty." George W. Patrick observed that one faction—O.K. Smith—had been left out. Then, as he had very rarely done, Clerk Anderson intervened, suggesting that a resolution to table would end the matter. Dougherty made the motion and the unusual compromise was tabled.[10]

Assemblyman A.W. Blair (R–Monterey) then entered the affray, stating, "I do think if we continue to go on this way, we shall soon come to be classed by the people, our constituents, with certain animals which are more distinguished for the length of ears and general stupidity, than for any great breadth of intellect." He offered a resolution that an entire slate of officers for the Assembly—all Republicans, with Fargo as Speaker—be elected. With fifty-five members voting "Yes" to table, the "Noes" were not even counted. Montgomery then brought up the so-called San Francisco Bulkhead Bill from the 1860 session. This bill, promoted by mining interests, appropriated $250,000 to build nine wagon roads over the mountains to the Washoe, financing it by a tax levy upon the "bulkheads" in San Francisco harbor. It was wildly unpopular in the state, with opponents viewing it as an impediment to commerce. When Governor John Downey had vetoed the bill, he became hugely popular overnight. Montgomery followed with a resolution that the Assembly not elect as Speaker any candidate who had voted for the bill—he referred to it as a "scheme"—during the 1860 session. He, of course, meant Conness. After some protests had been made, Anderson ruled Montgomery's proposal out of order. This ruling was appealed, but Anderson's decision was sustained by a vote of 57–14. Showalter's vote was among the minority.[11]

Finally, another ballot—the sixty-ninth—was taken. There was still no majority for Conness, with Showalter and Fargo trailing in that order. Charles W. Piercy then spoke. He said that neither of the two Democratic candidates could be elected and then nominated Murray Morrison (D–Los Angeles). It didn't change things much. Only one Conness and two Showalter supporters joined him in voting for Morrison. After identical results on the seventieth and seventy-first ballots, the Assembly adjourned until Monday with no Speaker and no prospect of breaking the deadlock in sight.[12]

On Monday, January 14, the seventy-second and seventy-third ballots resulted in Conness—31, Showalter—22, Fargo—18, and a few scattered votes. W.M. Buell (D–Del Norte and Klamath) rose to speak. He said, "I can no longer aid, by my vote, in prolonging this useless contest," and called upon the Breckinridge faction to state what Douglas man they could support with him joining them. Buell was the first "bolter" from any faction. This indication that finally a resolution of the impasse might be in sight was cheered by observers. William Childs (D–Calaveras) then stated that he would abandon his caucus and vote in a way to result in organization. P.H. Harris (D–Plumas) rose, said that he was tired of doing nothing and, to "test the sentiment of the House," nominated Aaron Wood (D–Plumas). John White (D–Shasta), citing $12,000 to $15,000 of public money spent to no purpose, concurred with Buell, Childs and Harris. Piercy then withdrew his nomination of Morrison. Dan Showalter then rose "for the purpose of withdrawing my name, ... The Name of Mr. Wood is perfectly acceptable." He urged his fellow members of the Breckinridge caucus to join him in supporting Wood to organize the Assembly and said he hoped Wood would be acceptable to the Douglas party as well.[13] Doubtless, observers wondered if a stampede had begun and that there would soon be a Speaker.

If so, the next speaker dispelled that notion. Patrick Munday (D–Placer) said that Conness was being "persecuted" and vowed that he would stand by him. Dougherty agreed with Munday. He said that Harris and the others were wrong, that persons elected as Democrats were "sowing the seeds of dissension," and that "the spirit of disunion, rebellion and treason now stalks forth." If they persisted in abandoning Conness, they would find themselves "on the side of those who are promoting a fratricidal war." Dr. D.P. Durst (D–Colusa and Tehama) was more conciliatory than Dougherty, but voiced his support for Conness. W.P. Tilden (D–Butte), in the longest oration of the day, defined positions of parties and factions, went into great detail on national politics (despite objections), and charged that the Breckinridge faction and the Republicans in the Assembly were determined to make no sacrifices. He concluded that he would "vote for Conness as long as he is our party nominee." Montgomery classified Tilden as a "political Rip Van Winkle" and protested the "calumny" which Tilden had hurled. Dougherty responded at great length, calling those who opposed his talking fearful of his investigation of their positions since they were "disunionists."[14] It only remained for the next ballot to determine if all of the "speechifying," the Douglasite bolters, the nomination of Wood, and the withdrawal of Showalter would have any effect.

The seventy-fourth ballot did produce different results—but no election. Wood, with the support of the Breckinridge faction and his fellow bolters from the Douglas faction, led with thirty votes. With twenty-six votes, Conness trailed for the first time. Fargo retained his solid eighteen Republican votes. Seven more ballots were conducted with "no choice." Adjournment finally occurred at 1:30 in the morning. Two quick ballots on Tuesday morning, when the Assembly was again called to order at 11:00 a.m., produced the same result—Wood, then Conness, then Fargo, and no Speaker elected. Assemblyman Cherry then moved a compromise resolution dividing the Assembly positions among all three factions: The Republicans would receive the Speakership (Fargo) and Enrolling Clerk; the Douglas faction would choose the Chief Clerk (Anderson), Assistant Clerk and Engrossing Clerk positions; and the Breckinridge faction would fill the positions of Sergeant-at-Arms and his assistant. A motion to table passed 56–19, with only the Republicans opposed (and favoring Cherry's compromise). An eighty-sixth ballot followed with no change in result. Charles Crocker then moved that both the Assembly and the Senate adjourn *sine die* on Wednesday, the following day, if no Speaker could be elected. He reasoned that the Assembly could not unite upon a Speaker because those of the Breckinridge faction would never give their votes to an anti–Lecompton Democrat and had vacillated among several candidates, and the Republicans were determined in adherence to their own candidate. He felt that the Senate would concur since no legislation could be enacted without the vote of both houses. The decision would then pass to the people, who would decide at the next (September 1861) election. After some discussion, Crocker's motion was tabled. White again nominated Wood of Plumas, explaining that he was a Douglas man, but was not pledged to any man or set of men, and that a Douglas Democrat would act for the good of the country and not for any faction. Four more ballots followed, all with virtually the same results as earlier that day.[15]

The next compromise motion, offered by Laspeyre, was unusual. He moved that all of the candidates withdraw and the Assembly then elect as Speaker some person who was not a member of the Assembly. He said there was nothing in the state constitution explicitly requiring the Speaker to be a member. Showalter then spoke in opposition to this motion by his friend and fellow "Breck." He said that if the Douglas men would not withdraw the name of Conness, there would be the same difficulty in electing an outsider as Speaker. He also felt that if the Assembly did seek an outsider for the post, Sacramento would be overrun with applicants. His motion to table carried. D.V. Waldron (D–Stanislaus) then moved that no member be permitted to speak more than five minutes on any one subject until a Speaker was chosen. There were numerous seconds to this probably long overdue motion and it passed with only one or two dissents. There was no change in results of the ninety-second and ninety-third ballots which followed. Munday moved that the rules be suspended and Aaron Wood of Plumas be unanimously elected. This motion was tabled by a 42–33 vote. At 12:45 a.m. on Wednesday, they adjourned until 11:00 a.m. the next day.[16]

Wednesday, January 16, was the ninth day of the Assembly. After Anderson announced that the regular order of business was to elect a Speaker, John Conness—perhaps to the surprise of many—rose to speak. After receiving "leave" of the house to do so, he explained his course over the past eight days. He said he had objected to organization of the house without the Democrats having had preliminary consultations. He acknowledged that "I cannot be Speaker of this body." He said that any differences that had arisen between himself and others were not personal, but differences of policy. He said he had never "importuned" any members to vote for him during the balloting and then arrived at the effect of his remarks. "The time has now arrived, …, when, in my opinion, I can retire from this combat," not driven from it, but no longer desired. Conness then placed into nomination the name of Ransom Burnell (D–Amador). Burnell was virtually unknown and had not spoken at all during the proceedings thus far. According to Conness, there were "no charges connected with antecedent action" that could be made against Burnell and no shadow of an excuse for any Democrat not to vote for him.[17] Conness had quit—perhaps now there was a chance to end the marathon balloting.

The only change resultant in the ninety-fourth ballot which followed was that the votes which Conness had been receiving now went for Burnell. Wood of Plumas remained atop with 33, followed by Burnell with 24 (including that of Conness), Fargo with his usual 18, and three miscellaneous scattered votes. Frank Fargo then attempted to break open the deadlock. He deplored the many days of balloting at a cost of probably $20,000 and said that some concessions had to be made by some party. He then withdrew his own name and nominated W.P. Tilden (D–Butte). Tilden responded that, as a loyal Douglas man, he could not accept the nomination. Fargo then withdrew both the nomination and his own withdrawal. Seven ballots followed without change in results. After the 101st ballot, F. Walters (D–Trinity) moved that a committee of seven, chosen as equally as possible from all factions, be appointed by the Chair (Clerk Anderson) to determine a basis by which organization could be accomplished. His motion was tabled. With no change after the 102nd ballot, D.B. Holman (B–Solano) moved that members be requested to vote only for those who were candidates—perhaps hoping that the "scattering" votes would fall to Wood, electing him. This motion also was tabled. A 103rd ballot was taken, yet again there was "no choice." William Childs (D–Calaveras), who had been voting for Wood, then moved that, on the next ballot, whichever candidate received the most votes be declared elected. As with an earlier, similar motion, this one was tabled. Following five more "no choice" ballots, the Assembly adjourned at thirty minutes past midnight.[18]

Immediately after the Assembly was reconvened on Thursday, January 17, Frank Fargo withdrew his name from nomination. He left the Republican members free to vote as they individually chose. The ballot which followed found most of them voting for Burnell, and there were no scattered votes. The result was Burnell—40, Wood—36. Burnell had a majority. After ten days of marathon ballots (109 in all), the Assembly had finally elected a Speaker. Wood and Fargo then escorted Burnell to the chair, where he relieved Clerk Anderson as presiding officer.[19]

With Burnell in the chair as Speaker, the Assembly then proceeded to complete its organization—with a lesser degree of factionalism. For Clerk, the Douglasites nominated none other than J.M. Anderson. The Brecks nominated one W.J. Hooten and the Republicans a Mr. Taylor. It took two ballots before Anderson was elected Clerk—a position that he certainly deserved with three years previous experience in the post and his trial as "acting Speaker" for almost two weeks. Only one ballot was required to elect the Douglasite candidate for Assistant Clerk. Subsequent balloting for Sergeant-at-Arms, Assistant Sergeant-at-Arms, Engrossing Clerk, and Enrolling Clerk required more. Supporters of the Douglas faction won all five of these positions, with the Breckinridge supporter placing second and the Republican last. The Breckinridge candidate for Sergeant-at-Arms, J.C. Mintern of Merced County, had been placed in nomination by Dan Showalter. It took four ballots to eliminate him.[20]

The House of Assembly of the State of California was now, finally, ready for business. The Clerk was instructed to so inform the Senate. A committee of three was appointed to, with representatives of the Senate, inform the governor that the legislature was ready to receive any communication from him. A resolution was adopted to form a select committee of five to formulate rules for the Assembly and, with a like committee from the Senate, rules for when the two houses met jointly. A resolution was adopted that the application of any legislative employee for a pay raise would be sufficient grounds for that employee's termination. The Assembly then adjourned at 2:00 p.m.[21]—about nine hours sooner than had been the case on previous days. The real work would begin on the morrow.

The activity in the Assembly the next day, Friday, January 18, was rather mundane—for a change. Speaker Burnell announced the appointment of four porters, four pages, a "Post Office Boy," and a "Paper Folder." There was a proposal to hire a Watchman at $5.00 per day. Showalter questioned the necessity for the position. Ensuing discussion involved the propriety of the appointment and the number of porters which had been appointed. Others joined Showalter in questioning the need for a watchman. He supported a motion permitting the Speaker to "lop off" some of the porter appointments. William Coleman (D–El Dorado) then moved that a special committee be created to recommend upon compensation for services rendered to the Assembly from its opening on January 7 until its organization. Others objected to paying them for two weeks when they had actually served only ten days. Showalter's only activity relating to this motion was to request it be read again and then opposing it being tabled. Coleman's motion then passed with an amendment that the employees be paid for only ten days. Showalter was part of a large majority that voted to appoint a Journal Clerk and a Minute Clerk.[22]

Matters then became more contentious when a resolution was offered by P.H. Harris that the Assembly and Senate meet jointly the following Monday to elect a United States Senator for a term of six years. Crocker moved that this motion should be tabled, and it was by a 51–23 vote, with Showalter in the opposition.[23] Legislative activity then ceased upon arrival of the governor's annual message, which was read. Afterwards, there was a proposal for a joint committee to study costs for printing and distributing the message of the governor. A motion to table the proposal passed, with Showalter again in the minority. Adjournment followed.[24]

When the Assembly convened again on Saturday the 19th, B.S. Lippincott (D–Calaveras) brought up the subject of electing a United States Senator. He moved that all of the candidates be invited to address both houses of the legislature in the Assembly chamber on Monday the 21st. Patrick immediately moved that the motion be tabled. In this he was supported by Showalter, the other "Brecks," and sufficient other members for his tabling motion to pass. Assemblyman D.V. Waldron (D–Stanislaus) then moved that the Assembly and Senate meet in joint convention on Friday the 25th for the purpose of electing a senator. Republican Cherry's motion to table passed 50–23, with the Breckinridgers and Showalter joining with the Republicans to do so.[25] Another potentially contentious matter was then brought up by O'Brein with introduction of a resolution to expunge the action of the 1859 legislature censuring then United States Senator David Broderick for failing to, as instructed by that session of the legislature, support the admission of Kansas as a state under the Lecompton Constitution. Debate on the subject was set for Thursday, January 24.[26]

Several other divisive resolutions were also introduced this date. One, by Breckinridger Patrick, avowed that "while anything exists worthy of being called an American Union, California will cling to it." This was in support of the governor's having included in his message comments that California was in a favorable position to mediate between the North and the South. Montgomery submitted that California was unready to pledge allegiance "to either a Northern or a Southern fragment" of a dismembered nation. Another resolution from Montgomery stated that "never will we consent to become the ally of one section in waging a fratricidal war against another section of our country." Republican Crocker also presented resolutions. One of his declared that the Constitution had established a government and that no state had a right to secede. The Douglas faction did not present any resolutions relating to the matter,[27] but it was obvious that controversy and contention would follow.

Tuesday, January 22, 1861, was also a day of "light" work in the Assembly. Speaker Burnell announced Standing Committees. Showalter was named to the important Ways and Means Committee along with two Douglas men (Crocker and N.C. Miller), two Republicans (Martin Baechtel of Mendocino County and Fargo), and two additional Breckinridge men (Laspeyre and Magruder). He was also named to the Internal Improvements Committee. Other members were Republicans Fargo and Tilton, Douglasite Murray Morrison, and fellow "Breck" F. Sorrel of Siskiyou County. Showalter was part of a losing 59–15 minority opposing assignment of a bill to transfer funds to a Committee on Swamp and Overflowed Lands. The Assembly then authorized the Ways and Means Committee to procure for itself a meeting room at a cost not to exceed $25.00 per month. Adjournment followed.[28]

On January 23, 1861, the Assembly reached its full membership when Abel Stearns (D–Los Angeles) finally appeared to take his seat. Assemblyman Munday (D–Placer) afterwards offered "Concurrent Resolutions on the State of the Union" that cited "unjust treatment of Southern States" and "unwholesome agitation of the question of negro slavery by evil-disposed persons at the North" and opposed coercion of seceded states. His resolution was referred to the Committee on Federal Relations. W.P. Tilden then moved that the Ladies' Washington National Monument Society be granted use of the Assembly chamber on February 22 for a lecture. This motion passed 45–23, with most of the Republicans, Showalter, and some other Breckinridge men opposed. There were lengthy speeches, to no result, regarding the hiring of a Fireman for the legislature. A motion to fix January 25 for a joint convention with the Senate to elect a United States Senator was again introduced and again tabled, 45–30, with Showalter again against postponing the convention. H.W. Briggs (R–Santa Clara) then moved that the Assembly chamber be used on the 26th for the U.S. Senate candidates to express their views. A Showalter motion to indefinitely table lost. He then voted in favor of a Blair motion to table, which also lost on a 31–41 vote. The original motion to invite the Senate candidates to speak on the 26th then came to a vote. It passed 39–35, with Showalter among the "noes." The final item of business was a report by the Committee on Swamp and Overflowed Lands on a bill to transfer $40,000 to the General Fund. The Committee recommended its passage. A motion by Conness to postpone action failed, 31–43. Showalter was among the losing "ayes." The Assembly then adjourned to the next day.[29]

Only two matters of note occupied the Assembly on Thursday, January 24. W.C. Wood (B–Yolo) moved that N.C. Miller (D–Nevada) be added to the Committee on Military Affairs. After Wood's motion failed, Showalter, in support, moved to suspend the rules for that purpose. His motion also lost. Then the really controversial matter came up. This was the "Concurrent Resolution to Expunge a Resolution of Censure of the Late David C. Broderick." (Resolutions of the 1859 legislature had instructed Senator Broderick to vote in the United States Senate for admission of Kansas as a free State. He had ignored those instructions and, in 1860, the legislature passed a resolution of censure against him. Assemblyman O'Brein, who had introduced the resolution to expunge, had been a strong friend of Broderick.[30]) There was considerable debate over the resolution featuring O'Brein, Conness, Laspeyre, Fleming Amyx (B–Tuolumne), and Munday among others. Thomas O'Brien moved that his resolution be referred to a special committee. His motion was defeated 34–37, with Showalter and the other Breckinridgers joining with the Republicans in voting it down. Then Conness moved to postpone the matter for two weeks. Briggs moved an amendment to postpone only for one week. Showalter demanded a roll call vote, and Briggs' amending motion failed 15–56, with Showalter part of the majority. Conness then withdrew his motion. A motion by John White (D–Shasta) to indefinitely postpone failed, 36–40, as did, by 32–43, a motion to reconsider that vote. Showalter had voted "No" in both cases.[31]

Assembly activity on Friday, January 25, began with Assemblyman Waldron reporting for the Select Committee on Mileage. Their report revealed that Showalter was due $624 for 320 miles travel.[32] Rules for the Assembly were then reported,[33] after which there was discussion on creating a state commission to work with a United States commissioner on locating and marking the boundary with the Nevada Territory.[34] The "Broderick Resolution" (officially Assembly Concurrent Resolution No. 6) arose again. Alex. Campbell (R–San Francisco), D.H. Haun (B–Yuba), Montgomery, Laspeyre, and, in particular, Conness all made lengthy remarks on the subject. Showalter was among the 17–53 majority against adjournment (which would have ended discussion). A motion to draw a line through the resolution and just insert wording that the censure was expunged by order of the Senate and Assembly was then offered and discussed. Showalter was one of thirty-two opposing passage, but forty-one members supported its passage.[35]

Saturday, January 26, began with the Assembly finally coming to agreement to appoint a watchman. Showalter's position was that *if* a watchman was necessary, one should be appointed.[36] A motion by Munday to fix the following Monday for a joint session with the Senate to elect a United States Senator was tabled, 49–20, with Showalter, the other Breckinridge men, and the Republicans in the majority. J.H. Morgan (R–Santa Clara) then proposed that the Committee on Public Morals inquire into and report on the propriety of electing a chaplain for the Assembly. Showalter's motion to indefinitely postpone failed, 30–36, but Aaron Wood's motion to table passed.[37] On Monday, January 28, D.B. Kurtz (D–San Diego) moved that the Assembly meet with the Senate on the first Monday in February to elect a United States Senator. Again this action was postponed, with Republican Alex Campbell's motion to table passing 38–30. Showalter again voted with the majority.[38] Nothing particularly controversial or significant came up in the Assembly on Tuesday.

On Wednesday, the 30th of January, Assemblyman W.M. Buell (D–Del Norte and Klamath) presented a "Joint Resolution for Election of a United States Senator." Republican Campbell's motion to table passed, 45–31, with Showalter with the minority.[39] Charles Crocker then moved that Dougherty, Showalter and himself, all members of the Committee of Ways and Means, be authorized to visit San Francisco to take testimony on the effectiveness of an act which appointed Inspectors of Pork, Beef and Other Salt Provisions. After a motion by Wood of Plumas to table failed, Conness moved that, instead of members of the Ways and Means Committee, members of the Committee on Commerce and Navigation be substituted in the authorization. The Conness motion passed, 44–32. Not surprisingly, Showalter, Crocker and Dougherty all voted against the substitution.[40] Showalter then exhibited his generally fiscally conservative inclination by opposing a Conness motion to amend Senate Bill 14, which would limit a legislator's appropriation for postage to $25. Conness felt that the limitation should be removed in case, as in the previous session, it not be enough. Showalter felt that $25 was sufficient and that, if the limitation were removed, there would be no assurance that some members might not draw even $50 or $100. He spoke to his experience during the 1857 session, observing that many did not draw their $25 worth of stamps while others had drawn the entire amount and would probably have drawn more if not for the limitation.[41] The bill was passed later in the session with the limitation intact.

Assembly debate on February 1 was dominated by discussion of recent actions on the floor of the United States Senate by Oregon Senator Edward D. Baker (a personal friend of President Abraham Lincoln and a former Californian who had been elected to the Senate by the Oregon legislature in 1860). Republican leader Frank Fargo introduced a resolution commending the Senator for a speech on January 2 that had appealed for federal union above party gain and political advancement. William Ross (B–Sonoma) moved that the resolution be tabled. Showalter then requested his fellow Breckinridge Democrat to withdraw the motion to table so that Assembly members could express their sentiments. P.H. Harris (D–Butte) then stated that he would move to postpone consideration of the resolution until February 9. Showalter's friend and fellow "Breck" Patrick then moved that Fargo's resolution be amended. Patrick's proposed amendment, completely altering the nature of the resolution, was that Senator Baker, "in voting to postpone indefinitely the Pacific Railroad Bill, did not represent the wishes of the Pacific coast." Ross then again made his motion to table the Baker resolution. Showalter was among the majority tabling the resolution by a vote of 45–27.[42] Even the mild debate about Baker's actions could not hide the fact that factionalism in the Assembly was a serious matter.

The business of the Assembly session on Saturday, February 2, began with reports from the Committee on Federal Relations on the so-called "Union Resolutions." The majority report of Conness (D), Thomas Wright (D–Sierra), Campbell (R), and Charles Ford (R–Santa Cruz) was presented by Conness. The purport of the committee majority was summarized by their third paragraph:

> The time has arrived in our history where every man must take position unmistakeably, and be for his country, for the Union and the Constitution as they are, or be against them.
> The heart of California beats true to the Union, …

A minority report by F. Sorrel (B–Siskiyou), John White (D–Shasta) and Lloyd Magruder (B–Yuba) opposed. The two reports were made "Special Order" for Wednesday the 6th— meaning that they would be debated and voted upon then.[43]

Fargo moved unsuccessfully to take up from the table the resolution regarding Senator Baker. Assemblyman Charles W. Piercy moved that it be "resolved, as the sense of this House, That the troubles existing in the Atlantic States are justly chargeable to the sectional doctrines advanced by the Republican party." Republican member Campbell immediately moved that Piercy's resolution be tabled. Dan Showalter then "moved the question," that is, that the Assembly vote on Piercy's resolution. A division of the house revealed only twenty-eight (including Showalter) favoring Piercy's resolution and forty-three opposed.[44]

The accusations of culpability in the national situation continued. John Conness moved an amended resolution stating "that the United States forts and arsenals recently taken at Charleston and elsewhere, have undoubtedly been taken by Black Republicans in disguise." Motions to first postpone consideration and then table this both failed. O'Brein proposed an amendment to Conness' amendment, to strike out reference to Black Republicans and insert instead "Republican and Breckinridge parties." Alex Campbell (R) moved a substitute for that, that it be "resolved, that we have an abiding confidence in the justice and patriotism of the people of the United States and that the unhappy domestic difficulties now existing between the North and the South is not chargeable to the great masses of the people of the United States, but is justly charge-able to the Abolitionists of the North and the secession leaders of the South." This motion was tabled. Doubtless weary of all of the bickering, the Assembly voted to adjourn until the next Tuesday.[45]

The following week's sessions saw continued factional contention. On Tuesday the 5th, a motion by William Childs (D–Calaveras) to "endorse the course of Hon. S.A. Douglas" (who was working and speaking for compromise) was tabled. Showalter and his

Breckinridge friends were among the twenty-nine voting against tabling it. Wednesday found consideration of "resolutions on the State of the Union" postponed a further two days. On Thursday, Douglasite Powell moved that the Assembly meet with the Senate on February 15 to elect a United States Senator. A motion to table by the leader of his faction, Conness, passed, 51–22. The postponement of difficult and contentious matters continued on Friday with another Powell motion to set a date (February 20) for election of a senator failing, 36–40, with all of the Breckinridge faction and Republicans voting "no."[46] Showalter explained on the floor his reasoning for continual postponements of the Senate election, saying "that is only wasting the time of the House, with no prospect or probability of electing a Senator this Winter" because all of the factions (he referred to them as "parties") were refusing to agree. His conclusion was that while the matter was hanging over the legislature, "it prevents us from performing the duties which the people demand of us."[47]

D.J. Williamson, Secretary of the Senate, on Saturday, February 9, brought the Assembly a communication that the Senate had passed a joint resolution for the election of a United States Senator. It was now only the Assembly that would be delaying this important matter. Various motions to postpone consideration of the Senate resolution failed, and then a 36–37 vote defeated action on the resolution itself. On the postponing amendments and the resolution, Dan Showalter had voted contrary to the others of the Breckinridge caucus. This was a legislative tactic. When the position of the "Brecks" did not prevail, Showalter, having voted with the majority, was able to give notice of reconsideration—in other words, a new vote on the same matter.[48] This he did on Monday, February 11. After a failed delaying amendment by Laspeyre, reconsideration of the vote itself failed, 26–33. The Assembly also voted once more to again postpone consideration of the Union resolutions.[49]

A new twist was added on Tuesday, February 12, when Aaron Wood (D–Plumas) moved that the legislature endorse the so-called Crittenden Plan by which, through compromise, national union would be preserved. A motion to refer this resolution to the Committee on Federal Relations by Dougherty passed, 38–34, Showalter voting "no."[50] This having failed, P.H. Harris moved a concurrent resolution endorsing "the course of John J. Crittenden, Stephen A. Douglas, and John C. Breckinridge." After failed motions to amend, postpone and table, the resolution passed, 44–29, although Conness gave notice of later reconsideration. Then consideration of the Resolution on the State of the Union was yet again postponed, this time to the next day.[51]

Wednesday the 13th, a five-member majority (including Showalter) of the Committee on Ways and Means reported favorably on Assembly Bill No. 1 to repeal a previous act that created the Inspectors of Pork, Beef and Salt Provisions. The Assembly then returned to more contentious matters when Conness moved reconsideration of the vote endorsing the Crittenden Compromise and the positions of Stephen A. Douglas and John C. Breckinridge. During discussion, Showalter asked Conness if he supported the Crittenden Compromise. Conness refused to state directly if he did or did not and withdrew his motion to reconsider.[52] Showalter then tried to renew the reconsideration motion, but was ruled out of order. He appealed this ruling, but Speaker Burnell was sustained by a 40–32 vote. Laspeyre then moved indefinite postponement of the matter. His motion failed, 36–40. Laspeyre then moved an amendment stating: "We, the Representatives of California in Senate and Assembly indorse [sic] the patriotism and wisdom of the Hon. John C. Breckinridge and Hon. Stephen A. Douglas, manifested by them in their endorsement of the compromise—and in their condemning the use of Military force to coerce the Southern States, which have seceded, or may secede, from the Federal Union—recommending conciliation and concession, rather than war, and compromise rather than disunion."[53] O.K. Smith, the lone Union Party member of the Assembly, immediately moved a substitution, stating, "And as the sense of the People of the State of California, be it further Resolved, that it is the duty of the people of all the States to assist the Federal Government in all its legitimate and Constitutional efforts to execute the Constitutional laws of Congress." Motions to postpone and to table failed, as did a motion by Haun (B) to take up the Resolutions on the State of the Union. Conness again tried to have reconsideration of the Crittenden Compromise matter. By a 39–38 vote, a Showalter motion to indefinitely postpone reconsideration passed.[54] Nothing accomplished, they adjourned until the next day.

The concurrent resolution to elect a United States Senator on February 20 was again taken up on Thursday the 14th. Republican Campbell's motion to table failed, 33–37, after which a motion by William Ross (B) to change the date from the 20th to the 25th was also defeated. The Assembly then voted on the resolution itself to elect a Senator on the 20th. With Showalter and his fellow Breckinridge men voting in the majority, the resolution lost, 34–39.[55] Assemblyman Dougherty (D) then spoke at length about concurrent resolutions on the State of the Union. He spoke strongly against secession and averred that the Federal government had the right to coerce, blockade, and collect revenues in the seceded states. Showalter asked if Dougherty proposed to take all forts by force of arms. Dougherty responded that the Constitution gave the government that power and that "the man who fired the cannon upon the *Star of the West* [a ship seeking to resupply Fort Sumter in December 1860] had voted for J.C. Breckinridge and was as devoted a supporter of the right of secession as his friend from Mariposa [Showalter]." He went on to state that it was the duty of the government to suppress rebellion and of Californians to oppose treasonable purposes on the Pacific coast. Dougherty then "supposed his friend [Showalter] was not opposed to the Pacific Republic plan." This was a proposal by two of California's congressmen that if the Union divided in the East, that the Pacific States and territories not take sides, but form their own republic. Showalter rose, saying that it was necessary for him to answer immediately, that he was not in favor of a Pacific Republic and that he had never contemplated any such thing. But he did go on to state that "when the great old States of Virginia, Kentucky, Pennsylvania and Ohio—when the representatives of those States no longer met together in Congress and not until then, was he in favor of a Pacific Republic." Postponement to the next day resulted.[56]

On the 15th, another effort to schedule election of a senator failed and consideration of the Union Resolutions were again postponed a day.[57] Activity on the 16th was relatively light. By a vote of 0–69, Showalter and his fellow assemblymen refused to override Governor John G. Downey's veto of a bill to fix compensation of the Calaveras County Judge. Repeal of the Pork, Beef and Salt Provisions Inspectors came up again. Showalter spoke for indefinite postponement, but, upon a motion by Sorrel, consideration was scheduled for the following Tuesday. Consideration of the State of the Union resolutions were deferred to Monday.[58] On Monday, it was again deferred to the next day.[59] Delay—neither action nor compromise—was the order for each day, for, on Tuesday, consideration of both the Pork, Beef and Salt Provision Inspectors and the Union Resolutions were postponed one day.[60] The next day, the 20th, both were postponed again—the Union Resolutions until the 21st and the Inspectors repeal until the 26th. Showalter gave notice that he intended to introduce a bill to grant right to lay railroad tracks on those streets of San Francisco not already tracked.[61] He did not introduce this bill the next day or any other day—however, he announced his support for a Senate bill having the same character and effect, and called for a vote soon upon it.[62]

Meanwhile, Democratic members of the legislature who favored the Crittenden Compromise had met in the Assembly chamber during the evenings of Monday, February 18, and Tuesday, February 19. Dan Showalter had been chosen to preside over the meeting. In addition to himself, nine state senators and twenty-six assemblymen attended. Senate Clerk George S. Evans and Assistant Assembly Clerk J.W. Scobey were also present and acted as secretaries for the meeting. A Mike Gray, Douglas Democrat, served as Sergeant-at-Arms. Showalter was not reported to have spoken much at all during the deliberations—as chairman, this would have been precluded. He stated that the purpose of the meeting was "reorganizing the Democratic party, by bringing the two wings of the party together on a common platform to meet a common enemy." He specified that the election of a United States Senator was not involved and ruled out of order a motion for a resolution that Lieutenant General Winfield Scott was acting in contravention to the Constitution. He also referred to the meetings as a "Convention." Nothing was settled during the meeting of these two days and a further meeting was set for Tuesday the 26th, and a committee of six appointed to call upon and invite other Democratic members of the Senate and Assembly.[63]

This convention, or "fusion meeting," reconvened after 8:00 p.m. on the 26th with forty-four senators and assemblymen attending. Reporters who were present did not report who was presiding, but, since Showalter is not mentioned, presumably it was again he. The delay in getting together had been caused by a caucus of the Breckinridge members beforehand. The Chair (Showalter?) advised that minutes of the previous meeting had been sent to the chairman of each County Central Committee. The chairmen of the Douglas and the Breckinridge State Central Committees were reported (by Morrison and Magruder, respectively) as having indicated willingness to confer. Resolutions were offered by Magruder which castigated the Republican Party for coercion of the seceded states and recommended that all Democrats unite, for "the preservation of our common country and the maintenance of the Federal Union," in endorsing the Crittenden Compromise. Two of those in attendance, D.L. Haun (B) and Charles Piercy (D), opposed. Piercy said he was "for the Union, and not for a war against Black Republicans," whereas Haun thought the resolutions concentrated too exclusively on the rights of Southern states. The resolutions were referred to a conference committee and then the meeting adjourned, to meet at the call of the chairman,[64] an event that never occurred.

The principal activity in the Assembly on Tuesday, February 26, was consideration on repealing the act which had created the Pork, Beef and Salt Provisions Inspectors. Showalter supported the repeal as "useful legislation" which should not involve "factious fight" and called the question (to repeal), which lost on a 29–29 tie vote. A new motion to indefinitely postpone the matter, which Showalter supported, failed, 31–33. The repeal legislation was then ordered engrossed by a 32–30 vote, with Showalter against.[65] It was more of the same on the 27th of February. T.M. Horrell (D–Amador) moved scheduling election of a United States Senator to March 2. Showalter was among those voting 38–30 to table Horrell's motion. The resolution on State of the Union was again postponed until the next day.[66] Then, on the last day of February, it was postponed until March 1.[67]

On February 28, Showalter spoke on a more mundane legislative matter. The Committee on Public Morals reported a Senate bill for a California Institute for the Deaf, Dumb and Blind, which would involve appropriation of $12,000 for new buildings. Haun and Conness spoke in favor of a smaller per annum sum per pupil. An amendment for a smaller appropriation was passed. Showalter, with his usual fiscal conservatism, moved an amendment to halve the new buildings appropriation. He felt that the one building already housing the Institute was good and that there was nothing indicating a need for an additional one. He said that he was willing to vote for a moderate sum, but not to "go it blind." Conness, in opposing Showalter's amendment, mentioned during his remarks that if Showalter should go blind, he would find at the school an institution for him. At this point, Showalter asked Conness if the latter's intention was to cast ridicule on himself. If it were, Showalter said, there was "a tribunal beyond the House to which he could appeal"—an obvious reference to a duel. Conness responded that he was glad "they had a schoolmaster here," but that Showalter had begun the "business" with his own attempt at wit and then went on to make a case for the larger appropriation. Haun spoke in support of Conness. Showalter's amendment was rejected.[68]

On March 1, the Senate endorsed the Crittenden Compromise.[69] It sent the Assembly a Joint Resolution calling for the election of the United States Senator to be accomplished on March 9. Initially, Showalter moved to table the resolution, but withdrew in making a new motion to consider it the next day. Joseph Powell (D–Sacramento) said he hoped the motion would not be pressed since a committee was to leave the next day to inspect the state prison at San Quentin. Showalter offered to pair his vote with that of any member of the committee. By a 22–48 vote, the Assembly did not schedule consideration. The resolution was then tabled, 27–24. Then the Union resolutions came up. C.H. Kungle (B–Yuba) spoke at great length about the resolution and the situation occasioning it. It was his opinion that states had entered the Union voluntarily and could therefore withdraw from it if they felt the need. He said the North was "making war" on slavery, thus giving them reason. He was opposed to coercion of seceded states and pointed out costs to the nation of blockade and/or war. He felt that it was therefore "absurdity" equaled by "its wickedness." Once Kungle's oration was concluded, Showalter moved to take up the Union Resolutions the next afternoon. Conness said he recognized a disposition to vote on these resolutions at an early time, but preferred Thursday of the next week. William Ross suggested that Saturday would be better, to which Showalter observed that many would be absent on a Saturday. Friday was a better day, he said. Conness accepted Friday as the date for a vote on the resolutions.[70]

Saturday, March 2, the Assembly voted 45–26 to concur with the Senate and schedule a vote for United States Senator for March 9. Success in finally scheduling the vote was possible because the previous evening the Breckinridge men had caucused and decided that on this matter each of its members should vote according to their own personal inclination. Even so, ten of them—and all of the Republicans—had voted against.[71] Matters taken up during the intervening days until then were comparatively routine and noncontentious. Zach Montgomery had taken the floor on March 4 to deny comments in the *Sacramento Daily Union* of that morning relating to him. He denied that the Breckinridge men were "out and out secessionists." He was for peace. Conness responded that he was for the preservation of the government.[72] On Tuesday the 5th, the Committee on Mines and Mining Interest reported negatively on a bill. Several members felt that the bill was necessary and proposed that it be referred to a special committee. At this point, Showalter spoke in opposition to what he called "a perfect mania to raise special committees," but a majority voted to so refer it.[73] The Pork, Beef and Salt Provisions Inspectors bill came up. B.S. Lippincott of Calaveras County wanted to postpone the matter indefinitely. Conness wanted to delay it until the next Tuesday. N.C. Miller said he thought postponing the bill would be no more harmful than discussing it for three hours. H.W. Briggs objected to voting on the 5th on such an important bill since some members were absent. Showalter observed that any absent members had been paired off. Lloyd Magruder said that too much time had already been taken up on the bill. He wanted to vote that very day. Finally, a vote was taken and the bill failed, 17–21.[74]

A different sort of bill resulted in considerable discussion when, on Thursday, March 7, the Judiciary Committee reported amendments to a Senate bill establishing a standard of weights and measures. Showalter made motion for an amendment that the bill should not take effect until January 1, 1862. He said that repealing the existing law on weights and measures immediately would be unfair to the sealers (of weights and measures) who had just recently been appointed and had spent large sums for their equipment. Montgomery argued that the bill should go into effect in the normal sixty days since it was for the benefit of the people and not for the benefit of the incumbent sealers. Showalter responded that he would vote for the bill if it were amended according to his motion. He felt that those sealers, appointed only three to four weeks prior for distant counties, would be unfairly treated after having just spent $400 to $500 for their standard measures. Sorrel opposed Showalter's contention, stating that replacement of the appointed sealers by county clerks with the clerks retaining payments for inspections would mean loss of monies to the state. Harris stated that the county clerks already had too many duties. Crocker differed, saying the present law was unjust, and the sooner it was repealed, the better. Showalter objected that, under the existing law, sealers received reimbursement in scrip (which was not worth its face value). Crocker wanted immediate effect of the bill's provisions. The bill, despite Showalter's efforts, was passed.[75] Also on this day, Showalter was appointed to a special committee of three to recommend on the transfer of Swamp Lands Fund monies to the General Fund. He would report the committee's favorable recommendation the next day.[76]

The motion on Union Resolutions finally came up on Friday, the 8th of March. It was decided, on a 41–24 vote pursuant to a motion by Piercy, to consider the preamble and each resolution separately. Showalter and the other "Brecks" all voted in the minority against the motion.[77] John White (D–Shasta) moved a substitute that "we cordially indorse the plan of Compromise for the difficulties now existing in the Atlantic States, by the Hon. John J. Crittenden, in the Senate of the United States; and that pending the existing difficulties, we condemn the use of force to coerce the people of the seceding States, and that we prefer compromise to war, and concession rather than disunion." He was ruled out of order by the Speaker, whose decision was sustained on appeal. The wording of Conness was then adopted. Montgomery moved that the first subdivision of the resolution be amended to read: "Except in cases where it becomes necessary for the protection of such State against infractions of the Federal Compact, each State has the right to judge for itself, as well of infractions of said compact, as of the mode and measure of relief." Showalter and all of the other Breckinridge faction voted for Montgomery's amendment, but it failed, 30–36. A minor amendment, also offered by Montgomery, to the second subdivision was carried and the amended subdivision also passed. Assemblyman P.H. Harris moved that the third subdivision be amended by striking out three lines. This amendment passed, 48–14, with only Breckinridge men (including Showalter) opposed.[78]

John Conness then moved to adopt the resolutions as negotiated by the Committee on Federal Relations. Zach Montgomery moved an amendment to add: "And we deprecate any attempt on the part of the General Government to maintain by force of arms the union of these States since to do so, would light the fire of civil war, and crush forever the last hope of reconciliation between the opposing sections." Frank Fargo moved an amendment to the amendment to add the words "unless it be necessary to vindicate its integrity" after the word "States." Kungle moved a substitute for the resolutions that included the words "reserving each State to itself the residuary means of right to their own self-government ... the government was not made the exclusive or final Judge ... each party has an equal right to judge for itself as well of Infractions as of the mode and measure of redress." A motion then made by Showalter for adjournment failed, 19–44. A motion to sustain the motion of Conness failed, 29–30, with Showalter casting a "No" vote. A motion by Crocker to take the matter up the following Monday failed, as did another Showalter motion to adjourn.[79]

Dan Showalter then made his own motion for amendment. It stated:

> Resolved, That the people of the State of California acknowledge neither the North nor the South, but the whole American Union as their common mother to whom they are united not merely by considerations of interest, but by the more enduring ties of blood and filial affection.
>
> Resolved, That as Californians we are willing to stand by the whole Union, hazarding if necessary our lives, and our fortunes, for her defense; but we are not prepared to pledge our allegiance to either a Northern or Southern fragment of a dismembered confederacy, nor will we ever consent to become the ally of one section in waging a fratricidal war against another section of our common country.

The vote on Showalter's amendment was relatively close, but it failed, 29–33.[80]

Fargo then withdrew his proposed amendment to Montgomery's amendment, which then failed on a 26–37 vote. Finally, the Assembly was ready to vote on the Union Resolutions. They passed, 40–22. Voting "Yes" with the Douglasites and Republicans was, surprisingly, Dan Showalter.[81] His reason for so voting with the majority for passage became apparent the next day—Saturday, March 9—when he moved reconsideration of the vote on Tuesday following. This would provide time for Union Resolutions foes to attempt to persuade others to join them in rejecting the resolutions. Conness immediately moved to postpone Showalter's reconsideration motion indefinitely. His motion passed, 41–30.[82] The resolutions and the debate upon them in the Assembly were summarized the next day in San Francisco's *Daily Alta California*: "The resolutions adopted by a decided majority are very conservative in their character, and yet their tenor cannot be misunderstood. They advocate the execution of the laws under the Federal Constitution and bitterly oppose Secessionism."[83] The California Assembly had weighed in on the side of the national government.

The Assembly then took up the matter of transferring money from the Swamp Lands Fund to the General Fund. There was some debate against the bill. Showalter spoke in its favor, saying that "I am not one of those who come here and talk of an act for the purpose of Buncombe" and that there was no good objection to passage of the bill. He pointed out that the money could not be used for swamp lands before November, so its use in the General Fund was opposed by speculators who were in the habit of buying up state obligations at discount. Others wished to postpone the matter, including N. Greene Curtis, who proposed sending it to the Committee on Ways and Means. Showalter pointed out that that committee, of which he was a member, were all in favor of the bill. Two of the committee (Magruder and Miller) disagreed, saying that they were opposed to it. After a motion to postpone failed, a 38–35 vote resulted in passage of the measure.[84]

"Buncombe" (more frequently spelled "bunkum" or simply "bunk" today) was then a relatively new term. Its first use had been in 1845 by North Carolina Congressman French Walker in defending one of his speeches by claiming he was "speaking to Buncombe [County]" and had already come to be understood as insincere speechmaking solely to please local constituents.

The members of the Senate then entered the chamber, and the joint convention to elect a United States Senator to the vacancy caused by the expiration of the term of Senator William Gwin finally began. The first nomination made was that of former Governor John B. Weller by Fleming Amyx of the Breckinridge caucus. The Republicans then nominated T.G. Phelps. The main portion of the Douglas caucus then nominated former Governor John A. McDougall. Two groups of dissident Douglasites placed in nomination the names of John Nugent and James W. Denver. G.W. Bowie, J.P. Hoge and N.E. Whitesides were also nominated. A ballot was then immediately taken with the following result: McDougall—27, Weller—27, Phelps—23, Denver—16, Nugent—9, Whitesides—5, Hoge—2, Bowie—2, and two scattered votes for Heacock and Creanor.[85] Four more ballots would be taken that day with no nominee receiving the necessary majority. The second ballot had McDougall leading with twenty-six votes, closely followed by Phelps and Weller, both with twenty-three votes. Denver had seventeen and Nugent eleven. The remaining eleven votes were scattered. Other than Weller falling slightly behind Phelps, there was little change on the third, fourth and fifth ballots. The responsibility for failure to elect largely rested with the factionalism of the Assembly members. Finally, the joint convention adjourned to meet again on Monday.[86]

When the Assembly returned to its sole deliberations, Showalter asked and received "leave" to change his vote on the Union Resolutions from "Yes" to "No," indicating that there was no chance of reconsideration changing the result to rejection of the resolutions. W.P. Tilden moved that John Housman, Clerk of the Assembly Committee on State Prisons, be paid $64 mileage per diem. The matter was referred to a special committee consisting of Showalter, A.W. Blair (R–Monterey) and Joseph Powell. The Assemblymen then adjourned for the day.[87]

On Monday, March 11, Showalter was part of a 6–49 majority that refused to override the governor's veto of an Assembly bill on the burning of bricks in San Francisco.[88] Then controversy reared its head again. Frank Fargo then moved the following resolution:

> Whereas, one of more members of this House are reported to have said, in the course of debate, upon this floor, that they recognize as being a sovereign confederacy those States presided over by Jefferson Davis, of Mississippi, and which were independent and sovereign in every respect; therefore,
> Resolved, That the Judiciary Committee be, and are hereby instructed to report to the House, at its earliest convenience, whether or not such sentiments are compatible with the constitutional obligations of members of the Legislature of California.

Upon the resolution's introduction, Showalter immediately moved that it be rejected. Fargo was given leave to withdraw his motion.[89] Thereafter, Showalter was part of a 44–23 majority voting to pass Assembly Bill 74, selling 500,000 acres of land granted to the state for school purposes and donating 72 acres for a Seminary of Learning.[90]

At noon, the Senate entered the Assembly chamber for resumption of the joint convention to elect a United States Senator. Five more ballots (numbers six through ten) were taken. McDougall stayed in the lead on all of these ballots, receiving from twenty-six to twenty-eight votes. The twenty Republicans remained steadfast for Phelps. Denver was ahead of Nugent by one vote on the sixth ballot, but then fell behind. Showalter, who had been voting for Weller, switched his vote to Denver. Weller's vote fell considerably, from nineteen down to only ten on the tenth ballot.[91] Once deliberations of the joint convention concluded for the day, the Assembly reconvened solely to adjourn itself until the next day.[92]

After the marathon balloting for Assembly Speaker in January, observers were beginning to wonder if the Senate election would be more of the same. On the morning of Tuesday, March 12, legislators were greeted by a "No United States Senator" headline in San Francisco's *Daily Alta California*. The brief article observed that "at 2 P.M. to-day the Convention will again go through the monstrous farce of voting for their favorites, not one of whom can come within thirty votes of an election." The writer opined that "no Senator can be elected this winter."[93] The impasse also resulted in a *Sacramento Daily Union* report entitled "A Remarkable Case of Fusion." It seems that the various factions had printed pamphlets, each advancing its candidate and positions. The materials for the pamphlets of the Breckinridge and the Republican factions had been sent to the same printer. Through error, the last half of Assemblyman Laspeyre's remarks for the Breckinridge faction had been printed as the last half of the comments of Frank Fargo in the Republican pamphlet. As a result, the published pamphlet had stalwart Republican Fargo stating, about reasons for the secession of the Southern states, that "before high Heaven, they are justifiable" and "I will now proceed to the task of proving that the Black Republican party [sic] are an Abolition party." When extracts of the erroneous pamphlet were read on the floor of the Assembly, they provoked roars of laughter. Douglas faction leader Conness remarked that they proved what he had said all along, "that these extreme parties have found their affinities."[94] Shortly thereafter the joint convention resumed its task and took three more ballots. McDougall retained his lead, followed by Phelps, Nugent and Denver. The number of scattered votes increased on the twelfth and thirteenth ballots. Showalter resumed voting for Weller on this day's ballots.[95] The prediction of the *Alta*'s reporter looked as if it might be so.

The Assembly session on Wednesday, March 13, began with lengthy "Personal Explanations" arising from newspaper reports on a long-running bill to change the venue of a trial of Horace Smith (for the murder one Samuel T. Newell[96]). Thomas Laspeyre stated that Alex. Campbell had used language in debate to which he had taken offense. He felt that Campbell's language had intimated that "lobby influence" was guiding members of the legislature on the bill and that a report in the *Sacramento Daily Union* had Campbell saying that Laspeyre was one of those influenced. Campbell responded that his remarks the previous day were to the effect that he opposed the bill to change venue because he felt the matter should be left to the judges, who were acquainted with the laws, rather than left to "the confusion always attendant upon legislative bodies to some extent; not surrounded by lobby members laboring to influence the feelings and bias the judgement of the Legislature." Campbell continued, "I did not suppose at that time I made the statement that I had said anything at which any member could possibly take personal offense. I did not suppose that any member of this House entertained for one moment the idea that I had charged corruption in reference to the bill." He felt that the remarks of Laspeyre were personal charges upon himself. Laspeyre stated that the *Union* had reported remarks of his correctly and wished Campbell to state if those remarks were untrue. Campbell said the reported remarks were not offensive, that he had understood Laspeyre differently. John Conness then intervened, remarking, "I do not know that I have any right to interfere in this matter, but it seems to me unnecessary to waste time about it, because everybody knows that lobby influence does not affect anybody here. I thought everybody understood that."[97] The laughter that resulted from the members and in the gallery resolved a potentially dangerous Laspeyre-Campbell dispute.

B.S. Lippencott then reported for a special committee on Senate Bill 18 to establish a Boundary Commission to cooperate with a United States Boundary Commission in locating and marking a portion of the boundary between California and the Territory of Nevada. The bill was passed with its appropriation reduced, by $2,000, to $10,000. Other "minor" matters were briefly discussed, and Showalter was appointed to a special committee to recommend upon paying $6.00 per diem to the Clerk of the Committee on State Prisons. This was followed by considerable debate over the matter of "apportionment" (today called "reapportionment") of the legislature according to the 1860 Federal Census. A special committee was appointed to investigate and research the matter and then provide recommendations. Showalter took no part in this debate—he had been absent, meeting with his special committee on the State Prison Clerk's per diem. His committee recommended the per diem be paid since the clerk, John Housman, had taken the job on the understanding that he would be paid per diem mileage. Showalter added that in the future he would oppose all such proposals to allow mileage to any committee clerk. The resolution passed. After a few other matters, the Assembly and Senate met again in joint convention. Only one ballot, the fourteenth, was taken for Senator. There was very little change, although Showalter again, on this ballot, case his vote for Denver.[98]

The *Daily Alta California* of Friday, March 15, complained that many legislators were paying "very little attention" to important matters and specifically that "there exists in the minds of some country Representatives a jealousy of San Francisco which has become not only bitter but chronic."[99] This was perhaps so. Among the actions taken that day in the Assembly was one to reduce the fare of passengers on street railcars, but they did pass Assembly Bill 57, providing railroad tracks in San Francisco for horse cars to run on.[100] This was followed by debate on a Senate bill appropriating money to pay the claims of some for transporting arms and munitions to the Carson Valley (there had been a campaign the previous summer against Indians in the area). Many seemed to feel that the governor's actions on the matter had been unconstitutional; others that, although unconstitutional, the claims were equitable. Showalter spoke against referring the bill to a special committee, saying that he was sure the House was tired of the matter and that, "whether the Governor went beyond his constitutional powers or not, the necessity of the case required it." He voted for the bill and it passed.[101]

Joint convention with the Senate followed. Two more ballots for U.S. Senator were conducted, with McDougall receiving twice the votes of any other Democratic candidate. Republican Phelps remained in second place. There was no election. For some reason, though he was present, Showalter did not cast his vote on either ballot. It was he, though, who moved the adjournment until Tuesday.[102] On March 17, the *Daily Alta California* correspondent reported that this adjournment was because "the Breckinridge men 'smelt a mice' when the disaffected [Douglasites] 'broke cover.'" The correspondent went on to state that they "knew very well that the twenty-four Republican votes would have gone over *en masse* for McDougall had another ballot been held." He predicted that "there will be a desperate struggle on Tuesday. The Breckinridgers are trying to get up a joint caucus."[103] Neither Saturday nor Monday saw any contention or controversy in the Assembly. It would seem that there were indeed various caucuses meeting about the Senate election.

Tuesday morning's Assembly activity centered around bills for a bridge in El Dorado County, a San Bruno turnpike with toll-gate between San Francisco and San Mateo Counties, and bills relating to the State Militia. The militia bills were quite lengthy and, upon a motion by Showalter, were considered by the Assembly as a Committee of the Whole. Officers of militia and funding occupied most of the discussion. No action was taken this day since the time arrived for the joint convention with the Senate.[104] Showalter immediately moved adjournment of the convention until 2:00 p.m. the next day. His motion failed, 48–62. Before balloting for Senator began, Assemblyman A.W. Blair (R–Monterey) rose and said that the people of California expected them to elect a United States Senator and that he was willing to vote for "any good Union man that could be elected," but would abstain from voting for the time being. Neither a seventeenth nor an eighteenth ballot resulted in election. After the balloting, Blair had his vote recorded for Phelps. A new candidate, former legislator (and future Confederate general) Joseph Lancaster Brent of Los Angeles, received four votes on each of these two ballots. Casting their votes for him were Senator Pio Pico (who had served as the last governor of Alta California under Mexican rule) and Assemblymen Piercy, Wood of Yolo, and Showalter.[105]

That night, March 19, the dissident anti–McDougall Douglas men and the Breckinridge men caucused together behind closed doors for what the correspondent of the *Daily Alta California*, to whom information had been leaked, called a "turbulent session." It took them thirty ballots to select a candidate for Senator—John Nugent (a San Francisco journalist, editor of the *San Francisco Herald*, and 1856 opponent of the Vigilance Committee[106]). The correspondent said that "at least four of the adherents of Denver and Weller will in no event vote for Nugent." He thought that the Republicans, though, would vote for no Democrat other than McDougall. He predicted that "there will be desperate rally for Nugent to-day [his report was printed the morning of Wednesday, March 20], but beyond his ardent personal friends, few really desire his election."[107]

The nineteenth ballot for United States Senator, taken when the joint convention reconvened on March 20, revealed that the dissidents and Breckinridge men had indeed come together on a candidate. Just prior to the taking of the ballot, Assemblyman Wood of Plumas rose and withdrew the nomination of Denver. When the votes were recorded, Nugent led with forty-five votes, McDougall had twenty-nine, and Phelps had twenty-three. Weller retained six votes and seven were scattered. After the ballot, Assemblyman Charles W. Piercy rose to explain his abstention. He acknowledged that he had taken part in the previous evening's "Nugent caucus," but he "could not endorse the sentiments entertained and enunciated by the nominee of that caucus." He further stated that "he owed greater allegiance to his country than to consistency, and he could not, therefore, sustain the nomination of Mr. Nugent." The twentieth and twenty-first ballots produced much the same results, but with Piercy casting his vote for Weller. The result of the twenty-second ballot was McDougall—56 (including those of the Republicans and of Piercy), Nugent—47, Weller—6, and four scattered votes for Assembly Clerk Anderson, Casserly, Creanor and Phelps. When the votes were tallied, those for Anderson and Casserly were omitted. This gave McDougall a majority, and certification of his election as United States Senator was signed by the President of the Senate and the Speaker of the Assembly and sent to the governor.[108]

The Senate election was not over, though. March 22's *Sacramento Daily Union,* under the headline "The Senatorial Imbroglio," reported that McDougall "still stands as the Senator elect." Its writer felt that it would be "difficult, if not impossible, to correct the official announcement of the President of the Convention, even if found erroneous." There was no journal of the convention (none was required by law). The paper believed that the certification of McDougall would stand. It concluded that "the error in the count and announcement, if made as alleged, is not chargeable to the friends of McDougall."[109] The *Daily Alta California* called the situation of the miscounted votes and certification of McDougall a "terrible muddle."[110] The situation even excited comment from the correspondent of the *New York Times*, whose report, appearing on April 19, noted that the Senate favored revising the vote, but the Assembly was refusing another joint convention. This writer's conclusion was that "the probabilities are that McDougall may be considered elected—at least so far as the present Legislature is concerned."[111]

Joint conventions of the Senate and Assembly were, in any case, not over. They had to meet together on Thursday, March 21, to elect a Resident Physician, a Visiting Physician, and two Trustees for the State Insane Asylum at Stockton. There were five nominees for Resident Physician, among them Assemblyman W.P. Tilden (D–Butte), who was a doctor. Six ballots were conducted with no doctor achieving the necessary majority. Showalter's preference, Dr. W.D. Aylette, led on all ballots, followed by Tilden with the other three trailing. Tilden's vote increased on each ballot after the first at the expense of the trailing three.[112]

On Friday, March 22, John Conness renewed a motion of the previous day by Thomas Laspeyre that a committee of three be appointed to meet with a similar committee of the Senate to investigate and report on "doubts as to the accuracy of the count of votes for the office of United States Senator." The motion passed, and Speaker Burnell appointed Conness, Laspeyre and Fargo to the committee.[113] Also on this day, the Assembly voted for the incorporation of the town of Hornitos in Mariposa County near the Horseshoe Bend residence of Showalter, received a committee report recommending the organization of Lake County, and the recommendation of the Committee on Public Morals for passage of Assembly Bill 51, "an Act to Prevent the Amalgamation of the Different Races." A majority, including Showalter, voted for construction of wharfs at the foot of several San Francisco streets.[114] Then the joint convention met again and took five more ballots without electing a Resident Physician for the insane asylum. The seventh through eleventh ballots were close, but with different leaders. Aylette led Tilden on the seventh ballot, Tilden led on the eighth through tenth ballots, and the eleventh was tied 36–36. With the other three doctors splitting the remaining votes, neither Tilden nor Aylette were ever close to victory.[115]

On Saturday, March 23, the Assembly refused to concur with Senate Resolution 26, to meet in joint convention to elect a United States Senator.[116] On Monday the 25th, Assembly Bill 280, to repeal a prior act to aid in construction of the Washington Monument, was referred to the Committee on Ways and Means.[117] Tuesday the 26th, Fargo reported that census data had been received from the Secretary of State, so apportionment of Senate and Assembly districts could proceed. A committee of one member of the Assembly from each senate district was approved (Showalter opposed). With Showalter in the chair, consideration of an Assembly bill to create Alturas County was postponed until the next day. The Assembly finally concurred with a Senate Resolution to elect a Boundary Commission.[118] Then the joint convention met again and took seven more ballots for Resident Physician. Aylette led on five, Tilden led on one, and one ballot was tied. Neither approached the necessary majority for election.[119]

On the 27th, Speaker Burnell announced his appointments to the Special Committee to Report a Bill of Apportionment. Assemblyman O.K. Smith was appointed for the senate district which included Fresno, Mariposa, Merced, and Tulare Counties.[120] After a few miscellaneous items of legislation, it was again time for the joint convention. Five more ballots for Insane Asylum Resident Physician were taken. Tilden led on all of them, but continued to fall short of a majority.[121] The Assembly's time on Thursday, March 28, was largely consumed by two joint conventions with the Senate. After a failed motion by O.K. Smith to exclude all but senators and assemblymen from the hall, three more ballots (the twenty-fourth through twenty-sixth) to elect a Resident Physician were taken. Tilden led on all three, but did not receive the necessary majority. Further balloting for the position was adjourned until Wednesday, April 3.[122]

The second joint convention of the day was for the purpose of electing a Boundary Commissioner, who would work with a Federal Commissioner to determine and mark the state's boundary with the Nevada Territory. There were four nominations made: R.P. Hammond of San Joaquin County, J.C. McKibben of Sierra County, R.C. Mathewson of San Francisco, and Ferris Forman of Sacramento, who was nominated by N. Greene Curtis. Forman, followed closely by McKibben, led on the first five ballots. "Scattering" votes made their appearance on the sixth ballot, including one for Showalter cast by Assemblyman Sorrel. Perhaps to the surprise of all, the seventh ballot resulted in an election. The final vote was Forman—60, McKibben—34, Mathewson—8, and Hammond—2. Showalter had voted for Forman on all seven ballots.[123] Forman was never to serve in the position to which he had been elected. The Interior Department cancelled its participation due to lack of appropriation by Congress of funds for the purpose.[124]

The protracted balloting of all the joint conventions provoked criticism in the press. In the March 29 edition of the *Daily Alta California*, its Sacramento correspondent commented that "the various Joint Conventions are interfering seriously with State legislation." He noted over ninety pending bills between the Senate and the Assembly, with some of them being "of vast importance."[125] Perhaps in reaction, the next few days were relatively quiet, with legislators devoting themselves to actual legislation. The Assembly addressed its backlog of bills on Friday the 29th by voting to convene its future sessions at 10:00 a.m. instead of 11:00 a.m.[126] On Saturday, March 30, the United States Senate election arose again. The question about the validity of McDougall's election would not go away. The Senate adopted an Assembly Concurrent Resolution to consider the March 20 vote. Yet another Assembly Concurrent Resolution (moved by Lippencott) to hold another joint convention on April 2 for the purpose of electing a senator passed, 38–32. Showalter had voted "No" on the resolution.[127]

Assembly proceedings on April 1 and the morning of the 2nd were devoted to routine legislation. Among the bills considered was Senate Bill 66, to appropriate state money for the support of the Ladies' Seamen's Friend Society of San Francisco. The society had in the past been supported by private charity. The Committee on Ways and Means, including Showalter, recommended indefinite postponement of a vote. Campbell, a San Franciscan, spoke against postponement, saying that it was a worthy purpose, and asked for the reasons for the committee's recommendation. Speaking for the committee, Magruder responded that the institution was laudable, but that the Assembly had not funded any kind of charity other than to orphans and deaf and dumb children and could not justify any other appropriations to charity. Amyx contended otherwise, to which Crocker replied that seamen were notoriously improvident and dissipated, and questioned where it would all end if the state started making such appropriations. He concluded his remarks stating that "there was another class, namely, broken down politicians, who were notoriously improvident and dissipated in their habits. It was just as necessary to establish an institution for them as for seamen." Showalter supported Crocker, stating the committee was unanimous in its recommendation. He then pointed out that the people of the mountains could just as well ask for an appropriation for broken down miners as the people of San Francisco could for broken down sailors. He said that, in the mountains, people contributed to help injured miners until they could work again and that was what the people of San Francisco should do. He believed approval of the bill would encourage idleness. After further lengthy discussion of the bill, it was finally approved by a 39–26 vote.[128]

The committee also recommended indefinitely postponing the next item, a Senate bill pertaining to San Francisco auctioneers, but postponement was voted down, 27–39. At this, Showalter gave notice that he would no longer serve on the Committee on Ways and Means since it was apparent to him that the committee was of "no use." Lloyd Magruder expressed the same sentiment, and the Assembly excused the both of them from the committee.[129] Some discussion of creating an Esmeralda County followed, and then it was time for the joint convention to meet and, hopefully, resolve the election of a United States Senator. A message from James A. McDougall was received and read. In it, he relinquished any right or claim he might have to election by the convention on March 20. He requested only that they proceed without further delay to elect a senator to represent the state. Laspeyre offered resolutions to cancel the election certificate which had been issued since they had convened without any official notice that no senator had been elected on the 20th. There was extensive debate on the appropriateness of Laspeyre's resolutions, the circumstances surrounding the vote on March 20, and McDougall's message. Showalter took only a small part in these discussions. Several motions to postpone failed. Finally, a ballot was taken. Its result was McDougall—57, Nugent—39, and scattered—8. This time, McDougall had an actual majority and was declared elected.[130]

On Wednesday, the 3rd of April, Showalter was among the 39–27 majority voting to reconsider passage of the bill regarding San Francisco auctioneers. The bill creating Esmeralda County was amended, changing the county's name to Mono. Yet another bill creating a county—Alturas—was passed by the Assembly.[131] Then it was time for yet another joint convention to continue the balloting for Resident Physician of the insane asylum. Three ballots were conducted, Showalter continuing to vote for Dr. Aylette on all of them, and, on the twenty-ninth ballot, Tilden was elected.[132] The convention proceeded immediately to election of the asylum's Visiting Physician. Seven doctors were nominated for the post, the seventh of which was a Dr. Limon of Mariposa, who was nominated by Showalter. A first ballot found Dr. Limon receiving only two votes (those of Showalter and his fellow Mariposan, Assemblyman Gregory) and his nomination was withdrawn before the next ballot. Only four ballots were necessary to elect Dr. Clark of El Dorado County.[133]

There was no controversy on the Assembly floor on Thursday, April 4. On this day, Dan Showalter introduced his first legislative bill of the session. This was an act to authorize construction of a wharf at the foot of Howard Street in San Francisco. After two readings, Showalter's bill was referred to the Committee on Commerce and Navigation.[134]

Then, on Friday there was another joint convention—this time to elect trustees for the State Insane Asylum. Perhaps the legislators were growing weary of continued voting on nominees in such conventions. After six nominations were made, it only took one ballot to elect three trustees. Showalter had voted for only one nominee, but that one, L.R. Bradley, was one of those elected.[135] The joint convention had, however, made another mistake: only two Trustee seats were to have been elected. Over the next four sessions, April 6 and April 8 through 10, legislation proceeded without controversy.

Then, on the 11th, controversy arose again. This time it was provoked by a relatively minor matter—amendment of a previous act granting the right to construct a dam and locks across Napa Creek. Showalter reported that the assemblyman from Napa County, Breckinridge Democrat J.B. Scott, was absent at home on important business and requested postponement until Scott's return. Long debate over postponement followed. Breckinridgers Laspeyre, Magruder, Munday and Sorrel all spoke in favor of postponing a vote on the amendment. Douglas Democrats Flanders, Dougherty and Conness all spoke for an immediate vote. Magruder mentioned that State Senator Henry Edgerton, who represented Napa, had been on the floor of the Assembly talking to members about the bill. John Conness then stated that some language in speaking of Edgerton was "unparliamentary and uncourteous." Laspeyre rose and said that if Conness was saying he (Laspeyre) had used such language, that "you tell what is false." Conness responded, "You are a dirty dog." At this, Laspeyre threw an inkstand at Conness, which struck the floor, splattering ink. Conness then threw his own inkstand at Laspeyre. It too spattered ink over several assemblymen. Laspeyre drew a Bowie knife and rushed toward Conness, who was headed toward him. Other assemblymen arose out of their seats to restrain them both. In the words of the *Sacramento Daily Union*'s reporter, who had observed the event from the gallery, "the utmost excitement prevailed." The Assembly's Sergeant at Arms was unable to effect an arrest, the lobby was filled, and order was not restored for several minutes. Conness then expressed his regrets for the incident, stating that he had not intended any insult or offense to anyone, but that he was justified in replying to a similar charge of discourtesy against himself. After some further discussion, Conness withdrew his objection to postponement of a vote on the amendment.[136]

It was during this period that there was a fracus between Dan Showalter and J.C. McKibben (a former congressman). One newspaper, the *Times*, reported that McKibben had gotten Showalter's head "in chancery" and that he had "whipped" Showalter. The *Mariposa Gazette* (Showalter's "hometown paper") of April 16 disputed this, writing: "We will bet the last dollar of our political perquisites now on hand, that Showalter can whip McKibben in just three minutes.... The facts are, it was a scrimmage, 'late at night,' and when the combatants closed, they were separated, without damage of consequence to either."[137]

At various times during the sessions, Speaker Burnell had temporarily been absent or relinquished the chair in order to address legislation himself. During those periods, he had asked various members of the Assembly, including Showalter a few times, to preside in his stead. When the Assembly convened on Friday, April 12, 1861, Showalter took the chair, stating that he was doing so at the request of Speaker Burnell, who was sick and confined to bed. He then called Andrew J. Gregory, his Mariposa County colleague, to take the chair. William Coleman (D–El Dorado) then moved that the Assembly elect a Speaker *pro tem*. The motion was passed. George W. Patrick (B–Tuolumne) then nominated Showalter for the post. J.M. Avery (R–Nevada) nominated Frank Fargo. There were sixty assemblymen present. The vote was Showalter—39, Fargo—12, O.K. Smith—6, Conness—1. The Assembly's *Journal* recorded:

> Mr. Showalter having received a majority of all votes cast, was declared duly elected Speaker *pro tem* for the remainder of the session.
> Messrs. Patrick and [N. M.] Gordon [B-Marin] were appointed a committee to conduct Mr. Showalter to the Chair.
> The oath of office was administered by the Chief Clerk.

Gregory then introduced Dan Showalter to the Assembly as its Speaker *pro tem*.[138]

Contrary to almost all previous balloting—for Speaker, for United States Senator, for Assembly patronage jobs, for insane asylum doctors—election of a Speaker *pro tem* took only one ballot and was non-factional. The members voting for Showalter comprised sixteen fellow Breckinridge Democrats, twenty Douglas Democrats, two Republicans, and the sole Union member. Fargo had received the votes of twelve Republicans and two Douglas Democrats, one of the Conness faction of Democrats. O.K. Smith's vote was from five Douglas Democrats and one Republican. One Republican cast his vote for Conness. As was customary in those days of "let the office seek the man," neither Showalter nor Fargo voted. A third non-voter was Charles W. Piercy.[139] It is not known why on this date, so far into the session, the Assembly decided to elect a Speaker *pro tem*. The fact that they did so and that they elected Showalter by the votes of members from all factions is probably an indication of the personal popularity of Dan Showalter among his fellow members, regardless of political and factional differences. Likewise, he had no doubt exhibited both ability and fairness when presiding.

One of the first official acts as Speaker *pro tem* that Showalter performed was to certify, on the 12th, the Assembly's concurrence in the Senate's April 10 override of an act granting the right for construction along the shore of San Francisco bay. This certification placed the act among the statutes of California.[140] The Assembly convened on Saturday, April 13, with the new Speaker *pro tem* in the chair. The short session of that day went smoothly, with no controversies or fights.[141] Burnell was back in the chair on Monday, April 15. The first item of business was a report by Fargo of the Committee on Apportionment on the results of the 1860 Federal Census. The committee believed that the total population of 380,015 reported for the state by the census was understated by 100,000. They also complained that, for the nine southernmost counties, the census made no distinction by race. After some discussion, vote on a bill of apportionment was scheduled for April 23.[142] The sessions on Tuesday and Wednesday progressed without any controversy. The only significant debate was about the dam on Napa Creek. Showalter argued that there were differences between the original bill and the one passed by the Senate on Tuesday previous. He said that time was needed to study the changes regarding the rate of tolls and the length of time for which the franchise for the dam was granted. He observed that the reporter for the *Napa Reporter* was "quite in the dark about it." His view prevailed, and a vote on the bill was postponed for one week.[143] The major item of legislation on Thursday the 18th was a vote on ratification of an amendment to the United States Constitution—the Crittenden Compromise. Showalter voted with the sixty-one member majority for ratification, with only nine Breckinridge Democrats opposed.[144]

Friday, April 19, went smoothly, and the Assembly adjourned to meet next on the following Monday. Saturday was not for all of the assemblymen an "off day," however.

An excursion was made to Folsom by the State Prison Committee to inspect the granite quarries. Afterwards, the chairman of the committee, Dr. Joseph Powell, requested that the *Sacramento Daily Union* state that "on the principle of honor to whom honor is due," Dan Showalter was "entitled to a full share of credit for the attentions paid to the excursionists." This the paper did in its issue of April 23, 1861.[145] Monday, Tuesday and Wednesday of the next week passed calmly in the Assembly. It was likewise on Thursday the 26th until debate on the appropriation for the State Reform School.

Certain "expressions" used in the debate by Assemblyman J.A. Banks (R–San Francisco) were found to be objectionable by Assemblyman D.L. Haun (B–Yuba). Shortly after adjournment that day and in the Assembly chamber, Haun struck Banks over the head with his cane. Other members interfered, ending the assault. Showalter was in the chair the next morning, when the Assembly convened. The very first item of business was introduction by Alex. Campbell of a resolution that a committee of five members be elected to inquire into the assault and report back the facts and their opinions. He compared the incident to the 1856 assault with his cane, inside the national capitol building, of South Carolina Representative Preston Brooks upon Massachusetts Senator Charles Sumner. Not surprisingly, much discussion followed. Fleming Amyx said the motion should be out of order since the incident did not occur during session. Wood of Plumas differed. Giving examples of incidents which had occurred in Congress and in the Missouri legislature, he felt that an investigating committee was appropriate. Magruder said that the Assembly had wisely overlooked "flagrant wrongs" upon its members in the past and should do so again. Campbell said that the Assembly had been lax in doing so. Amyx said the resolution was proper since Haun had no right to hold Banks accountable for words spoken during debate. Speaker *pro tem* Showalter intervened and suggested that the resolution should specify the time the incident occurred. Campbell then amended his resolution, specifying that the incident happened "after the adjournment of the House." The amended resolution passed, and Showalter appointed a committee of five: Amyx (B), Childs (D), Gregory (B), J.H. Harrison (B–Yuba), and O.F. Willey (R–San Francisco).[146] It would seem that with these appointments he sought a committee that would be favorable toward his fellow Breckinridger, Haun. If so, nobody objected to the appointments.

In other early action that day, Showalter appointed Conness, Sorrel, and Wood of Plumas a committee to report a substitute for Senate Bill 321, to distribute $400,000 *pro rata* among holders of Indian War Bonds.[147] News from the East that the Confederates had attacked the United States garrison at Fort Sumter in Charleston Harbor had very recently been received in California. John Conness introduced a bill to move up the 1861 elections for Congress to July. He said that the "extraordinary events" that had taken place necessitated an earlier election to fill vacancies in California's congressional delegation since President Lincoln had called for Congress to convene on July 4. Republican Campbell stated that he initially thought such action desirable, but that the expenses of two elections (only the congressional election would be moved up) in the same year would cripple the state financially. Zach Montgomery deplored "the strife that was going on in the Atlantic States" and said what was needed was a convention of delegates elected by the people of California to determine the state's position. Conness said that he did not wish sectional feeling to be involved and that he owed allegiance solely to the Union government and flag. The amendment to hold an early election of congressmen passed the Assembly by a substantial majority.[148]

Speaker Burnell then arrived and assumed the chair. Debate turned to the time to be permitted the Secretary of State to report the results of the election. George W. Patrick used this opportunity to speak against a tyranny, which he described as the "Union" of the majority in California. Alex. Campbell said that he "could see no reason for the terrible state of excitement [of Patrick]."[149] This line of debate was then interrupted by two members of the committee appointed to investigate the Haun-Banks affair announcing that they wished to be excused from the committee. Alex. Campbell said that even though he had proposed the committee be established, he too would not wish to serve on it. Montgomery moved that the committee be dissolved, and it was by a 24–22 vote in which Showalter voted with the majority.[150] Debate on reporting the congressional election then resumed. It turned to a substitute for the original bill that would move up elections of state officials to June and hold congressional elections at that same time. Showalter spoke at some length in opposition. He said that such an action would entail a cost of $75,000 to $100,000, which he believed the people would not wish to bear just to have representatives in a special session of the Congress. He said his fellow Democrats should consider that they were badly disorganized, while the Republicans in the State were united and were urging a June general election as a favorable opportunity for themselves. He did not want to hurry on and force a general election which the people were not prepared for. He questioned if two representatives from California would be of service, saying, "Could they save the country from ruin, or bring back the lost sheep of the flock? Would the two members from California restore peace and harmony to a distracted country?" He made the observation that the Republicans already had a large majority in Congress and didn't need two more. On the other hand, he said, if by some chance two Democrats were elected, their influence would hardly matter. Douglasite Munday said he was for the Union and believed that two California votes would have weight in Congress. He continued, "All party considerations should be thrown aside, and an election held as soon as practicable." Further debate revealed that Crocker (D) and Fargo (R) were opposed. Eventually the substitute for a general election instead of a special election for the two congressional seats passed, 37–23, with the Republicans in the minority.[151] As it turned out, the election bill did not gain favor in the Senate and the regularly scheduled general election was held on September 4, 1861.

Activity in the Assembly on Saturday the 27th was relatively light. A motion to reconsider the previous day's vote for a June election failed. Showalter introduced a resolution to grant a four months leave of absence for Judge E. Burke of the 13th Judicial District. O.K. Smith opposed the motion, saying he didn't know that the judge wanted a leave of absence, but did know there was a large backlog of judicial business in the court. Showalter responded that he wasn't certain that the judge would use a leave of absence, but that Mrs. Burke had recently gone east to the Atlantic States and that her health was in very critical condition. He said that Judge Burke would clear the court docket before he left and had made arrangements with another judge to cover his duties during any absence. William Ross said he was opposed to leaves of absence for judicial officers on general principles. Gregory moved an amendment, to which Showalter consented, that the judge should obtain another judge before he left. Smith moved an amendment that Judge Burke could not leave before September 1 and had to return by February 1. Showalter opposed that amendment, saying that the purpose of his motion was to allow the judge to go, if it should be necessary, when it should be necessary. C.W. Councilman (R–Nevada) and Magruder spoke in support of Showalter. John Conness questioned the power of the legislature to grant such a leave of absence. Finally, when a vote was taken, Showalter's motion with the Gregory amendment passed, 38-24.[152]

On Monday, April 29, the Assembly occupied itself with routine legislation. The "Act to Prevent Amalgamation of the Different Races of Men" was passed, 33-18, with Showalter and the other Breckinridge men, surprisingly and for an unknown reason, voting against it. Speaking for a special committee, Showalter reported favorably on an act to raise the salaries of judges of the 3rd and 13th Judicial Districts from $3,000 to $4,000 at the next term. After limited discussion, the bill was passed.[153] On April 30, Showalter was again in the chair when the Assembly convened. The only significant and potentially controversial matter handled by the assemblymen on Wednesday, May 1, was the motion of Conness to reconsider the act creating the special election for congressmen. He wanted the date advanced to the third Tuesday in May. Early in the debate, Showalter spoke twice, presenting the problems of timing that would prevent people in distant counties being able to vote. Finally, he made an impassioned speech in opposition:

> I do not think, in all the history of republican governments, an attempt of this kind has ever been placed upon record before. Certainly in all my knowledge of legislative enactments, I never saw one bearing with it the same enormity, the same wrong, the same great injustice upon a free people as this law which you passed yesterday. Not only did you pass that bill, but had it not been for the votes of a few here, you would have passed the bill in worse shape than it stands to-day. I regret that I found a majority of this body, of men who call themselves Republicans and free men, ready to thrust upon the people of this State a measure violative of the election franchise, a measure that would disenfranchise a large number, and that would elect members of Congress to represent us by a voice of but fourteen or fifteen counties of this State. I wish to say to gentlemen to-day, the bill has passed. It may be a capital thing as a party movement. It may place the gentleman from El Dorado [meaning Conness], or the gentleman from San Francisco [meaning Fargo], in Congress; but it does not do justice to a free and independent people. The very author of the bill here—and I charge it on the authority of the press, who attempted to bring on the election within twenty days, is himself a candidate for a high and honorable position, for a seat in our National Congress. It is strange that the gentleman should bring on this bill now. And how do gentlemen meet our arguments on this floor? They turn to you and cry traitor in your teeth. Traitor! I am ready to stand here and battle for the rights of my people! Traitor! Because I like to see right and justice extended to all! Well, Mr. Speaker, I may be a traitor. One thing is very certain, when this cry of war is raised, if he who raises his arm and his voice against it can be denounced as a traitor, then place me down as the arch-traitor of the band. I say this, here in an assembly of free men, and I care not where it goes. Let the press waft it forth throughout the land. I say, sir, if defending the rights of free men constitutes the act of treason, then, too, am I a traitor. These men who cry treason in this hall, have not the manliness to breathe it in the streets. This cry has been heard too often, Mr. Speaker, in order to carry measures through this body. I regret to hear it. I regret to hear men using the term. But I know that those who were denounced as traitors a century ago now live and will continue to live in the hearts of the American people. Gentlemen cannot deter me from what is right by crying treason, because I will not support what I believe to be a wrong—what I believe to be a rank outrage upon my people—this forcing an election upon them when they are illy prepared for it, and when you go about the streets organizing your Jacobin Clubs in order to foist upon the people representatives that they do not desire.[154]

John Conness immediately responded that he did not rise to make any reply, saying, "I find no argument in what he has said," but denying that he, himself, was a candidate for election to Congress. He said he was inclined to think that since Showalter had announced himself as "the arch-traitor ... not meaning a word of it, except that he was the ... leader of the party," he was doing nothing other than introducing himself as a candidate. To this, Conness stated he did not object and "I would say that there is not a gentleman in the State I would sooner have as an opposing candidate than the gentleman from Mariposa." Showalter answered that he had no such aspiration and "I have now reached the very height of my ambition—representing my people in the legislative hall of my State." Additional remarks were made by a few more and then a vote taken. The motion failed, 17–36, with Showalter and the remainder of the Breckinridge faction in the minority. Showalter was then given lead to change his original vote in favor to "No." He stated that he opposed the entire bill and had only voted for the amendment so as to make the entire bill as objectionable as possible.[155]

The Assembly (and the Senate, too) was trying to catch up on pending legislation in anticipation of its pending adjournment. On May 2 they discussed the census results, and, on the 4th, reapportionment for new Senate and Assembly districts was approved, 37–28, with Showalter in the minority.[156] On the 3rd, Showalter had risen "on privilege" to read reports which had appeared in the *San Francisco Call* and the *Sacramento Daily Bee* linking himself and others to "secession rioters" who had disrupted a meeting of U.S. Senator Milton Latham. The reports stated that they had "shouted and huzzaed in the St. George Hotel for Jeff. Davis." Showalter's response was that "I never have in all my life interrupted a public assembly" and that if he didn't like the purpose of some such assembly, he just left. He concluded, "I trust, sir, that the editor of the paper who first started this report without my authority, will do me justice to set me right. If not, I may set myself right."[157] Nothing pertaining to the then-existing war in the East was taken up by the Assembly until Saturday, May 11. On that date, John Conness moved an amendment to the state's Militia Act to provide that no commissions be issued in the militia unless the recipients took an oath administered by an officer of the United States Army in addition to the civil oath. The amendment would also require that those who already held commissions in the militia should take the same oath. The proposed amendment of the Militia Act was defeated on a 15–26 vote, with the Breckinridge faction, including Showalter, voting in the majority.[158] The militia was taken up again on the 13th with talk of an amendment that the salary of the State Adjutant General be increased and that the serving Adjutant General, William C. Kibbe, be removed from office. Showalter spoke in favor of increasing the salary, but for retaining Kibbe in the office.[159]

There was no little excitement in the Assembly chamber on Tuesday, May 14, when a drunken man named Calloway made his way to the desk of the correspondent of the *San Francisco Call* and commenced to loudly threaten him. He was about to draw a Bowie knife when he was removed from the hall on order from Showalter, who was at the time presiding.[160] The legislature met only very briefly on the morning of May 16 and then adjourned to participate and observe the laying of a cornerstone for the new State Capitol building.[161] The next day and a half was devoted to "routine" legislation—"catching up." Then on Friday, May 17, John Conness moved adoption of Senate Concurrent Resolution 78, which read: "Resolved, By the Senate, the Assembly concurring, That the people of California are devoted to the Constitution and Union of the United States, and will not fail in fidelity and fealty to that Constitution and Union now in the hour or trial and peril; that California is ready to maintain the rights and honor of the National Government at home and abroad, and at all times to respond to any request that may be made upon her to defend the Republic against foreign or domestic foes."

The resolution had been brought up somewhat unexpectedly and there was no debate, although several members sought the necessary unanimous consent of the Assembly to explain their votes as the roll was called. Fleming Amyx (B) received consent and explained his "No" vote as being so cast because "no such proceeding as that of Mr. Lincoln is authorized." There were objections to the next voter, A.W. Blair (R), doing so. D.L. Haun (B) managed an explanation, saying simply that Amyx was "my exponent" and voted "No." Laspeyre (B) asked leave to explain his vote. There were objections, but he claimed that a majority was in favor and unsuccessfully attempted to give his explanation. Patrick Munday (D), like Haun, worked his explanation into his vote, saying, "As a true American citizen I vote yes." Thomas O'Brein (D) desired to explain his vote, but did not since there were objections. He voted "Aye." When his turn came, George W. Patrick (B) said he would attempt to say something whether or not he was stopped. His remarks began with a statement that he was going to vote for the resolution because he felt fealty to the Constitution, "but not as Abraham Lincoln interprets that Constitution. I consider his acts as those of a traitor, and in future times he will be put down as such. I vote for the resolution. Yes."

When his turn to vote on the resolution arrived, Dan Showalter said, "I ask leave to explain my vote, and I want to see the gentleman that will rise and object." Immediately, Charles W. Piercy stated, "I make the objection." He gave as reason the fact that Blair had been refused that opportunity and concluded, "I do most emphatically object now to the gentleman form Mariposa explaining his vote." Blair interjected that he hoped Showalter would be heard. Showalter pointed out that he had never himself objected to any member explaining their vote. Piercy tried to interrupt, but Showalter continued, saying, "It is a right which I have always maintained, and I have nothing but contempt for any gentleman who does object. I concur in the sentiments which fell from the lips of the gentleman from Tuolumne [Amyx], and vote no." Piercy stated, "I do most emphatically object to the language of the gentleman from Mariposa.... At all events I object to the language of the gentleman. I meant no disrespect to him in objecting." Showalter still sought leave to explain, and Piercy again objected. At this, Showalter gave up struggling for leave and simply stated, "I vote emphatically NO, because I believe that Lincoln has violated the Constitution." F. Sorrel (B) endorsed the sentiments of Amyx and voted "No." P.H. Harris (D) endorsed the words of Patrick and voted "Yes." Lloyd Magruder (B) said Lincoln's gathering an army at Washington was not constitutional and voted "No." T.J. Chandler (B) remarked, "As a sworn member of this House to support the Constitution, and, as I know no other tie but that, I vote Aye." Thomas Laspeyre (B) moved that Blair (R) be given leave to explain his vote, but such was denied. The so-called "Union Resolution" passed, 48–12. The "Noes" were contributed solely by Showalter and other Breckinridgers. After conclusion of the vote, several members rose "on privilege." One of these was Piercy, who explained that he had objected to explanations of votes because he wanted the voting finished without delay. He asked if Showalter now wished to make an explanation. Showalter responded that if he had been in violation of the rules of the house, he regretted it, but, as applied to "the gentleman from San Bernardino," he had nothing to retract. Piercy angrily replied, "Then I hurl it back in his teeth, and with all the contempt that language can express; and I have not language enough to express it." The next day's *Sacramento Daily Union* applauded passage of the resolution in the Assembly and, of the verbal altercation between Piercy and Showalter, said that it "resulted harmlessly."[162]

Action on some important pending bills was finalized on Saturday, May 18. An "Act for a Better Sabbath" (a "blue law") was passed. Apportionment of Senate and Assembly districts was passed. Organization of the new Mono County was completed, along with passage of a bill to appoint an Assayer of Metals for it. C.H. Kungle (B-Yuba) introduced a resolution "Recognizing the Independence of the Confederate States of America." Kungle was appointed a committee of one to report on the resolution. This he did shortly later—recommending its passage. B.S. Lippincott (D-Calaveras) moved that the resolution be tabled. A 45-11 vote tabled the matter, ending the day's session.[163]

The Assembly and the Senate convened again on Monday, May 20, 1861, for the final day of their sessions. Z.L. Garwood presented a claim for payment of four months rent of committee rooms. Showalter spoke up, saying that Garwood, having already been paid for three months rent, was trying to swindle the state. Showalter said that Garwood should consequently suffer by not being paid even the one month's rent due. Conness agreed with Showalter, stating that Garwood had made deliberate misstatements. John White (D-Shasta) suggested that it would be an injustice to not pay the amount due to Garwood. A motion to pay Garwood was made and tabled. After disposition of a few minor matters, Aaron Wood moved a resolution of the Thanks of the House to Speaker Burnell for "the efficient, dignified, impartial and courteous manner in which he [had] discharged his duties as Speaker." It carried unanimously. Conness then offered a resolution, using the same terms, thanking Showalter for his performance as Speaker *pro tem*. This motion also passed unanimously. Speaker Burnell then spoke, thanking the members of the Assembly.[164] These valedictory remarks ordinarily would have been the final moments before adjournment *sine die* of the body. But being the 1861 Assembly, they were not.

John Conness rose and submitted a report by himself and a majority of a special committee on a petition from the people of Greenwood in El Dorado County. They wanted the state to pass an act to tender to the United States government the credit of the state to aid it in suppression of rebellion. Conness stated that the majority felt that no action was necessary on the petition since the concurrent resolution expressing devotion to the Union had already been passed. A minority report submitted by Montgomery and Kungle had averred that the military could not lawfully be used against the seceding states and that they could not be treated as a foreign power without declaration of war. Their report further stated that the blockade should be removed and that millions of dollars and hundreds of thousands of lives would be saved if Federal troops were removed from fortifications in the South. Their recommendation in regard to the petition was indefinite postponement of any action on it. Since both the committee majority and its minority recommended against action on the petition, albeit for entirely different reasons, the matter was dropped.[165]

Charles W. Piercy then rose with a "question of privilege." He said that upon his objecting to explanations of the vote on the Union Resolution, that "the gentleman from Mariposa" [Showalter] had used language that was "susceptible of being construed into a personal insult" and asked Showalter if that had been the intent of his language. O.K. Smith objected with a point of order that the Assembly had nothing to do with personal difficulties between members. Speaker Burnell thought Smith's point was "well taken." Showalter referred Piercy to reports in the *Union* and to his own explanation the following day. He finished saying, "The language was plain, and it was not susceptible of two constructions." N. Greene Curtis spoke up, reminding of Smith's point of order. The Speaker concurred, and the matter was dropped by the Assembly.[166] Piercy, however, rose and left the Assembly chamber. As he left, a friend said to him, as he passed, that he hoped nothing further would come of it. The somewhat ominous reply of Piercy was that "he acknowledged the code"—a reference to the code duello, a duel—and that he had no alternative.[167]

A resolution informing the governor that the legislature was ready to adjourn was adopted and three members appointed to inform the governor. Dan Showalter then rose and addressed the Speaker, saying:

> Mr. Speaker, I rise for the purpose of tendering to this House, through you, my warmest thanks for the kindness and courtesy extended to me during the time I have had the honor of presiding over your deliberations. I trust, sir, that if at times I may have been thought arbitrary, they will remember that when I took the position I said I would endeavor to maintain the honor and dignity of the House, and to treat all with strict impartiality. This has been my object since I have had the honor of presiding over your deliberations, and again I say if any one has thought me arbitrary at times, it must be remembered that only by preserving order and decorum can business be transacted with speed and promptness. Let me tender again my sincere thanks, and assure the gentlemen upon this floor that in after years I shall look back with pride upon my associations here.

This was followed by a message from Governor Downey that he had approved and signed certain bills, passage of a resolution of thanks to the employees of the Assembly, and, finally, several facetious resolutions of wit. Speaker Burnell then announced that the time agreed upon for adjournment had arrived and declared the Assembly of 1861 adjourned *sine die*.[168]

In anticipation of the adjournment, two days earlier the Sacramento correspondent of the *Alta* had written, "Day after tomorrow, thank Heaven, the twelfth session of the Legislature terminates its existence." He wrote that it had been overly active in doing things it ought not to have and left undone things it should have done. He said it had rendered itself "particularly unpopular" and that the state would not forget the great loss of time consumed by "factions wrangling over the election of Speaker, United States Senator, Insane Asylum Physicians, etc."[169] There can be no doubt but that the House of Assembly of the State of California of 1861 was probably the most factional and disputacious legislative body ever elected in the United States. Neither can it be doubted that the serious divisions in the body had been occasioned by the great crisis over slavery and secession that then plagued the nation as a whole and which resulted in the Civil War. The frontier conditions and attitudes prevalent in California at that time were also influences.

Dan Showalter cannot be absolved for his part in the rampant factionalism, although, like others, he doubtlessly acted out of sincere devotion to the principles which he held and upon which he had been elected. He loyally supported the stands of the caucus of Breckinridge Democrats. Though not its leader, he soon was considered one of its foremost members and, in the balloting for Speaker at the session's beginning, had become its substitute nominee and, as such, increased slightly their vote for the position. In debate, the major addresses by members of his faction were delivered by Montgomery and Laspeyre, but, as seen by his "arch-traitor" speech on April 29, he could be quite eloquent. He was consistently conservative in relation to expenditures and creation of new positions, but, where obligations of the state had already been made, insistent that they be met. Though representing a mining district, he had not been oblivious to the needs of other areas of the state, supporting wharfs, street railways and roads for the Republican stronghold of San Francisco. Though Showalter could be as hot-headed as any of his fellow assemblymen, he never directly insulted any of them nor resorted to inkwell, knife or cane. In electing him Speaker *pro tem*, his fellows recognized his abilities and fairness.

He was personally popular with members from all four factions. In his valedictory, he included a gracious apology for any perceived arbitrariness. Given the temper of the times and the frontier, he had done well. In all probability, Showalter was sincere, on April 29, when he stated that he had no further ambition in government. He had, according to the *Mariposa Gazette*, served "with credit to himself, and to the satisfaction of constitutents."[170]

Four

The Duel and Its Aftermath

Neither Dan Showalter nor Charles Piercy were optimistic that adjournment of the legislature on Monday, May 20, had ended their differences. In his letter of that evening to San Francisco's *Daily Evening Bulletin*, the paper's correspondent wrote that Showalter's valedictory speech had been delivered with considerable agitation. The correspondent felt that this was in part because he was about to retire permanently to private life and "partly, possibly—just possibly—in consideration of the fact that an undignified, ungentlemanly and unjustified expression of 'supreme contempt' for another member had placed him in a position where he would have to accept or refuse a demand for the 'satisfaction due to a gentleman.'"[1]

A gentleman signing his name "G.V.M.," from Healdsburg, Sonoma County, wrote to the *Sacramento Daily Union* on May 30 that, on Wednesday, May 22, he had been walking down J Street in Sacramento with a Colonel Wood (not otherwise identified) when they met Piercy. Piercy had previously told Wood "that he did not intend to return home until he could meet his constituents without dishonor." G.V.M. and Wood asked Piercy how the matter stood. Piercy's reply was simply, "It's all settled, but don't ask me any more questions, for I cannot tell you any more." G.V.M. wrote that he and Wood both understood that the difficulty had been arranged.[2] The difficulty had indeed been arranged, only not in the manner that G.V.M. and Wood had hoped and believed.

A duel had been arranged. Dueling, in California, was not at all unusual in those days. Historian Roger D. McGrath, in an essay entitled "A Violent Birth: Disorder, Crime and Law Enforcement" published in 2003, succinctly, but eloquently, summarized the situation: "Dueling also reflected the violent character of many Californians ... they often sacrificed their lives or at least their well-being for a highly developed sense of honor. Honor could not be bought, it had to be earned. An insult or a challenge meant a fight. There was no duty to retreat. A man stood his ground and fought—with fists, knives, or guns. The polished gentleman preferred a formal duel. During the 1850s more duels were fought in California than any other place in America, including the South." Professor McGrath went on to point out that dueling was so common that it was made illegal in 1854, but the law was ignored by most of an "honor-bound public." Lawyers, editors, judges, and politicians all dueled. Even the legislator who had drafted the law making dueling a criminal offense later participated in a duel, slaying his foe.[3]

Contemporary newspaper accounts, a later press account by a writer who interviewed witnesses, and a letter written by Dan Showalter to a brother soon after the event, taken together, present a fairly complete account of what happened. Immediately after the Assembly adjourned on May 20, a friend of Piercy called upon Showalter and asked him the name of a gentleman with whom he might confer in order to make arrangements for a duel.[4] Presumably the "friend" of Piercy was one of those who served as his seconds, either State Senator H.P. Watkins or Samuel B. Smith. Showalter's designated "gentleman" was perhaps Assemblyman Thomas Laspeyre, who was later one of his seconds. Marin County and the north shore of San Francisco Bay was selected as the site. That county had already been several times used for duels—to the disgust of many of its citizens.[5] The parties did not immediately proceed there, however. They were still in Sacramento on Wednesday, May 22, when G.V.M. and Colonel Wood encountered Piercy. His reluctance to speak with them about the matter indicated that efforts were being made to keep the illegal matter out of the public eye. If so, it was an open secret.

The two principals, along with other parties to the duel and perhaps some who just wished to witness it, apparently traveled to San Francisco, arriving sometime on Thursday, May 23.[6] There, if not previously, the arrangements were made as to where and when to conduct the duel. Soon after 9:00 a.m. on Friday, May 24, Piercy was seen at Meigg's Wharf at San Francisco's North Beach in the company of Senator H.P. Watkins and Frank Schell. Piercy had apparently traveled there alone, in an omnibus. He was met soon after by Schell, who was carrying a bundle later presumed to have contained Piercy's weapon. Watkins arrived later. They observed an acquaintance, whom they ignored. This person later reported that they had seemed "indifferent." Showalter, with a few friends, reportedly left San Francisco for Sausalito, from a point a little west of Meigg's Wharf, slightly before 9:00 a.m.[7] Piercy and his friends had used a Whitehall boat (a rowboat type resembling a Thames River water taxi or wherry[8]) to travel to San Quentin. Showalter and his friends had taken the steamer *Petaluma* to San Rafael, where he overnighted at the Marin Hotel.[9] Piercy and his companions were entertained overnight by the warden of the state prison at San Quentin.[10] Those who observed or heard about their activities on this day all presumed that they were leaving the city to fight a duel somewhere in Marin County on the 25th.[11] The citizenry of San Rafael were excited as it was "whispered around" that a duel was in the offing.[12]

Early the next morning, all involved—principals, seconds, doctors, and friends, plus would-be spectators—set off for the duel site.[13] McDathe's Ranch, about eight miles west of San Rafael in the Lagunitas Mountains, had been selected. Dan Showalter and his party arrived there about 10:45 a.m. Piercy, his seconds and advisers were nearing the site, but concealed themselves in some bushes when they saw the Marin County Sheriff approaching. Since dueling was an illegal activity, the arrangements were supposed to be secret. Even so, it seems almost everybody knew—there were just too many who had come to Marin County for it to be otherwise. One of those who indeed knew about the upcoming duel was Marin County District Attorney John H. Haralson, who filed a complaint that parties were intending to fight a duel. Acting on the complaint, Sheriff Valentine E. Doub performed his duty promptly. At about 11:00 a.m., he arrived, possibly assisted by a small posse. Alarm that the sheriff was near went out, and those assemblying for the duel scattered. Piercy and his party and those there in support of Showalter escaped into the bushes. Showalter was, however, arrested by the sheriff, who conveyed him to San Rafael, where he was soon taken before the county judge, R.B. Frink, and charged with intent to fight a duel. San Francisco attorney Cornelius M. Brosnan (later a member of the Nevada Constitutional Convention and a Justice of the Nevada Supreme Court[14]), who was apparently one of the many who had traveled from San Francisco to

The site of the Showalter-Piercy Duel is explained by one of its last witnesses, John Murray (center), to Dr. Thomas Snead (left) and an unidentified friend in this 1936 photograph from the Dr. Thomas Snead Collection. An open field at the time, the site is now a residential neighborhood of San Anselmo, California, at the intersection of Elm and San Anselmo Avenues (courtesy Fairfax Historical Society, Fairfax, California).

witness the affair, represented Showalter. For some reason, District Attorney Haralson did not appear. Brosnan therefore moved that since the complainant had not appeared and no cause had been shown for Showalter's further detention, the case be discharged. Judge Frink, who was not a lawyer, could have placed Showalter under a bond to preserve the peace, but instead delivered a brief discourse against violence. Showalter asked, "I am discharged from custody, am I, your Honor?" to which the judge replied he was. Showalter then left the courtroom with Brosnan and other friends and proceeded on foot to the ranch of Charles S. Fairfax, about three miles from San Rafael. Here all the other parties in the duel had already assembled.[15]

Charles Snowden Fairfax was one of those fascinating and unique characters that peopled the Old West. Born in Virginia in 1829, he had arrived in California via Panama in 1850. After a year in the goldfields, he turned to politics as a Democrat. In 1852 he had been elected a Justice of the Peace in Marysville and then was selected to serve on Yuba County's Court of Sessions as a judge. He was elected to the California Assembly each year from 1853 through 1855, serving as Speaker in 1854. Receiving more votes in California than anyone save James Buchanan in his successful presidential bid, in 1856 he won election as Clerk of the California Supreme Court, in which position he served through 1861. He had established his residence, called Bird's Nest Glen, in Marin County on a site now within the City of Fairfax, in 1855. By 1861, he was then and later sometimes referred to as "the most popular man in California." He had affiliated himself with the Breckinridge Democrats in that year, but maintained friendship with members of the Douglas faction. He was commonly known as "Lord Fairfax," having, in 1846, succeeded to the title of Lord Fairfax of Cameron as the tenth baron. He never assumed this title as he preferred to stay in America and retain his United States citizenship. He was also noted as an expert in the "code duello,"[16] which perhaps explains why Marin County had become, in those days, a preferred site for formal duels.

It had been previously arranged by the seconds that, if Showalter were released, the duel should immediately proceed. It now being sometime after noon and none having eaten, Fairfax provided a luncheon for Showalter, Piercy, their seconds and doctors, and others who had come to witness the event. There was apparent amity among all of his guests during the luncheon. Fairfax took the opportunity to unsuccessfully seek a peaceable reconciliation of the difficulty between the two principals. Showalter's position was that he had been challenged and so the matter was out of his hands. Piercy, claiming that he had been insulted, said that, under code duello, he had to have a retraction of the insult by Showalter. He knew that this Showalter would not do.[17]

After the luncheon, everyone proceeded to a new site selected for the duel. Fairfax's home has frequently, but erroneously, been cited as the site of the duel. The inscription on California Historical Landmark No. 679, "Site of Bird's Nest Glen," has even implied this with its wording: "Fairfax was involved in the last of California's historic political duels as host to the principals and friend of the two antagonists."[18] The actual site, however, was located one-third mile east, approximately at the present-day intersection of Elm and San Anselmo Avenues in the City of San Anselmo.[19] The property was then known as the McRae Ranch.[20] It was described by the *Daily Alta California* on May 26, 1861, as "an open grassy space of about five acres surrounded by thick chaparral, with the stream running through its center, which was crossed by a log serving as sort of a bridge. The valley, at some distance beyond the immediate ground, was surrounded by high hills, and the tall peak of Tamalpais bore to the southwest."[21] The *San Francisco Call* reported that "the ground was as level as a floor, and covered with a fair carpet of grass."[22] To reach the site from Fairfax's residence, it was necessary to cross San Anselmo Creek and then the leased farm of the William Murray family, which was then primarily open grazing land for livestock. The route across this farm was past Murray's dairy and then alongside a wooden rail fence Murray had built.[23]

As Showalter, Piercy, their seconds and doctors, friends and others crossed the creek and proceeded east across the Murray property, William Murray observed them, joined the procession, and called to his seven-year-old son, John, "Come on." A horrified Mrs. Murray, however, intervened. Many years later, John recalled: "She grabbed me by the arm and dragged me back toward the house. She was crying, I remember, and saying over and over, 'It's a terrible thing and no place for you.'"[24]

Even without the presence of young John Murray, a considerable group witnessed the duel. It was, according to Marin County journalist/historian James H. Wilkins, "a free show, with a thrill to it more intense than a boxing match for the heavyweight championship of the world." He wrote that the impending duel, its approximate time, and the originally-planned location on the side of Mt. Tamalpais had been given wide publicity and all kinds of watercraft had been used to carry spectators over from San Francisco the night before. Spectators included, according to Watkins, "lawyers, doctors, financiers, merchants, legislators, sports gamblers and other unclassified."[25] Estimates of the actual number present varied, being guessed at by various people as fifty, one hundred, or even two hundred.[26] According to witnesses interviewed by Wilkins, there were no women present.[27] Though no women may have been present on the field, some did view the duel. Young Ellen and Rose Murray watched with their brother John at a distance, from their hilltop home. There were perhaps some women included among those who had climbed the side of nearby Bald Hill to see.[28]

The names of thirty-three individuals who were present that day are known from the accounts given in the *Daily Alta California* of May 26 (the day after) and by Wilkins later.[29] These were:

Henry Baker—member of the Republican State Central Committee.[30]

Wake Brierly—Piercy's doctor.

W.H. Bruner—Showalter doctor. Resident of Sonora, Tuolumne County.[31]

Edward Byrne.

T.J. Chandler—Assemblyman (B–Tuolumne).

William Tell Coleman—Guest of Fairfax. Had been a leader of San Francisco Vigilance Committees in 1853 and 1856.[32]

Charles Snowden Fairfax.

Martin Flynn—San Francisco shipowner and pilot.[33]

P.A. Gallagher—State Senator (D–Calaveras). The *Alta* of May 31, 1861, disputed a May 28 report in the *San Francisco Times* that Piercy had slapped Gallagher in the face during the legislative session and that Gallagher was at the duel with Laspeyre as a Showalter sympathizer. The *Alta* reported that during the affair Gallagher had "acted as a peacemaker in the difficulty and was the trusted friend of Mr. Piercy."[34]

M.Y. Gillett—Assemblyman (B–Tuolumne). Attorney.

Andrew J. Gregory—Assemblyman (B–Mariposa)

William Hammond—Showalter doctor. San Francisco.

Thomas Hayes—Showalter second. San Francisco landowner. San Francisco's Hayes Street named after him. Had been second for David S. Terry in his duel with Senator Broderick.[35]

John Kelly—San Francisco Port Commissioner and proprietor of Hotel Brooklyn in San Francisco.[36]

Thomas Laspeyre—Showalter second. Assemblyman (B–San Joaquin).

Charles Minturn—Known as "The Ferryboat King," his Contra Costa Steam Navigation Company operated ferries on San Francisco Bay.[37]

James Moore.

William Murray—Fairfax neighbor.

Mike O'Brien.

James C. Pennie—Warden of San Quentin Prison. Later Public Administrator of San Francisco.[38]

Charles W. Piercy—Duelist.

H.M. Robee—Reporter, *Daily Alta California*.

Frank Schell—"well known about our Legislative assemblages."

Jacob Short—San Rafael resident.

Dan Showalter—Duelist.

Samuel B. Smith—Piercy second. Yuba County attorney. Indian War Bond Commissioner.

F. Sorrel—Assemblyman (B–Siskiyou). Showalter second?[39]

Alfred Taliaferro—San Rafael doctor. Substitute Piercy doctor. Later Assemblyman, State Senator and Prison Doctor at San Quentin.[40] He had agreed to assist in lieu of Piercy's original choice of a Dr. Murphy, who, for some unknown reason, had defaulted.[41]

Daniel T. Taylor—San Rafael resident and Marin County Clerk.[42]

Charles W. Tozer—Miner and fruit grower. Later a Nevada Territorial legislator.[43]

H.P. Watkins—Piercy second. State Senator (D–Yuba).

C.V. Williamson—State Senator (B–Stanislaus & Tuolumne).

D. J. Williamson—Assistant Secretary of the State Senate (D).

Though not mentioned in any accounts, Cornelius M. Brosnan, who had represented Showalter before Judge Frink, was likely also present. Several guards from San Quentin Prison were among the numerous local residents who turned out for the event.[44]

It was about 3:15 p.m. when the participants, their supporters, and the spectators arrived at the field.[45] Upon arrival, the agreed-upon rules for conduct of the duel were reviewed by the seconds and principals. The general conditions had been agreed upon back in Sacramento soon after Showalter had accepted Piercy's challenge and their seconds had conferred. Sheriff Doub's arrest of Showalter had, as seen, necessitated a change in location from the slopes of Mount Tamalpais to the McRae Ranch field. It also precluded fighting the duel in the morning, as had been planned. (Originally, the time set may have been 7:00 a.m. according to one speculation published on May 25.[46]) The challenged had the choice of weapons, and Showalter had chosen rifles. He knew that Piercy was "one of the best shots in the state with this weapon,"[47] but wished no undue advantage. Each selected their own weapon of a standard gauge to use. That of Showalter belonged to a Mr. Hayne.[48]

On arrival upon the field, the seconds tossed a coin for selection of positions on the ground. Showalter second Tom Hayes won, and the distance of forty paces was marked off.[49] This was done by Hayes and Watkins walking arm in arm, counting off the forty paces aloud as they went. Hayes chose Showalter's position "haphazardly, for the light was equally good in either."[50] Dan then "offered to exchange positions with him [Piercy] if he thought there was any difference in them," an offer which was apparently not accepted.[51] While this measuring was being done, Piercy walked on the other side of the creek with Warden Pennie, while Showalter paced the grass with Senator Williamson.[52] Both were chatting with their companions and calm. The seconds then measured off where they were to stand to the right of their principals. Spectators began to seat themselves on the grass.[53] During this time, a number of cattle—including two or three large bulls—were attracted by the crowd. According to the *Alta*'s reporter, their incessant lowing had to some of the crowd "a peculiarly ominous sound."[54]

Senator Watkins, one of Piercy's seconds, then read the articles of agreement for the duel. Upon taking his position, each principal could hold his rifle in whatever manner he desired; but upon the question "Gentlemen, are you ready?" they were to raise their weapons in a perpendicular position. Once both had responded affirmatively, the appointed second would then give the order, "Fire—one, two, three—stop." At "stop," both were to lower their weapons. This method of giving the firing order was slightly lengthier than normal and added seconds to the period during which fire was permitted.[55]

The rules specified that if either fired before the word "fire" or after the word "stop," he would then be shot by the seconds of the other.[56] Each principal was allowed the service of two seconds. Showalter was represented by Tom Hayes and Assemblyman Tom Laspeyre. Piercy's were Senator Watkins and Samuel Smith. Pending the start of the duel, Laspeyre held Showalter's rifle and Smith that of Piercy.[57]

Dan Showalter and Charles Piercy took their positions. The appearance of both at the time was described by Robee for the *Alta*: "Mr. Showalter is a native of Pennsylvania, a tall built man, with red whiskers and heavy hair, black eyes and a determined cast of countenance. Mr. Piercy was a rather light formed man, but tall. He had blue eyes and light auburn hair, and looked somewhat delicate owning to his recent illness, which had caused him to spit blood during the session. He was but twenty-four years of age and looked even younger than that. His face was immovable, and, like that of his opponent, showed unflinching courage." They were dressed similarly. Each wore a black hat and black clothing with their coats buttoned up to hide their collars or other prominent marks.[58]

Once in their positions, accounts differ as to whom it was—Watkins or Hayes—that asked if they were ready. Showalter responded, "Ready," as did Piercy about three seconds later. At the words, "Fire! One, two, three," Showalter fired at "one" and Piercy at "two." Neither shot struck his opponent.[59] Showalter had deliberately missed. He had told his friends that he would do so, "hoping that [Piercy] would be satisfied with one shot." Piercy's shot passed directly over Showalter's head, missing only by an inch or two.[60] (One account, gleaned later from witnesses, that Piercy's bullet had grazed Showalter's cheek[61] is not in agreement with Showalter's own statement that it missed him—barely.) As the challenger, Piercy now had the option to declare his honor satisfied or to proceed with the duel. Charles Fairfax attempted to play the peacemaker, saying, "For God's sake, Piercy, do not let this affair go further. You have behaved like a man of honor, and I will so proclaim it to all the world. Say you are satisfied." Piercy hesitated, but one of his friends approached, "laid his hand on [Piercy's] shoulder and pleaded, 'Have one more shot, Charlie.'" At this, Fairfax pulled the fellow's nose (a gross insult of the day, which usually led to a duel), at which the fellow yelled to Fairfax that he'd hear from him.[62] The chance to end the duel was lost. Showalter believed that it was "[Piercy's] bad advisers," like this fellow, who "were determined to have me killed or dishonored," who promoted and kept the duel going. When he saw the exchange and that Piercy would not withdraw the challenge, Showalter said, "Load the rifles again."[63]

As Piercy conversed with Dr. Brierly, Dr. Hammond reloaded Showalter's rifle. They resumed their places. Hayes asked if they were ready, but then immediately said, "Stop," and said to Piercy, "Hold your gun perpendicular, sir." Watkins protested Hayes' manner, which Hayes later acknowledged, with regret that it had not been different. Watkins, who did not wish his principal compromised by an accidental rules violation, conferred with Piercy and then returned to Hayes, stating that Piercy could "hold his gun as he pleases until the word 'ready' is given." When the question "Are you ready?" was again given by Hayes, Piercy anticipated the word "fire" and began to lower his weapon (both held their weapons with butt on their hips and muzzles pointed up), but, realizing his error, began to raise then lower the barrel again. When the word "fire" was given, Showalter fired his rifle at "one" and Piercy at "two." Piercy's having begun raising his weapon again and the extra movement may have thrown off his aim as well as causing the slight delay. Piercy missed; Showalter didn't. Dan had determined to make his shot "tell" this time, knowing that "one or both of us must fall at [this] next fire." Piercy's head flew back and he collapsed. The bullet, having struck him in the mouth a little on the right side, broke the vertebrae in his neck and went into the base of his brain.[64]

When Piercy fell, his seconds, his doctor, and bystanders all rushed over to him. His eyes were open, and there was slight nervous movement of his hands and one leg. He did not utter a sound. Showalter was affected by the horror of it all and exclaimed to his own physician, "Dr. Hammond, will you render every possible assistance to that poor man?" Hammond joined Dr. Brierly and Dr. Taliaferro. There was nothing that any of them could do. They were all of the opinion that death had been instantaneous.[65] Piercy's body was carried through a small valley overgrown with shrubs to the nearby home of Dr. Taliaferro. From there, a wagon brought from Fairfax's house then took the corpse to San Rafael.[66] The next day, Sunday, May 26, an inquest was held by Coroner T.K. Watson. A hastily assembled Coroner's Jury rendered its brief verdict, that Piercy "came to his death by a gun-shot wound inflicted by Dan'l. Showalter." The citizens of San Rafael had intended to bury Piercy there, but that evening a steamer arrived from San Francisco with some of his friends, who took possession of the body and escorted it back to San Francisco.[67]

A large number of friends and citizens attended his funeral, which was conducted from San Francisco's Metropolitan Hotel. The plate on his coffin read simply, "Charles W. Piercy, aged 26 years, He sleeps an honorable sleep." The Rev. G.B. Taylor of the Episcopal Mission School preached at graveside that government officials "need to be taught and corrected by that golden rule, which teaches us that forbearance and forgiveness are necessary—pre-eminently so in order to stay and control the unruly passions of our hearts." At the conclusion of the service, the body of "Charles W. Piercy was consigned to its final resting place in Lone Mountain Cemetery."[68] Although at the time Lone Mountain was San Francisco's principal burying place, it was not to remain so. In 1914, the City of San Francisco, ostensibly for reasons of public health, ordered all of its cemeteries closed, with remains removed. During the 1920s, the remains at Lone Mountain began to be removed to Cypress Lawn Memorial Park at Colma, California, south of San Francisco. This activity was completed by 1939. If Piercy ever had a memorial stone, it, like others at Lone Mountain, was used as facing for drain gutters at Buena Vista Park or dumped along the shoreline to reinforce seawalls.[69]

Piercy's real monument was to be remembered in the Union-oriented press of California as a martyr to the Union. The *Alta* summarized this sentiment in its report of the duel, concluding that "the universal feeling was, that his life had been sacrificed to his everlasting devotion to the Union, in defiant opposition to the Secession influence in the Legislature."[70] Opinion expressed in the Union-oriented California press was quite the reverse with respect to Showalter. At a minimum, they implied that somehow the duel was not fair to Piercy. The *Alta*'s report of the duel on the 26th claimed that "the large majority of those present at the duel were not friends of Mr. Piercy, were politically opposed to him, and most of them were of the party who had vowed vengeance upon him the moment when he broke the back of secession Senatorial influence."[71] In citing a report from a San Francisco paper on the "interference" of Hayes before the second firing, the *Sacramento Daily Union* believed it had distracted Piercy's aim and was thus unfair.[72] "Glaucus," in the *New York Times*, supported this contention, writing that all agreed the duel was "all fair, except, perhaps, the peremptory order of HAYES to PIERCY."[73] G.V.M. wrote that the feeling in San Francisco (a Republican stronghold) was "greatly against

Showalter, and the wish was frequently expressed that the loss of life had been that of the survivor." He said that opinion was strong that, "from a duelist's standpoint, the fight was not a fair one." The Sunday morning after the duel, G.V.M. said he heard a clergyman "pray that the mark of Cain might be upon the murderer's brow."[74] There was even criticism of the Reverend Taylor's funeral sermon for Piercy. Glaucus thought it sounded like an apology for Showalter rather than a eulogy for Piercy. He reported, "Perhaps a score of men said: 'So goes another good Union man.'—and a score more might have remarked: 'It was arranged evidently to kill him, and that is the game of the Chivs.'"[75]

The Reverend Taylor was not the only one to generally denounce the duel. The press was condemnatory. The *Daily Alta California*, in its May 25 report on the difficulty between Showalter and Piercy before the duel, referred to it as a "silly exhibition of barbarism."[76] After the fact, on the 26th, the same newspaper, in an editorial entitled "Another Victim to this Code," referred to dueling as "the brutal code of honor" and stated that "there was no plausible pretext for a hostile meeting," that the cause "certainly did not warrant either party in resorting to force to reconcile fancied or real insults," and concluded that "it only remains for us to set our seal of condemnation on the act, and to insist that the laws of this State be strictly enforced against the survivor."[77] Other papers took the same general line. The *Marin Weekly Journal* was particularly bitter that the duel had taken place there, referring to what it called "that ancient and barbarous *code*" under which each participant had "to show the world, that each had the courage to stand up in the face of day and of enlightened public opinion, in this nineteenth century, to blow out each others brains. We denounce the senseless duello;...."[78] The *Sacramento Daily Union*, in its regular "News of the Morning" column on May 27, referred to "the bloody demands of a false sentiment of honor and bastard chivalry."[79] The San Francisco correspondent of the *New York Times*, signing himself as "Glaucus," wrote his paper on June 1, calling Showalter and Piercy "two legislative simpletons." He opined that "the dead man will only be remembered as a suicide, the living will be henceforth an outcast, shunned and abhorred."[80]

Only one press report favorable to Dan Showalter survived. It was published in the *Mariposa Gazette* of June 4. Its editor wrote: "We do not know whether our old acquaintance and friend, SHOWALTER, is at his home at Horse-Shoe Bend, or not. We sympathize with him in his misfortune wherever he may be. Next to the one falling in a fatal duel, the survivor is entitled to the merciful consideration of all. Whatever of blame may be attached to him, we will not now speak of."

A few days after the duel, Dan wrote to his brother William A. Showalter a letter which explained much about both the duel and his intentions at that time:

Dear Brother; Inclosed you will find an account of that fatal duel between C.W. Piercy and myself deeply as I regret the necessity which compelled me to meet this man and kill him on the field, still I had to choose between that and disgrace and dishonor I could have killed him on the first fire but I told my friends that I would not do it hoping that he would be satisfied with one shot, but he had bad advisors who were determined to have me killed or dishonored when I say this I ordered the weapons to be loaded again. I knew from the precision of his first shot that one or both of us must fall at the next fire I determined to make mine tell, his last shot passed directly over my head and it could not have missed me more than an inch or two. To prove that I did not desire and advantage I chose rifles when I knew well that he my opponent was one of the best rifle shots in the state with this weapon and after the ground was measured off and I had won the position, I offered to exchange positions with him if he thot there was any difference in them. I am well satisfied that parties on the outside who had not courage to meet any honorable man in mortal

combat forced Mr. Piercy into the fight with the vain hope of disgracing me or the satisfaction of seeing me fall at the hand of my opponent, should fortune ever point out those men to me there shall be a day of reckoning. I know how you all view matters of this kind in the old states, there a man may without dishonor refuse to fight, but, here such a refusal would subject him to the insults of the whole community and the jeers of a corrupt press which apparently condemns dueling but always brands the man who refused to fight as a coward. I intend to return to Marin County and stand my trial and I have no fears for the results. I know that it will give me a great deal of trouble and cost me all and much more than I am worthy, but nevertheless I will not attempt to avoid a trial. I would not have written you about this unfortunate affair but I know very well that a account of it would reach you at some time. I would much sooner you should have the whole truth. Remember me kindly to all my friends.
Your Brother,
Dan Showalter[81]

William Showalter received from his brother Dan an exculpatory letter explaining the duel with Charles Piercy (courtesy Robert L. Showalter).

This letter to his brother was published in an unknown Pennsylvania newspaper under the headline "The Showalter Duel," which read:

> Our readers are already aware that Mr. Dan Showalter (A Westmore-lander by birth, and until recently a citizen of this county) was engaged in a duel with C. W. Piercy on the 25th of May last near San Francisco, California in which Mr. Piercy fell mortally wounded. As a number of contradictory statements have been published some of them reflecting upon Mr. Showalter we deem it but just to his numerous relatives and friends residing in this county to publish the following letter received by his brother Wm. A. Showwalter of Latrobe. From it will be seen that Mr. Showalter acted most honorably towards his antagonist and was willing to give him any advantage compatible with his sence of right.[82]

The majority of the spectators returned to San Francisco after the duel, leaving San Rafael about 6:30 p.m. on the steamer *Pride of the Bay*, the steamer *Marin*, and two Whitehall boats. They arrived at the San Francisco wharf about 9:00 p.m. and quickly spread news of the duel.[83] A rumor of yet another duel to come was also spread. Fairfax had pulled the nose of the man who encouraged Piercy to continue the duel. This subsequent duel, however, never took place. Fairfax, it seems, was widely known as the best shot in California with any firearm.[84] They left behind in Marin County fears of another duel. The editor of the *Marin County Journal* commented in the paper's next issue on this: "Rumor says that another 'affair of honor' is on the tapis [*sic*]"—arising out of the Showalter-Piercy duel.[85] Of the locals who had observed the duel (or part of its proceedings), two survived well into the 1900s. In 1936, John Murray, whose father had wanted to take him along, showed the site to local citizens. He told them that the next day he had visited the actual place where Piercy had fallen and had found blood-stained grass.[86] His sister Ellen was the last surviving witness. She died at Larkspur, Marin County, on April 29, 1956—only one and a half months shy of her hundredth birthday. The duel ninety-five years previous, she said, was one of her earliest memories.[87]

The Civil War had not really yet "gotten going" as far as battles went. The duel between Dan Showalter and Charles Piercy was therefore "big news." As seen, it had been carried to San Francisco the night of May 25. The next day it would have reached Sacramento by steamboat and telegraph. From there telegraphic reports reached the east and the report of Glaucus appearing in the *New York Times* was published on June 25. Showalter's letter to his brother had to have been published in a Pennsylvania newspaper at least soon after, if not before, the same time. In those days newspapers copied their news items from other papers, so the "hot" story of the duel would have then spread quite rapidly. By July 1, 1861, it had reached London, England, when the report of the San Francisco *Morning Call* was republished in the *Morning Chronicle*. From there, news of the duel spread west to Hampshire and on to Devon and north to Newcastle and Scotland. It had been told in newspapers all over Great Britain by the end of the month.[88] The report in the *Morning Call* also traveled across the Pacific Ocean to Australia, where it was republished in various papers. The *Sydney Morning Herald* carried it on August 12, followed by *The Empire* on the 14th. News of the duel reached Tasmania on the 17th (*Launceton Examiner*) and Perth, in far-off Western Australia, on August 20. The "Extraordinary Duel in California" was, according to *The Perth Gazette and Independent Journal of Politics and News*, "the principal topic of conversation."[89] Two legislators from small California towns had briefly achieved fame—or infamy—on the world stage.

After sending Dr. Hammond to try to assist the fallen Piercy, Showalter, seemingly affected, delivered a brief eulogy on the courage and coolness which his foe had displayed. He then left the field with his friends. It was not immediately known where he had gone.[90] G.V.M.'s May 30 letter from Healdsburg in Sonoma County stated that Showalter had arrived in Sonoma with one friend about two in the morning of Sunday, May 26, and had left that town before noon on the same day. G.V.M. added to his letter, "It is thought he has fled into Oregon."[91] As seen earlier, the *Mariposa Gazette* did not know whether or not he had returned to his Horseshoe Bend home. He was neither headed for Oregon nor back home. This is evidenced by the letter to his brother, which was dated "Sacramento May 28, 1861."[92] This is further supported by a brief report entitled "His Whereabouts" in the *Sacramento Daily Union* on Wednesday, May 29. It said: "The impression prevails over town that D. Showalter did not pass through the city on his way to Mariposa county, as rumored on the street, but that he is and has been at the residence of Humphrey Griffith, Washington, Yolo county, since Sunday night."[93] Yolo county was (and is) across the Sacramento River from the City of Sacramento. Griffith was obviously a friend of Showalter and had held several political offices, including Yolo county's clerk, assessor, and county judge, as well as one term as a State Senator during the 1850s.[94] In September of 1861, he was a candidate for office on the "Yolo County Secesh ticket."[95]

Dan Showalter appears to have mostly remained in the Sacramento area while awaiting indictment in Marin County. A trial for the slaying of Piercy never occurred.[96] He was in Sonora, Calaveras County, on June 6 according to a report in the *Columbia Courier*, which mentioned of him: "This notorious individual was around at the primary meeting of the Anti-Coercion party in Sonora, on the 6th inst. He seemed as unconcerned as if he had done [nothing] against the laws, and was well received by the friends of secession."[97]

The next definite report of Showalter's post-duel presence was contained in reports of the 4th of July celebrations in Sacramento. Under the headline, "Eighty-Fifth Festival of American Liberty," the day's events were extensively reported in the *Sacramento Daily*

Union of July 6, 1861. Union clubs marched, pyrotechnics were burned, the City Guard fired a salute, and notable citizens gave speeches. The paper proudly reported "the almost unanimous Union sentiment everywhere manifested throughout our city." There was one notable exception, however. This incident happened at the St. George Hotel soon after 10:00 p.m. The paper's report read:

> J.W. Bideman and Curtis Clark, on reaching Fourth and J streets, after the exhibition of fireworks at the Plaza had concluded, noticed in the hands of J.P. Gillis a flag entwined around a cane. Gillis was at the time standing on the corner in company with E.J. Sanders. Bideman concluded at once that the flag was not that of the Union, and remarked to Clark, "I'll bet ten dollars that that is a secession flag, and if it is I'm bound to take it if it is unfolded." In the course of a few moments Gillis unfolded the flag, which proved to be that of the Southern Confederacy, and raising it on his cane over his left shoulder marched up and down the sidewalk in front of the St. George. The most of those present appeared to be Secessionists by sympathy, and were pleased with the exhibition. Bideman and Clark followed, and the first named, on approaching Gillis, caught him with the left hand by the throat and with his right tore the flag from the cane and put it in his pocket. Gillis appealed to his companions for a knife, but no weapon was exhibited. Bideman stated that no such flag as that could be carried in this town in his presence, and left the ground with it. He and a large number of his friends returned to the St. George subsequently, and Frank Rhodes and A. Burns waved the flag and invited to the Secessionist present in the most pressing manner to come and take it. The invitation was not accepted. Major Gillis subsequently plead for its return very earnestly, but the flag was considered by its possessors as too valuable a trophy to voluntarily surrender it. It is made of silk; is two feet wide and four feet long; contains three stripes, two red and one white, and on the blue field were ten stars. When waved around by its captors one star fell off, which the boys concluded must be South Carolina.[98]

Less lengthy reports in other newspapers mention Dan Showalter as being connected to this incident. Glaucus, writing for the *New York Times* on July 11, described the incident—and the secession flag bearer—somewhat differently.

> At Sacramento, SHOWALTER, whose neck ought to be stretched for murdering PIERCY, his fellow Assemblyman, in a duel, aided by Major GILLIS and E.J. SAUNDERS, ventured to stick a secession flag, tied on a cane, out of a window of the St. George Hotel. Andraman [meaning Bideman], lately in the employ of Leland Stanford (who is going to be our next Governor, D.V., and I guess he is,) seized the valiant Major by the throat with one hand, and with the other wrested away the flag. The three Secessionists called on the crowd for the loan of any small weapon. The crowd laughed and cheered the drayman [Bideman].[99]

The report on July 5 in the San Francisco *Bulletin* was shorter, but varied only slightly from that in the *Times*:

> Major Gillis, E.J. Saunders and D. Showalter (the duelist) raised a Secession flag on a walking-cane, and displayed the same at the front of the St. George Hotel last evening. Mr. Deiderman [sic], a drayman, lately employed by Leland Stanford, seized Gillis by the throat with one hand, and wrested the flag away with the other, amid a great deal of loud swearing on the part of Gillis and associates. The affair created considerable excitement, but the three Secessionists did not seem inclined to do anything more desperate than to call on the crowd to lend them weapons, without any response except laughter and hisses. There is talk of giving Showalter notice to quit town within 24 hours. He ought to be arrested by orders from the San Francisco police for his crime of dueling.[100]

The next day, the *Bulletin* carried a brief notice, stating, "E.J. Sanders and D.R. Showalter deny that they had anything to do with raising the Secession flag on the evening of the 4th, as telegraphed yesterday."[101] The *New York Times* correspondent seemed to disbelieve this when he reported: "Now SHOWALTER denies that he had anything to do with the rag."[102] Whether or not he had something to do with displaying this First National Flag of the Confederacy, his denials of involvement establish Showalter as being in Sacramento on and around July 4, 1861.

The following September, J.W. "Jack" Biderman (such was his actual and full name) exhibited to friends his captured flag taken from James Gillis at the State Fair in Sacramento. A number of Union men mistook its appearance as a display of loyalty and a riot involving several hundred resulted. The police and fairgrounds employees were unable to suppress the riot and it lasted until Biderman and his friends—with the flag—were finally ejected from the fairgrounds.[103] Biderman received a job as a day watchman at the passenger station of the Central Pacific Railroad and then operated the Silver Palace Eating Stand (later Restaurant) there.[104] Perhaps he kept his prized capture there for a while. His employment relationship to railroad magnate and Unionist California Governor Leland Stanford perhaps led to the flag becoming a possession of the State of California. There is no record of when or how this happened, but the "Gillis" or "Biderman Flag" is now exhibited at the State Capitol Museum in Sacramento as "the only known Confederate flag captured in California during the Civil War."[105]

The Gillis-Biderman Flag in the collection of the California State Capitol Museum is the only Confederate flag captured in California. It was taken on the evening of July 4, 1861, in downtown Sacramento by J.W. Biderman from J.P. Gillis who was accompanied by Showalter at the time (sketch by Devin Cook).

After the exciting 4th of July in Sacramento, there is a gap of almost three months before there was any mention of Dan Showalter. What was he doing? Perhaps he was "laying low" while expecting an indictment from Marin County. Five months later, he was to try and lead a small group of fellow-minded Californians overland to the Confederacy. If this was his intent, why did he not leave the Pacific Coast immediately? The motivation may have been that he was awaiting the results of the California General Election to be held on September 4. It is known that "after the election, a number of southern sympathizers left the state to join the confederate army."[106] Showalter's known movements and activities fit this pattern. It is probably during the summer of 1861 that he decided to make his way to the South. He had already recognized that a political career in California was now no longer possible. Roundly denounced because of his pro–Southern stance in the state legislature and because of his duel with Piercy, and because the 1861 election had swung the state into the Union camp, California no longer had much to hold him.

Dan Showalter next appeared in Nevada. An October 8, 1861, letter from Carson City, about activities in the Nevada Territorial Legislature, to the *Sacramento Daily Union* concluded with the brief line: "D. Showalter has arrived from Virginia City."[107] That he had earlier been in the Aurora mining district is likely since the *Esmeralda Star* of Aug. 23, 1862, reminded its readers of this in a brief diatribe: "There are traitors in our midst who helped to fit out Showalter and his party; they have also helped to fit out others and given the rebels aid and comfort; but their game is now up, and they are closely watched. Traitors have come in here from other quarters, but they will find this to be too hot a Union community for any of their kind, and the sooner they got out of it the better it will be for them."[108] Additional evidence of his presence in the Aurora area was a letter he wrote in November 1861 to a G.H. Crenshaw asking him to write "Scott and Montre at Aurora for me."[109]

Now long a ghost town, Aurora was a prosperous community in those days with both gold and silver mining. When Dan Showalter was there, it was also a county seat—of both Mono County, California, and Esmeralda County, Nevada Territory, with two sets of county officers. The exact location of the California-Nevada boundary was uncertain and Aurora was thought to be in each. It was not until 1863 that surveyors declared that it was three miles inside Nevada.[110] In the next month (November 1861), four men from Mono County would associate themselves with Showalter and accompany him to Southern California for a journey to Texas and the Confederacy.

When Dan Showalter left Nevada sometime in late September of 1861, he probably took a wagon road over the mountains back to California. There were reports in the *Marin County Journal* of October 4 and the *Visalia Delta* of September 26 that he had, the previous week, left Murphy's in Calaveras County "to go down on the other side of the Sierras, through the Tejon Pass to Los Angeles." The writer seemed to not believe, but related anyway, stories that Judge Terry and 270 men were with him.[111] The tales of large numbers of men (and Judge Terry) with Showalter were greatly exaggerated. Showalter was, however, indeed bound for the Los Angeles area of Southern California. Though of dates later than the events, his route to Southern California can be traced by news reports of his passing. There is no record of Dan Showalter passing through Mariposa County—his home "diggings"—during his journey south, but, after leaving Calaveras County, he would have had to have passed through the county on the way. That he did so is perhaps verified by the fact that by November he had with him four residents of the county.

Showalter was next reported in Visalia, with the *Mariposa Gazette* of November 19 citing from an earlier item in the *Visalia Post* and printing "Dan Showalter and one or two others passed through there a few days ago—'going to Texas.'"[112] Since Visalia is located on the eastern side of the San Joaquin Valley, an item in the *Sacramento Daily Union* during the first week of October 1861 may well apply—though once again numbers were greatly exaggerated. The item stated that "a report gained currency that David S. Terry, Dan Showalter and a few other leading lights of the secession Democracy had gathered in the San Joaquin Valley and foothill counties adjoining several hundred desperate men and started overland to join the Southern troops."[113] The truth about some who actually were not Showalter's companions on the trip appeared in the October 3, 1861, edition of the *Union* in a brief item titled "Still at Home." It stated that "Judge Terry and T. Laspeyre, whom the Visalia *Delta* referred to lately as being on their way South to carry out secessionism into practice, are still at Stockton, as we learn from the papers of that city."[114]

Dan Showalter and those with him on the trip south—whomever or however many they were—did not take the direct route south through Tejon Pass to Los Angeles. The pass was the site of a Union garrison at Fort Tejon. Additionally, there were stronger Union forces in Los Angeles itself. Instead, at the southern end of the San Joaquin Valley, he turned east across the low Tehachapi Mountains and then along the northern foothills of the San Gabriel Mountains (and the southern end of the Mojave Desert), making his way to Cajon Pass. There he camped in Cleghorn Canyon[115] and sent "emissaries" to the miners in the nearby Holcomb Valley (now the Big Bear resort area) to seek recruits.[116] Though the miners plied his agents with whiskey and gave them a small amount of gold, none of them enlisted.[117] One later-day account stated that Showalter then planned to raid the town of San Bernardino for supplies, but this was aborted when citizens learned of the plan and fortified themselves in the brick Catholic Church.[118] Actually, there was no such plan by Showalter. It was "a band of filibusters, recruited in Visalia for the Confederate Army, [which] was to raid San Bernardino, but this party proceeded quietly through on their way to Texas, and it is doubtful if they ever had any intention of molesting the citizens."[119] Dan and those with him rode west through Reche Canyon to the San Gabriel Valley and into the town of El Monte.[120]

Five

The Showalter Party

Upon arrival in Southern California, Dan Showalter would have found himself in relatively friendly territory. Although former Southerners and others sympathetic to them (such as Showalter) had settled in mining districts all over California, there were large concentrations in the southern portion of the state. Federal authorities had early recognized that Southern California could become a problem. Writing about Los Angeles on June 10, 1861, Brigadier General E.V. Sumner, then commanding the Department of the Pacific, had advised the Army's Adjutant General in Washington that "there is more danger of disaffection at this place than any other in the State."[1] The nearby communities of El Monte and San Bernardino, east of Los Angeles, and the Holcomb Valley mining district north of San Bernardino were also considered to be strong centers of Secessionist support. The Federal authorities therefore acted quickly to station loyal volunteer units raised in the central and northern portions of the state in the southern region. This prevented any overt actions for the Confederacy, but did nothing to reduce sympathy for the South or to prevent small parties from leaving the area for Texas.

Thirteen miles east of Los Angeles, El Monte seemed to be particularly pro-secession. On May 7, 1861, Captain Winfield Scott Hancock, then Assistant Quartermaster at Los Angeles, wrote Department headquarters that, on May 4, a Bear Flag had been paraded through the streets of the town escorted by forty to seventy horsemen.[2] The Knights of the Golden Circle was also active in El Monte and surrounding areas. They met frequently in the homes of members,[3] which tends to indicate that they were not nearly so numerous as often stated in press reports based on rumors. Obviously, not everyone in El Monte was pro–Southern. The postmaster there would hide issues of *The Southern News*, a pro-slavery, pro–Confederate newspaper, and not deliver them until the news in its issues was old.[4] Another Unionist of the town was Jonathan Tibbett, around whose home the Bear Flag had been paraded.[5] Nevertheless, it was a likely community for Dan Showalter and like-minded others to gather for a projected journey across the Southwestern deserts to Texas and the Confederacy.

The pro–Confederates were a vocal group, and their loud and frequent pronouncements gave the appearance that they were more numerous than they actually were. It is not determinable whether their exaggerations of their strength was to boost their own confidence, wishful thinking, or to frighten their opponents. According to General Sumner in June 1861, "the leaders of the party claim to be acting by authority from the Montgomery Government which gives them some weight in the country."[6] There is no record, official or otherwise, that the Knights of the Golden Circle ever accomplished anything in California for the Confederacy other than to circulate rumors disturbing the state's loyal citizens and, to a lesser extent, Federal officials. For all of its vaunted significance, the Knights of the Golden Circle (elsewhere as well as in California) appears to have been a very ineffective organization. They were "all talk and no do."

Resultant from Dan Showalter's brief sojourn in El Monte and known activity of the Knights of the Golden Circle in that area, reports associating him with that organization later arose. The earliest such published "historical" report appeared in a single paragraph in the "Historical Department" column of the September 1950 issue of *The United Daughters of the Confederacy Magazine*. A paragraph on secret societies formed to support the Confederacy stated that the Knights of the Golden Circle was said to have had 24,000 members in California. Then, the article continued, "San Gabriel had its own group, under Dan Showalter, who paraded regularly...."[7] The next published article connecting Showalter to the Knights appeared in 1959. This was a brief article by John Crippen, Jr., entitled "The Golden Knights of Dan Showalter," which appeared in the monthly *Westways* magazine of the Automobile Club of Southern California. This article had the Knights selecting San Bernardino as their temporary headquarters, where, after several hundred had gathered there, Showalter revealed his plan to travel in small groups to Texas.[8] The *UDC Magazine* article then mentioned Showalter's capture and imprisonment at Yuma. The Crippen article then proceeded to a fairly accurate account of Showalter's capture, although inserting contrived conversations. Neither of these articles provided either footnotes or bibliography. Their sources are therefore unknown. Both accounts seem to be suppositions based on accounts of the Knights in Southern California and the fact that Showalter was in the area at about the time of these accounts or perhaps gleaned from an 1892 romance novel, *The Little Lady of Lagunitas: A Franco-Californian Romance*, authored by a Union veteran.[9] Though it might be said that there would be no record of Showalter's membership in the Knights since it was a secret society, in addition to absolutely no official records of such a connection (and in the *Official Records* there are fairly extensive Union reports of secessionist activity during the period in the area), there are no news reports or later reminiscences mentioning it. Showalter himself, in February 1862, wrote a letter stating that there was no organization.[10] That he was a Knight of the Golden Circle does not seem likely at all.

Those who would become known as "the Showalter Party" camped in an open field on the southern side of El Monte and supposedly drilled along the Rio Hondo (a parallel channel of the San Gabriel River).[11] Two false legends arose about the Showalter Party at El Monte. One was that Dan Showalter contacted Confederate General Henry Hopkins Sibley, who had recently captured Albuquerque and Santa Fe, New Mexico, and was instructed by the general to organize a force of cavalry at El Monte and, when it was trained, join him in New Mexico. The other was that Showalter's band was known as the "California Volunteers, El Monte Battalion, Confederate Army."[12] The earliest published account presenting these two "facts" was an unsigned article, "El Monte and the Confederacy," published in the September 1961 issue of the bulletin of the El Monte Historical Society. This article neither gave citations of sources nor provided a bibliography. A blending of these two legends led to yet another—that Dan Showalter, when he set out with his party for the Confederacy in November of 1861, possessed a commission in the Confederate Army.

The historical facts easily refute these false legends. Dan Showalter could not, in the period July–November 1861, have contacted General Sibley. The general did not arrive at Fort Bliss in the El Paso, Texas, area until December 14, 1861.[13] Albuquerque was not taken by the Confederates until March 2, 1862,[14] and Santa Fe until March 10.[15] Lieutenant Colonel John Robert Baylor had reached Fort Bliss with a small Confederate force earlier, on July 13, 1861.[16] As a general, Sibley had authority to appoint volunteer aides at officer rank, but Baylor did not. In any event, there is no record that either ever appointed any person as an officer. Although throughout the stated period there was traffic in both directions on the Butterfield Overland Stage Route between California and the El Paso area, such a journey took a month one way, leaving little, if any, time for Showalter to communicate with El Paso and receive a response. Also, there were neither contemporary press reports (or rumors) nor reports in the *Official Records* of Showalter holding any commissioned rank in Confederate forces in November 1861, when he set out from El Monte for Texas.

The "El Monte Battalion" also does not measure up historically. The "El Monte and the Confederacy" article itself stated that Showalter had eighteen men with him in El Monte.[17] In those days, the minimum complement of a company was sixty men, and a battalion would require at least two, but, generally, three or more companies. Except for perhaps propaganda purposes, calling Showalter and his small party a battalion would be patently incorrect. It is possible, however, that such an impression could have been created by one H.H. Dickey. The *Los Angeles News* had reported, on November 27, 1861, that "on the morning of the 23rd instant, a party of men, who have for sometime past been encamped in the Monte, left there on their way to Texas. There are various estimates as to the number of men in the party, but we have been informed, on what we consider reliable authority, that they numbered, all told, forty-four." Dickey had approached the paper on the 23rd, bragging that "the party was 175 strong; that they had organized themselves into three companies, by electing a captain to each, as follows: Captains, Dan. Showalter, H.H. Dickey, and Wilson…. Dan. Showalter was their commander-in-chief. We have also been informed that these men were regularly enlisted soldiers in the Southern army."[18] The number alleged by the boastful Dickey would have minimally been sufficient for a small battalion.

The story of Dan Showalter—and perhaps others of his party—having commissions in the Confederate Army while still in California has been clarified by the preceding two paragraphs. There was neither opportunity nor time for General Sibley to have been approached and to have issued a commission, nor any contemporary report of such being done other than the interview given by Dickey. In his boast to the Los Angeles newspaper, he himself stated that the party had elected its captains. "Captain," in those days, was the frequent, informal, courtesy title given to the leader of any traveling group and in no way implied more than election or consent by the group. Neither Showalter nor any other members of his party who eventually reached Texas ever claimed rank by virtue of any previous commission.

Even without all the publicity and rumors of secessionists gathered at El Monte and San Bernardino, the probability that pro–Confederate individuals or small groups would endeavor to reach Texas and the Confederacy via the overland route was not, of course, unknown to the Union authorities. In late June 1861, members of the Los Angeles Mounted Rifles, a California militia unit, and some resigned United States Army officers, including Albert Sidney Johnston—about thirty in total—had made their way to Warner's Ranch on the Butterfield Overland Mail Route to Texas. They left Warner's on June 27, reached the Colorado River at Yuma on July 4, crossed the river on the 7th, and finally reached

Confederate forces on the Rio Grande at Dona Ana (north of El Paso) on July 27.[19] Other small groups continued to use this route. Hezekiah Cable, a Union sympathizer who operated a tavern at the Oak Grove stage station, informed Lieutenant Turner of the 4th United States Infantry in late September that "parties of armed men were constantly passing through."[20] One party of Californians reached Dona Ana in late October.[21] In order to secure this route to Fort Yuma for movement of Union forces east into New Mexico Territory and to intercept would-be Confederates, General Sumner advised the War Department, on September 17, 1861, that he would "establish a strong camp at Warner's Ranch, on the road to Fort Yuma, which will support the post, [and] prevent the gathering of Rebels in that vicinity."[22] Camp Wright (named after Brigadier General George Wright, who assumed command of the Department of the Pacific on October 21, 1861) was established at Warner's Ranch on October 16. At a high altitude, it was exposed to cold and to high winds, which blew out campfires. It was therefore moved, on November 23, about sixteen miles west, along the trail to the station at Oak Grove.[23]

The commander of Camp Wright in late November of 1861 was Major Edwin A. Rigg of the 1st California Infantry Volunteers.[24] Under his command, at Camp Wright and nearby Warner's Ranch, were Companies D, G and F, 1st California Infantry, and a detachment from Co. B, 1st California Cavalry Volunteers, under Second Lieutenant Chauncey R. Wellman.[25] Rigg knew that Dan Showalter was coming that way with a group. On November 11, Jonathan T. Warner, former owner of Warner's Ranch, had written Colonel James H. Carleton in Los Angeles, "I believe there is a party of twenty-five men now at El Monte. They have been there some days, waiting the arrival of Showalter and others to proceed on to the Colorado."[26] Carleton daily sent letters to Rigg informing him of activities and movements of Showalter and his men. Roads near the camp were guarded strictly, scouts sent out in the area, and signal stations erected on peaks.[27] Ramon Carillo, husband of the then owner of Warner's Ranch, had set local Cahuilla Indians to hunting about the mountains as spies.[28] Rigg sent his mobile force out on long patrols. A patrol comprised of Lieutenant Wellman with his detachment, from the 20th through 22nd, checked the valleys south of the camp and the road to San Diego. Wellman sent an Indian servant of Francisco Ocampo (manager of Rancho Santa Ysabel) to Temecula and back. No one was encountered or heard

2nd Lt. Chauncey R. Wellman (1829–1910) of the 1st California Cavalry was Showalter's captor at Minter's Ranch in November 1861. Prewar he had been a Sergeant of Dragoons and rose to the rank of Captain during the Civil War (courtesy Shirley Ann Wellman South).

of making their way east.²⁹ As yet, there was no reliable information. The strength of Showalter and his party was variously reported, sometimes asserted to be as many as one hundred men. Other reports had the group breaking up into smaller detachments taking different routes.³⁰

As mentioned, Dan Showalter and those with him had left El Monte on November 23. The trail was southeasterly through the Chino Hills and Temescal to Temecula, which was reached on the evening of November 27, 1861.³¹ At that time, there were only two white persons resident at Temecula—John Magee and his employee, E.M. Morgan.³² Magee had opened a store at Little Temecula Rancho, where the road from San Bernardino to San Diego crossed the Southern Emigrant Trial (also known as the Butterfield Overland Mail Route) in 1849. The first post office in inland Southern California had been established at his store in 1859.³³ Magee was a strong Unionist, but his assistant, Morgan, was a secessionist, according to Second Lieutenant Thomas E. Turner of the 4th United States Infantry, who passed through Temecula in September. Morgan seems to have been somewhat of a braggart—certainly careless and loose-lipped. He told Turner that he was a Knight of the Golden Circle and showed the lieutenant what he said was a badge of the order—a gold ring with St. Andrew's cross—which he wore upon his breast.³⁴ The Unionism of postmaster Magee and the braggadocio of Morgan would both play a significant role in what soon transpired for Showalter and his companions.

The post office provided Dan Showalter and other members of the party with a last opportunity to address letters to others not with them. Their letters, which would soon come into possession of Major Rigg, revealed their current situation and short-term plans and hinted at their purposes. Charles Benbrook wrote a friend named Frank, telling him that there were nineteen in the party—eleven of whom Frank knew, but who were not named as Benbrook did not think it "policy" to do so. Benbrook wrote that they all were in good spirits and would cross the Colorado River in Sonora to avoid Fort Yuma. He was optimistic, stating, "Perhaps the chances are tough, though I think we will make it."³⁵ T.L. Roberts wrote his brother, telling him that "we had quite a pleasant trip" and also mentioned the plan to cross the Colorado below Fort Yuma to avoid the troops stationed there, where some difficulty was expected.³⁶

Dan Showalter himself wrote definitely three and probably four letters while at Temecula. To "Friend Coulter" he wrote that all of the party were in good health and spirits and their animals in good condition (Showalter himself had three), and that there were "no fears of getting through." He advised Coulter they would cross the Colorado about thirty miles below Fort Yuma in order to avoid trouble, but "after that, if they annoy us, we will make the best fight we can."³⁷ Of G.H. Crenshaw he asked, "Write to Scott and Montre at Aurora for me," stating that he hadn't the time to do so himself. He included word about a mutual acquaintance named Baker, who was well and sent his "kind wishes." Crenshaw was also told the group would cross the Colorado "on the Mexican side to avoid trouble at Fort Yuma."³⁸ Two friends, "Allison and Powell," were written to jointly, telling them that he had waited to hear from them at Los Angeles. He told these two that he had expected to have fifty to one hundred men, but there were only twenty, although twenty more from San Bernardino were expected to overtake his party. The final two sentences of this letter told of plans to cross the Colorado at Gonzalez' Ferry in Sonora, below Fort Yuma, where "no one can pass that point now without submitting to be searched or taking the oath." He asked them why a man named "Gilbert" had not come, and told them, if they were soon ready to come, to "communicate with

Sam. Brooks at Sacramento."[39] The fourth letter, signed only "On the Way," but probably by Showalter himself, was addressed to "Hon. Samuel Brooks" (Brooks was at that time California's Secretary of State), who was addressed as "My Dear Friend." The writer mentioned that he had received a letter at Los Angeles from Brooks, but had been busy and forgotten to reply. He told Brooks of the plan to cross the Colorado thirty miles below Fort Yuma on the Sonora side "as no one can pass that point without submitting to a search. This, of course, would not suit me." Brooks was also told that if he should take the same road during the winter, to travel to Los Angeles by water and outfit himself there so the animals would be fresh. This letter concluded with the words "Remember me kindly to all friends" and the closing "Very truly, your friend."[40] These letters all indicated that Dan Showalter was making a journey which would not be approved by Union authorities—yet he was determined to do so.

At Temecula, the party decided to alter its route east to avoid Camp Wright. A letter to a friend by Charles Benbrook explained, "We will leave the road at this place to avoid the troops at that place, as they are aware we are coming and are looking for us, and the chances are that we would have some trouble with them."[41] Levi Rogers later told his Union captors that they saw Morgan at Temecula and that he had told them they would be arrested if they followed the road.[42] Henry Crowell expanded on this—that it was Morgan and a man named Ritchie at Temecula, who "seemed to take a good deal of interest in the matter," who recommended they instead take the trail to Santa Ysabel and from there the overland route at Carrizo Creek.[43] In his letter from Temecula, T.L. Roberts had written that they needed to avoid two hundred troops and thirty dragoons at Warner's Ranch, so would use a trail.[44] Dan Showalter himself was opposed to leaving the road. Under questioning, he later told Major Rigg that "taking the trail from Temecula was very much against my wish; a majority of the party were in favor of it, and I acceded to it."[45] Their trail would lead south from Temecula to the valley of the San Luis Rey River, up that valley to Santa Ysabel, and then via an overland trail to Carrizo Creek, by which they could rejoin the road. This was the route recommended by Ritchie and Morgan.[46]

Some members of the party had been sent out separately to scout the routes. T.A. Wilson wrote E.B. Sumner from Temecula the evening he arrived there (the copy in War Department files is misdated as December 30, 1861, but it was enclosed with a November 27 letter): "I have hired a man to go after you, and I want you to start back as soon as he gets to where you are, and also bring Mr. Chum with you, and look sharp he don't play you some trick. He is a bad man for us, and we want him back as soon as possible. There are eighteen of us here. Say nothing to him about what I have written, but tell him we want men, and we are going another road. I have no time to write more."[47] This letter was given to Mr. Cable by E.M. Morgan, who requested, "You will please deliver the inclosed letter to Mr. Sumner, the gentleman who came to your place with Mr. Warner, and tell him to hurry up, and oblige," adding, "P.S.—Please deliver immediately at any expense."[48] Warner had Cable give the note and enclosed letter to Major Rigg on the morning of November 27. Sumner and Chum had not yet arrived at Camp Wright, having stopped at the ranch of a man named Geftareus (referred to as "the Dutchman"). When they arrived at Camp Wright at about 10:00 a.m., they were promptly arrested by Rigg. Wilson's letter gave the major good reason to believe that they were the advance of the party he had been looking for.[49] The letter to Sumner and his arrest along with Chum set the pursuit in progress.

Captain Henry A. Greene was ordered out, with his Company G of the 1st California

Infantry, to the San Jose Valley. There he was to detach twenty men under Lieutenant Whitman B. Smith to guard the valley, where several trails entered. Greene was then to proceed with the rest of his command to Francisco Ocampo's at Santa Ysabel. Rigg sent a note to Ocampo directing him to send someone through on the trail to Temecula.[50] Company D of the regiment, under First Lieutenant DeWitt C. Vestal and accompanied by Major Rigg, marched with two days rations and sixty rounds of ball cartridge to close trails out of the valley. Captain Hugh A. Gorley of Company D was left in command at Camp Wright.[51] Lieutenant Wellman and his cavalry detachment was sent out from Camp Wright on a patrol to Temecula on November 27 by Major Rigg. On the way there, at the ranch of Geftareus, they encountered William Hamilton. They found nothing when he was searched, but, upon questioning him, were told that Hamilton was looking for a man, whose name he did not know, who had taken his horse. Hamilton told the cavalrymen that this man was in the company of another named Sumner.[52] Apparently, Wellman had Hamilton taken along with his patrol. There is no record to the contrary, and the man was a few days later included with the Showalter party prisoners.

On the afternoon of November 28, from Warner's Ranch, Major Rigg sent Captain Gorley the message that he needed Wellman's detachment "as soon as possible, and before daylight if he can get here." If Wellman had not returned from his scout, Gorley was to have Second Lieutenant Edward G. Taylor get a mule and ride to Temecula after him. He wrote Gorley, "The party we want are on the road from Temecula to San Jose Valley, and will be in to-night if they are not alarmed." Gorley was to keep this information to himself except for explaining to Lieutenant Taylor what he was to do. If Taylor discovered that Wellman was on the right trail, he was to let him proceed to the San Jose Valley by it, but sent the cavalryman a message that the party had been seen at Pomona on the trail at 10:00 a.m. Taylor was unable to make connection with Wellman and returned to Camp Wright, and so informed Gorley, but advised that Wellman's route would drive the party into the San Jose Valley unless he captured them in the mountains. By daylight of the 29th, this news had been passed on to Major Rigg and Gorley had deployed Company D to cover trails out of the mountains.[53]

Dan Showalter and his companions had left Temecula early on November 28. They reached the San Luis Rey River valley at Pala and then turned upstream (southeasterly). They reached the ranch of John Minter, at the base of Angel Mountain at Mesa Grande, that evening and encamped. This information was communicated to Rigg by Ocampo at midnight. Ocampo promised to advise in the morning which way the party went from Minter's.[54] Born in Kentucky and raised in Missouri, John S. Minter was an early American settler in California, having come to the state as part of the expedition of John C. Frémont. After some time in Stockton, he moved to San Diego County, where he purchased his ranch and married (1859) into the Machado family.[55] It is not known if Minter was at home when the Showalter party arrived. If he were, it is likewise not known whether he welcomed them or not. More than likely, he probably reacted as most would do if approached at their out-of-the-way home at night by a large group of heavily armed men—by being cooperative. Meanwhile, having followed the party's trail from Temecula, Lieutenant Wellman and his cavalry detachment camped about a quarter of a mile away, without water or forage, at 8:30 p.m. on the 28th.[56] The noose was almost closed.

When Wellman awoke early on the morning of the 29th, he discovered that the party he was searching for were camped at Minter's ranch. He immediately saddled up his detachment and led it to the camp. He questioned the group "as to their business, destination, and purpose." Their reply was that they were headed to Sonora, Mexico, that they were peaceable, and they had taken the route they were on to "avoid any unpleasant difficulty with the troops of the Government." Wellman then asked them if they would accompany him to Oak Grove and undergo examination there. The response was detailed by Wellman in his report: "The most of them appeared willing. There were two or three that demurred. Showalter was one of them. He [Showalter] said he did not see why they could not be allowed to proceed quietly, as other parties had, and as for himself he should

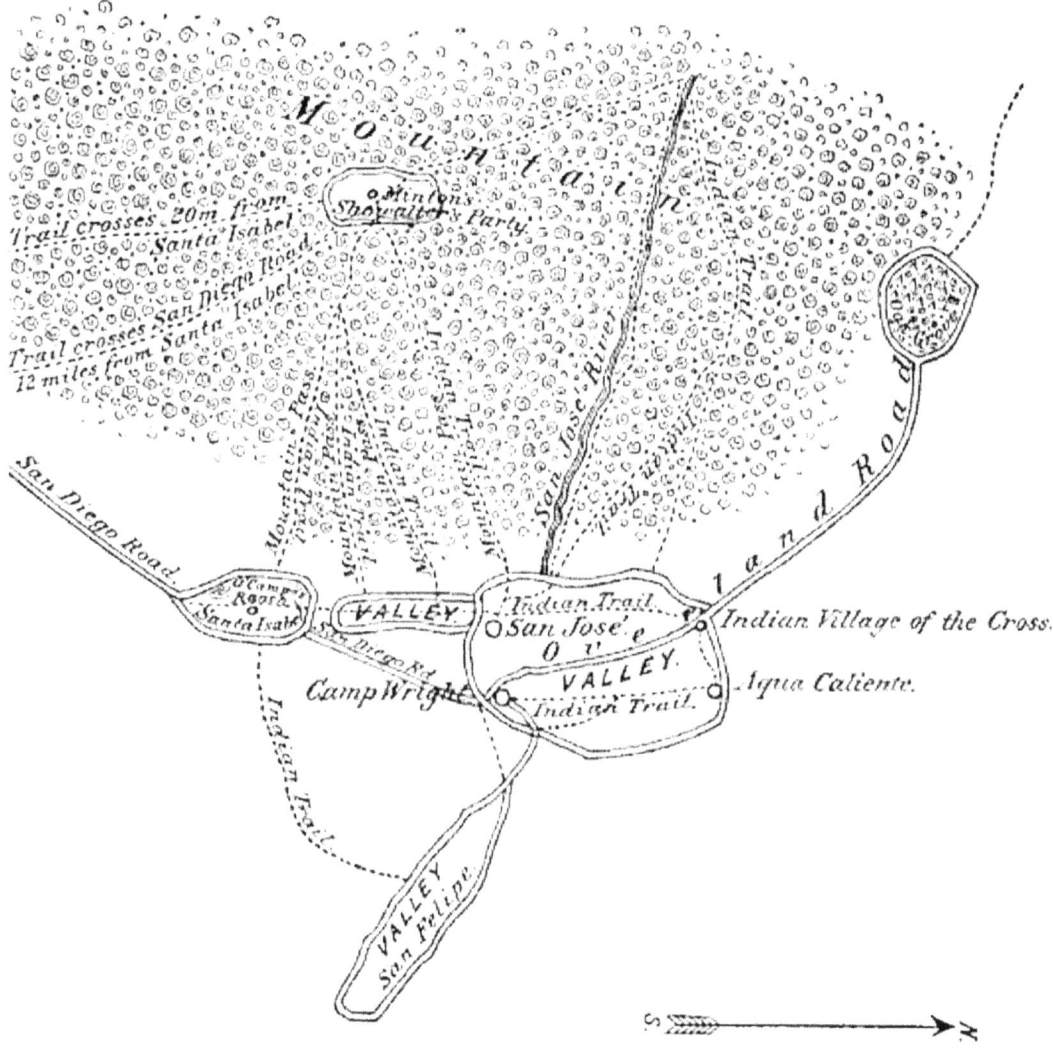

Lt. Wellman included this map of the Minter Ranch area with his report to Major Rigg. The map, drawn with north to the right and a lack of scale, can be confusing. Still, the map sketching ability of Wellman is evident. The location marked "Camp Wright" is its original location at Warner's Ranch. It had only recently been moved to Oak Grove which is the darker area encircled by a road at the upper right. The "San Jose River" is now known as the San Luis Rey River (*Official Records of the Union and Confederate Armies*, Series I, Vol. 50, Part II, p. 45).

say no decidedly, and he would take the consequences, but finally said that he would abide by the decision of the company. The company wanted that I should pledge my word that if nothing—no evidence of treason or disloyalty—against them that they would or should be released and allowed to go about their business." To this, Wellman assented— as well he might, the Showalter Party being armed and equal in number to his detachment.[57]

During the discussion, Lieutenant Wellman sent a message to Major Rigg at Warner's Ranch, informing him that he had made the arrest, was proceeding slowly to Oak Grove, and requesting that he be sent some assistance. The detachment and their captives moved out through Buena Vista, Drycke's Ranch, and La Puerta. When they reached La Puebla de los Indians, the assistance Wellman had requested joined up—Lieutenant DeWitt C. Vestal with twenty men of Company D, 1st California Infantry. Major Rigg also met Wellman at the Indian village. The column finally reached Camp Wright at 6:00 p.m.[58] Taking advantage of the departure of Jose Sepulveda, brother-in-law of Ramon Carillo, the Major immediately sent a message to Colonel Carleton informing him of the arrest of Showalter and his party, totaling sixteen. He provided the colonel with the names of those taken by Wellman and of the two captured on the 27th. He said he believed these two to be an advance party—it having been reported to him by unknown persons that eighty more were getting ready and on the road. Rigg requested instructions on what to do with Showalter and the other captives.[59] The requested instructions were sent by Richard C. Drum, Assistant Adjutant General at department headquarters in San Francisco, on December 9, 1861. They were: "The general commanding the department [Wright] desires you to hold and keep securely guarded the state prisoners, Showalter and party, until further notice."[60]

Hugh Gorley, who had been left in command at Camp Wright, gave a different account of the capture in 1893 to the California Commandery of the Military Order of the Loyal Legion of the United States (MOLLUS: an organization of former Union officers and their descendants). He related that, on the morning of November 29, Wellman had approached the party with his handkerchief on his sword and demanded their surrender, which Showalter refused. Wellman then stated that his orders were to arrest and take them to Camp Wright, which he preferred to do peaceably. Two hours were consumed in the negotiation, according to Gorley. During this time, Showalter had his men shelter their animals out of the line of fire. He then told Wellman that he and his party would not go to Camp Wright unless by force compelled to do so. At this point, Gorley's account diverged significantly. He had Wellman's bugler sounding "Dismount," then "Deploy," and finally "Advance." Gorley said a battle was avoided at this point only by the arrival of Lieutenant Vestal and his men under the eye of Major Rigg. The Company D infantrymen deployed as skirmishers and moved up the hill toward the ranch. Seeing himself between two fires, Showalter then raised a white flag and surrendered.[61] Perhaps after thirty-two years Gorley's memory of events as told to him was poor. Perhaps he was— as so many had done at the time and later—embellishing the story to make it more interesting. In either event, his rendering of the capture was at variance with the contemporary reports of Wellman and Rigg both as to circumstances and as to when Vestal's infantry appeared.

Other variations on the events of the capture of Showalter and his party appeared in the press. On December 14, San Francisco's *Daily Alta California* cited reports from the *San Bernardino Patriot*. One of these reports gave as its sources a "Capt. Wilks" and a U.U. Tyler, who had arrived in San Bernardino the Sunday after the capture. These two told the paper that five men of the party had in some way become separated, that the arrest was made "at or near Temecula," and that all of the captured men said they were traveling to Texas to look after property. A fuller account from the *Patriot* was occasioned "by the arrival of a gentleman on Thursday direct from Temecula." This unknown gentleman's story followed Wellman's report closely, even naming Minter's ranch as the site of the capture. It diverged greatly in regard to the actual capture, however. The informant told the *Patriot* that the infantry was in position south of Warner's, allowed the party to come within range, and then surrounded them. He noted that there were about twenty-five and that "they were not commanded by Showalter, as is generally supposed, but by Capt. Wilson, an old Texan ranger."[62] This same account was republished later (December 24) by the *Mariposa Gazette*.[63] The news was no doubt of startling interest to Showalter's old neighbors.

Though then and later the captives were referred to as "the Showalter Party," it seems that, in fact, Dan Showalter was not its leader. The statement by Dickey to the Los Angeles paper, the fact that the only captured letter from Temecula that gave instructions to a member of the party was by the hand of Wilson, and the unknown gentleman's report in the *San Bernardino Patriot* all would support the fact that T.A. Wilson was the actual leader of the group. To this evidence must be added a comment by Major David Fergusson of the 1st California Cavalry. Fergusson had been sent to Chihuahua, Mexico, to obtain intelligence of possible movements of Texans toward New Mexico and Arizona. In his report, dated February 13, 1863, at Mesilla, Arizona (now New Mexico, bordering Las Cruces), he noted that "Nelson [meaning Wilson], the captain of Showalter's party, ... [was] in Chihuahua when I arrived."[64] It has already been seen that though Showalter had opposed both taking the trail that led to Minter's Ranch and surrendering to Wellman's patrol, he had to give in to the majority of the party, who thought otherwise. An actual officer would not have had to submit to a vote on these matters. If indeed Wilson was a former Texan, he would have had more knowledge of trails to Texas and conditions along them than Showalter, who had never been through the area to be traversed. It would have been more logical for Wilson to be the leader of the expedition. Wilson stated the fact of the matter to Major Rigg: "I was elected foreman of the party traveling with me for the purpose of selecting camping places and the like."[65] Dan Showalter was an influential member of the party and its most prominent member, and so the group was called after his name. T.A. Wilson was its leader.

There is evidence giving some credence to the reports in the *Patriot* that there were twenty-five men in the party with Showalter and that, as alleged by Wilks and Tyler, five of them had become separated. On January 31, 1862, Haywood Dickey (the same who had boasted to the Los Angeles newspaper in November) was captured at Pilot Knob near Fort Yuma. He said that he had intended to overtake and accompany Showalter on the journey east, but, due to illness, was unable to do so. He later went to San Diego and crossed into Mexico, where he was provided with an Indian guide named Marto la Cruz by Baja California governor Jose Matias Moreno. The guide led Dickey to the Colorado River and then, on the instructions of Governor Moreno, informed Major Rigg (now commanding at Fort Yuma), who had Dickey arrested. Dickey acknowledged that he personally knew Showalter and the nineteen captured with him. He told the Major: "I saw one of the Showalter party that you did not get. I saw some of them at San Diego. The names of them I do not know, although I had some conversation with them." He further stated that he had left Stockton with several men, one of whom named Ward was, at the time of Dickey's statement, confined at Fort Yuma.[66] Showalter himself had written in November that he had expected twenty more from San Bernardino to join him.[67] It seems possible, if not probable, that the additional men expected, as reported to the *Patriot*, and those seen by Dickey were part of the San Bernardino contingent that never linked up with Showalter.

As Officer of the Day, Gorley, assisted by First Lieutenant Joseph P. Hargrave (Company F), who was Officer of the Guard, disarmed Showalter and his party, taking down a record of their names along with the number and description of their arms. Of this, Gorley said, "They were the best armed men I ever saw, or expect to see." The weapons were of the latest pattern, and their ammunition was carried in a manner to facilitate rapid loading and firing. Besides their repeating rifles, Gorley said they were loaded down with pistols and knives. Gorley and Hargrave missed one weapon—a knife a foot and a half-long belonging to T. L. Roberts, who was described as six feet tall with coal-black eyes, broad shoulders, and a full black beard. Roberts, however, informed the two officers of the weapon, which he had hanging down his back. The prisoners' horses were placed in a corral.[68]

Major Rigg questioned all of the prisoners, taking statements from each of them.

THE SHOWALTER PARTY
AS INTERROGATED BY MAJOR RIGG

Name	Age	Originally From	To Calif.	Residence County
Benbrook, Charles	?	Simpson Co., KY	1850	Mariposa
Chum, F. N.	30	Choctaw Co., MS	1856	Los Angeles
Crowell, Henry	24	Erie Co., PA	1851	Mariposa
Edwards, William	22	Arkansas	1854	Mono
Hamilton, William	51	near Lexington, KY	1850	Mono
King, A.	35	Carroll Co., TN	1854	Mono
Lawrence, James	23	Washington Co, AR	1853	Mono
Roberts, T. L.	30	Fairfield, SC	1860	Placer
Rogers, Levi	25	Alabama	1858	Sacramento
Rogers, S. A.	??	Warren Co., TN	1854	Sacramento
Sampson, J. M.	35	Louisville, KY	1850	Mariposa
Sands, William	40	Wilson Co., TN	1849	Mariposa
Showalter, Dan	30	Greene Co., PA	1852	Mariposa
Sumner, Charles	34	Perquimans Co., NC	1849	Mariposa
Turner, William	22	Cass Co., GA	1849	Amador
Ward, R. H.	27	Jackson, MS	1852	Merced
Wilson, T. A.	29	Tennessee	1852	Mariposa
Woods, T. W.	?	Bedford Co., VA	1852	Placer
Woods, William	30	Clay Co., MO	1850	Los Angeles

The members of the Showalter Party were identified by statements given to Major Rigg (chart prepared by Gene C. Armistead).

The nineteen men were asked their age, place of birth, date they arrived in California, and California residence. The Major also inquired how they came to become members of the party, the purpose of their trip, their stand on secession and the war, and if they would take an oath of allegiance. There were some minor discrepancies between the individual, signed statements, but all of them purported to be headed to Sonora, Mexico, to mine (at least initially), were loyal citizens not thinking of taking up arms against the government, and perfectly willing to take an oath of allegiance.[69] Curiously, the *San Bernardino Patriot* erroneously reported the names of two others as being members of the party—Hugh Miller of San Bernardino and Charles Murray of Mono.[70]

Major Rigg did not have at hand any form for an oath of allegiance, so he drew up one himself.[71] Assisted by Lieutenant Hargrave, he administered the following oath to all of the prisoners:

> I, _____ _____, do solemnly swear that I will bear true allegiance to the Government of the United States, that I will serve them honestly and faithfully against all their enemies and opposers whatsoever, and that I will support, maintain, and defend the supremacy of the Constitution of the United States, and all laws of Congress made in pursuance thereof, and that I will in all things well and faithfully discharge the duties of a citizen of the United States to the best of my ability. So help me God.
> Subscribed and sworn to me before this 1st day of December 1861.
> Camp Wright, Oak Grove Station, San Diego County, Southern California.[72]

While writing his report to Colonel Carleton on December 3, Rigg changed its tenor three-quarters of the way through. He added to it on the 4th, "I had concluded to discharge them, and informed them that I would, but Lieutenant Wellman has just returned from another scout.... He has intercepted many letters ... which, in my opinion clearly proves that a regular organization exists, and that his party with a few exceptions is in it." He continued that it was suspicious that they were all Southerners (an error; Showalter and Crowell were originally from Pennsylvania) headed for the Sonora mines. He thought that all miners, irrespective of section, would be attracted to the mines if they were good miners.[73] The letters "intercepted" were those that Showalter and others had left behind at the post office in Temecula to be forwarded. Wellman had led eight men of his detachment out of Camp Wright at 11:00 p.m., December 1, and gone to Temecula, where they arrived an hour before daylight the next morning. Here, they made a "thorough but fruitless search for the parties in question." Mr. Ritchie told them two men had been encamped there, but had left and gone back to San Bernardino, while Morgan had gone to San Luis Rey. After "screening" the letters he thought of suspicious character and taking them, Wellman and his men pursued Morgan. They arrived at San Luis Rey about 6:00 p.m., found Morgan at the nearby ranch of a Mr. Tibbett and arrested him. Wellman had the letters and Morgan back with him at Camp Wright by about 9:45 p.m. on December 3.[74] One of the suspicious letters taken by Wellman—that set him off in pursuit of Morgan—was indeed suspicious:

> Temecula, Cal., November 30, 1861.
> Friend Wild: Times have changed so that I feel it will be impossible for me to get to my friends in the East, and therefore have half resolved to stay in the God-forsaken country, provided I can get a situation in a place where I will be satisfied. Now I think that if I could get a place with Jeagers, at the Colorado River, I might be contented for a few years. When you go out I wish you would speak to Jaegers or some one at the river in my behalf. I will be satisfied with any agreement that you may make, so I am well paid. I hear nothing of interest from the States.

Yours, truly, E.M. Morgan

P.S.—I would write more, but am afraid that I might spin off on a subject that would not be acceptable to some people, provided this did not reach you in safety.

Yours, &c., E.M.M.[75]

In his report, Major Rigg justly and forthrightly complimented the captor, writing, "I cannot close this without testifying to Lieutenant Wellman's merits as an officer, and to the good behavior of his men. He is fast earning the name of the fox hound. He has had two long scouts, and in both instances fulfilled his errand." Rigg's report, enclosing three by Wellman, one by Captain Greene, a sketch map of the area by Wellman, the captured letters, the statements made by nineteen prisoners, and the signed oaths, was completed and sent on December 4. Rigg had orders to take command at Fort Yuma, leaving the prisoners with Gorley, who was instructed to not release them until either Colonel Carleton or his second in command, Lieutenant Colonel Joseph West, gave orders to do so.[76]

According to Gorley, the first day he was in command of Camp Wright he was given a note from Showalter requesting permission to speak to him on business. An interesting conversation followed when Showalter was brought to the Captain under guard. Showalter told Gorley that his name was familiar. To this, Gorley responded that there were Showalters in his home county in Pennsylvania. Further conversation brought out that Showalter was familiar with Gorley's home town and that he had known Gorley as a "tow-headed boy." Gorley recalled Showalter as a young man attending Madison College. In the intervening years, the appearance of both had changed, making immediate recognition of each other impossible. Showalter brought Gorley up to date on his life, relating "his early and daring exploits in California, his political career as a legislator, and his trouble with a fellow member by the name of Piercy, the victim of his duel."[77]

This pleasant reminiscing was concluded when Showalter brought up his business. He demanded that he and his party be sent to Los Angeles for trial by civil authorities. This was, of course, against Gorley's orders and he refused. At this "[Showalter] raged and threatened, cried and cursed, all at the same time, and at last brought his fist down upon the table with an oath that he would take a desperate chance in the face of the guard, and go." Gorley ordered him returned to quarters and doubled the guard. Gorley later told his fellow members of the Military Order of the Loyal Legion of the United States that, up to that time, there was "no proof positive" that Showalter and his party were Confederates or that they were on their way to join the Confederacy. About the 10th of December, Gorley received instructions from headquarters to permit Showalter and the others to depart, taking with them their horses and arms. He told them the date they would be released and gave them freedom of the camp to make preparations for their journey. Gorley said that "they appeared to be very happy in anticipation of their freedom, and made themselves at home among the soldiers, engaging in foot-racing, ball-playing, joking and laughing.[78] The Showalter party also enjoyed with the troops the comical antics of "Tom," pet cat of Company D, with the pet crow of Company G.[79]

The day before their release, however, the cavalry (Wellman's) brought in a captured mailbag. In this captured mail were several letters from Showalter to friends in San Francisco that he had written several days before his capture. Gorley claimed that one of these letters reveled that "[Showalter] and most of his party were commissioned officers in the Confederate army." This letter closed: "We understand that a force of United States troops are stationed at Camp Wright, about twenty-six miles east of here. We intend to evade them by taking a trail over the mountains, south of their camp, strike the Colorado river below Fort Yuma, and when once on the other side, if they follow us, we will give them hell." Gorley sent for Showalter, read him the letters, and told him that, under these new circumstances, he was going to hold the party as prisoners of war pending communication with Colonel Carleton. Gorley told his fellow MOLLUS members that he made copies of the letters and sent the originals to Colonel Carleton along with a request for instructions. Within a few days, he had his instructions: to hold Showalter and his party "at all hazards" and await further orders.[80] It is important to note that the *Official Records of the Union and Confederate Armies in the War of the Rebellion* contain neither correspondence between Gorley and Carleton nor captured Showalter letters supposedly stating that he and others had Confederate commissions. Was Gorley "adding to memory" with allegations from rumors published in the press?

Orders regarding disposition of Showalter and those captured with him were not long in coming. Richard C. Drum, on December 10, wrote Colonel Carleton that "the general commanding the department desires you to send Showalter and party under a competent guard to Fort Yuma, there to be held securely guarded until further notice."[81]

On the 13th of December, Carleton in turn ordered Lieutenant Colonel Edward E. Eyre, commanding the 1st California Cavalry, to move Showalter and his party to the fort. The guard was to be both infantry and cavalry as far as Carrizo Creek, after which, if Eyre deemed it safe, infantry alone the rest of the way.[82] On December 16, 1861, Second Lieutenant James Barrett, Company I, 1st California Cavalry, was detached from duty to escort, under guard, Showalter and the others to Fort Yuma. Using wagons as transport, Barrett had the prisoners safely at Fort Yuma on December 28.[83]

Federal authorities had sometime before considered what should be done with California secessionists who might seek to leave the state for the Confederacy. Back on November 4, Colonel Carleton had written Lieutenant Colonel Eyre, "If Showalter comes to San Bernardino, or where you can get hold of him, have him swear allegiance to the Government. If he refuse, hold him good. I will send him to Alcatraz; same of Judge Terry."[84] As an island in the middle of a bay and garrisoned by Federal troops, Alcatraz was even then considered to be an inescapable site. On December 11, the *Daily Alta California* had speculated that "it is not at all unlikely that Alcatraz island may speedily become the 'Fort Lafayette' of the Pacific coast."[85] (Fort Lafayette was an island fort located in the narrows of New York Harbor. During the Civil War, it was used as a prison for both Confederate prisoners of war and northern politicians detained for opposing war policies.[86]) The *Mariposa Gazette* also speculated that Showalter would "probably be taken to San Francisco, and perhaps confined in the fort at Alcatraz."[87] Since news traveled slowly in those days, as late as December 27 there was speculation as to where Showalter would be imprisoned. The San Francisco *Evening Bulletin* of that date published a letter from an "occasional correspondent," signing himself as "L," from Los Angeles. "L" wrote that for several days the rumor was that Showalter and his party would be taken to Los Angeles. "L" reported that upon hearing someone shout, "Here they come!" people would rush out into the street to view them.[88]

The timing of the orders to send the Showalter party to Fort Yuma may have been influenced by rumors of a rescue attempt. Early on the evening of December 10, C.E. Bennett of San Bernardino, a former army officer, had approached Captain Emil Fritz of the 1st California Cavalry near San Bernardino. Bennett told Fritz that seventy-five or eighty men were fitting out at El Monte and San Bernardino to attack Camp Wright and release Showalter and those captured with him. These men, according to Bennett, were armed with revolvers and shotguns and bound by oath to each other. They planned to attack Camp Wright at night. Captain Fritz was unsure if this report was factual or rumor, but, at 10:00 p.m., sent the information on to his superior, Eyre, at Camp Carleton.[89] Eyre responded on the morning of the 11th, telling Fritz to relay the rumor to Major Fergusson at Camp Wright and, if he thought the rumor reliable, that he should send a captain and two lieutenants with fifty picked men to Camp Wright.[90] Fritz, as ordered, on the 11th sent a message to Fergusson informing him of the reported plan to rescue Showalter. He was careful to alert Fergusson that this was just a rumor, writing, "It may be true or false."[91] Fritz obviously thought it just a false rumor—he did not send reinforcements to the Camp.

Fort Yuma was not considered by the press to be an ideal location for the confinement of prisoners like Showalter. The *San Francisco Bulletin* considered the fort "the most insecure place for political prisoners in all of California." It pointed out that the fort was located over 150 miles away from reinforcement and that Confederates could march across the New Mexico Territory, cross the Colorado River on pontoon bridges, and take the fort.[92] Indeed, in early December there had been reports that the Confederate force of Colonel John R. Baylor was or soon would be threatening Fort Yuma.[93] There had also been rumors that the fort's garrison was not reliable, with two of the three companies stationed there having mutinied. The editor of the *Daily Alta California* wrote, "It is surmised that they have been tampered with by Southern agents. Lieut. Col. West is fearful of being attacked by a large Confederate force, now assembling somewhere along the Colorado River."[94] Later, the same paper's opinion was that "something more than infantry or artillery appears to be required at that point."[95] The then extreme isolation amid a barren landscape seemed not to have been taken into account by the protesters, but not all comment was that the fort was an unsuitable place for prisoners. As early as December 12, a commentator in the *Alta* had stated, "We learn that Fort Yuma is to be strongly garrisoned, and to be made the 'Fort Lafayette' for California. Showalter and party will probably be the first boarders."[96]

This Colt Navy .36-calibre Revolver, Serial No. 62467, was issued to and used by Private Thomas Hooper, Company C, 1st California Cavalry, while a participant in the capture of the Showalter Party. This pistol is now in the collection of a member of the Showalter family (courtesy Dr. John J. Kudlik).

The horses and weapons of the Showalter Party were not to accompany them to Fort Yuma. An order from Colonel Carleton to Lieutenant Colonel Eyre on December 13, 1861, had specified he have the Showalter Party transfer all of their horses, mules, ammunition, equipage and provisions to Eyre, who was to give each man a receipt and to have a memorandum made and certified by each man. When Eyre returned to Los Angeles from Camp Wright, he was to bring all of the animals and other items with him.[97] The *Los Angeles Star* of January 18, 1862, reported that Second Lieutenant James Barrett had arrived at Camp Carleton, near San Bernardino, on January 14 with twenty-nine horses belonging to the party. According to the correspondent, "Civis," the other property consisted of "several carbines, a number of shotguns, Colt's revolvers and rifles; one of the latter was used by Showalter in the duel with Piercy," and valued by him at "several thousand dollars."[98] The property and animals were apparently then taken to San Pedro (now the port of Los Angeles) for, on February 18, Major David Fergusson, commanding at Camp Carleton, received correspondence from district headquarters directing him, "If Lieutenant Wellman has not taken all the property and animals belonging to the Showalter party to San Pedro, send the remainder to him without delay."[99] Apparently Cutler didn't know that Wellman had already arrived at San Pedro by February 17 and the horses had been taken to Camp Drum (now Drum Barracks Civil War Museum, Wilmington).[100] The regimental return of the 1st California Cavalry dated March 1, 1862, indicates that Wellman had been detached for this purpose on February 16th.[101] Shortly thereafter, Colonel Carleton sent the invoices of effects to department headquarters in San Francisco. In his letter of transmittal, he advised "as the Government is responsible for these animals and arms, and is obliged to feed the animals, I am now using and shall use them in the public service."[102]

Major David Fergusson arrived at Camp Wright on January 8, 1862. On the 11th, he gave Captain Gorley orders to take half of his company, the general prisoners (military offenders) and "also the two civilian prisoners, William Hamilton and M. Morgan, and proceed to Fort Yuma." Gorley was told to maintain a strong guard over his prisoners. In his 1893 address to his MOLLUS companions, Gorley referred to these men as "the remnants of Showalter's party." They left Camp Wright on January 12 during a heavy rainstorm.[103] There is no account of the trip, under guard, of Dan Showalter and the other men across the mountains and the Imperial Desert to Fort Yuma. Their journey would not have been dissimilar from the trip a few weeks later by Gorley, his half company (thirty men), and his eleven prisoners, which serves well to illustrate the conditions and hazards of the trip. Gorley's general description of the trip was "a dreary one, indeed—a desert of sand, destitute of vegetation, scarcity of wood, and but little water." Just six miles east of Camp Wright, the little command halted at a spring, where Gorley inspected canteens. He emptied out on the ground liquor that he found in some and had the canteens refilled with spring water. After nine more miles, they reached San Felipe, where they camped. The next day's march of twenty miles to Vallecitos was through heavy sand under a scorching sun. The third day's march took them twenty miles to Carizzo Creek. The heat was so bad (and this was in January) that they left there at midnight to avoid daytime heat. Gorley said that his men were in good spirits because they had been promised a good rest when they reached Sackett's Wells. Their progress was interrupted by a brief sandstorm that covered them with several inches of sand and, when they at last reached the wells, they found them dry. They had no choice but to continue another twenty-five miles to Indian Wells, arriving there at 2:00 p.m. on the fifth day. The water supply here was sparse and they had to wait long intervals for it to gather in the wells. The next morning they moved on to Pilot Knob, home of the chief of the Yuma Indians and located on the Colorado River. After spending the night there, it was a short march the next day to Fort Yuma, in total 180 miles from Camp Wright.[104]

Fort Yuma was, to say the least, not the nicest place to spend captivity. Sylvester Mowry, later a noted Arizona secessionist, had been stationed there in 1855 as a young

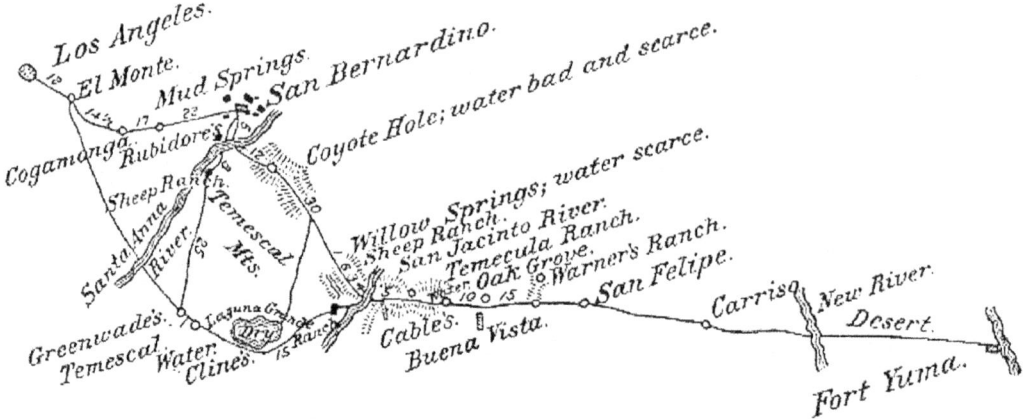

Road from San Bernardino to Warner's ranch by way of Willow Springs and Temescal.
NOTE.—At most of these camps wood and grass is very scarce; water is abundant, excepting at Coyote Hole and Willow Springs. The road through Temescal is the best.

This map of 1861 route between Los Angeles and Fort Yuma shows the various stations along the trail. The Showalter Party used the western loop from El Monte to Temecula. The "New River" shown on the map was not so large as implied—it was only a dry water course in the desert leading to the Salton Sink (now the Salton Sea). Between this river an Fort Yuma, the trail dipped south through Mexico (*Official Records of the Union and Confederate Armies*, Series I, Vol. 50, p. 31).

second lieutenant. His opinion was that "Fort Yuma is a hell of a place. More than 200 miles from anywhere in the midst of Indian country—hotter than hell—and not a sign of anything for amusement."[105] Another officer who served there, Lieutenant Edward Tuttle, called it "a perfect Sahara without an oasis."[106] J.D. Lauderdale, post doctor at the fort during the 1870s, stated that it was the "hottest military post in the United States," and complained that it was overrun with ants and, when the river was in flood, mosquitos. The only drinking water was from the Colorado. Lauderdale called this water "too muddy to drink and too thin to plow." He also mentioned that the site was subject to periodic desert storms.[107] Without supplies, travel from Fort Yuma in any direction was virtual suicide.[108] Anyone desperate enough to try to desert or escape the post had another problem: The army paid local Indians for each fugitive they caught.[109]

Some of the press in California reported that Showalter and his band would be confined at Yuma as prisoners of war.[110] Their actual status was that of political prisoners, as was evidenced by numerous such references to them and other captives by Colonel Carleton in official records.[111] When Lieutenant Wellman was placed on detached service at San Pedro on February 16, it was "in charge of property of political prisoners known as Daniel Showalter's party."[112] Prisoners of war could not be assigned any duties by their captors—they were simply kept confined. Showalter and the other Fort Yuma prisoners had to work. Fort Yuma had no walls. The volunteer soldiers at the fort had been working five hours per day on fortifications.[113] They were doubtless happy when Showalter and the other political prisoners were put to work on the construction of earthworks. Carleton's instructions were to "have all the brush and undergrowth cleared off and burnt, so as to have the ground clear for at least 600 yards in all directions from the fort," followed by specific direction that political prisoners could do this work.[114] A brief article, "Well Set to Work," appearing in the *Sacramento Daily Union* on February 4, 1862, reported that "Major Rigg at Fort Yuma, has set Dan Showalter and his party at work with the shovel, pick and spade throwing up earthworks."[115] Such work was their daily task.[116] Even in late winter and early spring, the weather in the area was both hot and dry. One volunteer soldier, apparently from Mariposa County and knowing some of the prisoners, on April 16, 1862, wrote J.M. Van Dyke of that county. His letter, which Van Dyke provided to the *Mariposa Gazette*, said of the prisoners and their work, "They take it pretty hard."[117] Despite having to perform hard work, treatment of the prisoners at Fort Yuma was otherwise described as "kind and hospitable" by a correspondent to the *Los Angeles Star*.[118]

Despite a strict guard, the combination of confinement, hard labor and heat probably led to two of Showalter's party attempting to escape. On March 2, 1862, Major Rigg reported to District Headquarters in Los Angeles that two political prisoners, Chum and Edwards, had escaped.[119] They had left during the night. One of them headed up the Colorado and the other went west. Both were recaptured, one at Carrizo Creek 120 miles west of the fort and the other 100 miles up the river.[120] The response of Colonel Carleton to their escape and recapture was communicated to Major Rigg by his Acting Assistant Adjutant General, First Lieutenant Ben C. Cutler, on March 15. The orders were: "Upon receipt of this letter, the political prisoners, Edwards and Chum, are to be securely ironed, and are to be kept in irons until further orders. Their irons must be carefully inspected by the officer of the guard every time the relief is changed. The colonel commanding directs you to say to all the political prisoners, that, although he is unwilling to do so, yet, if another one of them even attempts to escape, the entire party will at once be placed in irons."[121] There were no more escape attempts.

Dan Showalter and his party would not be the only political prisoners at Fort Yuma. On Dec. 23, 1861, Colonel Carleton had ordered that "all persons who have been arrested or who may be arrested as secessionists or traitors to the country will be kept in confinement at Fort Yuma."[122] Showalter and his party would soon be joined by others. The case of Haywood Dickey has already been mentioned. In early February 1862, they were joined by two men, named Gilbert and Samuels, transported there from Los Angeles.[123] It is possible that this Gilbert was the same whom Showalter inquired about in his letter from Temecula to Allison and Powell. Calvin M. Chriswell of San Bernardino, in the fall of 1861, had proposed a toast to the health of Confederate President Jefferson Davis. This resulted in his being knocked down by a Union soldier. He apparently continued to voice his support for the Confederacy since he was arrested in late February 1862 and sent to Fort Yuma.[124] In mid–March 1862, Captain Nathaniel J. Pishon was ordered with Company D, 1st California Cavalry, from Los Angels to Fort Yuma. He was given secret orders to arrest along the way a Mr. Greenwade of Temescal and take him along to the fort.[125] Curiously, this Greenwade was the man who had engineered Piercy's fraudulent election to the Assembly in 1860. There were many others, although occasionally some of those who had been arrested from the countryside surrounding the fort were released on orders.

In addition to no possibility of escape, there was little chance of release due to process of law. As early as December 1861, Colonel Carleton had written Major Rigg at Fort Yuma that he was "to obey no writs of habeas corpus issued for Showalter or either of his party, or for any other secessionist who has been or who may be taken prisoner and confined at your point."[126] Brigadier General George Wright, commander of the Department of the Pacific, was in full agreement, but sought clarification from higher headquarters, writing on December 28, "Can I disregard writs of habeas corpus in case of political or State prisoners?"[127] This course of action was, of course, not disapproved. It coincided with policies the Lincoln administration had been enforcing in the eastern states. Secretary of State William H. Seward had advised Secretary of War Edwin M. Stanton that suspending the writ of habeas corpus was expedient for counteracting secessionists.[128]

Colonel Carleton was unsure if this was enough. In early February 1862, he confided to Major Rigg that "we shall be obliged, I fear, to hang some of these fellows before they [secessionist sympathizers] can be awakened to the fact that the Government forces on the Pacific Coast are in earnest." In the same letter to Rigg, he told the Major that if someone was found guilty beyond a doubt of a violation of trust, "Shoot him."[129] On February 20, the Colonel advised Major Fergusson at San Bernardino to arrest a man and, if a writ of habeas corpus should somehow be served upon him to show cause why the prisoner was being held, to reply that the prisoner was being held by order of Colonel Carleton and under no circumstances obey the writ.[130] The practice of ignoring writs of habeas corpus would continue in the department throughout the war as Federal officials felt needed. This policy was made well-known. It was emphasized by instructions to commanders that "the department commander desires you to let the people understand generally that the order of the President suspending the writ of habeas corpus and directing the arrest of all persons guilty of disloyal practices will be rigidly enforced."[131]

Some were able to make humor out of Showalter's imprisonment at Fort Yuma. In late 1861, the *London Times* had commented that the Lincoln administration's suspension of habeas corpus was illegal as regards United States citizens. The *Sacramento Daily Union* commented on this in its December 20 edition, stating that "The *Times* will be pleased to learn that.... Dan Showalter concur[s] in its opinion upon the habeas corpus business."[132] Later arrests of secession-minded persons were referred to in the press as "recruits for Fort Yuma" and "reinforcements for Genl. Showalter's command."[133] This is probably the source for some later mistaken statements by a few "historians" that Dan Showalter was a general. Then there was the unknown joker in San Francisco who registered himself, in early March 1862, at the Union Hotel in San Francisco as "Dan Showalter," giving his residence as "Fort Yuma." Reports of this prank appeared in three newspapers.[134]

There was, of course, no humor in the situation on the part of Dan Showalter. He and the other political prisoners were not denied the privilege of the United States mails. On February 27, 1863, Showalter wrote Brigadier General George Wright. This letter survives—in a faint and barely readable condition—in the historical papers collected for H.H. Bancroft during the late 1800s and maintained at the Bancroft Library of the University of California at Berkeley. In this letter, Showalter informed the General that the letters taken at Temecula and in Wright's possession were the only basis for imprisonment of himself and those with him. He said that in regard to the contents of those letters, he could muster his defense "when brought before the people." He denied that they were an organized group since "every individual member of the party was perfectly free to act for himself." The barely legible letter seems also to include a denial by Showalter that he had a commission from the Confederacy. He stated that if an investigation could be had, "That not a shadow of testimony could be addressed upon which to detain" them. He concluded that "in order that justice may be done to these men who have already suffered three months imprisonment, I most respectfully ask you to order an investigation at the

Post before such officers as you may choose to select."¹³⁵ In short, he argued that there was no real evidence against himself or those who had been with him and, significantly, he held that an investigation would only be justice to his men.

It would be two more months before Showalter and the members of his party would be released. There is no information to indicate whether or not his letter to General Wright influenced their release. In fact, there are no definite indications of the reason(s) for the release of any of the political prisoners held at Fort Yuma during the spring of 1862. They were definitely not released in response to an amnesty proclamation of President Lincoln, as stated in a biography of General Wright.¹³⁶ This proclamation was not issued until December 8, 1863—long after Showalter had been released. Nor were they released or exchanged as prisoners of war, as some early accounts stated.¹³⁷ In the case of Dan Showalter and his party, it is possible that pressure upon General Wright by "important political friends in the California legislature" for their release may have been involved.¹³⁸ Certainly "persons in sympathy with the rebellion" had "made a great deal of talk and noise at the time" that the capture and imprisonment was "an infringement on the constitutional rights of the citizens to molest them when they were quietly proceeding along the highway."¹³⁹ The fact was that there actually was "no positive incriminating evidence" against Dan Showalter or those with him.¹⁴⁰ The principal argument for release of the prisoners was probably that there was by then, in the southern region of California, danger from neither Confederates nor California "secesher" since the "California Column" (a small Federal brigade under Colonel Carleton) was at Fort Yuma and progressing east across Arizona. General Wright summed up this situation to the Adjutant General of the Army on April 30, 1862, stating that he had "no apprehension as to the result in any conflict with the rebels this side of the Rio Grande" and, although there were "many men on this coast who are traitors at heart, ... they are harmless now, because so greatly in the minority." Wright advised that he was sending more troops to Southern California and they would be "ever ready to crush any attempt to raise the standard of rebellion on the Pacific."¹⁴¹ Dan Showalter was just no longer viewed as a threat to California.

Though the specific reasoning for Dan Showalter's release is not known, the actual circumstances are. On April 3, 1862, Colonel Carleton, from his district headquarters in Los Angeles, wrote Major Rigg, commanding at Fort Yuma:

> Keep H.C. Minor in arrest, as well as all other of the political prisoners, until you have sent to these headquarters the oath of allegiance signed by each on a separate sheet of paper, and sworn to in the presence of all the officers and men for duty in your command on the parade, and until you have heard from me what disposition to make of them. I inclose a copy of a form for the oath. Let the officers witness the signature of each man. Then, if afterward we find any of these men in the ranks of the enemy, or giving aid, intelligence and comfort to him, we shall have an abundance of witnesses to their oath and shall have according to the rules of war, a just right to hang them up without further ceremony. They should understand this....

In the same letter, Rigg was instructed to collect any horses, mules and equipage held at the fort and send them to Captain M.A. McLaughlin, 2nd California Cavalry, near Temecula.¹⁴²

The oath prescribed for the prisoners read:

> I do solemnly swear that I will support, protect, and defend, the Constitution and Government of the United States against all enemies, whether domestic or foreign, and that I will bear true faith, allegiance and loyalty to the same, any ordinance, resolution or law of any State Convention or

Legislature to the contrary notwithstanding; and that I will render no aid, intelligence or comfort to enemies in hostility to the United States; and further, that I do this with a full determination, pledge, and purpose, without any mental reservation or evasion whatsoever, so help me God.[143]

In a diary entry dated April 13—a Sunday—Sergeant George Hand, Company G, 1st California Infantry, noted that, at dress parade that day, the officer of the day marched the Showalter party to the center of the parade ground, where this oath was administered to them. Hand wrote that "it was a strong oath and if there was a Secesher in the party it must have been a bitter pill."[144] "Civis," the Camp Wright based sometime correspondent of the *Los Angeles Star*, wrote that Showalter and the others took the oath because they were "disgusted with their board and lodging at Fort Yuma."[145] There was no other way for the prisoners to gain their release.

Specific orders for release were sent to Major Rigg from district headquarters on April 22:

> As soon as this letter reaches you, send Theodore A. Wilson, Henry Crowell, William Wood, Oliver Woods, T.L. Roberts, A. King, E. Sumner, James Lawrence, and R.H. Ward, political prisoners to Camp Wright, where they will be released. They will be furnished for the transportation of their effects with one six-mule team: they are to have ten days rations issued to them at Fort Yuma, and instructions will be given to the commanding officer at Camp Wright, to give them ten days rations when they are released, on which to enable them to reach Los Angeles.
>
> You will furnish the commanding officer at Camp Wright a list of the property received from these persons when they were arrested. At Camp Wright they will find most of the horses, mules, horse equipage, pack saddles, etc., of the Showalter party, so called. The commanding officer at Camp Wright will be instructed to deliver the proper owners, such of those horses, mules and equipage as may belong to them.
>
> You will be careful to return to Camp Wright by these prisoners such of the Showalter animals as may be at Fort Yuma. If these men want shoes or other clothing, see that they are supplied with all that may be necessary.
>
> The arms and equipments of the so called Showalter party are in the possession of First Lieutenant T.A. Morgan, Fifth Infantry, California Volunteers, depot Quartermaster, at New San Pedro, California. You will give each of the above named prisoners a written order that it is done by the direction of the District Commander. It is possible that some of the animals belonging to these men may be up the Gila river; as soon as such fact (if it exists) is ascertained, the person whose horse or mule is so absent shall be furnished with another at the Government's expense, of equal value. Give Mr. Wilson a certified copy of this letter.
>
> This party need have no other guard than their word of honor that they will move with the wagon to Camp Wright. All this is by direction of the Colonel commanding the district.

On the same date, a similar letter was sent to Rigg to send other prisoners to Camp Wright "under charge of Dan Showalter." These other prisoners were William Turner, William Hamilton, Charles M. Benbroke, Joseph M. Sampson, Hayward H. Dickey, Edward M. Morgan, William Sands, William Edwards, Calvin M. Criswell, Levi Rogers, Simon A. Rogers, Frank D. Gilbert, John R. Samuels and Hugh C. Minor.[146]

The wagons with Showalter, Wilson and others arrived at Camp Wright on May 7, 1862. "Civis," the *Star*'s correspondent there, reported that they all looked "remarkably well" despite a fatiguing journey across the desert. From Colonel George W. Bowie of the 5th California Infantry they received their horses and equipment, and also rations and forage for the horses. They then set out for Los Angeles.[147] Upon arrival there, they likely received back all the rest of their property.

Very little is known regarding the activities of Dan Showalter or any of his party after they arrived in Los Angeles. Some probably returned to their California homes, as did Charles Benbrook and William Sands, who were back at Hornitos in Mariposa County by May 26, 1862.[148] Others perhaps made their way to the Confederacy. As shall be seen later, such is the case of T.A. Wilson and Henry Crowell, who eventually reached Texas, where they joined the 4th Regiment, Arizona Brigade of Texas Cavalry. On June 11, a correspondent writing to the *Sacramento Daily Union* stated that two members of the Showalter Party had passed through Fort Yuma on their way to mines beyond the Colorado River. They were among many seeking to make their fortunes at these new mines.[149] Writing from La Paz, New Mexico Territory (Arizona Territory was not established until 1863), on the Colorado River, on November 6, 1862, to the commanding officer at Fort Yuma, Herman Ehrenberg reported that some fifty horses had been stolen from ranches in the area on November 4. He wrote that "persons here who seem to have been privy, state that these horse thieves are secessionists." He enclosed with his letter a list of the names of those whom he could discover, "amongst which is one of the Showalter party."[150] Unfortunately, his list of names was not included in the published *Official Records*, so exactly which member of the Showalter Party was among the suspected thieves is not determinable.

There is a strong probability that William Edwards was this man or one of the two known to have crossed the river to the new mines. In any event, Edwards is definitely known to have been in the La Paz area a year later, when he murdered two Union soldiers and seriously wounded another. At this time, Edwards was described as "about six feet high, light complexion, light hair, wears a light mustache, no beard, is slightly built, and answers to the name of 'Frog,' but has quite a number of aliases."[151] It was believed that he was originally a gambler from Visalia.[152] The circumstances surrounding the murders by Edwards were explained by E.B. Tuttle in the July 1928 issue of the *Arizona Historical Review*. At the time of the incident, Tuttle was a lieutenant and in charge of the quartermaster depot at Fort Yuma. He had chartered the steamer *Cocopah* from the Colorado Steam Navigation Company to transport supplies to Fort Mojave (now a suburb of Bullhead City, Arizona, across the Colorado River from Laughlin, Nevada). Lieutenant James A. Hale and a detachment from the 4th California Infantry made the trip as escort for the supplies. During the return from Fort Mohave, the *Cocopah* stopped at La Paz to overnight—it was considered an unsafe practice to run boats on this river at night. Lieutenant Hale permitted some of his men to go into town for individual supplies.[153]

It was a dark night, but, since no trouble was expected, the soldiers left their arms behind when they left the boat and went into the town. After shopping, about 10:00 p.m. (or perhaps 9:00 p.m.[154]), they gathered in front of B. Cohn's store to return to the boat.[155] The unsuspecting soldiers, reported to be of "sober habits, attentive to their duties, and of the better class of soldiers," were attacked from ambush. Yelling, "Git you sons of b[itche]s, git," Edwards fired four shots at them while they were standing in the street.[156] The first shot hit Private Thomas Gainor in the knee, shattering the bone. The second shot struck Private C.L. Wentworth in the chest. The third hit Private Ferdinand Behn in the abdomen, passed through his body, and hit a nearby Mexican in the head.[157] Witnesses called it "the most cold-blooded and cowardly murders ever perpetuated."[158] Lieutenant Hale, on hearing the disturbance, ordered his remaining men to fall in and search the town, but Edwards was gone. Privates Behn and Wentworth died aboard the *Cocopah* on the way downriver to Fort Yuma.[159] Though severely wounded, Private Gainor evidently recovered since he was mustered out on December 31, 1864, at the conclusion of his three-year term of service.[160] Edwards' flight, due to his precipitate action, was made unprepared for the desert. He apparently attempted to make his way to Sonora, Mexico, but was found dead in the desert of thirst and starvation.[161]

When Dan Showalter arrived in Los Angeles in May 1862, the Union commander at Camp Latham was Colonel Ferris Forman, a Sacramento acquaintance and commander of the 4th California Infantry. Through June, Showalter visited with him. An unknown correspondent to the *Sacramento Daily Union* commented on this from Camp Latham on September 10, 1862:

> This man [Showalter], who was taken *flagrente delicta*, and made to take the oath, I say visited Colonel Forman, and was treated by him with all the cordiality and courtesy he could extend to any person. More than this, all the privileges of camp were allowed him, his horses fed at the Government expense, etc.

This and presumed lack of vigorous response to "secessionist" activities in the Los Angeles area occasioned the writer's severe castigation of Colonel Forman.[162] Nevertheless, Colonel Forman remained in command of the post at Los Angeles until October of 1862, when he was transferred to command the post at Benecia on San Francisco Bay. On April 10, 1863, he was ordered back to Los Angeles to command the Southern District of California. When his regiment was ordered consolidated in early July 1863, he was without orders and resigned on August 15 after twenty-two months' service.

The next report of Dan Showalter was by the *Daily Alta California*'s resident correspondent in San Diego. He wrote the paper, on August 8, 1862, that "Dan Showalter and his party of fifteen men passes through San Quintuc on the 15th of last month." (By San Quintuc is meant San Quintin, Baja California, located on a bay just south of Ensenada, Mexico.) The writer said that four of the fifteen with Showalter were deserters from the U.S. Army, who had horses branded "U.S." All of the group were said to have been well mounted, armed, and having "plenty of money." Showalter ordered the horses left at San Quintuc to prevent trouble since they had the "U.S." brand. Their intention was to cross the Gulf of California to Guaymas, Sonora, Mexico, where they would be joined by others and proceed on to Texas.[163]

Guaymas is located in the southwestern portion of Sonora, about 242 miles from the border with the United States. Then, as now, it was the principal port of the Mexican State of Sonora and the entrepot for miners. Sonora was then noted for its mining, with both gold and, particularly, silver being attractive. Many Californians made their way to the mines of Sonora via Guaymas during the Civil War period—a convenient excuse for other Californians making their way to Texas and the Confederacy. By early 1863, the national press reported "a large emigration" there. The reports also mentioned that "several hundred Secessionists" had already or soon would leave California for Guaymas and from there cross Sonora and Chihuahua to Texas. One party, "including Judge Shatweck and Dan. Showalter," was reported as having already taken this route to Texas.[164] The "Judge Shatweck" in the company of Showalter was probably David Olcott Shattuck, a former Mississippi District Judge, unsuccessful Whig gubernatorial candidate, and Louisiana college president, who had emigrated to California in 1850. He purchased a farming estate in Sonoma County and practiced law in San Francisco, where he became a San Francisco Superior Court Judge. In 1861, he was defeated in a race for Congress as a Breckinridge Democrat. During the Civil War, he went to Mexico and raised cotton there before returning to California after three years. He died in 1893.[165] A son of his,

John S. Shattuck, is known to have gone from California to Texas about that period and served as a Captain of Confederate cavalry.[166]

In November 1862, Showalter was reported as having been "in Ures, the Capital of the State of Sonora, in company with a noted Secessionist from Mariposa, named Sumner. They were en route to Dixie."[167] Presumably, the mentioned Sumner was the same E.B. Sumner who had been with the party captured with Dan Showalter at Minter's Ranch. A report by Major David Fergusson dated February 13, 1863, to Brigadier General Joseph R. West (Commander, District of Arizona) on his gathering of "intelligence" in Chihuahua, Mexico, mentioned that many secessionists from California were making their way in small parties through that city to Texas. Significantly, he stated "Dan Showalter, David Douglas, late secretary of state of California, and some seven or eight more, passed two months previous." Fergusson also reported that, when he arrived in Chihuahua, "Nelson, the captain of Showalter's party, and three or four more of his band, with Yancy, late of Tucson, and about ten more of the same brood, were in Chihuahua when I arrived."[168] This would have placed Showalter in Chihuahua probably in November 1862. By "Nelson," T.A. Wilson is obviously meant, but the "three or four more" of Showalter's party are not identifiable except for perhaps Henry Crowell, who was later carried on the rolls of Wilson's company of the 4th Cavalry, Arizona Brigade. They would have been in Chihuahua about January 1863.

Dan Showalter's 1862 route from California to Texas and the Confederacy would have been by horseback from Los Angeles, via San Diego, to San Quintin, Baja California, and from there by steamship to Guaymas. The shortest and most direct route from there would have been north to Hermosillo and then east to Ures. From Ures to Chihuahua would have been by a particularly difficult road east across the Sierra Made. Even today, there are no major highways for this route. In those days, it would have been little more than a rough trail. During the summer of 1865, Showalter indicated to others a familiarity with Parras, Durango, Mexico.[169] This would indicate that from Guaymas he had traveled south to the Mazatlan area and then east to Parras along a more-frequented road. At Parras, he would have discovered that Union forces were in control of the lower Rio Grande Valley and so would have had to divert north to Chihuahua instead of going on from Parras to Eagle Pass or Brownsville in Texas. A near-contemporary press report stating that he had taken "the northern route,"[170] however, strongly implies that his trip was via Ures to Chihuahua. After a stop in Chihuahua, he and his companions would have taken a poor road roughly paralleling the Rio Concho north to Presidio del Norte (now Ojinaga, Mexico). There they would have crossed the Rio Grande into Texas, near the site of Fort Leaton (now Presidio, Texas). San Antonio, Texas, would have then been a relatively easy trip along well-known trails. Showalter's arrival in San Antonio would have been in late November or early December of 1862. Finally, slightly more than a year after he initially set out from El Monte, Dan Showalter had reached Texas and the Confederacy.

Six

Texas and the Indian Territory, 1863

Upon his arrival at San Antonio, Dan Showalter found himself "a stranger in a strange land." Fortunately he "soon met with Capt. George L. Patrick of Tuolumne."[1] George L. Patrick was the son of George W. Patrick, with whom Showalter had served in the Assembly of 1861. The younger Patrick had left California early during the war and, on November 1, 1861, at Dona Ana, Arizona (New Mexico Territory; immediately north of present-day Las Cruces), enrolled as a Private in the 2nd Texas Mounted Rifles (later designated as 2nd Texas Cavalry). He was elected Captain of Company D of the regiment at Gila City, Arizona, on July 1, 1862. When Sibley's invasion of New Mexico ended, he remained with the unit upon its return to Texas.[2] It was known in California that he was in the Confederate Army as late as May of 1862, when a report in the Memphis *Appeal* was republished in the *Sonora Democrat* and then the *Mariposa Gazette*.[3] Soon after Showalter's joining Patrick's company, the regiment was transferred to Galveston, Texas, and Dan was soon serving otherwise. With the regiment for less than a month, Private Showalter does not appear on any roster or return of the 2nd Texas Cavalry.[4]

Showalter's first month's service with the Confederate Army found him involved in some significant—even exciting—events. Like so much of his life, there are few specific details of his personal involvement in these events. Clues are provided by a few brief lines in his 1864 letter to Anna Forman and two equally brief newspaper articles. He wrote Anna that he "had the honor of participating in the battle of Galveston, and soon after in the naval engagement off Sabine Pass, ... My name was favorably mentioned in the reports of both those fights."[5] San Francisco's *Evening Bulletin* of March 11, 1863, in a two-sentence "Secesh for Texas" article's second sentence, read: "Showalter, who took the northern route [across Mexico to Texas], distinguished himself in command of a gun at the capture of Galveston."[6] The *Daily Alta California* of the same city, on March 13, 1863, devoted its entire two-sentence article "In Texas" to Showalter. It read, "Dan Showalter is said to be figuring extensively in Texas as a Captain of Artillery, or rather with the rank as such, but acting as an Aid to John B. Magruder. Showalter was present at the fight when the Union gunboat *Harriet Lane* was basely surrendered."[7] Taken all together, these three brief accounts, when fitted with reports of the mentioned events, provide a reasonable depiction of Showalter's role in the events.

Major General John Bankhead Magruder had distinguished himself during the defense of Yorktown, Virginia, at the beginning of McClellan's 1862 Peninsula Campaign, but then, at the Battle of Malvern Hill, lost the confidence of R.E. Lee, new commander of what became the Confederate Army of Northern Virginia. He, like so many other

Confederate generals (Beauregard, J.E. Johnston, Theophilius Holmes and E. Kirby Smith) who in one way or the other came to displease Lee or President Jefferson Davis, was "exiled" to the west. In October of 1862, he was assigned to command the District of Texas, New Mexico and Arizona, replacing Brigadier General Paul O. Hebert, who was disliked by both his Texas soldiers and Governor Lubbock of Texas. Magruder arrived at Houston in November 1862 and assumed command. Like all generals in those days, he had discretion to appoint to his staff, with a courtesy rank, Aides-de-Camp. In the armies of the Confederacy especially, these staff aides were volunteers and frequently prominent personages. Dan Showalter met these criteria. Newspapers in the east had reported his pro-secession comments while a member of the California Assembly and reports of the duel with Piercy had emphasized this. It is therefore probable that General Magruder was quite happy to appoint and have on his staff a California legislator and gave him the courtesy rank (necessary in order to transmit orders for the general and to command upon occasion) of Captain of Artillery.

Upon assuming command of the District, Magruder set about to rectify the matter that had led to General Hebert's unpopularity: Galveston. The island port city was the largest in Texas when the Civil War began. Hebert had ordered Confederate forces out and the city evacuated when confronted by a Union fleet in October. (The city was not really defensible.) The city had not been occupied—three companies of the 52nd Massachusetts Infantry were stationed on a wharf in the harbor on Christmas Day. He began to organize forces for retaking the city. A principal difficulty was in obtaining enough soldiers to do so. This problem he largely resolved by appropriating the brigade which General Sibley had led in New Mexico. His plan was for a midnight attack, during which troops would be sent across a railroad bridge to Galveston Island with artillery to attack the small Federal force on the wharf. Once this action had commenced, the Union fleet inside the harbor, occupied in supporting the Federal troops on the wharf, would be attacked by armed riverboats loaded with soldiers. The use of riverboats in this manner had been suggested to him by local river men. Given that Showalter was appointed a Captain of Artillery and was present when the Federal ship *Harriet Lane* was taken, it seems likely that his duties were as a "gun captain" or assistant on one of the riverboats.

The "naval" element of Magruder's force was placed under the command of Leon Smith, a former steamship captain. His rank was as Major in the Marine Department of the District, but he was frequently referred to as "Captain" or "Commodore" because of his naval activities on the Texas coast. He fitted out his fleet in the Trinity River and on Galveston Bay. The river packet-boat *Bayou City* was "fortified" with cotton bales and armed with one 32-pound rifled gun on its bow. This gun was under the command of Captain A.R. Weir. One hundred soldiers from the Sibley Brigade were put aboard as "sharpshooters." It was captained during the action to follow by Henry Lubbock, brother of the Texas governor. The *Neptune*, another river packet, was also "cotton-clad." Its sharpshooters were about 150 men from the 7th Texas Cavalry. The armament of the *Neptune* was two howitzers. The commanders of its guns were a Captain Harby and Lieutenant Harvey Clark. It would seem that Dan Showalter was perhaps assisting one of these three gun captains. These two cotton-clad gunboats were to be accompanied by two tenders, the *John F. Carr*, with more soldiers aboard, and the *Lady Gwinn*, loaded with armed spectators.

The infantry and artillery movement onto Galveston Island and their attack on the Massachusetts troops on Kuhn's Wharf began on schedule at midnight of December 31,

1862. With Smith's "naval" force not in sight, they were on the point of withdrawal when the *Bayou City* and the *Neptune* came into view in the bay. The Federal naval force in the harbor and bay consisted of four vessels. Closest to shore was the *Harriet Lane*, a steam-powered, sidewheel Revenue Service cutter armed with a four-inch rifled Parrott gun, a nine-inch Dahlgen gun, two eight-inch Columbiads and two 24-pound brass howitzers. Its captain was naval Commander Jonathan M. Wainwright and its executive officer was naval Lieutenant Commander Edward Lea. In somewhat deeper water was the *Westfield*, a converted ferryboat, which served as the flagship. Its captain (and "commodore" of the fleet) was Commander William B. Renshaw. The other components of the Federal "fleet" were the *Owasco* (another converted ferryboat) and the small gunboat *Clifton*.

The nearest ship to the approaching Confederate vessels was the *Harriet Lane*. Smith, aboard the *Bayou City*, therefore moved to attack it. Its gun fired twice, the second round of which struck the *Harriet Lane* behind the wheelhouse, resulting in a large hole. As it fired again, the gun exploded, killing Weir. Now gunless, the *Bayou City* moved to ram the Federal ship so that its soldiers could board. It struck a glancing blow near the port wheelhouse. Meanwhile, the *Neptune* approached the *Harriet Lane* on its starboard side and, ramming, stove in its own bow. The *Bayou City* turned and, with steam up again, rammed the *Harriet Lane*. This time she struck a little behind the larboard wheelhouse, pushing her bow far under the gunwale. The two vessels were now stuck together, and the Confederate riflemen opened up on the Union ship's decks with a heavy fire from close quarters. Commander Wainwright was struck several times, then killed instantly by a musket ball through the brain. Lieutenant Commander Edward Lea received five wounds in his side and abdomen. The crew raised a white flag and fled below decks. The Confederates boarded from the *Bayou City* and the *Neptune* and quickly took control of their capture. The United States gunboat *Owasco* had attempted to aid the *Harriet Lane*, but was driven off. A report—apparently given to the paper by John Robert Baylor (governor of the Confederate Territory of Arizona, who served, like Showalter, as a volunteer)—in Houston's *Tri-Weekly Telegraph* on January 7 provides the only details of Dan Showalter's participation in this battle. He was aboard the *Bayou City* and from it boarded the *Harriet Lane*. With one of its guns, "Governor J. R. Baylor fired the last shot at the *Owasso* as she sailed off. He fired six shots from a rifled cannon, four of which took effect. Capt. Shoalwater [sic], late member of the Legislature in California, assisted the Governor in working the gun, as did three privates whose names the Governor does not recollect."[8]

Subsequent to the capture of the *Harriet Lane*, Edward Lea died of his wounds, the badly leaking *Neptune* made it to the channel and sank in eight feet of water, the Union flagship *Westfield* ran aground on a bar and its commander and several others were killed in the explosion when he ordered it blown up to avoid capture, and the Massachusetts infantry on the wharf surrendered when the *Owasco* and the *Clifton* left, abandoning them. The guns of the *Harriet Lane* would prove useful to Texas Confederates in the future. The *Harriet Lane* itself would be deemed not useful as a naval vessel and was used as a blockade runner. The Texans were elated. General Magruder sent notice to Commodore H. H. Bell, commander of the Union's West Gulf Blockading Squadron, that the blockade of Galveston had been lifted. This was not strictly true since the Union thereafter maintained a strong, offshore blockade of the port.[9]

After Galveston, Dan Showalter was sent to Sabine Pass on the Louisiana border, where he shortly would become involved in what was called by *Confederate Military History* "one of the most extraordinary and hazardous naval exploits during the war."[10] Though extraordinary, this event has been almost completely overshadowed by two later ship-versus-shore battles at the same general location. Again, the exact nature of Showalter's participation in the battle is not known. It is possible only to relate what occurred with the understanding that he was directly involved in a portion of it and cognizant of the balance.

General Magruder's energies had not been directed solely toward the recapture of Galveston and ending the blockade there. Concurrently with his planning for that action, he had also begun preparations for similar activity at Sabine Pass.[11] The Sabine River, then as now, served as the boundary between the states of Texas and Louisiana, from where its course turned south to the Gulf of Mexico. The last seventeen miles of its course take the form of seven-mile-wide Sabine Lake, into which also outflows the Neches River. Finally, there is a four-mile narrow egress into the Gulf named Sabine Pass. Steamboating began on the lake and river in 1843, bringing cotton raised in east Texas downriver. The town of Sabine Pass, located on the western side and near the upper reach of the lake, became an important port for the export of cotton.

In early December of 1862, General Magruder instructed Captain Charles Fowler, a Texas river boatman, to proceed to the Sabine, where he was to select two or three river steamers and fit them out as gunboats for the purpose of attacking the United States naval ships blockading the pass. Fowler was given authority to impress such vessels and materials as necessary to accomplish this purpose. After examining the boats available, he selected two, the *Josiah H. Bell* and the *Uncle Ben,* as best for the purpose. The *Josiah H. Bell* was about 180 feet long, and the *Uncle Ben* 130 feet. Both were about ten years old, but in fairly good condition. Soldiers were detailed to the work of converting them into gunboats. They constructed breastworks to protect sharpshooters on the decks by sinking 14-by-14-inch timbers through the decks and fastening them to the floor timbers in the hold.[12] Bales of cotton completed the protection of soldiers who would be assigned as sharpshooters aboard the steamboats.[13] The *Josiah H. Bell* was armed with one 64-pound rifled cannon and the *Uncle* Ben with two 32-pound cannons.[14] This conversion of the boats to "cotton-clads" was accomplished at Port Orange at the north end of the lake.[15]

General Magruder sent Major Oscar M. Watkins to the Sabine to command the operation. Beginning as Captain of a company of the 2nd Louisiana Infantry, he had served in charge of conscripts in the district and was now on Magruder's staff. According to Texas Governor Lubbock, Watkins was "an efficient staff officer."[16] He was also a favorite of Magruder's. His assignment to command the expedition incensed Lieutenant Colonel Ashley W. Spaight, who was both senior to Watkins and in command of the 11th Texas Battalion (a mixed infantry, artillery and cavalry unit) stationed in the area, and some of whose men would be used in the effort. Spaight therefore submitted his resignation to Magruder's adjutant. After an argument with Spaight, Magruder forwarded the resignation to Richmond, where it was later rejected. Meanwhile, Spaight had no part in the operations off the Sabine.[17] The Davis Guard (Company F of the 1st Texas Heavy Artillery), commanded by Captain Frederick H. Odlum, was transferred from Houston to the Sabine for Watkins' use.[18] Two members of Magruder's staff—an engineer, Captain Heriot, and Captain Dan Showalter—were assigned to assist the Major.[19]

Watkins headquartered himself aboard the *Josiah H. Bell,* which, in his detailed report of January 23, 1861, he referred to as "Flagship, Second Squadron, Magruder Fleet."[20] His aides, Captains Heriot and Dan Showalter, were with Watkins aboard the *Josiah H. Bell*, where, according to the Major, they rendered him "invaluable assistance in communicating my orders." The boat was captained by Fowler. Her single gun was commanded by Captain Odlum, with Lieutenant Dick Dowling at the gun. Captain Matt Nolan of Pyron's 2nd Texas Cavalry Regiment commanded its sharpshooters. The *Uncle Ben*'s captain was William Johnson. Its two guns were commanded by Captain Kosciuszko Dewitt Keith of the artillery company ("B") of Spaight's battalion. The sharpshooters aboard it were also from Spaight's battalion and commanded by Captain George W. O'Bryan. There were about 150 sharpshooters aboard each boat—the soldiers of the units had drawn lots for the privilege.

The Federal blockading force off Sabine Pass at the time consisted of only two sailing ships, the ship *Morning Light* and the schooner *Velocity*. Acting Master John Dillingham, captain of the *Morning Light*, had been assigned to command the blockade station by Commodore Henry H. Bell on January 18, 1863. At that time, he had been ordered to detach a third ship, the *Rachel Seaman*, to the Federal naval station at Pensacola, Florida, to be caulked, since it was leaking very badly.[21] The *Morning Light* was only slightly larger than the *Josiah H. Bell*, carried a crew of just over one hundred, and was armed with eight 32-pound guns and one small breech-loading rifle. The *Velocity* was a small schooner with a crew of only about a dozen. It had been captured by the Federal navy in September 1862, while trying to run the blockade into Sabine Lake, and taken into service. It was armed with only two brass howitzers. It was not in particularly good condition. It had been described to Rear Admiral David G. Farragut, by Commodore Bell in a letter of January 18, 1863, as "a miserable little craft, badly found, and scarcely able to keep the sea [out]."[22] Knowing the vulnerability of sailing ships to steam-powered craft, Dillingham had solicited addition of a steam gunboat for his force, but none had been assigned.[23]

The improvised Confederate squadron under Major Watkins set out down the river on their mission, but were delayed when they found their boats could not pass out of the river into Sabine Lake due to obstructions the Confederacy had installed there to keep the Federal navy out of the river. They were enabled to proceed on January 18, when the tide was raised just enough by a strong wind out of the southeast for them to pass over. Then an icy Texas "norther" struck, making Sabine Lake too choppy and conditions aboard the boats severe for the men. This storm began to clear on the 20th, and, finally, early on the morning of the 21st, the squadron moved out across the lake and out of the pass to attack the blockaders.

Almost all accounts (not including those published in *Official Records of the Union and Confederate Navies in the War of the Rebellion*) of the engagement that followed contended that Major Watkins was drunk the entire time and actual command was exercised by Captain Fowler. Testimony of this is found in statements of four veterans of the battle. First Sergeant H.N. Connor recorded in his diary that there was "too much whisky aboard of Maj. Watkins."[24] Captain K.D. Keith wrote in 1883 that the major "had imbibed so freely of General Magruder's hospital stores as to be totally unfit to command."[25] Keith, however, is definitely known to have been aboard the *Uncle Ben*,[26] so his testimony would have had to have been made on observations before the boats set sail. Abel Coffin, Jr., a civilian engineer, noted, in the flyleaf of a copy of Macaulay's *Essays* that he had taken as a share of the "spoils," "We proceeded to attack the blockaders under the nominal command of a drunken military officer."²⁷ The fourth witness was John A. Drummond of the Davis Guard. Almost forty years later, he claimed that, during the engagement, he had been standing close to Watkins, who was "so drunk he was disgusting and no order of his was obeyed."²⁸ One recollection was that Watkins had remarked to Captain Fowler "jocularly" that he had never smelled any gunpowder. To this, Fowler responded, "I'll give you a chance to smell some to-day."²⁹ Perhaps this was an effort to excuse his inebriation.

Whomever was actually giving the orders, the Confederate cotton-clads steamed out of the pass at daylight, the *Josiah H. Bell* in the lead. Shallow-draft river boats, slow with minimal keels and high decks, were far from ideal at sea, unable to steer so easily, and the high decks an impediment against a wind. Their steam propulsion, however, gave them an advantage in maneuverability over sailing ships. The *Morning Light* and the *Velocity* were at anchor with sails furled. When they saw the two Confederate boats coming, they immediately set sails to flee. Unfortunately for them, the wind was very light that morning. The riverboats pursued the blockaders for twenty miles before closing in at about cannon range (about two miles). The official report by Acting Assistant Surgeon J.W. Sherfy, later made for Acting Master Dillingham of the *Morning Light*, stated that this was at about 8:30 a.m. The report of Major Watkins said it was at about 10:00 a.m. Both pursuers and pursued had their guns ready for action. The *Josiah H. Bell* fired twice upon its enemy, each shot being replied to by a four-gun broadside. The *Bell*'s gun jammed. After some effort, the Davis Guards artillerymen were able to push into position a shell that had lodged in the barrel and resume fire. The cannon fire of neither side was very effective—passing over or falling short—until a shell from the *Bell*'s gun exploded on the deck of the *Morning Light*, dismounting its forward port gun.

The *Uncle Ben* had been ordered to close to the port side of the *Bell* so that, when the time came, the Federal ship could be boarded from both sides. Soon after, the opposing ships were within a thousand yards of each other. At this range, the numerous infantrymen and cavalrymen aboard the Confederate vessels were able to open fire with their Enfield rifles. The elevated deckhouses of the riverboats here was a significant advantage for them. They were able to sweep the decks and rigging of the Federal ship effectively. Its upper decks were "completely riddled" and four of its five boats destroyed. Dillingham's crew were forced below decks by the severe rifle fire. Using its steam power, the *Bell* was able to maneuver behind the stern of the Federal ship. The *Morning Light* was unable to train its aft guns on its pursuers, even with intent to fire through its own cabin. After about two hours, eighty rounds of shot and shell fired, unable to maneuver, flanked, and outnumbered, about twenty-eight miles southwest of Sabine Pass, Dillingham, who had remained on deck throughout the action, reluctantly surrendered after his crew threw their small arms overboard. The small *Velocity*, whose steady fire had been ignored by the Confederates, then also surrendered.

There were no Confederate casualties reported. Aboard the *Morning Light*, there was one seaman killed in action, one or two (reports differ) mortally wounded, and several slightly wounded. One hundred and nine prisoners of war were taken. All of these, except twenty-nine who were "contrabands," were well-treated and sent to Houston two days later. The captures were taken to Sabine Pass. The *Velocity* was escorted to Sabine City, but, due to its deep draft, the Confederates were unable to get the *Morning Light* over the bar at its entrance. It was left at the bar under command of an Army Lieutenant, Eugene Aiken, with a small crew, until it could be divested of its guns and stores. This did not happen. The next day, January 22, the USS *Tennessee* approached and hailed the *Morning Light*. The Confederates aboard, unable to lure the *Tennessee*'s commander into capture, admitted it was now under Confederate command. The *Tennessee* then sped off to Galveston to notify the large Federal blockading fleet there. Although the bar was soft mud and several local river boatmen believed they could coax it over into the lake, Major Watkins ordered his largest prize destroyed. He was criticized as being drunk at the time. In an April 1863 supplemental report, he wrote that his "wish was to take our fine prizes into the Pacific and operate against the commerce of the enemy there, but this was impracticable, for want of supplies and seamen."[30] Due to the recent (January 11) destruction of the USS *Hatteras* by the CSS *Alabama* in nearby waters, Watkins knew that the Federals would soon send more strongly armed ships than he had to the area. Aiken had consequently been instructed to burn the ship and take his men ashore, which he did. The Confederates were unable to dismount and take ashore the guns of the *Morning Light* and retrieved only about half of her stores.[31]

In his detailed report of the action, dated January 23, "on Board Steamer Bell," Major Watkins complimented the steamers' captains and engineers, the artillery, cavalry and infantry officers commanding soldiers aboard the vessels (including his greatest detractor, K.D. Keith), the captains of two support boats, the surgeons of the command, and wrote that "Captains Heriot and Showalter rendered invaluable assistance in communicating my orders."[32] His brief initial report of the victory on January 21 had also mentioned Showalter in its last sentence (edited out when *Official Records* was published): "Cap. Dan Showalter, whom I have appointed a captain of artillery, in accordance with the orders of the Major General commanding, and assigned him to duty as commander of Shell-Bank Battery."[33] This battery was located on the Louisiana side of Sabine Pass. It seems doubtful that Showalter ever actually exercised any command of this battery since he was soon after the battle in Houston. On January 26, 1863, the editor of the *Houston Tri-Weekly Telegraph* published an article, "The Victory Off Sabine!" with the attribution that "the arrival of Capt. Schowalter from Sabine, brings us some particulars of the brilliant victory of Maj. Watkins and his gallant comrades off Sabine."[34] Major Watkins himself was in Houston by Saturday, January 31, when he was seen and spoken with by the paper's editor. Among those that Watkins "particularly mentioned" was "Capt. Showalter."[35] Drunk or not, Major Watkins was not remiss in commending those, including Dan Showalter, who had served under him. Dan Showalter was soon to receive another assignment in the Confederate Army.

After Sibley's Confederate Army of New Mexico (actually just a brigade) had retreated, in the summer of 1862, from the Rio Grande valley in New Mexico Territory, many retained hopes of one day recovering the region. In May 1862, Confederate Secretary of War George W. Randolph had authorized Colonel John Robert Baylor, governor of the Confederate Arizona Territory, to raise five battalions of partisan rangers of six companies each. Randolph's order specified that "these troops will be under your command as Governor of Arizona."[36] Baylor was, however, dismissed as governor and cashiered from the army when President Jefferson Davis learned of an order issued by him, in March 1862, to call in bands of Apache Indians for peace talks, then get them drunk, kill all of the adults, and sell the children as slaves. The organization of what would be known as the Arizona Brigade continued, however. On February 21, 1863, Special Order No. 81, issued by Headquarters, District of Texas, New Mexico, and Arizona, consolidated the battalions into three regiments: the first under Colonel William P. Hardeman, the second under Colonel George W. Baylor (former Governor Baylor's brother), and the third under Colonel Joseph Phillips.[37]

John Baylor was not the only person interested in forming a force to retake Arizona. When Sibley's Texans had withdrawn, numerous pro–Confederate citizens of Arizona and New Mexico had gone to Texas with them. Among these was Spruce McCoy Baird. A lawyer, he had been appointed Judge of Texas' new Santa Fe County in 1848. The area was separated from Texas in 1850, but Baird remained behind, becoming a large landowner in northern New Mexico and practicing law. In 1860, he was appointed Attorney General of the New Mexico Territory.[38] Once in Texas in 1862, he had agitated for a force to retake the territory. His efforts had not gone unnoticed. From San Antonio, John R. Baylor wrote General Magruder recommending him:

> I would respectfully suggest that if Judge S. M. Baird, for fifteen years a resident of that country [New Mexico and Arizona], and by far the most popular and influential man among the natives, was authorized to raise one or more regiments of Mexicans in New Mexico and Arizona, he could do so, and he could keep up the disaffection and stimulate the people to hold out against our enemies until such time as you could send a force to retake the country. I have conversed with Judge Baird and he is willing to undertake the raising of one regiment of citizens, composed of men now resisting the U.S. authorities. The most influential citizens of that country would join Judge Baird.[39]

The previously mentioned Special Order No. 81 also stated that a "Fourth Regiment of this brigade is to be formed in Arizona and New Mexico." Baird was designated as Colonel of the regiment and "Dan. Showalter, lieutenant-colonel."[40] Showalter was commissioned at this rank on February 13, 1863, per a roster of the brigade's officers made at Columbus, Texas, on March 1.[41] Three regimental rosters made in 1864, however, indicated that he was so appointed or elected on March 9, 1863.[42] The list of the brigade's officers would seem to be the more accurate. General Magruder, district commander, later explained that the decision to form the fourth regiment was subsequent to the first three and due to "a favorable opportunity to invade Arizona" having been presented to him. He authorized Baird "to raise a regiment, if he could, of New Mexicans, Arizonians, Californians, and others not subject to conscription."[43]

The designation of this regiment seems to officially have been "Regiment, Cavalry, Fourth Regiment, Arizona Brigade," which was how it was listed in a list of district commands by Magruder's headquarters in June of 1863.[44] "4th Regt., Arizona Brigade," however, was how it was most frequently referred to in correspondence by its superiors, John S. Ford in 1864 and Brigadier General James E. Slaughter in 1865. The Adjutant and Inspector General's office in Rich-

New Mexico attorney Spruce McCoy Baird was Colonel of the 4th Arizona Cavalry though its active command was primarily exercised by Lieutenant Colonel Dan Showalter (courtesy Don E. Baird).

mond, Virginia, even used this designation upon occasion.⁴⁵ Its own commanders, Baird and later Showalter, in their correspondence almost invariably referred to it as "4th Regiment Arizona Brigade" though occasionally simply as the "4th Arizona." Veterans of the regiment in later years called it the "4th Arizona Cavalry" or, less frequently, the "4th Texas Cavalry." Other appellations which have been given to the unit have been the "4th Arizona-Texas," the "4th Texas-Arizona," and the "4th Texas Cavalry, Arizona Brigade." Since there was actually a 4th Texas Cavalry, use of this designation is inappropriate and confusing. Of course, like all so many Confederate units, they were also referred to after the name of their commander: "Baird's Cavalry" and, subsequently, "Showalter's Cavalry." All of these designations and the existence of other organizations having a similar designation, as shall be seen, led to confusion. For the sake of simplicity, to reduce confusion and for consistency, the authors have henceforward used "4th Arizona" in referring to the regiment.

The regiments were formed and organized at a camp at Eagle Lake, Texas (about halfway between San Antonio and Houston). The first three regiments were recruited and organized in Texas by their Texan commanders with relatively little difficulty. Department of the Trans-Mississippi commander General E. Kirby Smith, on April 5, 1863, had written to General Magruder that no troops could be withdrawn for an expedition to Arizona since western Louisiana, Arkansas and eastern Texas were threatened.⁴⁶ By the middle of 1863, the first three regiments had been sent east to serve in Louisiana and Arkansas. It was customary during the Civil War for volunteer units to have prominent men recruit and then organize them. These men then became the field officers of the regiment. Despite the laudatory comments of Baylor to Magruder, Baird's name proved to not be so well known as to attract many recruits. Showalter, however, had a more well-known name from his service in the California legislature, the duel with Piercy, and his capture at Minter's Ranch—news reports of all three having been republished in the eastern states, including Texas. That and, no doubt, his performance at Galveston and off Sabine Pass accounted for his appointment and his success in recruiting men for the regiment.

It seems that, like Dan Showalter himself, many Californians who had made their way to the Confederacy arrived at San Antonio. Among these—perhaps one to two months later than Showalter—was Theodore A. Wilson. Having served in 1850 and 1851 as Quartermaster Sergeant of the "Mariposa Battalion" (actually a company) of California militia volunteers in a war against Indians of California's Central Valley,⁴⁷ he had military experience and became Captain of Company A of the regiment. At least two others who had been part of the Showalter Party became members of this company: Henry Crowell ("Krowell" in most regimental records) and A. King. It is not known if these two came together or separately, with Showalter, Wilson, or otherwise. It is possible, if not probable, that other California refugees in the San Antonio area during this time joined this company. A second company, B, was assigned to the regiment at about the same time under Captain William S. Rather of Bell County. This company had a number of men from that central Texas county in it and had been organized in the summer of 1862, but not previously assigned to a regiment.⁴⁸ These would be the only two companies until the early summer of 1863. The displeasure of General Magruder with Baird's lack of success in raising the regiment was hinted at in a letter to Lieutenant General E. Kirby Smith, Commander of the Confederate Department of the Trans-Mississippi, on June 26, 1863, stating that there were only two companies "of the Fourth Regiment, Colonel Baird commanding,

Showalter's signature and clear handwriting—and his hopes of recruiting Californians into his regiment—are illustrated in this June 3, 1863, report to General Magruder's Assistant Adjutant General (compiled Service Record of Dan Showalter in the National Archives and Records Administration).

which regiment was to have been raised in New Mexico and Arizona, but is still incomplete."[49]

Obtaining men—and equipment for them—impeded completion of the 4th Arizona's organization for most of the year. Reporting for an absent Colonel Baird, Dan Showalter advised Magruder's headquarters, on June 3, 1863, that the regiment was not ready for duty. He advised that "there are several men out on recruiting Service, who I expect to hear from in a few days, and I fully expect that they will bring in a number of recruits."[50]

In a June 22, 1863, report to district headquarters, Major A.G. Dickinson, commander of the Post of San Antonio, mentioned the two companies: "The fourth Regt Arizona Brigade consists of two companies numbering about 40 men each under Command of Lt Col. Shoalwalter, and stationed about 5 miles above this Post, they are without arms and entirely without discipline. Complaints are being made continually by the stock raisers in the vicinity of The camp of the manner in which their property is abused. And whenever a number of them visit this city a row or disturbance is usually the consequence." Dickinson went on to write that "Shoalwalter" had applied for assignment to the command of General S.P. Bankhead. Dickinson wanted to use them as scouts between San Antonio and Eagle Pass, which was an escape route for deserters, but noted that they would have to be first armed.[51] Baird pleaded to Magruder's headquarters that it be "filled up from any troops unattached" so that it could operate with the first three regiments of the brigade, which by then were on the way to service in Louisiana. He specifically asked for a company of a Captain Navarro that was in the area, but still unattached. Despite this plea, he stated, "We are recruiting with considerable success, but would like to be filled as soon as possible."[52] Navarro's company, however, would never be added to the regiment. The colonel had no way of knowing then that his regiment would never serve with or as part of the rest of the Arizona Brigade. On May 5, he reported that thirty wagons had brought in some supplies—flour, shoes, and blankets—from Chihuahua. In the same letter, he optimistically advised that with these supplies and "30,000 Confederates in the State of California," according to a source, Fort Yuma could be captured and California taken for the Confederacy.[53]

On July 11, from "Camp Mariposa" near San Antonio, Showalter reported that the regiment was getting recruits from California and Arizona, but they were arriving destitute and needed equipping.[54] Citizens of San Antonio were not generous with the arriving Californians, as one newspaper commented:

> A short time since a brigade of Arizonians composed mostly of loyal Californians, passed through San Antonio, Texas. Being in want of clothes and other things, some of them went about among the hucksters and shopkeepers of the town, displaying an unusual amount of coin. So great was the cupidity of some of the shopkeepers to get possession of the specie, that they made an extraordinary difference in the specie price and the Confederate note price of an article—The Californians after getting the specie price and the Confederate note price of what they wished, would take possession of the same and pay for it in Confederate notes. This of course caused a row at once. The soldiers, however, came off victorious.[55]

Soon after, Company C would be assigned to special duty in San Antonio. Baird, seeking greater success in recruiting, moved his efforts west, to near the Pecos River, which had become sort of a "no man's land" between Confederate Texas and Union-held New Mexico. Available recruits from this area consisted of conscription evaders and deserters and other less desirable men.[56]

Amzi Bradshaw, a lawyer who had been District Attorney of Ellis County, had represented that county in the Texas Secession Convention (voting for secession), and then joined the 19th Texas Cavalry as a private. He was discharged in May 1863, after participation in the Battle of Cape Girardeau in Missouri, and then raised and captained his own company, which was assigned to the 4th Arizona, as Company D, in early August.[57] Company E was also enrolled or joined to the 4th Arizona in July and August of 1863.[58] Its commander was Captain Henry LeKaester or LeKoester.[59] Two more companies, F and G, were added during the fall. On October 12, 1863, the independent company of

Captain Pablo B. Alderete was ordered from San Antonio to Baird at Austin. At the same time, Lieutenant Colonel A.G. Dickinson, commanding the post at San Antonio, inquired of headquarters in Houston, "Please instruct me in regard to Captain Conway's company [Company C]. They are without horses or arms."[60] During the war, a total of 980 men would serve in the 4th Arizona for various periods. As late as October 10, the complement of organized companies was still incomplete when Baird wrote from Austin to the same headquarters that, although his staff appointments were all full, he was "forwarding all recruits to Lt. Col. Showalter as soon as procured and consequently do not design organizing any company at this place."[61]

The Confederate situation had changed north of Texas. In April of 1863, Major General James G. Blunt, with his small Federal Army of the Frontier from Kansas, had driven Confederate Indian troops from Fort Gibson, ninety miles upriver from Fort Smith, Arkansas. Confederate Brigadier General Douglas H. Cooper withdrew his force of Indians and Texans thirty miles south to Honey Springs, just north of the Canadian River. The advance of the route of the Federal Army toward north Texas seemed to be succeeding. Brigadier General William Steele, commander of the District of Western Arkansas and the Indian Territory, had assumed that command the prior January, with his headquarters at Fort Smith. He had no more than 5,000 soldiers—on paper. Some of his Indian units were unreliable, the countryside was stripped of supplies, the populace was demoralized, and pro-union "jawhawkers" were in the majority.[62] At the same time, the Comanche and Kiowa Indians of the plains presented a threat to the small communities and farms along the Red River border of Texas. The principal forces in the Confederate Trans-Mississippi Department were needed to protect the Arkansas River Valley, the Red River Valley of Louisiana, and the Texas coast. Additionally, it was hoped that they could render some assistance in relieving Union pressure on the Confederate bastion of Vicksburg on the Mississippi River. The partially completed 4th Arizona was one of the few available units that could be sent to north Texas to meet the dual threats of Indians and Federals.

On May 29, 1863, General Magruder established a new northern subdistrict within the northeastern corner of his District of Texas, New Mexico, and Arizona. Its headquarters were to be established at Bonham, a few miles south of the Red River, with its quartermaster and commissary depots to be at Paris. Magruder proposed to supply Brigadier General William Steele, commander of Confederate forces in western Arkansas, from there. He felt that having a subdistrict in the area would enable better protection for the gathering of wheat in that region. His plan was to send three regiments and a battalion to the area with Colonel Smith P. Bankhead, his chief of artillery, in command as Acting Brigadier General.[63] Magruder's Special Order No. 145 of May 30 ordered four regiments and one battery to Bonham to report to Bankhead. Among these was Colonel William P. Hardeman's First Regiment of the Arizona Brigade and the 17th Texas Field Battery of Captain William B. Krumbhaar.[64] Most of the men in Krumbhaar's Battery had been recruited from Company F of Hardeman's 1st Arizona.[65] At least one of the regiments named in the order never arrived, but one other unit made its appearance in Bankhead's command—a battalion of the 4th Arizona under command of Dan Showalter. The service of Showalter's battalion along the Red River, in the Indian Territory, and in Arkansas during 1863 would be the only time that any portion of the 4th Arizona would ever serve with any of the rest of the Arizona Brigade.

To reinforce the Confederates under Bankhead, that portion of Baird's 4th Arizona that was sufficiently organized—Companies A, B, and D—was sent under the command of Lieutenant Colonel Dan Showalter to Bonham. While in northeastern Texas, a fourth Company E would be raised and organized, as is attested by Bankhead, that one company (of what he referred to as the "4th Texas," at which time the actual 4th Texas Cavalry was serving in Louisiana) was from north Texas.[66] Showalter left San Antonio on July 19, 1863, with Companies A and B[67] and probably arrived at Bonham three to four weeks later. Bankhead himself did not arrive at Bonham to take command until July 9.[68] The situation in the Indian Territory had by that time worsened. General Blunt's Federals attacked the Confederate Texans and Indians at Honey Springs on July 17, driving them further south to Perryville. Steele had yet to receive any reinforcements from south of the Red River and his powder was defective. Blunt received reinforcements, but turned toward Fort Smith. Steele, on July 11, was pressing for Bankhead to move his force northwest of Fort Gibson and attack Fort Scott in Kansas.[69] On this same date, Bankhead was reporting to his higher headquarters that his "command is at present so inadequate to accomplish anything." He reported having only 350 men effective in the one regiment he had received, with two (including the 1st Arizona) expected and one unheard from.[70] There was, at this time, no mention of Showalter's battalion as being either present or expected. For the balance of July, Steele, in the western Arkansas/Indian Territory subdistrict, continued to plead for Bankhead to reinforce him.

General Steele continued to wait and hope for Bankhead's assistance throughout early August. Finally, on August 11, General Magruder advised the Department's Chief of Staff that he had ordered Bankhead to report to Steele at Fort Smith with the regiments of Hardeman and Colonel Edward J. Gurley (13th Texas Cavalry), a company of light artillery (probably meaning Krumbhaar's battery), and "any other forces he may have in hand." One of the regiments that had been intended for Bankhead—Terrell's—had been sent elsewhere.[71] Since Dan Showalter later advised Anna Forman that he had been involved in "engagements" in the Indian Territory and Arkansas, it seems possible, if not likely, that it was at about this time that he and his battalion appeared in north Texas, as part of the "any other force in hand" and perhaps as replacements for Terrell's regiment. Bankhead did not yet leave to reinforce Steele, however. During the first part of the month, there had been a wave of Indian attacks in the western portion of his subdistrict. He had to send a portion of the Confederate States Border Regiment of Colonel James G. Bourland through the region. (This regiment was in the subdistrict, but operated on both sides of the Red River and not specifically under Bankhead's command.) At the same time, he had to disarm a company of the 4th composed of men from that region who were beginning to desert to go defend their families on the frontier.[72]

After only a short time, Bankhead was already growing weary of his command. In correspondence to General Magruder and Captain Edmund P. Turner (Magruder's Assistant Adjutant General) on August 9 and August 16, he made his feelings clear. He began by reporting that when Magruder assigned him to the position, that "neither of us had any idea of the trying position I had to occupy. On my arrival I found everything perfectly chaotic." His litany of complaints included the area being "overrun" by agents acting for "every army" at cross-purposes, exorbitant prices, problems collecting taxes, a disaffected populace, lack of cooperation by militia officers, lack of supplies since "cut off" by quartermasters from depleted stores, deficient officers in his units, numerous petitions for relief from Indian attacks, and no information regarding the Frontier Regiment. Bankhead was very frank in calling his assigned subdistrict "this God-foresaken country" and stating, "I wish myself anywhere but here." A postscript after his signature to the first letter asked, "Is my appointment as brigadier to be confirmed by the President of not? If not, please relieve me in time."[73] The acting brigadier obviously realized that he was "in over his head," but he "soldiered on," as did those in his command—Dan Showalter included—in the coming months.

On August 17, 1863, Blunt attacked the Confederates at Honey Springs. After defeat there, Steele withdrew with Brigadier General William L. Cabell's Arkansas brigade to Fort Smith, General Cooper pulling back his Texas and Choctaw troops south to Perryville in the Choctaw Nation, and the Creek Indian troops' two regiments moving west to the headwaters of the Canadian River.[74] Bankhead had meanwhile moved his force into the Indian Territory to a point (which he called "Camp Bankhead") seventeen miles north of Boggy Depot, where Steele had kept his stores. He reported, "My command is now uncovered."[75] Three days later, he was still at that point with a total of 1,200 men, including those of Showalter and some of Bourland's. He complained that he had needed to arm Showalter's battalion with "Texas-made guns [that] are so indifferent that I would not use them if I had shot-guns or the ordinary hunting rifles." It was a matter of "take this poor apology for a weapon or leave these troops behind." He had left Colonel Samuel A. Roberts in command of the subdistrict while he led the brigade.[76] By the 27th, Bankhead had his headquarters at Blue River, a few miles south of Boggy Depot. There were only about 800 men with him. Showalter and his battalion were apparently elsewhere at this time since Bankhead's total number is reduced by 400 and he mentions other elements of his brigade, but not the command of Showalter. He said he would march all night to join with General Steele in twenty-four hours time.[77]

He did soon join with Steele since that general reported, on August 30, that, having been forced to retreat from Perryville by a much superior force, he was on the Middle Boggy River in the Choctaw Nation and had been joined by Bankhead with 1,100 well-armed men (Showalter must have rejoined the brigade). Steele wrote that he would move in the direction of Fort Smith to assist Cabell. His words to Cabell were, "I will push forward Bankhead to your assistance."[78] Leaving for Fort Smith on September 1,[79] Bankhead, Showalter, et al., would be too late. Greatly outnumbered, Cabell was attacked by Blunt on August 31 and had to abandon the city and withdraw to a hill range, known as the "Devils' Backbone," south of the city about halfway along the road to Walden, Arkansas. Here, the next day, he was able to repulse another Federal attack.[80] Meanwhile, Department headquarters assigned Brigadier General Henry E. McCulloch to command the Northern Subdistrict of Texas, instead of Bankhead, "in the field."[81] When McCulloch arrived at Bonham on September 17, 1863, he encountered the same problems that Bankhead had faced: the anomalous command relationship to Bourland's Border Regiment, the Frontier Regiment under state control, difficulties in enforcing the conscription law, and Plains Indians in the western counties of the district. The new commander would devote his primary attention to the Indian Territory, advising, in an address given at Bonham upon his arrival, that his priority would be to protect the subdistrict from "Lincoln's dastard hirelings."[82] Showalter and his men would remain north of the Red River with Bankhead for a period longer.

Bankhead and his force were, by September 11, about fifteen miles from Waldron. Unfortunately, Cabell had not withdrawn along the expected road, so a juncture of the two did not occur.[83] On the 13th, Steele dispatched a message to Bankhead to confine his observations on the line of the Fort Smith Road and that "the road to Waldron is to be specially avoided" whether or not he succeeded in joining with Cabell. The road south from Waldron was extremely rough and the road to Towson "almost impassable," even for light vehicles. Steele feared that, if superior numbers forced Bankhead back, he would have to return to Steele's command by a roundabout detour along the Red River.[84] Two days later, Steele chastised Cabell for not having joined with Bankhead and directed him to take the shortest road possible to Boggy Depot or Camp Watie.[85] That same day, Bankhead wrote from "Eden's, 25 miles west of Waldron, on the Line" (that is, the Arkansas/Indian Territory border line) to advise Steele of his recent activity:

> I marched from Waldron yesterday to this place. I heard on Monday night that the enemy was moving down in two columns to attack me—one by the Lookout Gap road, and the other by the Waldron road. Believing that I could take both, I marched out to Lookout Gap by daylight yesterday, and waited until 2 p.m. The enemy, however, failed to make his appearance, and I am inclined to believe that he has no such purpose, and has not the force at his command. I shall leave a small party here to gather up the cattle left by the herders, and move on to Holston's to-day.... I shall hope to receive further instructions at Holston's or Riddle's.[86]

It is probable that Showalter and his men were part of the "small party" left behind to bring in the cattle since, on October 10, 1863, Private John W. Hill of Company A was captured near Waldron.[87]

Steele's Assistant Adjutant General, Captain J.F. Crosby, referring to an earlier communication from Bankhead, on September 17 noted, "Your movements, prompt action, and the judgment displayed by you adds to the confidence the commanding general had already entertained." He advised that a company of Choctaw with knowledge of the countryside Bankhead would be operating in were being sent him and another regiment would carry supplies to him. Flour would be sent from Boggy Depot to Bankhead at Riddle's. Bankhead was cautioned to "avoid the contingency of being forced off the Boggy road" and to keep vigilant watch on both the Fort Smith and the Waldron roads as far in advance of his position at Riddle's as his judgment allowed. No engagement was being planned by Steele until reinforced.[88] By this, it is evident that Showalter and his battalion, as part of Bankhead's small brigade, were now holding the advanced position of the Confederate forces in the Indian Territory.

On September 19, 1863, Crosby wrote Bankhead again. Steele had apparently ordered some sort of advance by Bankhead since Crosby's letter indicated "the commanding general will be glad to know of your prompt action on the receipt of orders heretofore sent to you. With regard to your movements in your advance, I am directed by General Steele to state that reliance is had upon the exercise of your judgment and discretion." A request by Bankhead to send his brigade quartermaster to Bonham for some supplies was authorized. Crosby confided that he thought force movements in the Indian Territory would in some respects be determined by the recent fall of Little Rock to Federal forces. That Bankhead had some concern regarding his exposed position was probably indicated by Crosby's closing "that everything possible will be done by the commanding general to render your position satisfactory to yourself and useful to the country."[89]

A message was sent to General McCulloch from Magruder's headquarters at Sabine Pass, Texas, on September 22. Bankhead's desire was that, if possible, McCulloch combine the commands of Steele, Bankhead, Cooper and Cabell and retake Fort Gibson and Fort Smith—if McCulloch thought it practicable.[90] McCulloch obviously did not think it practicable since neither such a combination of forces nor campaign were undertaken. Indeed, on the 23rd, Steele left for Department headquarters for ten days, leaving General Cooper in command in the Indian Territory until his return. The headquarters of the district were to be moved to Camp Washita. At this time, there was no information of any reinforcing troops on the way to Bonham. Moreover, Steele was of the belief that some troops which had been on the way had been stopped.[91] During an early October absence of Steele, Cooper took his and Bankhead's brigades (about 3,000 men, of whom 500 were unarmed) up the Butterfield mail route toward Fort Smith as far as Brazil Creek—apparently intending to attack it. Steele returned in time to forestall any such attack, which Steele doubted that Cooper had really intended since the Federal force at Fort Smith was well-armed and composed of disciplined troops with artillery.[92]

It was probably about this time and unknown to Steele or Cooper that Bankhead curiously received an order from the headquarters of the District of Arkansas at Arkadelphia, Arkansas, that he, in the future, act under instructions from those headquarters, keeping in communication with Major General Sterling Price (acting as district commander in the absence of Lieutenant General Theophilus H. Holmes). Bankhead was to stay at Waldron, guarding approaches to Arkadelphia.[93] This order was never really effected as Lieutenant General E. Kirby Smith, the Department Commander, visited the Northern District of Texas late that month, where he found affairs "involving difficulties beyond my expectation." Smith had noted 2,500 to 2,800 armed deserters in the region and decided that "Bankhead's force is ordered there to prevent their organization being perfected." Holmes was directed to order Bankhead and his brigade to Bonham, to report to General McCulloch.[94] Execution of these orders did not apparently, for unknown reason or reasons, take place immediately. On October 13, Steele wrote McCulloch from Camp Sabine, where his headquarters were then located, that a regiment was being transferred to him and mentioning that "as General Bankhead goes to Bonham," he would make explanations.[95]

As of November 10, 1863, Bankhead, with one regiment and Krumbhaar's Battery, were back in the District of the Indian Territory.[96] Showalter and his battalion must have returned very soon after, because later that month, on November 30, the Acting Assistant General of the District of the Indian Territory, Lieutenant B.G. Duval, wrote from Doaksville to Brigadier General Richard M. Gano, now commanding all cavalry in the Department, that "in pursuance of instructions from department headquarters, that Lieutenant-Colonel Showalter be ordered to report in person with his battalion to Brig. Gen. H.E. McCulloch, commanding Northern Sub-District of Texas." A detachment of at least thirty men from the battalion was to be sent to Fort Washita as guards for some prisoners (military offenders, deserters, or conscription-evaders?) to be moved from there to Bonham.[97] There is no indication, in the published records or any other source, of exactly how many or what skirmishes or other small engagements Dan Showalter participated in during this period under the command of Bankhead, Steele or Gano in Arkansas or the Indian Territory. No doubt it was arduous, and their service was appreciated by General Steele, who parted with them reluctantly. He wrote to Gano from Doaksville, on December 3, "I regret that Lieutenant-Colonel Showalter's command has been withdrawn at this time, but I believe in obeying orders."[98] Steele himself would, at his own request, be relieved of command in the Indian Territory on December 11 and be replaced by Brigadier General S.B. Maxey.[99]

Dan Showalter and his battalion were needed back in the Subdistrict of Northern Texas. There were estimated to still be one thousand anti–Confederate men hiding in the brush,[100] and Plains Indians had again raided its western counties in October.[101] Soon after Showalter had his battalion back in the subdistrict, the Plains Indians struck again with their largest and most devastating raid of 1863, terrorizing Montague and Cooke counties.[102] On December 21, about three hundred Comanche crossed the Red River into Montague County and rushed to Illinois Bend, on the border with Cooke County, where they killed one man, two women and a child while burning homes. They recrossed the Red River only to return into Texas the next morning. They killed several whites fleeing from the Elmore settlement, more at the Potter settlement, and raided Elm Creek, which was only six miles west of Gainesville, where they devastated more farms. After a total of thirteen whites were killed and thirteen more taken captive, the Comanche headed back toward the Red River.[103] At every place that they struck, the Indians left hanging, as a taunt, a blanket marked "U.S." Over one thousand, including Chickasaw Indians, left the next day in pursuit, but were unable to catch them. On December 23, Showalter and his battalion were sent from Bonham to join the pursuit.[104] Brown, then a member of General McCulloch's staff and later a noted Texas journalist, historian and politician,[105] soon after wrote of this pursuit, during which he accompanied Showalter and the companies of Captains Rather, Wilson and Carpenter of the 4th Arizona.[106] According to Brown they "rode day and night for 26 hours, all eager for a tilt with the barbarians, but their precipitate flight disappointed all."[107] The battalion arrived back in Bonham the evening of Christmas.[108] This was the last action by the 4th Arizona's battalion under Showalter in the vicinity of the Red River.

The need and usefulness of Dan Showalter and his battalion in the Red River country of North Texas was not the reason he had been ordered there from the Indian Territory. It was just a stop along the way to a new field of service. On December 15, 1863, the regiment's commander, S.M. Baird, had been sent the following from Headquarters, District of Texas, then at McNeel's, Brazoria County, Texas:

> Colonel: I am instructed by Major-General Magruder to say that you will collect all the men of your command, including Colonel Showalter's companies in the Indian Territory, and proceed without the least delay to San Antonio, taking post at that place with your whole regiment until further orders. The enemy is threatening all quarters in large force, and it is expected that every man who has enlisted in your regiment and who may be absent from any cause, whether detailed or not, will join his command at once. You will, therefore, give the necessary orders to bring all your men in.
>
> A copy of this letter will be sent to Brigadier-General Steele, who is requested to send down every available man who can be spared from his command, to repel the enemy, now threatening all along the coast.
>
> Please acknowledge receipt of this letter, and state when you will be at San Antonio with your command.
>
> I am, &c.,
> Edmund P. Turner,
> Assistant Adjutant-General.[109]

The last week of December and into January, the weather in Bonham was severe cold with rain, sleet and hail. On January 5, Showalter received his orders to march for San Antonio. Fires had to be made around the tents in order to melt sufficient ice that they could be struck and folded for the journey. The battalion was doubtless glad to be leaving for reasons other than the weather. Mrs. Rose Ellen Dryden, wife of Assistant Surgeon Robert Dryden, thought that the people of the area had been inhospitable, writing that they wanted soldiers to fight and protect their property, but would not accept Confederate money. (Five of the seven Red River counties had voted against secession in early 1861.) Upon leaving, she wished "that the Yankees would make a raid on them and clean them all out or that the bulk of our own army might encamp among them and eat them out of house and home." The winter march, during a northeaster, was a particularly hard march for Showalter and his battalion. Mud in the roads was sometimes up to the wagon hubs. Each morning, half-frozen teamsters had to grope about in the snow for stiffened harnesses for the mules, which had to be overnighted in the timber of river bottoms for some protection. Riders and horses were soon covered with coats of ice. Baggage had to be removed from wagons so four-mule teams could pull them through the heavy snow. The men had to dismount to push vehicles up steep creek banks. Unable to bear the cold, the soldiers would depart for a time to warm themselves at isolated houses. Some froze by the roadside. Firewood had to be dug out of the ice and snow. The trials of Showalter and his battalion's winter march to rejoin the balance of the 4th Arizona lessened the further south they proceeded, and when they reached Waxahachie in Ellis County they also found themselves in friendlier country. Here they met another company—Amzi Bradshaw's Company E—of the regiment, which had returned to this, their home county, to recruit.[110]

During the time of the battalion's march, District Headquarters issued General Orders No. 217, dividing military units in Texas among divisions and brigades. Paragraph IV of the order specified: "Colonel Baird, with such companies of his regiment as he has raised or may raise, will report to Brigadier-General Bee, commanding Western Sub-District. This regiment will be brigaded with Colonels Darden's and Richardson's regiments, and will be known as the Third Brigade of Cavalry, First Division."[111] This assignment was but temporary. General Magruder already had other plans for the 4th Arizona.

SEVEN

On the Rio Grande, 1864

Texas forces led by John Salmon Ford had taken control of the lower Rio Grande Valley soon after the state's secession in early 1861. After the Federal Navy implemented its blockade of Southern ports, it was never able to stop Confederate trade out of Brownsville, Texas. The city was located on the Rio Grande about thirty miles inland and across from Matamoros, Mexico. Since the river was an international boundary, traffic into and up it to Brownsville could not be blocked. Cargoes only had to be declared for Matamoros. Cotton trade through the city became a major asset for the Confederacy. In 1863, the French intervened in Mexico and soon an emperor, Maximilian of Austria, was installed on a Mexican throne. Both the trade and concern about the French in Mexico impelled the United States to make an effort to capture the port. Major General Nathaniel P. Banks, commander of the United States Department of the Gulf headquartered at New Orleans, sent a 6,000-man force to the mouth of the Rio Grande in November of 1863. There were less than four Confederate companies in the area to resist. They evacuated Brownsville, and it was occupied by the Federal forces on November 6, 1863. Confederate trade had to be sent to Eagle Pass, Texas, almost three hundred miles further up the river, to be crossed into Mexico and then carted to Matamoros—at considerable additional expense and delay. By the turn of the year, there were some indications and rumors that the Federals would move inland to take Eagle Pass. There were also rumors that California forces in New Mexico would be moving east to connect with them. General Magruder needed to do something to relieve the situation.

On December 22, 1863, he had his Assistant Adjutant General, Captain Edmund P. Turner, write to John Salmon Ford at Austin, Texas, who was then serving as the principal conscription officer in Texas. Ford was requested to go to San Antonio "at once" and take command of all troops there, organizing them into a force. He was informed that Colonel Baird "has been ordered to report to you and accompany you with all the forces he may have or may raise." He was to give the impression that his force was intended for use on the Texas coast, keeping secret its actual destination, the Rio Grande. Upon his approach to the Rio Grande, the Confederate regiment of Colonel Santos Benavides at Laredo and the battalion of Lieutenant Colonel George Henry Giddings at Eagle Pass were to become part of his command. The post at San Antonio was to provide him with logistical support to the extent of everything it had. All available conscripts gathered would be given to him to fill out his force.[1] Magruder realized that Ford did not at the time hold a Confederate commission. "Embarrassed in ordering officers to report to [Ford] lest they may legally decline doing so," he therefore petitioned Texas Governor Pendleton Murrah to

An unidentified recruiting party and new recruits of the Ellis County Bengal Tigers (Company D of the 4th Arizona) were photographed—probably by Assistant Surgeon Robert Dryden—in the spring of 1864 at Waxahachie, Texas. In this, the only known surviving photograph of a Confederate unit in Texas, the men wear brogans instead of boots and carry rifles instead of sabers. Presumably, Dan Showalter's Confederate uniform was similar to that of the officers pictured center and at the right (courtesy Ellis County Museum, Waxahachie, Texas).

give Ford a commission as a State Brigadier General.[2] Magruder proceeded with his plans for Ford to command both Confederate and State forces west and south of San Antonio. Governor Murrah did appoint Ford as Brigadier General for Texas' First District of State Troops on March 1, 1864.[3] Ford never used his State rank and always signed his communiqués as "Colonel, Commanding Expeditionary Force." He did not expect any difficulty due to his State rank versus Confederate rank. In a letter to Magruder's headquarters on January 6, 1864, he had included, almost in closing, the comment "There will be no difficulty about rank between Colonel Baird and myself."[4] Ford was to initially call his new organization the "Cavalry of the West,"[5] but thereafter referred to it as the "Expeditionary Force." The "Cavalry of the West" has, however, become its popular appellation in literature.

On January 17, 1864, information was received at San Antonio that some Federal troops had taken Fort Lancaster on the Pecos River. Spruce Baird, who had arrived in late December,[6] took this as meaning that the Federals would be moving eastward and, "availing myself of a latitude conceded me ... suggesting cooperation and consultation," proceeded by letter to make suggestions probably both unexpected and unwanted by Ford. Baird immediately proposed "that any attempt to retake Fort Brown be suspended." His opinion was that Brownsville could not be taken "without the loss of more men than we can spare in view of the advantage to be gained as the enemy could reinforce so promptly that we could not expect to hold it any great length of time." He suggested that a portion of the force being gathered for the Rio Grande expedition instead be used to hold the line from San Antonio to Laredo and Eagle Pass. Baird's proposal also said that portions of the Frontier Regiment (a state organization charged with protecting the frontier areas against Indians) should campaign against Indians toward the Pecos and in the direction of Kansas. Those campaigning toward Kansas could cut Federal communications and supplies passing along the Santa Fe Trail. Baird then suggested what was probably his real intention—"an adequate force" to operate in front of Federal forces in western Texas. The units which would compose this force were clear to Baird: "My Regiment with Col. Darden and Richardson's can do this." At the same time, an agent would be sent through Sonora, Mexico, "to open communications with our friends in California, New Mexico and Arizona, and aid such, as may desire it, to join us of which there is at least a reasonable prospect and if a sufficient force can be mustered, to expel the enemy from those Territories." Baird wrote that this would protect the Texas frontier against Indians and the trade with Mexico. He concluded that "this expedition against Brownsville can be made after we have defeated the enemy from above."[7]

Dan Showalter and the companies with him had marched from Bonham for Austin by January 6.[8] They arrived in San Antonio on February 8. Here he was delighted to encounter an acquaintance from California, the wife of Judge David S. Terry, who had arrived there the day before.[9] Terry had been a Justice of the California Supreme Court and had traveled via Mazatlan, Mexico, to Texas in February and March of 1863. Cornelia Runnels Terry traveled separately with four small sons—one of them a baby—to join her husband. The baby died in Mexico along the way.[10] She was, no doubt, equally delighted to find a familiar face in San Antonio. She gave Showalter a message from Anna Forman back in California.[11]

Dan's response to Miss Forman was the moving letter cited in full in the Introduction to this book. He sent at least one further letter to California from San Antonio, the final portion of which was published in the July 23, 1864, issue of the *Sonoma County Democrat* under the heading "Letter from Dan Showalter." He jubilantly relayed news of the Confederate defeat of Union forces during the Red River Campaign which had concluded in late May. He wrote of Confederate resolve to "continue the contest with redoubled vigor," even in the event of the fall of Richmond, Virginia, "as long as we hold territory enough to bury invaders on." He invited his friends in California to "address me at San Antonio, Texas, through the Mexican mail, care of C. S. Collector, at Eagle Pass." This letter was signed "Dan Showalter, Lt-Col. Com. 4th Arizona, C.S.A."[12]

On January 20, Ford reported that he had ordered that they encamp in the valley of either the San Marcos or Guadalupe River, where forage was available, when they arrived.[13] On February 1, Ford reported that Baird had been instructed to move via Helena (seventy miles southeast of San Antonio) toward Fort Merrill on the Nueces River (fifty miles from its mouth near Corpus Christi). Baird had been at San Patricio—120 miles southeast of San Antonio—until January 31. He and a Reverend Chamberlain arrived in San Antonio on February 5.[14] It would seem that Baird had in some manner disobeyed Ford's order—perhaps in going to San Antonio without orders to do so. In any event, that same date Ford sent a letter to Baird stating the difficulty:

> Colonel [Baird]: You decline receiving orders from me until the question of rank is decided between us. You disclaim anything personal. I accept the disclaimer, and in the same spirit demand of you not to interfere with or give orders to any of my command, and not to use supplies purchased, stored, or secured for its use by contract. In doing this you will simply accord what is just. If your regiment is not under my command you can certainly not ask me to supply it with articles procured for the use of my troops. The question of rank has once been decided by the major-general com-

manding the district, but as I am not in possession of a copy of his decision you can, of course, arbitrate it as long as you think proper, or until special instructions are received from district headquarters.[15]

(The Confederacy had, on March 6, 1861, adopted the United States Army Regulations of 1857, which specified in Article 62 that command of a unit fell to the senior officer present regardless of whether that officer was militia, regular or volunteer.) Instructions on Ford's command authority did arrive, for, on February 18, Ford addressed a letter to "Lt. Col. Showalter, Comdg, 4th Az. Reg. Ar Brig" in which he made reference to "your regiment" and to "your officers" and asked that Showalter visit his headquarters as soon as he could.[16] And by February 21, the 4th Arizona was being referred to by Colonel Ford, in correspondence to Captain Theodore Heerman, an Aide-de-Camp of General Magruder, as "Lieutenant-Colonel Showalter's regiment."[17]

Though the regiment was referred to as his, Dan Showalter was notably not named as Colonel of the 4th Arizona. Baird was now out of the picture, but exactly when in February is not known. He did, as commander of the regiment, make a speech in San Antonio sometime during the month accepting presentation of a flag to the regiment.[18]

Baird had not been relieved as Colonel of the regiment, but rather detached and given another assignment. The regiment was listed as "Baird's regiment cavalry" with headquarters in the "Northwest Frontier" in the return of the District of Texas for April 1864.[19] Yet, it appeared with the same description in the organization charts of the Department in the southern part of the state for September[20] and December of 1864.[21] The anomalous situation was obviously confusing, even to headquarters! Baird was evidently eased out of Ford's way by resurrecting and acceding to part of his December 1863 proposal. On June 6, 1864, General Magruder wrote Brigadier General William R. Boggs, E. Kirby Smith's Chief of Staff, that he had received a referral from General Smith to take necessary steps to arrange it. Magruder advised that if permission was received, he would authorize Baird to enlist one hundred men not eligible for conscription for frontier service and furnish Baird with some Confederate funds, ox teams or pack mules, and one hundred Enfield rifles.[22] Baird issued a recruiting circular at Austin on July 28, 1864, stating, "I am authorized by Gen. E. Kirby Smith, to raise six New Companies in addition to my present Regiment, from the Frontier Counties; and to form a part of the Light-Horse of the Plains, and the Frontier Expedition under my command." Significantly, he signed the circular as "S.M. Baird, Col. 4th Reg't Arizona Brigade."[23] Thus, there was no vacancy in the regiment's colonelcy for Showalter to fill. Baird would never be able to raise his six companies to disrupt traffic on the Santa Fe Trail.[24] Those he did raise and command would, in the future, however, become confused with the actual 4th Arizona Regiment.

Colonel or not, Dan Showalter was now in command of the 4th Arizona. On February 26, 1864, orders were sent to march the portion of the regiment that was in the San Antonio area to Helena "at once"[25]—apparently the order that Baird had refused to obey. An exception was Captain Cotton's Company C, which was placed on temporary artillery duty in San Antonio on the 28th.[26] In a communication to Magruder's headquarters on March 9, Ford noted, in a tone that seems relieved, that "Lieutenant-Colonel Showalter is moving."[27] Showalter wrote to Ford, on March 10, that he had arrived at Prairie Lea, Texas, but would not be able to leave there for six days as many of his horses were unfit to travel until shod with horseshoes. Interestingly, Showalter dated his letter as at "Camp Baird."[28] From there, on the 19th, Showalter submitted a requisition to District Headquarters in Houston for a supply of muster rolls and regimental returns.[29] Shortly later, on the 25th, Showalter had to write the District Adjutant General, Major Alston, at Houston, acknowledging "receipt of Genl. Order No. 239 with note accompanying stating that no return has ever been received from the 4th Regt. Arizona Brigade." He went on to advise that he had submitted one on March 6, which was probably received at headquarters after the note from Alston.[30] Apparently Baird had been remiss in his administrative duties and Showalter had to catch them up.

On March 22, Ford reported that he expected Showalter at Banquete, twenty-three miles west of Corpus Christi, within two days.[31] The concentration of Ford's force near the coast had changed within two days. Trouble had arisen on the "Line of the Rio Grande" when, on March 19, some two hundred of the Federal 1st Texas Cavalry attacked the town of Laredo with intent to burn cotton stored there.[32] With less than fifty men, Colonel Santos Benavides succeeded in repulsing the Federal cavalry, which withdrew downriver the next day. Benavides wrote to Ford, on the 21st, that he expected a reinforced Federal force to return, and requested reinforcements, weapons and ammunition within ten days.[33] On March 24, 1863, Major A.G. Dickinson, post commander at San Antonio, wrote Brigadier General James E. Slaughter, Chief of Staff of the subdistrict's commander, informing him of Benavides' report and that Ford was "moving with all rapidity possible" in an attempt to take the Federals in the rear. Dickinson had sent a dispatch to Showalter, who was then "in rapid march to join Colonel Ford."[34] Dan Showalter arrived with the five companies he'd had with him on the San Fernando River near present-day Bishop, Texas, and joined Ford on March 31, 1864.[35] The 1864 Rio Grande Campaign and the 4th Arizona's first unified activity under the command of Dan Showalter was about to begin.

Ford, with Showalter's command and four other companies, left Camp Patterson, on the San Fernando River near San Antonio, on April 9, 1864, for Los Ojuelos on the trade route to Laredo, where he planned to join forces with Benavides. Los Ojuelos was chosen since it was 100 miles from Rio Grande City and far enough inland to prevent any Federal force's gaining an interior or flanking position.[36] A severe drought during 1863 and 1864 that had dried up grass and water made this inland route necessary. Although men and animals suffered once they reached the Rio Grande near Laredo, they would have a supply of water as they moved south to Brownsville.[37] Ford reached Laredo on April 15 with his force following behind—Showalter and his regiment were about ninety-five miles back on the trail, within a dozen miles of Los Angeles, Texas.[38]

This late in the war, the matter of supplies was a problem for all Confederate forces, including Showalter's 4th Arizona. On June 15, 1864, he wrote Colonel Ford, in response to a Special Orders No. 93 he had just received, that

> the number of pack saddles allotted to this command is entirely inadequate. I have reported to you three hundred men ready to move at the shortest possible notice, and you must know that seven pack animals would not carry more than two days supplies. I see that other commands are allowed more than twice the transportation that I am for the same number of men. Why is this done, If I am to be crippled in every movement. Don't place me under seeming [obligations?]. I can move and subsist for ten days in number without pack animals, and unless I can get what is actually missing I don't want any.[39]

The very next day, Colonel Ford responded by letter:

> I have given your command every thing I could. I gave them one hundred Enfield rifles and more [?]. I must be allowed to judge of what different commands need. I may err in judgement, but not from partiality.
> The line of march for your command is the shortest of any by one third.

You can take a wagon to the neighborhood of the Salt Lake.

Your constant complaints are not in my opinion founded in justice. Your regiment when they reported to me for duty were badly armed, and supplied, and if I had been disposed to do them injustice could I not have withheld many things?

If you need, and have needed pack saddles so badly why have not you and your [?] taken steps to [?] them? The saddles in question were bargained for by myself for a specific purpose. I shall exercise the right to dispose of them to suit my own views, and my action is no concern of yours. Were I purchasing pack saddles to permanently fit out the command then you might complain if you failed to receive your [?] but until that is the case I shall ask you to cease complaining.[40]

The Salt Lake mentioned by Ford was ninety miles northerly of Brownsville.[41]

This was not the last difficulty Showalter had with his commander over equipment or munitions. On July 12, Showalter notified Ford that he had arrested a man of Captain Carrington's command for attempting to purchase arms from members of the 4th Arizona with money the man said Ford had turned over to Carrington for that purpose. Ford responded the same date, through his adjutant, that he had no knowledge of any such intention by Carrington and had referred the matter to Carrington. He did state that he had given money to Carrington to purchase arms in Mexico and affirmed that no soldier had any right to sell his arms. Apparently, Showalter had also sent notice of the incident direct to District headquarters since the response concluded, "The Colonel insists that you will in all your official communications to District HdQtrs, direct through these HdQtrs."[42] Fortunately, to the credit of them both, these disputes over equipment did not result in any difficulty between Ford and Showalter in cooperating during the campaign.

With 225 men, Showalter left on a scout in the direction of Brownsville.[43] On June 20, 1864, Ford reported from Young's Ranch—forty miles upriver from Brownsville—that, via a Colonel J.J. Fisher, he was negotiating with Mexican Liberal General Juan Cortina to purchase from him rifled cannon, arms and ammunition.[44] From Young's Ranch, Ford moved the command toward Brownsville via Santa Rosa, Tampacuas, Tio Cano (now La Feria), and Cotitlo to Rancho Como se Llama, where he joined with Showalter and the 4th Arizona. The entire force paused a day here to dry beef for rations. The best conditioned of the horses were selected, with the rest sent back to Edinburg. Then it was across the Arroyo Colorado (River) at Paso del Gigante to the military road running between Rio Grande City and Brownsville, striking the road about twenty-five miles north of Brownsville between the Carricitos and Las Rucias ranches. Some captured Mexicans informed Ford that Federals were at Rancho Las Rucias thirty miles upriver from Brownsville. Ford was able to approach within a few hundred yards of the Federal pickets by using an obscure trail through the chaparral.[45]

On the evening of June 25, the Federal picket at Rancho Las Rucias was attacked and driven in. Major General Francis J. Herron, commander of all the Federal forces along the Rio Grande, reported a loss of fifteen to twenty killed and wounded, including one captain of the 1st Texas Cavalry. Herron believed that Ford had about 1,800 men along the river downstream from Ringgold Barracks and that General Slaughter had 5,000 more men at San Antonio. He was "sorry to state that the Mexicans on this side of the river are co-operating heartily with Ford."[46] Ford's own report of the battle was more complete. A small party was sent forward to determine the Federal position, but encountered the foe sooner than expected and gunfire broke out. Captain Dunn, leader of the scouting party, charged the more numerous Federals. Dan Showalter promptly led in the 4th Arizona in support. The Federals took cover in Mexican houses, a large brick building, and behind a large pile of bricks. Soon after, two additional Confederate companies—those of Captain Tom Cater and Captain Refugio Benavides—joined in the attack. The Federals fell back to the bank of a large laguna (lake) and maintained a heavy fire, which, however, had little effect. Benavides was directed by Ford to lead his battalion to the bank of the lake and flank the Federal right. Instead, misunderstanding the order, Benavides moved his men to the Confederate extreme right and, because of the lake barrier, made two ineffective horseback charges on the Federal left. Showalter and Cater then led their men on foot against the Federal front. Benavides dismounted his men and joined them. Thirty-six of the Federals surrendered, while some escaped across the lake and others swam the Rio Grande into Mexico and hid in canebrakes. Ford reported the Federal loss as twenty-something killed and a dozen wounded. In addition to the thirty-six prisoners, two wagons with teams, thirty-eight horses, and some badly needed saddles were captured. A "brisk rain" prevented destruction of some Federal stores, which could not be transported away. Additionally, some of the Federal wounded drowned trying to escape across the lake. Their commander, Captain Temple, "left early." Orders and correspondence of his left behind revealed that half of the 1st Texas Cavalry had recently embarked for New Orleans and that orders to leave Texas had produced some insubordination among the Federal cavalrymen. Of 250 Confederates engaged, there were three killed and four wounded. One of those killed was Sergeant S.B. Cockerel, Company B, 4th Arizona. In his report of the battle, Ford complimented Dan Showalter thrice: for promptly supporting the advance, for leading his men gallantly, and for having "acted well."[47]

A lack of grass for his horses on the Arroyo Colorado compelled Colonel Ford to withdraw his force to Edinburg, where he awaited a Federal attack that never came. The Expeditionary Force was to remain there for several days.[48] Meanwhile, on June 26, in Special Order No. 178, General Magruder created a Western Subdistrict of Texas consisting of all of Texas west of the Colorado River, naming Brigadier General Thomas F. Drayton as its commander. Under him, Ford was to command everything south of San Antonio and west of the San Antonio River.[49] General Herron, the Federal commander, was aware of Ford's location and that Ford had received word that Brownsville was being evacuated. He used his cavalry (two companies of the 1st Texas Cavalry) to picket the roads, but, feeling it would be useless to send his infantry after the Confederates, his "intention [was] to let Ford come in and attack if he sees proper."[50] Thus, for the time, both commanders were awaiting the other to attack. Herron was in the process of withdrawing most of his force from the Rio Grande Valley and had no incentive to do so. Ford was encountering conflict with Colonel Benavides, difficulties in obtaining supplies, and loss of the service of some of his staff officers and units through transfers.[51] Also, the lack of grass between the Arroyo Colorado and Brownsville on which to forage his horses was a serious obstacle to operations.[52] These problems—particularly difficulty with Benavides and loss of units and personnel from his command—continued to bedevil Ford.

On July 7, he wrote a third time within a week to Magruder's Chief of Staff in Houston about the situation. One complaint was that apparently some of his communications to district headquarters had been delayed "by Col. S. Benavides, at whose headquarters they appear to have remained some time." Ford also protested an order restricting his recruiting. He pointed out that "the troops reporting here for duty were raised originally for my command or for the Fourth Arizona Regiment." He stated that withdrawal of exempts (from conscription) from his force and others who were absent without leave made it necessary for him to recruit replacements to fill his companies. He also sought to explain his use of deserters in his force. Many men who had deserted other Confederate units had, under authority, joined his command on promise they could serve under him. He reported that many of these men were not disposed to return to their original commands and would cross the Rio Grande into Mexico rather than do so. Others took advantage of this policy, but never joined Ford's expeditionary force. Ford stated that it was "not the time nor the place for the execution of the order with any hope of remedying the evil." He needed the men in his force and obviously felt that the Confederacy would not regain their service in their original units if he tried to enforce the directive. The Colonel also presented his difficulties of supply. The Confederate Cotton Bureau was not turning over cotton or money for purchase of supplies, so it was necessary for him to use cotton reclaimed by his command—he had, after all, protected the commerce in cotton and was "able to remain here only by means of the supplies for which the cotton was sold." His force was manufacturing both ammunition and cartridge boxes.[53] Two days later, he wrote again to protest the ordering of a company which had been raised, by his order, to report to Brigadier General Drayton rather than to his force. Likewise, he protested interference from a Lieutenant Colonel Steele.[54]

The time at Edinburg was used to replenish the Expeditionary Force's munitions and other supplies. Ford obtained all serviceable guns that he could and had ammunition manufactured for the different calibers of weapons available. Provisions were gathered, and all that could be carried with the force placed on wagons or packed on mules.[55] On July 4, Ford wrote Dan Showalter, informing him that fresh musket cartridges had been received from Banquete and that cartridges were being manufactured for Enfield and Sharpe's rifles. He concluded this letter with the words "Your regiment has performed most efficient service, and it will afford me great pleasure to supply them with every thing the law allows."[56] In the short time since joining Ford's expedition, Dan Showalter and his men had earned the respect and reliance of Colonel Ford. The force moved out toward Brownsville on July 19, 1864.[57] The distance to Brownsville was about one hundred miles via the only feasible route—the Military (or River) Road along the left bank of the Rio Grande—since, due to the severe drought, there was little grass available. General Juan N. Cortina, the Mexican Liberal governor of the State of Tamaulipas, was friendly with the Federals and would not permit supplies to be crossed over the Rio Grande to the Confederates at any point downriver from Edinburg. By the time Ford's force reached Carricitos, twenty-four miles upriver from Brownsville, this had caused great difficulty in forwarding the supplies to Ford's force.[58]

On July 22, 1864, the Confederates encountered a Mexican who informed them that Federals were at Ebonal Ranch. Exactly where these Federals were located was unknown, and an advance party was sent ahead to find out. Not knowing the strength of the Federals, Ford followed with 800 men. He endeavored to send a detachment on foot through the chaparral to pass around the Federals, but the dense underbrush presented more difficulty than expected. When it was time for Ford's main body (presumably including Showalter and his men) to attack, "they raised the Texas yell, and went in. The Federals opened fire." Finding out that they would be surrounded, many of them mounted and fled. A hot pursuit was made to within sight of the outer limits of Brownsville. At Ramirena's ranch within sight of the city, some prisoners, horses and a wagon with its team were captured. By now the command was scattered, so the advance was halted briefly. When no Federal counterattack developed, Ford's men moved slowly forward. The Confederates had no casualties and the Federals only several wounded. Pulling back slightly, Ford's rear guard was attacked. Ford positioned a company across the road, which repulsed the Federals with heavy fire. Ford had a line formed and prepared to give battle. No attack came and the Confederates went into camp.[59]

The next day, Ford stationed a picket near the road and moved the rest of his command back to Carricitos. This withdrawal was deemed necessary to shorten the line of supply from Edinburg and to render any enemy advance out of reach of reinforcements from Brownsville.[60] The Federal picket line was a mile and a half upriver from the city.[61] Over the next few days, there was firing between the pickets. A sick Ford (he had to be helped on his horse on the 22nd), not having any artillery, felt his force was too small to engage the Federals close to their prepared defenses. On July 25, Ford sent a battalion (not of the 4th Arizona) forward to combat the Federals at long range. The line was formed in a depression known as Dead Man's Hollow just outside the city limits. The Federals were driven back into the town with a loss of fifteen to twenty wounded and several horses lost. They refused to leave the city and give battle, and Ford would not move his men further forward, where they would come under artillery fire. Of this affair Ford wrote, "I am indebted to Lt. Col. Showalter and Lt. Col. Fisher for much valuable assistance."[62] On July 26, Showalter led a portion of the 4th Arizona, along with parts of Giddings' and Cater's battalions, in a vigorous attack on the Federal pickets at the Estephana Ranch less than twelve miles outside of Brownsville. In what was reported as "a sharp affair," the Federal infantry picket left, "running like blases, to get into town." They were followed to about one and a half miles outside of the town. Showalter returned with a captured wagon, six mules, and three prisoners.[63] It was subsequently learned that the Federals had planned an ambush in the town with infantry, cavalry and artillery. Fortunately for Ford's Confederates, they had not fallen into it. Ford had not seen any sense in taking the risk when the planned evacuation of his enemy was known to be soon. This skirmish had occurred on July 27.[64]

Brigadier General Francis J. Herron had been in command of Federal forces on the Rio Grande, with headquarters at Brownsville, since January 1864.[65] After the defeat and collapse of his Red River Campaign in the spring of 1864, Major General Nathanial P. Banks was relieved by Major General E.R.S. Canby. Canby was faced by a need to create a reserve force and to reinforce General Frederick Steele's Federal forces in Arkansas. For this purpose, Federal positions along the lower Texas coast were being evacuated by June. On July 5, 1864, Canby directed that "Fort Brown and its dependencies on the Rio Grande be abandoned," "and the troops now in Texas and not required for the occupation and defense of Brazos Santiago be ordered to [New Orleans]. A force of 1,200 men of alarms will be sufficient for the defense of that island against any force that can be brought against it."[66] Under these circumstances, it is apparent why Herron also did not wish to initiate a battle.

On July 30, 1864, Dan Showalter led the 4th Arizona into the city and Fort Brown. The rest of Ford's command followed. The Federals were gone (they had left on July 28[67]) and the city was in possession of its citizens.[68] Fort Brown had been left in good condition, and the city also—much better than had been expected.[69] He sent a company of Giddings' battalion on a scout that found the Federal rear guard about fifteen miles below Brownsville and drove them back onto the Federal main body, killing two and capturing two more.[70] This August 2 action against the 1st Texas Cavalry is known as the Skirmish at White Ranch.[71] Showalter set out pickets to watch and guard against any possible Federal return. These actions were taken by Showalter, who was commanding in the field for the still sick Ford.[72] The Federal forces withdrew to Brazos Island, about eight miles north of the mouth of the Rio Grande. General Herron had left behind at that place about 1,500 men under command of Colonel Henry M. Day of the 91st Illinois Infantry.[73] Day's force was composed of his own 91st Illinois Infantry, the 81st United States Colored Infantry, three companies of the 1st Texas Cavalry, Battery B of the 1st Missouri Light Artillery, three companies of the 19th Iowa Infantry until August 16, and, until November, two companies of the 18th New York Cavalry.[74] This force was considered—and proved to be—sufficient to support the Federal Navy's blockade squadron off the mouth of the Rio Grande.

Ford did not pursue the withdrawing Federals, seeing no reason to take the risk of being trapped in the cul-de-sac formed by the river and the coast.[75] Ford was still sick, but sent out a strong scout under command of Dan Showalter. When they approached the camp of the Federals, Showalter ordered Captain Refugio Benavides, with his company of the 33rd Texas Cavalry, forward to feel out or "develop" the enemy's strength. Captain Benavides exceeded his orders and charged, driving the Federals away from several wagons, which were captured. At this point, Benavides said, "I looked for Colonel Showalter, and saw his command going the other way, about a mile and a half off." The wagons had to be abandoned. Though admitting in his *Memoirs* that he remembered nothing more about the report, Ford wrote that "the unfortunate failing of Colonel Showalter had stood between him and success."[76] Ford did not make clear just what this failing was.

Throughout the month of August and most of the first week of September 1864, Ford remained sick and was unable to command in the field. Dan Showalter, his senior Lieutenant Colonel, exercised field command of what was referred to in their correspondence as the "Advance Force," deployed in the area south of Brownsville along the Rio Grande to the Gulf of Mexico.[77] The river formed the southern bounds of the area. It was in those days "a narrow crooked stream, and only deep water a small part of the year for small boats." Whirlpools in the river made it dangerous.[78] Along the coast to Point Isabel and including Brazos Santiago Island, where the Federals were based, there were sand mounds up to thirty feet high. The bay separating the island from the mainland was two to four feet deep and a half mile wide. The area in which operations took place was covered with chaparral, thorn bushes and cactus—so thick that one veteran of the 91st Illinois Infantry recalled it as "jungles." Roads through the thorny brush were bad—actually narrow and winding paths—and the thorns often injured soldiers moving along them. Wolves were not unknown in the area.[79] Serving on the border, with access to vessels trading with the United States, permitted Showalter to write to family in Pennsylvania. His sister Elizabeth apparently received more than one letter on single sheets of heavy paper, folded and sealed with wax. In one letter—"from some old battlefield of the Mexican war"—he wrote of quiet and peace at night in his bivouac along a river.[80]

Jackrabbits were also plentiful and described as "fat and fine." To supplement their fresh meat, the soldiers also resorted to armadillo. Corporal James M. Beverly of the 91st Illinois Infantry later described its preparation: "catch, kill, place in a hole in the ground that had been made red hot by burning wood in it, cover with earth and red-hot coals for an hour, remove the earth, and there was your meat done to a turn."[81] One Union veteran who served on the island of Brazos Santiago, where the Federal force was based, described it tersely: "Brazos Santiago is a sand-bar with no vegetable life and nothing good about it, if I except the breeze."[82] Although these descriptions were made by Federal soldiers who served in the area, Dan Showalter and his command served there at the same time and would have had the same experiences with the terrain, vegetation, and fauna.

Colonel Ford remained sick throughout August and into September. During this period, the "Advance Force"[83] was commanded by Dan Showalter. Ford reported that "the operations in front have been active. Lt. Col. Showalter has had several brisk skirmishes. He is encamped within seven miles of Brazos Island. Almost daily he runs in the enemy's pickets." In addition to the 4th Arizona, he also had under his command in the area the company of Captain Refugio Benavides and, from Giddings' battalion, that of Lieutenant W.N. Robinson.[84] Giddings, with the balance of his battalion, was ordered to join Showalter with "every man" on August 8.[85] Showalter's picket activity was vigorous. He maintained fifty men out on picket duty daily. This was trying on the horses of the command. He reported to Ford, on August 10, that he was resting his horses that day since they were "badly broken down, not more than 150 fit for action."[86] The Advance Force skirmished at White's Ranch with the 1st Texas Cavalry on August 2, with the 81st United States Colored Infantry at Point Isabel on the 9th, and, at Clarksville, a settlement right at the mouth of the Rio Grande, with the 18th New York Cavalry on the 14th. They also opposed the 19th Iowa Infantry during this period.[87] The fighting on August 9 at Point Isabel was by Giddings' battalion and failed when a Federal boat brought two hundred more soldiers to the skirmish. The report of this incident was made by Giddings to Showalter on the 10th; Showalter forwarded it to Ford on the same date.[88]

With what an early Texas historian referred to as a "bold and adroit movement," Dan Showalter captured a steamboat on the Rio Grande.[89] Although a report of this capture had been made by Showalter and enclosed by Colonel Ford with his August 16 report to higher headquarters, it was not found when the *Official Records* were compiled.[90] Fortunately, Colonel Ford wrote about the incident in his *Memoirs*. The steamer *Ark*, while proceeding up the river with a load of lumber and supplies, ran aground on the Texas shore at Cobb's Ranch near the White House on August 6, 1864. It had been seen entering the river flying a United States flag, but, when approached by Showalter and his men, was not flying any flag. The steamer's captain hid his United States flag. The captain told Showalter that he had no flag and refused to send a boat ashore. Having no forage for his horses, Showalter had to return to his camp at Palmito Ranch, but left a strong guard ashore, opposite the boat, to prevent its moving. Showalter returned the morning of August 7 and found the boat flying a Mexican flag. Showalter thereupon took possession of the boat and held its crew as prisoners of war. About ten o'clock in the morning, some three hundred Federals appeared in the distance, but, after three hours of skirmishing, were driven back to the works near Brazos Santiago Island.

Colonel Ford was notified. Anticipating that Federal forces would try to take the grounded ship, he, as mentioned previously, ordered Giddings to join Showalter with all of his men. Showalter was advised of the coming reinforcements and told, "You will hold the boat as long as you can, and if the enemy comes in too great force, you will retreat up the river, after burning the boat." Ford himself soon arrived and, after initially directing that the boat and its crew be released by its captors, was informed that the boat had been flying the United States flag when it entered the river. Over the next few days, the crew became friendly with the Confederates. Either upon promises by Ford to free the crew if they told where the United States colors were hidden or upon the boat's captain confessing—during a drinking bout—the true colors under which he sailed, after three days the United States flag was produced and Ford concluded to keep the boat. Lieutenant Henry De Wolf, Company A, 4th Arizona, was placed in command of the vessel.

The cargo of lumber had to be removed from the *Ark* in order to refloat her. Once freed from its grounding, the lumber was reloaded on August 26. Under command of Lieutenant De Wolf, it steamed into Brownsville on September 1. There was some talk of fitting it out to ply the shallow waters of the mouth of the river as a makeshift gunboat. This would have been expensive and probably beyond Confederate capabilities at Brownsville. It was instead used on the Rio Grande for transporting supplies and forage.[91] On September 25, 1864, General Drayton directed that it be sold "for the benefit of the Government, upon the most favorable terms."[92] Eventually the *Ark* was "libeled and condemned" by Judge Thomas Jefferson Devine, one of the two Confederate Circuit Judges in Texas. As a legal prize, the boat was then sold to someone in Matamoros.[93]

Meanwhile, the Mexican political and military situation had closed in on Matamoros and was about to impact Ford's Expeditionary Force and the life of Dan Showalter. Since its independence from Spain in 1821, Mexico had been plagued by a struggle between Liberals, who wanted a federal government that limited the influence of the military and the Catholic Church, and Conservatives, who favored a centralist government that protected the traditional powers and influence of the military and the Church. In control of the government, in 1857 the Liberals issued the Plan of Tacubaya, which would strip the Church of its rights, property and power, and limit the military. A Conservative revolt resulted. The Liberals controlled the Mexican states on the Gulf of Mexico, the Conservatives the central portion of the country, and the distant northwestern states were virtually independent under their governors. By 1860, the Liberals had won the war and regained control of the government. The Conservatives continued guerrilla opposition in the countryside. The president was now Benito Juarez. His government had incurred large debts to European financiers, and, in 1861, the British, Spanish and French invaded to secure payment. The British and Spanish soon withdrew, but the French remained and reinforced their forces. The Conservatives conspired with French Emperor Napoleon III to establish a monarchy. Its principal army defeated by the French in May 1863, the Juarez government fled north to El Paso del Norte (now Ciudad Juarez). In January of 1864, the Austrian Archduke Maximilian arrived in Mexico and became Emperor.

Matamoros and the State of Tamaulipas, like most other northern areas of Mexico, remained loyal to the Liberal, or Republican, government of Juarez. The Federal blockade of the Confederacy's coast proved beneficial to the Juarez government. Duties at Matamoros on cotton and goods traveling between the Confederacy and evaders of the blockade became the principal financial income of the Liberals.[94] Juan Nepomuceno Cortina was a native of the Mexican town of Camargo on the Rio Grande, but his family also owned lands on the Texas side of the river. He served in irregular cavalry during the Mexican-American War. Afterwards he resided north of the Rio Grande and, by the 1850s, had become a leader against Americans who were expropriating land from the Mexican citizens of the state. In 1859, Cortina shot the Brownsville marshal for brutality in arresting a Mexican, whom he freed. On September 25, 1859, he led eighty men into Brownsville and seized control of it. Responding to an appeal by leading citizens of the city, an influential citizen of Matamoros crossed the river and persuaded Cortina to leave the city. An armed struggle, known as the "Cortina War," resulted. Cortina was defeated in battle at Rio Grande City in December and retreated into Mexico. A small United States regular force was assisted by a Texas Ranger force in suppressing Cortina. During the War of the Reform and the early French intervention, Cortina supported the Liberal government. In 1863, he proclaimed himself Governor of Tamaulipas and Benito Juarez promoted him to General.[95]

The leader of the Texas Ranger force which had fought Cortina in 1859 was John Salmon Ford. Although both could be and often were personally kind to each other and respectful of citizens of the two countries, there was little love lost between the two. On September 3, 1864, in a report to subdistrict headquarters, Ford stated that "[Cortina] hates Americans, particularly Texans. He has an old and deep-seated grudge against Brownsville."[96] Cortina probably completely agreed with the Mexican Congressional Commission which reported, in 1873, about "Captain John S. Ford, whose conduct during the whole course of his life has ever been absolutely hostile to Mexico."[97]

In June 1864, the French and Imperials had controlled only the port of Tampico within the State of Tamaulipas. Cortina, who was governor and commander-in-chief, resided at Matamoros and had about two thousand men scattered about the state.[98] Cortina had renounced the Imperial Mexican government (which he said he had accepted to save his army and protect the residents) on April 1 and took Matamoros on the 11th.[99] Cortina placed his brother, Jose Maria Cortina, in charge of the city as Military Commandant of the Line of the Bravo (in Mexico, the Rio Grande is called the Rio Bravo)[100] as he operated inland, where the Imperial commandant, General Tomas Mejia, was approaching with a larger force.[101] Threatened by superior Imperial forces inland, with the French on the coast (who shelled Bagdad on August 22[102]), and needing income from the proceeds of cross-border trade between Matamoros and Brownsville, Cortina felt, according to Ford, "compelled to be more or less friendly. The immense trade existing between Mexico and the Confederate States was the prevailing reason."[103] Ford also needed to maintain the cross-border trade, both to supply his own forces and in recognition of its importance to the Confederacy. On August 10, he had written Cortina, expressing his "sincere desire to cultivate friendly relations, and to do all in my power to render our intercourse officially, commercially, and otherwise pleasant and mutually advantageous."[104]

In the interest of maintaining good relations, Ford, on August 19, even pled with District Chief of Staff Brigadier General James E. Slaughter that enforcement of a paragraph of Order No. 139 prohibiting the crossing of beef to the Mexican side of the river would not be in accordance with arrangements made with Cortina, would be disastrous for people whose livelihood depended upon the crossing of small herds and Mexicans needing the beef for food, and would "produce serious dissatisfaction with the Mexican authorities."[105] Despite Ford's efforts, Cortina was troublesome for the Confederates, giving what Ford termed "clear indications of an unfriendly character." The Mexican general made all of the ferries across the river remain on the Mexican side from early in the evening until the next day. He impeded navigation on the Rio Grande. Communications from Confederate officials to Cortina or his officials remained unanswered for long periods. Cortina also instituted a forced loan upon the people in Matamoros and arrested foreign consuls and citizens for non-payment. He even complained, on September 1, to Ford that Showalter's men had fired shots across the river—which, according to Ford, "Col. Showalter denied emphatically." This was probably Cortina's retort to Ford's report of shots fired from Matamoros, on August 30, upon the Confederate camp.[106] Desperate for artillery, since early August Ford had been negotiating to purchase artillery from Cortina,[107] but not getting anywhere. Although Cortina acted as though he was quite receptive to Ford's purchase order, he told Mifflin Kennedy he would see every last piece of his artillery destroyed before he would let the Confederates have any.[108] It is possible that Cortina also was negotiating to give the French his artillery if they would accept him as an ally.[109]

Thereafter, the volatile situation along the lower Rio Grande quickly came to a head. About the end of August, General Cortina had called, at Matamoros, a council of war with the commanders of his four battalions. He told them that they were surrounded on all sides and needed an alliance with the United States forces at Brazos Santiago in order to save their men, artillery, and supplies. Major Jose A. Puente of the "Faithful of Tamaulipas Battalion" said that he did not believe that either the United States consul in Matamoros nor Colonel Day at Brazos Santiago had the authority to make such an agreement. Cortina's response was that he had anticipated everything and that the council was a pure formality. He said his officers ought to accept his measures. Colonel Julian Cerda, senior colonel of Cortina's brigade, and Lieutenant Colonel Miguel Echazarrete[110] were named as a committee, with Puente, to record the basis of Cortina's agreement with the Federals. These three officers at first resisted Cortina's willingness to attack Brownsville if the United States attacked at the same time. All of the officers at the council felt that they should communicate at once with both the Federals and the Confederates. Puente was to translate the agreement into English for presentation to the United States consul. After the meeting, four officers—Colonel Cerda, Colonel Mariano G. Cerda, Colonel Mariano G. Hidalgo, and Major Puente—met privately and decided for the time to appear to conform to Cortina's wishes. A few days later, the "agreement" was presented to the United States consul, who told the Mexicans that neither he nor Day had the power to make a treaty, but that Cortina's force would be "well-received." Colonels Canales, Cerda and Hidalgo were, unknown to Cortina, determined "not to take a single step in the measure."[111] By September 3, Ford was fully aware of developments regarding Cortina and reported that the American consul was trying to persuade Cortina to cross the river and attack him. Stating that Mexican officers and others had so warned him, he wrote, "There is enough to place us on alert." Ford again pointed out his need for some artillery. Unfortunately, a communication to Showalter, a copy of which was included with this report, was not found when the *Official Records* were compiled.[112]

During this period, Ford, of course, communicated with the French commander at Bagdad, naval Captain A. Veron. On August 24, 1864, he had written asking Veron to allow the passage of supplies to him at Brownsville past French lines and—when the French occupied Matamoros—to respect "persons and property covered by the flag of the Confederate States of America."[113] Veron responded the next day from Bagdad, stating that the Confederates would "not suffer in anything on account of [the French] presence." As to French actions should they take Matamoros, the French captain's response was that Ford could "rest assured that I shall see that all persons and property covered by the flag of your nation are duly respected."[114] Veron's answer was pleasing to Ford, who wrote superior headquarters then at Columbus, Texas, on August 26, that he intended "to have the Confederate flag flying when the French enter Matamoros, and by that means to bring about a virtual recognition by the French authorities if possible."[115] It would seem that Ford, as part of his effort to establish good relations with the French force across the river from him, also agreed to sell cattle to the French. The French would need fresh meat, and Ford, as ever during his campaigning on the Rio Grande, needed income with which to purchase needed supplies of various types for his force. It was reported to

Colonel H.M. Day, commanding the Federal force at Brazos Santiago, that a small detachment of Benavides' 33rd Texas Cavalry under Captain Richard Taylor was herding cattle to the French at Bagdad. On September 5, 1864, Day crossed 300 men of the 91st Illinois Infantry and a cannon of the 1st Missouri Light Artillery to the mainland. Twelve miles above the mouth of the river, near Palmito Ranch, they encountered Taylor and his men. The Confederates were forced to withdraw up river and the cattle were taken by the Federals. The next day, Showalter and the 4th Arizona moved out to recapture the cattle.[116] Day's purpose was to drive the cattle into his camp "for the sustenance of [his own] command."[117]

Dan Showalter, of course, was not unaware of the complicated situation across the river in Mexico. On August 31, Colonel Ford wrote Showalter that he had "plausible, but not fully authenticated reports, that Cortina meditates crossing the Rio Grande, and forcing his way through our lines to the Yankees." According to the rumors, Cortina would cross his force at two locations—nine miles above Brownsville and twelve miles below (where Showalter's Advance Force was). He told Showalter that there was sufficient consistency in the rumors to "use the utmost watchfulness."[118] On September 1, Ford had written him that he (Ford) was satisfied that there was an understanding between Cortina and the Federals. Then, on September 3, Cortina stopped passage of forage up the river to Brownsville. Ford informed Showalter that he'd made arrangements to obtain a temporary supply from Boca del Rio (the mouth of the river).[119] On the 5th, Showalter wrote Ford that Cortina was at Burrita (a small Mexican settlement a few miles further south) with 300 men and two pieces of artillery, and another force of 300 was across the river, about two miles north of his (Showalter's) position. The boat he'd sent to the river mouth for forage had returned without any problem. He also told Ford that he'd had reports that the Federal force had been "reinforced with 1,000 Negro infantry."[120] Later that same day, Showalter again wrote Ford. This time he reported that a boat he'd sent down river for more forage had been stopped on orders of Cortina. He advised that he would send another boat and "I will have forage and supplies or a fight with the Mexicans," and requested that Ford send him reinforcements and send down the *Ark* to test the right of navigation on the river.[121]

Then on September 6, 1864, a small battle created quite a sensation. Then—and ever since—what happened has been surrounded in confusion, contradiction and controversy. Its events, along with those of the following five days, became intermingled in both reports (official and otherwise) of the time and in later accounts. In addition to the hyperbole so often common in those days, there were misstatements and outright falsehoods in reports by self-serving participants. As time went by, historians began to "read into" or "interpret" in the contemporary reports and accounts "facts" that were simply not there. As early as September 30, United States Secretary of State William H. Seward felt compelled to write Major General E.R.S. Canby, the Federal Department commander, that "the [newspaper] reports are contradictory and apparently entirely unreliable."[122] As to the negotiations and plans involving Cortina, a Mexican Congressional Commission in 1873—only eight years after the event—that interviewed many Mexicans of the area reported that it had been "unable to precisely ascertain the tenor of these negotiations."[123] Unofficial contemporary reports were limited to a few anonymous letters (the correspondents used pen names) to newspapers and were either self-glorifying or sensationalistic. The only person directly involved in the events who wrote about them in memoirs was John S. Ford. Unfortunately, his organization of memoirs of the events was not sequential and, being written thirty years later, subject to lapses and coloration of memory. It is instructive to first view the events as they were revealed, then, before attempting to reconstruct the actuality.

The *New York Times* of September 9, 1864, carried, under the headline "Reported Defeat of Mejia by Gen. Cortinas," a report from the (New Orleans) *True Delta* of August 28 that concluded: "It is rumored that the gallant Cortinas [sic] with his victorious army is now making forced marches back on Matamoras to contest the advance of the French up the Rio Grande. Celerity of movement is a distinguished feature in the operations of Gen. Cortinas, and we may expect to hear some stormy news from the State of Tamaulipas in a few days."[124] Readers of the *Times* were therefore not at all surprised to read in it, on September 20, three articles that were nothing less than sensational. The first reported: "We have reliable information that by the latest arrival from the Rio Grande of the gunboat Clinton, it is ascertained that Cortinas [sic] has crossed the river with his whole force of 2,000 men and sixteen pieces of artillery, and occupied Brownsville, driving out the Confederates under Col. Ford. He has hoisted the United States flag, and has offered his services, through the United States command at the Brazos, to that Government."[125]

The second article, which immediately followed, repeated the above news in substantially the same manner, citing news received via the steamer *Continental* from New Orleans. It then presented a much more lengthy and detailed report:

Sergeant F.S. Clarke, of the 91st Illinois infantry, who was a passenger by the steamer Belle to Cairo, gives the following statement of the affair:

It appears that on the morning of the 6th inst., the French moved out of Bagdad, with a force of 5,000, and commenced the ascent of the Rio Grande, with the purpose of attacking Matamoras. They were uninterrupted until reaching a point opposite White Ranche, where they met Cortinas with a Mexican force prepared to contest their approach.

A terrific artillery duel ensued, when the French were compelled to fall back in confusion, closely followed for three miles, when coming to a piece of chapparal [sic] they made a stand.

Cortinas [sic] on the Imperialists with shot and shell.

While engaged at this point the rebel commander at Brownsville, Col. Ford, came down from Texas on the Rio Grande with a large drove of cattle for the French, and seeing they were engaged with Cortinas promptly espoused the cause of the French and opened on the Mexican rear.

Seeing this, the Imperial army made an attempt to turn the tide of battle, and charged the Mexicans with bayonet determined to conquer or die. They were, however, driven back in disorder to the cover of the chapparal.

Cortinas then brought to bear two pieces of artillery on Ford's force, obliging him to retire. About this time the Ninety-first Illinois, stationed at Brazos Santiago, hearing the firing on the Rio Grande, were ordered to march to the scene to witness the repulse of the rebels. The gallant "Sucker" boys then pitched into Ford, drove him five miles, capturing his camp equipage and about thirty stand of arms.

Meantime Cortinas succeeded in putting the Imperials to flight, and then drove them to Bayo Del Rio. As his artillery could not compete with their heavy ordnance on ship board, he withdrew his forces to White Ranche [sic] and crossed five hundred men into Texas, where they lay on their arms during the night of the 6th, by the side of the American troops.

On the 9th Cortinas followed Ford to the old battle field Resaca de la Palma, where he rested his troops for the night, while Ford fell back to Brownsville. Cortinas dispatched couriers to Matamoras to order forces there to prepare to move away. Early on the morning of the 8th, 500 Mexicans moved up the Rio Grande, crossing the river and came down the Texas side, attacking Brownsville simultaneous with Cortinas. The struggle for Brownsville was brief, and resulted in the defeat of the Rebels, who were driven from the town. Cortinas took possession. The exit of the rebels was so hasty they left their flags floating on the Court-House and other public buildings, which were soon torn down and the stars and stripes hoisted amid the shouts of the citizens and Mexican soldiers, who were almost as proud of the starry banner as our brave boys.

The headline for this article, "Exciting News from the Rio Grande," was certainly consistent with its content.[126] After these accounts, readers probably missed the third article, "Later from New-Orleans," which had arrived on September 13 and began "There is much dispute over the Mexican news. It is not generally believed, but some who ought to know assert positively that it is true."[127] Among those "who ought to know" was presumably Sergeant Fletcher S. Clark of Company G, 91st Illinois Infantry.[128]

Sergeant Clark's story became the early news of the events of September 6 through 11. Washington's *Daily National Intelligencer* of the same date carried the exact same report.[129] The 20th's *New York Tribune* also reported on Cortina's capture of Brownsville, but in a shorter, less effusive article, stating that "the accounts of the events which preceded and led to the capture of Brownsville, differ." It reported, "based on the statements of two Mexican officers," that Ford had crossed the river into Mexico to aid the French. The *Tribune* concluded that there was "no doubt that the French and the Rebels had come to a perfect understanding about the opening of the Rio Grande," which Cortina had effectively blocked.[130] These reports were "copied" or restated in reduced form by other papers. One, the *Oswego* (New York) *Palladium*, even stated that "the reports of Cortinaz's [sic] operations in Texas are fully confirmed."[131]

Juan Nepomuceno Cortina as sketched 1864 by C.E.H. Bonwill for *Frank Leslie's Illustrated Newspaper*. He was for years an important Mexican leader in the lower Rio Grande Valley. During the Civil War and French intervention in Mexico, he trod a fine and confusing line between apparent alliances with the Union, the Confederacy, the French and Mexican Republicans. The involvement of some of his troops in the September 1864 skirmish with Showalter's command at Palmito Ranch led to "wild" reports of that battle (Library of Congress).

The "news" reached the west coast at about the same time. The *Sacramento Daily Union* gave it a little different and perhaps more exciting "spin" on September 20:

> By way of New Orleans we have an account of a grand free fight on the Rio Grande, in which French, Mexican, Unionists, and Confederates were mixed up with a splendid result. The French, five thousand strong, started to capture Matamoras. Cortinas met them with a republican army and drove them back. A rebel regiment coming up, pitched in on the side of the French. An Illinois regiment, stationed at Brazos Santiago, "snuffing the battle afar off," marched to the scene of action and, catching a glimpse of the rebel flag, went in on the side of the Mexicans. The rebels were cleared out and the French put to flight. Cortinas then went up the Rio Grande, brought over reinforcements, hoisted the stars and stripes and, with the aid of the Illinois troops, drove the rebels out of Brownsville. After the victory the Union boys and the Mexicans fraternized and had a good time generally. Cortinas has tendered his services to our Government.[132]

Another article, four columns over on the same page, dated September 19 in Chicago and citing the *New Orleans Picayune*, claimed that Cortina had crossed "his whole force and sixteen pieces of artillery."[133]

From newspapers exchanged across the lines by soldiers in Virginia, the Southern press picked up the story. On October 7, 1864, the *Richmond Whig and Public Advertiser*, in a first page article, "From the Rio Grande," cited "our Northern files" and provided its readers with additional information. Its article named Colonel Day as the Federal commander on the scene and even stated "it was undoubtedly the duty of Colonel Day to put a stop to such contraband traffic," referring to the cattle herd Ford was sending to the French. It pointed out that the combined Federal and Mexican force outnumbered the Confederates two to one. Then, after reporting Federal discharge of cannon, it mentioned Showalter and his regiment in generally creditable terms:

> The effect was electrical. The rebels were the best men in Ford's command, being Lieutenant Colonel Showalter's Californians, and they are brave men. They had dismounted and sent their horses to the rear, and were undoubtedly determined, upon a desperate fight, and their superior numbers made them confident of their success. But they never fought with artillery, and a cannon has more terror for them than ten thousand rifles and all the Commanches on the plains of Texas. At first glimpse of the shining brass monsters there was a visible wavering in the determined front of the enemy [from a Northern report—meaning Showalter's men], and as the shells came screaming over their heads, the [?] was complete. They broke rank, fled for their horses, scrambled on the first, that came to hand, and skedadled in the direction of Brownsville.

This portion of the account was obviously drawn from a different source since it gave Showalter a superior force, whereas the preceding paragraph had clearly stated he had been outnumbered two to one. The *Whig*'s account went on to relate Cortina's crossing the river and taking Brownsville. It concluded that the incident would have to be "handled with great care by those in power in this city and in Washington," and credited Cortina's action as "a most brilliant, bold and dashing one."[134]

Confusion and contradiction about the incident continued for a few weeks. On September 27, the *New York Herald*, on its first page, carried two separate reports on the matter. In "The Latest News From the Rio Grande" it reported:

> The reports from the Rio Grande received yesterday do not confirm previous advices. A passenger who came by a previous steamer [?] me that Cortinas had certainly captured and occupied Brownsville, and that with other portions of his forces he held Laredo, Texas, and Matamoros. This gentleman was direct from Matamoros and Brazos Santiago, and he ought not to have been mistaken in the details of the information, though he may have there. There has either been elegant romancing, greatly to the perversion of the facts, or very many have been mistaken to the supposition that Cortina had captured Brownsville and fought under the Stars and Stripes.[135]

The other report, "Important From the Rio Grande," included two items of correspondence from Brazos Santiago. One dated September 12 was fairly straightforward. The other, dated September 13, began, "It is now stated that there was an error in the report that Cortina had occupied Brownsville and raised the Union flag. It is true, however, that the rebels evacuated the town on the 6th inst., but returned after discovering that neither Mexican nor Union force occupied it."[136]

Confused accounts of the early September 1864 events on the lower Rio Grande have even been written into history. The Adjutant General of the State of Illinois, in his 1886 report, said little of the incident except that it was "quite a fight" and "it was said at the time a squadron of French troops forded the Rio Grande to help the rebels."[137] The Adjutant General's comments were repeated verbatim in the only history of the regiment.[138] That the supposed capture of Brownsville by Cortina made it into nineteenth century history books is even more surprising. Hubert Howe Bancroft, using numerous research assistants, collected a myriad of letters, documents and statements related to the history of the Pacific coast and the western states, from which he compiled and wrote a history of the region which was published between 1874 and 1890 in thirty-nine volumes entitled *The Works of Hubert Howe Bancroft*. Two volumes were devoted to the northern Mexican states and Texas. In Vol. II (Vol. XVI of the whole), covering the years 1861 through 1889, published in 1889, he wrote about the September 1864 events on the Rio Grande. Although many of the principal actors—including Cortina, Ford, and George H. Giddings—in those events were then still alive, unfortunately, neither Bancroft nor any of his researchers contacted them for details. Instead, the account which he published followed the early, erroneous newspaper accounts. He had Ford crossing the Rio Grande to attack Cortina's rear during an engagement with the French and Cortina later crossing the river, driving the Confederates from Brownsville, and raising the United States flag over the city.[139] Ford had considered the newspaper reports of Cortina's capturing Brownsville as having possibly been written by Leonard Pierce, the United States consul in Matamoros, and indicative of Pierce's confidence in the success of such an agreement.[140] He was also disgusted with Bancroft's history. He wrote in his *Memoirs*:

> Strange as it may appear this man [Cortina] is the hero of Mr. Bancroft in his bungling and untruthful history of Texas. How completely does the narrative of the distinguished officers of Mexico disprove the allegations of Mr. Bancroft, to say nothing of the reports of Confederate officers...? Mr. Bancroft has the ill-starred credit of publishing as true, as veracious history, the untruthful allegations of a mendacious Mexican, whose name is not given, and of giving the world an account of the capture of Brownsville by his criminal hero, Cortina, an event which never happened in the Confederate war, and is now disputed by Gen. Cortina himself. The author now bids adieu to Mr. Bancroft's effort to convert the baseless, lying, and scurrilous productions of tricksters into history.[141]

At the time, Bancroft was already noted as a—if not the—great historian of the American west. In this case, at least, he (or his writers who used his name) erred grievously and merited Ford's criticism.

Most "modern" accounts of the affair are also equally inaccurate. The versions found in recent histories specifically cast Dan Showalter in a very negative light. This is not at all surprising since they are all loosely based upon the memoirs of John Salmon Ford—a valuable source, but written over a period of years during Ford's later years and in no specific chronological order. Most modern historians also "interpreted" some of what was contained in Ford's *Memoirs*—and, to a lesser extent, the little available in the *Official Records*—in a manner which was not so evident in Ford's writing. These versions of events, all published by reputable historians and publishers, have subsequently been repeated on various internet sites. It is instructive to review what some of these accounts said.

> Showalter, "as chivalrous a man who ever drew a sword [when] not under the influence of liquor," had recourse to the bottle during the battle.[142]
>
> Day struck Showalter on September 6, 1864. As the Federal attack developed, Cortina's artillery suddenly hurled shells into the Confederate ranks. This surprise fire from Mexico caused the 4th Arizona to panic, primarily because Showalter, as the subsequent courts-martial revealed, was in no condition to command. Once too often he had tried to wash away unpleasant memories in alcohol.
>
> George Giddings came up behind Palmito to find the Confedederates "flying in confusion." He relieved Showalter on the spot, and finally stabilized a defense ...[143]
>
> Showalter, Ford's senior lieutenant colonel, had assumed temporary command of field operations, but he too now claimed an illness and was replaced on the last day of July.

A footnote to the preceding statement added,

> In view of later developments, it is not amiss to speculate that Showalter's illness was of the kind which may follow too free recourse to strong drink.[144]
>
> On September 6 ... Giddings arrived in time to rally the broken regiment several miles above Palmito. Once too often Dan Showalter had tried to wash away with liquor the memories of an unfortunate love affair. Ford relieved him of command, a move later sustained by Showalter's court martial ...[145]
>
> Cortina's guns fired on Showalter's camp from across the river on the morning of September 6, ... As Day wrote, "the last seen of [Showalter] he was flying in confusion back to Brownsville." Giddings arrived and, despite being peppered with Mexican shells, stabilized a defensive line by nightfall, ...[146]
>
> ... while Ford waited in Fort Brown, Showalter, "who had recourse to the bottle" used the cover of darkness to retreat from Palmito Ranch and move his company to within eight miles of Fort Brown. "He came to town in a maudlin condition" Ford recalled.[147]
>
> On the way the Arizonians encountered Giddings' Battalion that Ford had sent south to reinforce Palmito Hill. When George Giddings came up to the flying Confederates he was able to stabilize a defense. He relieved Showalter, who had alcohol problems, on the spot. Dan Showalter apparently used liquor to remove memories of his unfortunate love affair.[148]
>
> Showalter, who had been drinking heavily that day, was unnerved by the assault. The Federal commander reported his foe as "flying in confusion." Fortunately, Ford had expected an attack from the coast and sent reinforcements to Palmito. These soldiers, under Capt. G. H. Giddings, relieved Showalter and established a new defensive position.[149]

All of these renderings of the story compress the events into a single day and credit George Giddings with retrieving the situation. Most of them imply, if not actually so state, that Dan Showalter was drunk during the battle. Not all modern historians have fallen into similar errors regarding the events at Palmito Ranch. Notable exceptions are Frank Cushman Pierce in 1917[150] and Dr. Jerry D. Thompson in two books.[151]

It all began with the herd of cattle. The cattle were supervised and guarded by detached soldiers from Ford's command—including some members of the 4th Arizona—under command of Captain Richard Taylor of the 33rd Texas Cavalry.[152] On September 8, Colonel Day, at Brazos Santiago, reported what he called "a slight engagement" had taken place on the 6th at Palmetto (Palmito) ranch on the Rio Grande River, about sixteen miles from his headquarters. His scouts had learned that "a large number of cattle" were in a bend of the river just above White's ranch. After what he referred to as "mature deliberation," Day decided to try and capture the animals and, at the same time, push back the Confederates, who had been annoying his force the past few days. He sent a squadron of the 1st Texas Cavalry, along with one 12-pound howitzer of the 1st Missouri Light Artillery under Major E.J. Noyes, to accomplish the task. Noyes advanced with skirmishers on his flanks. The Confederates retreated slowly to Palmito Ranch, where they made a stand, and "brisk firing" resulted. Noyes' main body soon arrived, as did Confederates from above the ranch. Day reported that "a fair prospect of a heavy engagement was apparent," but then his artillery opened up with shell, which dispersed the Confederates, who Day said were last seen "flying in confusion." A detachment of the 91st Illinois Infantry was sent to reinforce Noyes, but was not needed that day. The entire Federal force returned to their camp on the morning of the 7th. Day considered his "expedition" a success, with "a lot" of cattle captured and brought to his camp.[153] The fleeing, confused Confederates were apparently only those detached to guard the cattle. Day's report certainly made him "look good" to his superiors and was a bit bombastic. It was also not the entire story of what happened that day. To have reported all that happened on that day would have opened him up to criticism for involving the Federal force in diplomatic complications.

Also that morning and at the same time as Noyes' advance, Cortina's men, according to Colonel Ford in his *Memoirs*, "opened fire on camp Palmito with three pieces of artillery, and small arms." Dan Showalter's morning communication of this information to Ford also requested reinforcements. To this, later on the 6th, Ford responded that George Giddings had been ordered to his support with what troops he had beneath Brownsville. Ford's response continued: "From information received from the other side we learn that some six hundred men (Mexicans) have gone up the river, consequently we cannot spare more men from the garrison. You will hold your position as long as you can, and will fall back slowly, if you are over-powered." Ford did not seem optimistic about Showalter's prospects and added that he'd received information that the French would give no assistance (against Cortina). Ford did send out pickets on the road from Point Isabel (on the mainland north of Brazos Santiago) and so informed Showalter. He felt that this would protect Showalter's inland flank whether or not he received "timely notice and aid."[154]

Then, on the morning of September 7, Dan Showalter sent the following communication to Ford: "The Mexicans have opened on our Camp from above & are now shelling us. I expect the Yankees on us every moment, I shall move my wagons above. The Mexicans have not yet crossed the River."[155] Unmentioned in Showalter's communication was that the Cortinista cannonade was returned by the 4th Arizona with small arms fire. Several of the Mexican cannoneers were killed.[156] This concise and clear report reveals a Showalter who was alert to possibilities, taking precautions and keeping his commander informed.

Then, according to Ford in his *Memoirs*—which he mistakenly recorded as happening on the 6th—Showalter remained in his position until late in the evening

> when the Federals advanced, then Showalter retreated, without having lost a man. Ford heard of his untimely retreat. His command was camped about eight miles below Brownsville. He reached town awhile after dark. Reported verbally that he had lost from 15 to 150 men. According to his account large parties of Mexicans and Federals were advancing by the Point Isabel road, and a heavy body of Mexicans had been sighted on the bank of the Rio Grande. One thing was certain the Federals and Mexicans were in force in Texas. They evidently intended to take Brownsville. Our opposing force had given way, was demoralized, and their commander was incapable of performing his duty.[157]

In this case, Ford's memory of the event must have been confused, for he also wrote of it that "the Confederates silenced the cannon of the Mexicans on several occasions and fought well." Then, in the very next paragraph, Ford wrote that "every thing was done that night that could be. Every measure was adopted that possibly could be to restore the morale of Showalter's men."[158]

A more complete—and evidently more accurate—report of the events of that day was shortly later sent to the *Weekly State Gazette* in Austin by a soldier signing himself as "Ranger." The details given in this report, "Extracts from the Journal of a Murrah Ranger, on the Rio Grande," which was published on October 19, tend to imply that its writer was Captain W.H.D. Carrington. This rather lengthy report began:

> I was walking leisurely down the street, immediately on the banks of the river, in Brownsville, in front of the houses where Carrington's company was quartered, on the morning of 7th Sept., when a commotion was observed among the soldiers on the brink of the river. It was stated by a Texan, who had succeeded in crossing the river, that Cortinas had sent four pieces of artillery to the banks

**Order of Battle
Skirmish at Palmito Ranch, Texas
On Sept. 6 and 7, 1864**

CONFEDERATE FORCE
Lt. Col. Daniel Showalter

4th Arizona Cavalry (Showalter)
1 Company, 33rd Texas Cavalry (Capt. Refugio Benevides)
Reinforcement on Sept. 7:
"Murrah Rangers" Company, Giddings' Battalion (Lt. Carrington)*

FEDERAL & MEXICAN FORCE
Col. Henry Martyn Day

91st Illinois Volunteer Infantry (Day)
2 Companies, 1st Texas Volunteer Cavalry (Maj. Edward Noyes)
Section, Provisional Heavy Artillery (2nd Lt. Andrew Hils)
Exploradores del Bravo Battalion (Col. Miguel Echazarrete)**
Section, Artillery with Exploradores del Bravo**
Section, Artillery, gunfire support from South Bank of Rio Grande**

*Not reporting to or under command of Showalter.
**Mexican Republican Army units operating with the Federals.

Order of Battle, Skirmish at Palmito Ranch, Texas, on September 6 and 7, 1864 (prepared by Gene C. Armistead from official and news reports).

of the river—masked at various points—all bearing upon Brownsville. Half an hour later a courier arrived from our front, from Lieut. Col. Dan E. Showalter, bringing the astonishing news that the Yankees, in strong force, with infantry, cavalry and artillery, were pressing upon his front and left; and that Cortinas was shelling him from the other side of the river. Col. S. called for immediate relief. The order was immediately given for 300 men to saddle their horses, and go to his assistance. Unfortunately, however, our horses had all been sent out to graze, and at least two or three hours must elapse before they could be brought in. Before this was done, other courier arrived from the front.

Unfortunately, several lines at the bottom of the column of Ranger's letter are now missing. It seems that the company (Carrington's) did move out to reinforce several hours later and, on the way to the scene, apparently met Showalter himself, with "the information that 200 Yankees, in two bodies had flanked him from the Point Isabel road and that he had with difficulty brought off his men."[159]

Ranger went on to relate that his company proceeded down the road "in such a rain as has not fallen before since the days of Noah," with water up to the saddle-girths of their animals, to "Showalter's old camp." He noted that, upon arrival, they set an ambush into which they were unsuccessful in drawing the Federals and Mexicans. The next day (the 8th), they skirmished several hours with their foes. The company maintained its position the next day "until 3 o'clock P.M., when we were informed that Col. Giddings was approaching with 200 or 300 cavalry reinforcements."[160] This report makes it clear that Showalter was on the field in command until at least the afternoon of the 7th and that Giddings did not arrive until the afternoon of the 9th. Further, on September 8, Ford reported to General Drayton, "I have sent a strong party under command of Capt. Carrington to ascertain the position and strength of the enemy."[161] A note by Giddings to Captain Maddon of his command, dated September 7, mentions that Captain Carrington's company had been sent down the Point Isabel Road. Giddings then ordered Maddon to take his company down the road to "ascertain hesitantly" if a force reported on the road was Carrington's or not.[162] The first report to Ford written by George Giddings as commanding the "Advance Force" was a brief note on September 8, which stated that he had received from Ford a dispatch at 8:30 p.m.[163] It would not have, therefore, been possible for Giddings to have relieved Showalter "on the spot" on September 6.

In his report about skirmishing on the morning of the 6th, Colonel Day had not made any mention of Mexican soldiers being with his force. Such a secret could not have been kept. On September 6, Ford had already communicated to the French commander at Bagdad, naval Captain A. Veron, his information that Cortina's Mexican force was going to attack in cooperation with the Federals.[164] He wrote Veron again, on the 8th, on Cortinista involvement in the attack on Showalter and stated, "I am confident the Commander of the French forces at Bagdad was not apprized of this movement on the part of Cortina, else in compliance with the assurances, previously given, steps would have been taken to prevent it."[165] Colonel Day, on September 8, had written to headquarters of the Federal Department of the Gulf about the Mexicans: "an armed body of Mexican troops have landed on the American shore of the Rio Grande River, about fifteen miles from [Brazos Santiago]. These troops are commanded by General Cortina, Governor of Tamaulipas, whom I have seen in person, and from him learn that it is his desire to receive protection from the U.S. authorities. An order has been sent to him, demanding the immediate surrender of his ordinance and ordinance stores to my command, after which I shall give him the protection that he desires."[166]

This report of Day's did not match the report of the United States consul at Matamoros to General Herron. Consul L. Pierce, Jr., wrote the general on the same day that Day had written to his higher headquarters. He said Cortina desired to cross to the United States with 1,500 men and twenty pieces of artillery, but that

> [Day] did not feel justified in moving any men from Brazos without orders. Finally it was arranged in this way: Cortina was to go down to a point about two miles this side of the White Ranch, cross the river with 800 men and four pieces of artillery, and then move up and drive the rebs from Brownsville, and thus get an opening for the passage of the remainder. At the time appointed, I sent a messenger to Colonel Day, who sent out some few troops, who chased the rebs half way up the river, and, the coast being thus clear, Cortina got safely over, and is now encamped about nine miles this side of the Boca, where there were also some 500 of our troops.

Pierce also expressed the hope that Day would hire the Mexican soldiers as beef hunters or muster them in as rangers.[167]

Although Day had stated, on September 8, that he personally had seen Cortina, he retracted that in a later communication to his department headquarters. On the 14th, he reported that he'd sent Major Noyes to the site of the Mexican crossing of the river on the 8th to demand surrender of their arms and offer protection, and then that "I also instructed him that if he found it necessary in order to defend himself against the rebels to allow the refugees to temporarily resume their arms." After stating Mexican compliance with these terms, Day wrote:

They were not commanded by Governor Cortina, as I was at first informed, and hence reported to you, but by Col. Miguel Echazarrete Cortina not having moved his headquarters to this side of the river. Shortly after The surrender had been effected our forces were attacked by the rebels with nearly double their number, and according to my instructions the refugees were allowed to resume their arms and fought bravely with our men. After a short engagement, in which one piece of Mexican artillery was used, the rebels were repulsed with great loss. They rallied and again attacked and were again repulsed, so a third time, after which Major Noyes, being short of ammunition, fell back two miles and took a stronger position.[168]

Twelve Mexican soldiers were captured by the Confederates between the 6th and the 11th, and Ford wrote Federal commander Day, on the 12th: "In the recent affairs between your troops and those of my command, between the 6th and 12th instant, 12 Mexicans of the Exploradores del Bravo of Colonel Echarzarrete's corps, General Juan N. Cortina's brigade, were taken prisoners. I desire to know if they were at the time of capture in the service of the Government of the United States?"[169] Day responded to Ford the next day, writing: "I have the honor to acknowledge the receipt of your communication dated the 12th instant, relative to 12 Mexicans who were taken prisoner by your forces and who were formerly under the command of Colonel Echazarete [sic], Juan N. Cortina's brigade. In reply I have the honor to state that those men were in the service of the United States and fighting under the U.S. flag."[170] A newspaper report by "Carlos," a regular correspondent from the expeditionary force to the Houston *Daily Telegraph*, published in that paper on September 12, falsely added that Day had informed Ford that "Col. Echazareta [sic] held a commission as a Colonel, and that Juan N. Corona held the commission of Brigadier General."[171] In two days' time, Day had changed the status of the Mexicans fighting with his force from refugees armed in an emergency to U.S. soldiers. It was reported that Colonel Echazaretta crossed with thirteen officers and 200 men and turned over to Day 249 rifles of three types plus a 12-pound cannon.[172] Rearming so many Mexicans with so many arms while under attack must have been quite an achievement— or was it really so? Colonel Day still had them with him as late as October 9, when he referred to them again as "refugees" and reported that many were enlisting for one year's service, but that most desired to return to Mexico.[173]

Prior to that time, stories of the Mexican involvement had reached Military Division of West Mississippi headquarters at New Orleans. Major General E.R.S. Canby, commanding the army, wrote Major General N.P. Banks, commander of the Federal Department of the Gulf, that he had received correspondence from Day, and "Colonel Day's action, so far as is known here, accords with out neutral obligations and is approved." Canby explained that the "Mexican refugees" were entitled to asylum when they delivered up their arms and munitions. Further, he stated that "they will not be received into the service of the United States for service on the Rio Grande frontier, but may be enlisted for the general service." In this case, they would be sent to New Orleans to be enlisted, organized, and armed.[174] Obviously, Day had misinformed Canby and likely lied to Ford. In any event, his letter to Ford at least gained the prisoners status as prisoners of war rather than as bandits.

Ford's superior, General Thomas F. Drayton, had arrived at Brownsville on September 10.[175] Four days later, he had his adjutant, Alexander P. Root, write his own superior that "on the 6th, before we arrived, while Colonel Giddings was engaging the Yankees in front, Cortina opened upon our troops with three pieces of artillery and shelled for some time, but without material damage." Drayton used this communication to request that artillery be sent with "all haste" to the Confederates on the Rio Grande.[176] In a letter the following day, Drayton again praised "the gallantry of our troops under Lieutenant-Colonel Giddings."[177] It is unknown why Drayton's letter was inaccurate regarding who was in command and engaging the enemy on the 6th. There had certainly been sufficient time to ascertain the facts. Exactly what the facts were is somewhat difficult to ascertain after so much time due to lack of official reports, inaccurate official reports, a plethora of confusing newspaper reports, and more modern-day "interpretations" and "insertions" of information as fact. As best as can be determined by your authors, what follows is actually what happened during and immediately after Dan Showalter's command of the Confederate force at Palmito Ranch in September of 1864.

It all began when, on the morning of September 6, 1864, Federal cavalry, with at least one artillery piece attached, attacked Confederates guarding the herd of cattle at or near Palmito Ranch. The Confederates were driven off to their main camp at Palmito, where Dan Showalter was in command of the 4th Arizona cavalry. (Showalter may have moved out his entire force in an effort to retake the cattle.[178]) At least four pieces of Mexican artillery opened fire on the Confederates from across the Rio. At the same time (about 6:00 p.m.[179]), approximately three hundred soldiers of Colonel Miguel Echazarrete's Exploradores del Bravo regiment of Cortina's command crossed the river and joined with the Federals in the attack. Showalter sent a message to Ford, informing him that he (Showalter) was under attack by a superior force. Ford, fearing a coordinated attack by Cortinistas across the river above Brownsville, responded that he could not spare men to send as reinforcements. Of the early part of the battle, Ford later commented that Showalter's command "behaved well" and even on several occasions were able to silence the Mexican artillery and kill about forty of their Mexican opponents.[180] Probably not long after, the Federal infantry of the 91st Illinois joined the assault on Showalter's men. Since he had reported a Federal force approaching along the Point Isabel road, they probably approached via this route. Showalter had been instructed by Ford to withdraw slowly, if he had to. Late in the evening[181] (about one in the morning[182]), he did this, retreating about halfway to Brownsville, to a point about eight miles below the town. That night it rained heavily.

The morning of September 7, 1864, found Showalter and his men in a blocking position eight miles from Brownsville. Another courier from Showalter reached Brownsville that morning. His message called for relief, as he was being pressed on both his front and his left, and shelling from the Mexican shore was continuing. Since Ranger was "walking leisurely down the street," it would seem that this was not early in the morning. Within thirty minutes, three hundred men were ordered to saddle up and go to the assistance of the 4th. Incredibly, despite the fighting of the previous day and strong rumors that Cortina would cross above the town with a strong force, there was no force ready to respond and at least two or three hours would be needed to gather in the horses, which had been set out to graze. Meanwhile, other couriers arrived from Showalter's front to advise Ford of the progress of the battle.[183] Later that day, Captain Carrington's Company C of Giddings' Battalion was sent out. Along the way, they met someone who informed them that the Federals (with their attached Mexican soldiers) had flanked the Confederates on two sides. Carrington's force, traveling through heavy rain, proceeded to Showalter's old camp without encountering any foes, who had perhaps withdrawn due to the rain and the resultant quagmire.

Ranger did mention that they did meet on their way a "stampede company"[184] and that it was on the evening of the 7th that Showalter himself reached Brownsville. In his *Memoirs*, Ford reported that "[Showalter] reached town awhile after dark. Reported verbally that he had lost from 15 to 150 men." He further stated about Showalter and his men that they were demoralized, and "their commander was incapable of performing his duty."[185] Ford subsequently, in his memoir, wrote again about the matter. This time he stated, "Unfortunately, Colonel Showalter had recourse to the bottle. In the evening he retreated. His command moved to within eight miles of Fort Brown. He came to town in a maudlin condition, claimed to have lost from 15 to 150 men."[186] Why he left his command eight miles below town is not known, but perhaps to personally appeal that the situation merited reinforcement. Obviously, Giddings did not "relieve Showalter on the spot." Showalter had gone to Brownsville on his own initiative on the second day of almost continuous skirmishing. Additionally, as shall be seen, Giddings did not take out his reinforcements until the 8th. Unfortunately, there is nothing to contest that Dan Showalter was inebriated on the evening of September 7, but he had held off, without reinforcement, for two days a force of infantry, cavalry and artillery that was more than twice the size of his own force (800 against his own 250[187]). In any event, his command of the 4th Arizona was, for a time, over.

Before examining what next transpired with Dan Showalter, it would be better to first summarize what happened during the ensuing days in regard to the Federal/Mexican advance. Showalter did not return to his command, but was apparently retained in town. In his absence, command of the 4th Arizona fell to the regiment's Major, Finis Ewing Kavanaugh.[188] The Missouri-born Kavanaugh was a physician in New Mexico Territory when the Civil War began and had traveled to Texas with Sibley's retreating Confederates in late 1862. When organization of the 4th Arizona began in 1863, he was appointed its Surgeon. The original Major of the regiment, Edward Riordan (a former Houston and Galveston slave trader), was reassigned, in early 1864, as Lieutenant Colonel of Hardeman's Texas Cavalry. Kavanaugh was then appointed, on March 1, 1864, to replace him.[189]

The first instance in which George Giddings signed himself to a report as "Commanding, Advance Force" was at 8:30 p.m. on September 8, and it is clear that, from no later than that moment, he had assumed command of the Confederate force in the field, opposing Day's Federals and Echazarrete's Mexicans.[190] Major Kavanaugh and the men of the 4th Arizona served under Giddings' command during the ensuing days while the Federal/Mexican force was pushed back. They were the larger element of the troops that Giddings led out on the 9th.[191] The series of skirmishes that began on the 6th continued for several days and included action on the grounds of the Mexican War battlefield of Palo Alto. Giddings was reinforced by the company of Captain Benavides on the afternoon of that day. Their ammunition being almost exhausted, Giddings camped his main force on Palo Alto prairie that night, but left Major Kavanaugh and his men on the field of battle as pickets. Day's force retreated overnight to Palmito. There were no large-scale skirmishes on the 10th as Giddings advanced to within one mile of Palmito. On the 11th, the Confederates advanced past Palmito. At this time, Giddings did not have over 350 cavalry and estimated his foes as being 300 Mexicans, 400 Federal infantry, 150 Federal cavalry, and four pieces of artillery, with 250 infantry reinforcements aboard a boat ready to land. Even with the proclivity of most Civil War commanders for overstating the numbers of their foe, the Confederates were probably outnumbered two to one (as had been Showalter on the 6th and 7th). Giddings hesitated to attack so strong a force, so left some men to harass the enemy and withdrew his main force to Palmito. The next day, the 12th, the Federals withdrew to the coast and crossed the Bolsa Chica to Brazos Santiago. Giddings had followed, but did not pursue when a Federal gunboat off the coast shelled his men.[192] Within three days, all that had been lost to the Federal/Mexican force had been recovered.

On September 22, the French moved up the Rio Grande and General Mejia advanced his Imperial force from the countryside. Matamoros fell on the 26th,[193] with Cortina changing his allegiance to the Mexican Empire, a loyalty he would then keep only until Maximilian's empire began to collapse. Ford (and Drayton) established cordial relations with the French and Imperialists, which ended any further difficulties for Confederate trade on or across the river.[194] Almost as soon as he arrived at Brownsville, General Drayton began crying for some artillery, and a battery soon arrived for the Confederate force. The Federals were discouraged. Federal Brigadier General William A. Pile commanded at Brazos Santiago during late 1864. He reported himself as "almost helpless, so far as expeditions on the mainland are concerned, for want of cavalry and pontoons with which to cross the Boca Chica Pass."[195] His successor, Colonel R.B. Jones, was more optimistic. With a few hundred cavalry, two pieces of artillery, and orders or permission to do so, he believed he could take Brownsville, but cautioned that "were I to occupy Brownsville it could only be temporarily." His counsel was that, due to lack of men to garrison the place, he would be compelled to abandon it almost immediately.[196] Not until May of 1865 would there be any Federal advance onto the mainland and toward Brownsville.

Dan Showalter, however, did not participate in any of these activities after the 7th of September. According to Ford, when Showalter came into Brownsville that night he was under the influence of liquor and had, in the streets, given voice to having lost fifteen to 150 men. Public comments of this sort could well have been demoralizing and no doubt gave occasion for relieving or suspending Showalter from command of the 4th Arizona. There exist absolutely no records of the charges and specifications of his court martial. Records regarding Confederate court martials are extremely sparse except for those of the Army of Northern Virginia. The testimony of Ford in his *Memoirs* and notations from regimental returns in Showalter's compiled service records provide the sole testimony to the fact that Dan Showalter faced a court martial. The reason for his intoxicated state is, of course, unknown. Some latter-day histories have stated that it was because he was in a "maudlin condition" over his "love affair"[197] with Anna Forman. The use of the word "maudlin" in this context is confusing. The most frequent definition for this word is "weakly and effusively sentimental," but, in the Showalter context, the variant definition of "drunk enough to be emotionally silly" seems to be meant. Neither definition indicates a "falling down drunk" condition. This does not seem likely since Showalter was a very strong-minded man and had, for at least one day (the 6th) and likely most of two, been involved in a creditable defense against double his number. Perhaps, when his defense had stabilized eight miles below Brownsville, he did imbibe—frustrated over the lack of any reinforcements. But it did happen, and he did at that time lose his command.

That he was not "falling down drunk" seems obvious by his reaction to being removed from command of his troops in the field. In his *Memoirs*, Ford recorded: "Lt. Col. Showalter was very mad when he found he was confined to the limits of Brownsville. Col. Ford sent word to him, through a friend, that personally he had nothing against him. He was compelled to refer his case to a Court martial. Gen. Drayton was acquainted with all the facts in his case, and he would have preferred charges against Ford, if he allowed Col. Showalter's case to pass without calling him to account."[198] There is no information regarding how General Drayton learned of the case or became involved in it. Drayton was yet another of those Confederate generals found wanting in Virginia (Robert E. Lee assigned the regiments of his brigade to others, depriving him of command after a particularly poor performance during the Antietam campaign[199]) and sent west to the Trans-Mississippi Department. The fact that Ford was compelled by Drayton to prefer charges against Showalter indicates that the Colonel did not consider the transgression to be all that serious. It was not, as stated by Richard B. McCaslin in his book *Fighting Stock: John S. "Rip" Ford of Texas*, a case of "he was also drunk, a sin Ford would not forgive."[200] (Ford had been a temperance campaigner.[201])

General Drayton left Brownsville on October 6.[202] On September 26, 1864, three members of the 4th Arizona—Privates F.S. Fritter, A. King and H. Krowell (actually Crowell)—were assigned to escort Showalter to San Antonio.[203] Perhaps it was their long association with Showalter that prompted it, since two of these men, King and Crowell, had been among those captured with him in November 1861 at Minter's Ranch in California. Showalter and his escort apparently reached San Antonio in late October since the Austin *State Gazette,* in its November 2 issue, noted, "The following additional news we find in the San Antonio Herald, which has been informed by Lt. Col. Showalter, who is just up from Brownsville."[204]

Meanwhile, a defense of Dan Showalter had appeared in Houston's *Tri-Weekly Telegraph* on November 4, 1864, under the headline "Letter from the Rio Grande":

Lower Rio Grande, Oct. 5, 1861.

    Ed. Telegraph:–While your correspondents on the Rio Grande have been lavish in their praise of Colonel Ford and his command, and while every officer connected with the "expeditionary forces" has been mentioned in print, either in official reports or by correspondents, never yet has any officer or man, connected with the 4th regiment of the Arizona Brigade, commanded by Lieut. Col. Dan. Showalter been mentioned. This is the usual reward of such troops—While they have stood constantly in the front, always the first in every engagement and generally the only ones, other troops and other officers have received the credit and all the honor of the campaign. A braver and nobler set of men never fought a battle. Col. Showalter (than whom no more gallant officer lives) has been maliciously, falsely and most basely maligned by certain interested parties, who have always been trying to keep him in a position where he could gain no credit and do no justice to himself. This regiment has fought its way in advance of all other troops of that command from Laredo to the mouth of the Rio Grande, where it now stands twenty miles in advance of the balance of the command alone; keeping back the foe. To it falls the lot of the picket duty, being the only regiment engaged in that duty, requiring half the regiment at a time, while other troops are back in Brownsville, quietly enjoying the fruits of the 4th regiment's victories—doing nothing.

    This is the regiment that fought Cortina's and the Federal forces combined at Palmetto, and because they were forced to retire before a force of 800 Yankees and Mexicans, with two batteries of artillery, while Col. S. had only 250 available men with no artillery, were accused of running from a hundred Yankees, and no one would believe that there had been any artillery used against them. No reinforcements were sent to aid them, although the rest of the "expeditionary force" were back in Brownsville doing nothing.

    Now comes the next fight; the gallant 4th under another leader (God knows not of their choosing) were held in reserve, at first, in order that other troops might steal their dearly purchased laurels. But mark the alter course. The commanding officer soon commenced calling on the 4th for detachments, and soon the entire regiment was absorbed into another command, fighting under Captains of another regiment. And now, when the battle fought and the victory won (by the 4th regiment) the balance of the command is marched back to Brownsville to be lionized and feted, while the unfortunate 4th—cowards, as they are, and not worthy of such things—are left to their old drudgery, of watching the front. Again placed in their old position at Palmito, 9 miles from Boca del Rio, and 20 miles in advance of any other force.

Other troops and other commanders receive all the praise and glory. Let justice be done though the Heavens fall. Honor to whom honor is due, and though I ascribe to all due praise and honor, yet let it be remembered that there is some other officers on the Rio Grande besides Col. John S. Ford, and let Carlos, or any other man, remember that where praise is due, there should praise be given.

NACION[205]

It is not possible to determine who "Nacion" was. His eloquence and facility with the pen indicate that he was a man of some education, and his point of view that he was, if not a member of the 4th Arizona, certainly a friend and partisan of it and Showalter. If not for the comment that no more gallant an officer than Showalter lived, it would be tempting to believe that Nacion was Showalter himself. Likewise, the identity of the mentioned "Carlos" is unknown. Carlos had been a frequent correspondent to the *Telegraph* throughout Ford's campaign from San Antonio to Brownsville and shortly after. He had mentioned Showalter only once in his letters—in a July 29 letter, and in conjunction with the names of Giddings, a Captain Cate, and a Captain Saunders at Las Rucias.[206] His letters of September 7 and September 12 reported the events that month at and about Palmito, but not once mentioned either the 4th Arizona or Showalter—Ford and Giddings received all the notice.[207] Since Ford was the overall commander, it is perhaps not suspicious that he received much credit—but to give Giddings commentary to the exclusion of Showalter is. The fact that Showalter was the only non-Texan commander in Ford's Expeditionary Force is perhaps the explanation, even though for over a month he had been commanding in the field while Ford was sick with his long-time recurring malarial fevers.

Nacion, however, was not the only observer who commented favorably about the 4th Arizona. In a "Letter From Brownsville" published April 28, 1865, a correspondent signing himself as "Confederate," in reviewing the 1864 campaign along the Rio Grande, weighed in with the comment that the regiment was "as good troopers we can desire to have and have done good service," and commented that for their service in that campaign they "[had] not received the credit they deserve."[208]

It apparently took some time to convene in San Antonio[209] a court martial panel to try Showalter. This would probably have been since its members had to be equal to or greater in rank than he. The trial evidently began or was held during December 1864, when Captain T.A. Wilson was noted, on the regimental return, as being absent at San Antonio as "witness in case of Lt. Col. Showalter."[210] Several other officers of the 4th Arizona had also been summoned to San Antonio as witnesses during the last quarter of 1864—presumably as witnesses on behalf of Showalter. Colonel John S. Ford was also called as a witness in the case. He refused to go. The only report as to the result of this court martial was that given by Ford in his *Memoirs*—"Showalter was cleared."[211] That he was cleared or acquitted of charges is also attested to by the fact that 1865 would find Dan Showalter again in command of the 4th Arizona.

Eight

Arch Rebel to the End

During Showalter's absence, the 4th Arizona had been commanded by Major F.E. Kavanaugh except for the month of December, when the Major was sick.[1] Finis Ewing Kavanaugh was a native of Missouri and graduate of the St. Louis Medical College who had settled in Santa Fe, New Mexico.[2] The fall of 1861 found him the contract surgeon at the Union post at Fort Fauntleroy in the Navajo country. In September of that year, many Navajo journeyed to the fort to receive an issue of rations. A horserace was organized between an Indian pony and a thoroughbred owned by Dr. Kavanaugh, which he had raced frequently over the preceding summer without a loss. Kavanaugh's horse won—apparently because someone had sabotaged the Navajos' entrant in the race by cutting its bridal. The Navajo, of course, protested, but were denied a rematch. Later that day, some angry Navajo attacked a guard post and the Union soldiers responded with gunfire and cannon, killing or wounding many Navajo men, women and children. A war with the Navajo ensued, which would not end until late during the Civil War.[3] On March 3, 1862, upon news of General Sibley's Confederate invasion of New Mexico, Kavanaugh led a group of civilians in the capture of the Union post at Cubero. Shortly thereafter, he was employed, along with others, by Sibley's quartermaster as a member of a group known as "The Brigands." This company, though never enlisted in the Confederate Army, served as scouts and guides for Sibley's force. Dr. Kavanaugh left this service in May.[4] He went to Texas and, when the 4th Arizona was organized, became its Surgeon. When the regiment's original Major, Major Edward H. Riordan, became Lieutenant Colonel of the 31st Texas Cavalry in February 1864, General Magruder appointed Kavanaugh to replace him.[5]

During Showalter's enforced absence, the 4th Arizona remained in the lower Rio Grande Valley, first at Camp Wilson near Fort Brown in October,[6] then, from November 27, 1864, at a site referred to as Camp Hood.[7] In late December, they were ordered to a point below Palmito to meet a reported Federal advance up the river. Upon their arrival in the area, they found that the Federals had returned to their base at Brazos Santiago and so returned to their own camp.[8] Then, on January 31 of the new year, General Slaughter issued Special Order No. 27 to Colonel Ford, directing that he "issue necessary orders to the 4th Reg Ariz Brigd to hold itself in readiness to march first [sic] practicable moment."[9] The general followed this order up, on February 8, with a letter to Ford directing Ford to order the regiment to march "at once" to Houston via Banquete and Goliad to Alleyton. Ford was told that arrangements had been made for "a fresh supply of Beef on hoof" at Goliad and also that orders had been issued for accumulation of ten days' rations. Slaughter concluded that Ford should advise him of the unit's probable departure date and to guard against any desertions of its members.[10] On the 11th, Special Order No. 36 by Ford directed that all members of the 4th Arizona on detached service be relieved from such service, return to the regiment, and prepare to take up the line of march for Houston.[11]

John Salmon "Rip" Ford figured large in Texas history and commanded the 1864 expedition to the Rio Grande in which Showalter and the 4th Arizona took part. This photograph was by Louis de Planque & Co. Photographic Studio of Brownsville and Matamoros and is in the Lawrence T. Jones III Collection, Series 2, Box 2 (courtesy DeGolyer Library, Southern Methodist University, Lawrence T. Jones, III Texas Photographs, Dallas, Texas).

The next that is known of the regiment was a complaint on March 1 by Thomas H. O'Callaghan, Chief Justice of San Patricio County, to General John G. Walker, now commanding the District of Texas. Judge O'Callaghan wrote:

> On Sunday last [February 25] the Regiment of Cavalry known as "Showalters Regt" marched through this place en route from Brownsville; I only say "marched" thru habit, not that the manner in which they passed through here in the least merited that technical term.
> I understand their entire route from Brownsville hence has been marked with plunder of private property and the abuse of citizens as if a Regiment of the enemy troops and not our own, had invaded us.

O'Callaghan went on to write that houses had been broken into and plundered of money and goods. Further, that horses were taken in the presence of owners who dared not protest against the robbery. Members of the regiment had two to five horses each with all of the horses in the neighborhood taken. The house of the ferryman at Santa Margarita was broken into and a barrel of whiskey, a sack of coffee, and other provisions taken. The women and children of the community had to crouch on the floor of their homes to avoid "bullets fired at random at chickens dogs and houses." But those "desperate characters" who committed the plundering did not consist of the entire body of the regiment. According to Judge O'Callaghan, they were 160 men who objected to orders that they go to Corpus Christi. Another 150 men obeyed the order and were "not to be held responsible in any manner for the acts of their fellows."[12] Another account, published in the Shreveport (Louisiana) Semi-Weekly News of April 1, reported that it was "some two hundred men" who refused the order, but that they had passed through Goliad "in a quiet and orderly manner." The paper condemned their disobedience of orders. This splitting apart of the regiment at San Patricio came to be referred to as "the burst-up" by the press.[13]

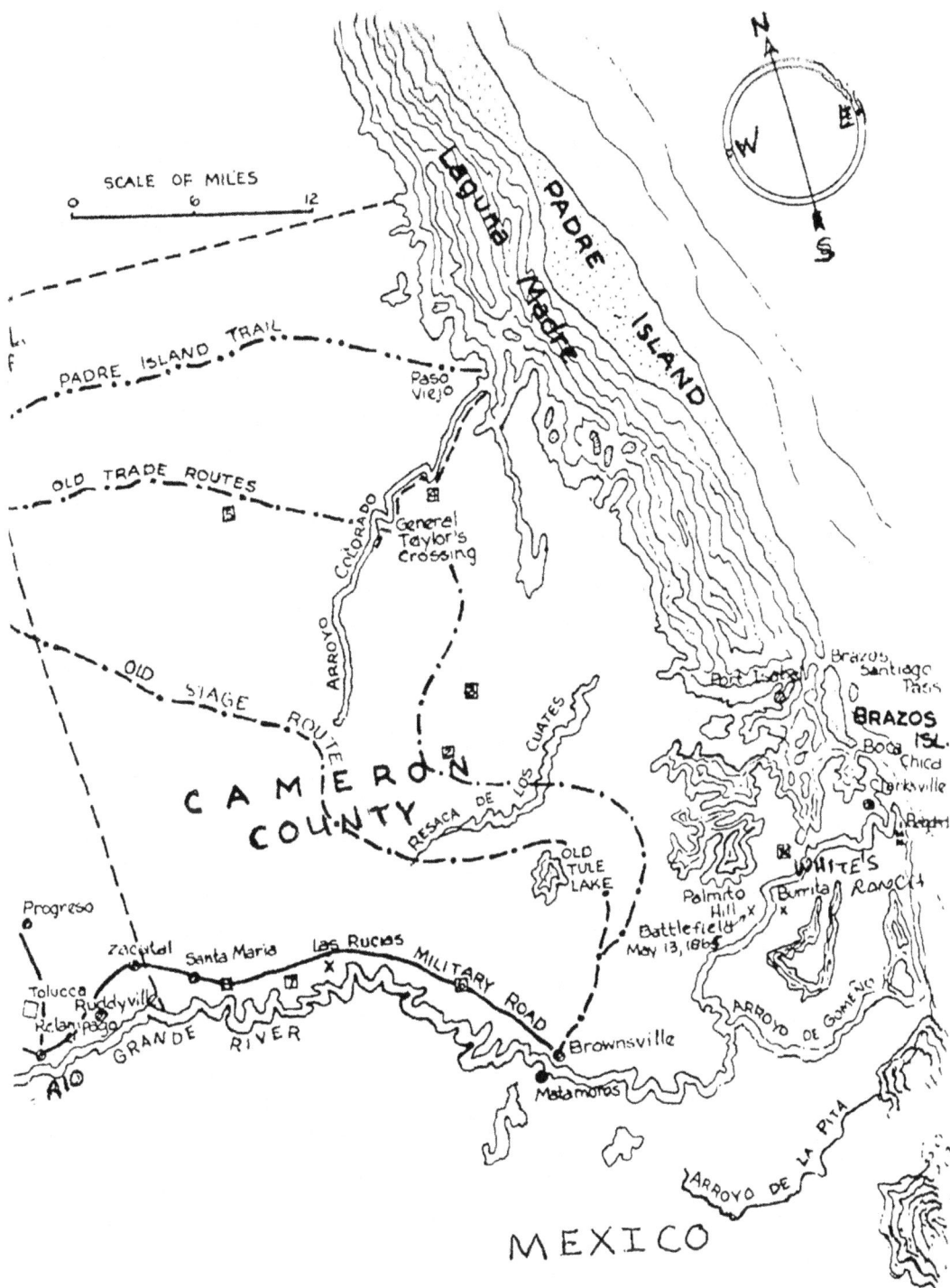

The 4th Arizona Cavalry's area of operations in the Lower Rio Grande Valley as depicted on page 1 of the *New York Herald* of November 23, 1863.

Dan Showalter was neither with nor in command of the regiment at this time—his court martial was apparently not yet dismissed or otherwise settled. He was reported to have been seen in San Antonio on January 19 by a correspondent to the Houston newspaper.[14] He was still in San Antonio and figured prominently in an evening meeting held at the county courthouse on Thursday, March 2, of "citizens of Arizona, New Mexico and El Paso Co." The purpose of this meeting was "to take into consideration the propriety of taking immediate steps to retake possession of our Western Territories and open a way to California."[15]

Showalter's name had frequently been attached to such proposals, which were believed by Union authorities in California to be "a pet scheme" of Showalter and others.[16] Rumors of his involvement in schemes or plans of this type had begun as early as January 1863, when he had just arrived in Texas to join the Confederates. On January 29, the *Sacramento Daily Union* quoted the San Diego correspondent of San Francisco's *Daily Alta California*, writing: "It is reported here that Daniel Showalter has turned up again, with a large party of armed men, who have joined him from this State, in Sonora. At last accounts, and which may be considered authentic and correct, he was at the city of Magdalena, Sonora, with from five to six hundred men.... Showalter has command of the whole force, and is said to be very popular with them, as well as being well supplied with the needful sinews of war,... A raid on Tucson or some other post on that line may be expected at any time, as that is to be his field of operations for the present."

This was but a rumor, but, by the next month, actual plans for such were developed. On March 2, General Magruder forwarded to Confederate Adjutant General Samuel Cooper a copy of his February 21 Special Orders No. 81 organizing the Arizona Brigade, mentioning in his cover letter that such had been "directed by the Secretary of War to take steps to recover Arizona."[17] This purpose of the Arizona Brigade was, of course, rescinded by the Trans-Mississippi Department commander early the following April due to "exigencies of the service."[18] Yet, by June 3, Magruder's Assistant Adjutant General, Edmund P. Turner, was reporting to Cooper that, at the request of Arizona Territorial Governor Baylor, S.M. Baird had been authorized to raise a regiment of "New Mexicans, Arizonians, Californians, and others not subject to conscription, to proceed and make a lodgement in that country."[19] As seen earlier, Dan Showalter was designated Lieutenant Colonel of this regiment.

An October 1863 plan to capture California for the Confederacy was submitted to Confederate President Jefferson Davis. This proposal, by Judge Lansford W. Hastings of California, was, in the absence of the President in Georgia, forwarded by the Secretary of War to General E.K. Smith. Smith was advised to determine his qualifications and character. Hastings believed that he could raise three thousand to five thousand men in California with which he could infiltrate Arizona and take possession and hold that territory for the Confederacy. Hastings' proposal was endorsed by several Arizonians in Richmond. General Smith, however, reported that he was not satisfied that Hastings could be trusted with such a mission and that he did not believe the plan feasible. Hastings resubmitted his proposal to Davis on January 11, 1864, but nothing ever developed to implement the plan.[20] Although Judge Hastings did not specifically mention Dan Showalter in his proposal, it would be more than highly likely that Showalter would have fitted into this expedition if it had been approved and implemented.

Colonel Baird's January 1864 proposal that he be given two other regiments along with his own for this purpose has already been discussed. Union authorities, of course, received knowledge of Confederate proposals of this type. From Mesilla, a J.A. Roberts wrote Union General J.H. Carleton that, in March of 1864, he was in Houston when David S. Terry arrived there from Richmond with authority to raise a brigade of about five thousand men. Roberts told Carleton that Terry thought he could, if he got through to California, have an army of 25,000 to 30,000 men. Roberts concluded his epistle stating that "I also learned that Colonel Showalter, Colonel [Sherrod] Hunter, Major Kirk, Major Darg, Captain Swoup, and Doctor Madison had been sent to California to assist Terry in his plans. Since my arrival here I learn that these men have been seen traveling through Mexico to California."[21] In almost all aspects, this citizen report to Union authorities was false.

Editors and citizens in the far west also knew of plans and rumors for a Confederate attempt to retake Arizona and move on to California. From this information, further rumors arose. The Gold Hill, Nevada Territory, *News* of September 7, 1864, reported that "suspicious individuals" had been seen in the mountains and remarked, "That such bands are to-day hidden away in unfrequented fastnesses in this Territory is established beyond a doubt. It will be seen, therefore, that the quiet organization of our Home Guard and its arming and equipment in the most serviceable manner has been a wise and necessary precaution. Several hundred stand of the finest arms and a sufficiency of ammunition are now in the hands of reliable men in this county, and Dan. Showalter, 'or any other man' in his line of business, can trot along up this way whenever he feels in the mood."[22] A November 29, 1864, letter from a man named M.O. Davidson to General Irvin McDowell, commanding the Union Department of the Pacific, reported a group assembling in the Mexican State of Sonora. That rumors and citizen reports of this type received credence is that, citing this report, General McDowell requested and received attachment of the Territory of Arizona to his Department.[23]

John Robert Baylor, former Arizona territorial governor and Confederate congressman, on December 21, 1864, submitted a plan to Confederate Secretary of War James A. Seddon. Acknowledging that the resources of the Confederacy were much exhausted, he suggested that the only areas in which Southern men could be recruited in large numbers were Southern California and New Mexico. He stated that he was "governed by the opinion of prominent men from that country, who are well acquainted with the sentiment of the people, such as Judge Terry, Colonel Showalter, and many others, who assert that from 15,000 to 20,000 men could be raised." Although thus indicating that, to him at least, Terry and Showalter were the most prominent of California Confederates, Baylor disagreed with their estimates of the number of men that could be raised. He felt that only 10,000 to 15,000 could be secured and that it would take an expedition of 2,500 men. He also believed that additional men could be had in Mexico. Baylor was sure that although the western men would not serve in Louisiana, Arkansas or places east, they would join for this particular service. On December 30, Seddon forwarded Baylor's proposal to President Davis for consideration along with his observation that it would be preferable to bring to the east of the Mississippi River all of the Trans-Mississippi forces or at least use them to create a diversion. Davis responded to Seddon on January 5, 1865, that the decision should be left to the commander of the Trans-Mississippi Department, who could better judge the propriety of detaching any of his forces for Baylor's proposed expedition. Davis also stated that if "a large force would be requisite that it would be impracticable to spare it."[24]

Although nothing further developed from this proposal, Major Sherrod Hunter of the 3rd Arizona Cavalry had, the previous April, sent a recruiting officer to California. This recruiting officer, Captain H. Kennedy, returned to San Antonio, Texas, in early 1865 and submitted a report of his trip to Colonel C.L. Pyron, then commanding the Western Sub-District of Texas. Traveling via Mexico, he had reached San Francisco in mid–July. He traveled through San Francisco and Stockton to Virginia City, Nevada, where he made arrangements to form a party to march overland to the Confederacy. This plan had been betrayed to Union authorities, and Kennedy was able to bring off but a few men from there due to inability to obtain sufficient horses and supplies on short notice. For a month, Kennedy had to hide in the Sierra Nevada. He found it impossible to travel to the southern portion of California, but was able to sail from San Francisco with a few men, on October 5, for Mazatlan, Mexico. Here he was joined by men previously sent there and collected by a Captain Jeff Standifer. Traveling across Mexico with thirty men, they crossed the Rio Grande into Texas on January 19, 1865. Two days later, they were attacked by Union forces numbering about 130 at Cibolo. After losing four killed and six missing, Kennedy's small command escaped to the east and soon reached San Antonio. Kennedy told Pyron that he had found many in California, Nevada, and northern Mexico who were anxious to join the Confederate Army, but were prevented by lack of the means to do so.[25] Standifer's men, along with some others, were enrolled in the Confederate Army as Company A, First California Battalion of Cavalry.[26]

Captain Kennedy's arrival in San Antonio and the results of his recruiting trip were soon well known in San Antonio and of particular interest to the California and Arizona exiles. On Thursday, March 2, these, along with Texan citizens of El Paso County, met to consider steps to be taken to retake possession of Arizona and open the way to California. James Wiley Magoffin, a prominent El Paso citizen often referred to as "Governor" or "General" even though he never held said offices, was appointed president of the meeting, and B.C. Murray (of Tucson) as Secretary. Magoffin's explanation of the purpose of the meeting was followed by "interesting and highly favorable remarks" by Dan Showalter. He was followed by former Californian Bethel Coopwood and Dr. Lewis S. Owings, the Confederate governor of Arizona Territory. "The Speakers were all strongly in favor of the earliest possible steps being taken to open a way to California to secure a safe passage for our numerous friends now in that State, besides a large number in Western Arizona." Showalter and the other speakers believed that ten thousand men could be raised for the Confederate Army in those areas and that one thousand men and a "reasonable supply of Confederate Treasury notes" would suffice for the purpose. A committee of Showalter, Coopwood, Owings, and Captain Kennedy was appointed to devise resolutions on the subject. The meeting adjourned until the following Saturday at 7:00 p.m. At that second meeting, the resolutions were unanimously adopted and a committee selected to confer with the Commanding General of the Trans-Mississippi Department. With Showalter on this committee were Magoffin, Coopwood, Kennedy, Owings, and a Major Jackson.[27] Showalter and Kennedy were appointed by the committee to represent them and present the resolutions to General Walker at Houston.[28]

For Showalter to have been able to travel to Houston to meet the district commander, all proceedings of his court martial must have by now been concluded. It is unknown exactly where the 4th Arizona Regiment was. Indeed, some Texans of the time wondered about this, with one newspaper, the *LaGrange Patriot* in Fayette County, even printing an inquiry so asking.[29] As of March 29, a detachment under command of Captain William S. Rather was still in camp near Brownsville when the captain reported that they were ready to march as soon as rations could be collected.[30] The balance of the regiment was then under command of Captain T.D. Sanders of Company H. From near Richmond, Texas, he wrote District Headquarters on April 8, 1865, stating that a portion of the regiment—Companies D, E, and H, along with parts of Companies C, F, and G—had arrived there on the 7th. (Rather's detachment must have, therefore, consisted of Companies A and B, and the three companies represented as with Sanders only in part must have been those that had plundered San Patricio County.) Sanders requested permission to remain there, where he could obtain forage and "recruit" his teams. Sanders also reported that about sixty deserted men had returned to the command and that, if given ten or fifteen days, nearly all of them would be back. This letter was signed by Sanders as "Commanding" the regiment,[31] so Showalter must, as of that date, still been in Houston and not with the regiment.

That Dan Showalter was in Houston is attested by an April 15, 1865, letter of William T. Robinson from there to a "Mr. Murry" in San Antonio (this was the B.C. Murray who had been secretary of the San Antonio meeting). At the end of this letter, he noted "Col. Showalter is here." Robinson had previously been a Colonel of Texas State troops and had recently returned to Texas from California. He had been authorized by General E. Kirby Smith to organize Californians (including some to be recruited at Mazatlan, Mexico) into a regiment, but feared General Magruder might cancel the commission.[32] Meanwhile, back in Brownsville, Private Robert J. Burney of the regiment, on April 1, had been sentenced to be shot by firing squad for the murder of an unarmed private of Giddings' battalion. His execution was carried out on April 17.[33]

By the first days of May, the 4th Arizona was nearing unification in the Houston area under Showalter. The Houston *Tri-Weekly Telegraph*, on May 10, reported all save Company G were at Harrisburg, with that company due to arrive there in a few days. The regiment's morning report showed 318 men present for duty, with another fifty coming in Company G. Nearly all of those who left in the "burst-up" two months previous had returned.[34] A separate article in the same newspaper noted: "We have noticed the fact of Col. Showalter's regiment, of the old Arizona Brigade, filling up rapidly to its full standard, from deserters, absentees without leave, and others returning to their colors, and this in the face of late disastrous news from the other side." This article credited a proclamation by General Robert E. Lee giving pardon to all deserters who returned to their commands.[35] One cannot help but believe that the restoration of Showalter, Wilson, and other officers to the regiment after conclusion of the court martial proceedings in San Antonio also played a part in many of the men's return to the regiment. The "disastrous news" mentioned included information regarding the surrender of the Army of Northern Virginia by General Robert E. Lee in April. Despite the disastrous news, Showalter was apparently still optimistic. During the first week of May, he wrote the Department's Assistant Adjutant General in Houston, requesting copies of recent Department orders and for a supply of blank forms, including fifty company monthly returns.[36]

There exist on the internet other reports of the regiment during this same period that have it operating in north Texas. One such message states that its members "roamed through north Texas committing robbery and murder" and that "the war ended with the rif-raff of the 4th Regiment being pursued through north Texas by other Confederate soldiers."[37] Like all legends and oral history, all internet messages seem to have some basis in fact. In this case, the basis has been greatly exaggerated, based upon incomplete examination of available records and reports, and this was not, in fact, the 4th Regiment,

Arizona Brigade, but rather the second command raised and commanded by Colonel Spruce M. Baird. The attribution of this to the 4th Arizona commanded at that time by Dan Showalter merits and requires explanation and clarification.

After being detached from—but not relieved as Colonel—of the 4th Arizona to serve on the Examining Board for Officers in Houston, Baird was, in the summer of 1864, authorized by General E. Kirby Smith to raise six new companies from the frontier counties of Texas "to form a part of the Light-Horse of the Plains" and a Frontier Expedition under his command. Recruiting headquarters were established at Austin, Texas, where unenrolled men of the frontier counties and any exempts (to conscription) were to report singly or in squads. Alternative reporting sites were at Camp Slaughter near Dallas or at Fort Belknap in northern Texas, near the Red River. Notices to this effect were signed by Baird as "Col 4th Reg't Arizona Brigade, Comd'g Frontier Expedition."[38] It is therefore obvious how this second command of Col. Baird could and did become confused with the 4th Arizona—especially when later referred to simply as "Baird's command."

Apparently Baird had difficulty recruiting his Light-Horse or Frontier Expedition force to the necessary strength because, in late 1864, Major Milton W. Sims was appointed Lieutenant Colonel and directed to increase Baird's battalion to a regiment. He was authorized to organize into companies all men in Texas on furlough from Confederate commands east of the Mississippi River.[39] The last company of this battalion was organized on October 24, 1864, and it was considered "completed" on March 14, 1865. One commentator at that time called it "the finest Regiment that has been raised in this State since Terry's Rangers—composed of the best material."[40] The battalion had originally assembled at Camp McCulloch, about six miles above Waco.[41] On February 17, 1865, by Special Orders No. 43, Sims and his battalion were ordered to Bonham, Texas, where they would report to Brigadier General Henry E. McCulloch.

This battalion of Baird's command—if not all of the "Frontier Expedition"—was in the Red River country of north Texas by April. On April 6, a complaint was sworn out before Confederate Commissioner John D. Elliott charging that men who "admitted that they were members of Baird's Command" had committed crimes in Falls County on the Brazos River. Among the crimes were assassination of planter J.D. McKissick, threatening families, and the theft of property by force. Commissioner Elliott stated that this command had moved on from the area.[42] Activities of this sort continued. Upon order of General Magruder, General Bee dispatched "two regiments to catch Baird's command," which had marched for Cooke County on the Red River.[43] A lengthy report of this pursuit was published in the *Tri-Weekly Telegraph* on May 21, 1865. It identifies the two regiments as Waller's (13th Texas Cavalry) and Brown's (35th Texas Cavalry), and is signed by "W." The signature and the text indicate that the writer was Col. Edwin Waller himself. The writer confided that the two regiments marched together from Owenville, Texas, with the objective of their march kept secret, although it soon became generally known that "the prime [object] was the capture of Baird's command which was encamped in Cook county." According to "W," the men of the regiments were "a little soured" at this news. Their route passed through Fort Worth on May 1 and, after a sixty-mile march, arrived in the vicinity of Gainsville, the seat of Cooke County, the evening of the 2nd. "W" stated that the men of Baird's command had heard rumors of the advance against them, but awoke the next morning to find themselves surrounded and "gave up almost without a murmer." According to "W": "The general opinion among our boys, is that these men have been censured for many things of which they were ignorant to this day. I do not exempt all of them from bad conduct. I would not exempt all of any regiment from blame entirely. But I do believe the community at large, are mistaken as it regards the character of these men generally. They are men of as affable manners as any to be found, submissive, polite, and men of good countenances." The writer felt that the mistake leading to this incident was the granting of permission to raise a regiment for a special purpose whose men, when the purpose was changed, became demoralized.[44] Not only were the culprits not Showalter's 4th Arizona, apparently their transgressions were not as bad as believed.

Dan Showalter was definitely with and in command of the regiment by May, when he wrote the District Assistant Adjutant General, Captain E.P. Turner, on May 2 and 3, requesting copies of department orders for the last three months and for a supply of blank forms.[45] Then the following item appeared on the first page of the Houston *Tri-Weekly Telegraph* of Friday, May 19, 1865:

> At a meeting held by the 4th Arizona Regt. of Cavalry, Col. Showalter commanding on Wednesday the 16th day of May 1865, on motion, Col. Showalter was elected President, and W. C. Sevier Secretary.
>
> Col. Showalter, on assuming the duties of the Chair, and in response to the request of the regiment, delivered an able, patriotic and eloquent speech, the sentiments of which were responded to by frequent and heartfelt applause from the men of his command, after which, on motion, the following resolutions were adopted by acclamation without a dissenting voice.
>
> Whereas, We have recently learned with painful regret of the surrender of most, if not all, of the armies of the Confederacy east of the Mississippi river, and deeply deploring as we do the disposition now manifested by many citizens and soldiers in the Trans-Mississippi Department, to tamely submit to the reestablishment of peace, upon degrading conditions of an absolute and unconditional surrender and a consequent return to the Federal Union, with most, if not all, of our essential and cardinal rights as sovereign States ruthlessly torn from us, since the commencement of the war, by sectional and fanatical legislation on the part of Congress and the military edicts and proclmations of the President of the United States
>
> Therefore, be it
>
> Resolved, That we, as members of the 4th Arizona Regiment of Cavalry, comprised of Californians, Texans and Missourians, in view of the perilous condition of the country, and relying on the justice of our cause, will stand by the military authorities of the Trans-Mississippi Department to the last, in defense of our country against the brutal and tyrannical foe who, flushed with their recent successes East of the Mississippi River now threaten this Department, and seek by one fell blow of arms, or through the cowardly submission of our soldiery, to conquer and hold us by military force, nominally as co-members of the Federal Union but really as a subjugated Province, to be governed by military satraps, under the absolute decree of a military dictator.
>
> Resolved, That in view of the surrender of the troops to the Trans-Mississippi Department, we do not hold that we are bound by any stipulations which may compromise our *Liberties*, and that as free agents and true Southern soldiers we will maintain our freedom at all hazards—remain in open warfare against any Yankee rule, and fight the enemy as long as life lasts—follow our commanders into the last trench—denying the right to be surrendered to the hateful foe who is now approaching our sacred threshold for the purpose of confiscation, tyranny and death.
>
> Resolved, That this regiment will stand by and remain true to Texas and the Confederacy to the last great and final struggle for freedom against tyranny, which existing facts indicate is about to transpire upon her soil—so long as her sons evince a determination to achieve their independence or go down to honorable graves—and if forced to retire from the soil we have so long defended we will take with us the battle flag of our Regiment, presented to us by the ladies of Texas and under its folds will if necessary cut our way through to some defensible locality, where cherishing the principles of which it is the consecrated emblem will repel the foe who dare assail us or perish in the attempt.
>
> Dan. Showalter
> Lt. Col. Comd'g, Président.
> W.C. Sevier, Secretary.[46]

These resolutions, not surprisingly, reflect the eloquence and feeling which Showalter had exhibited in some of his speeches to the California legislature in 1861. No other commander or regiment of the Confederate Army left behind such a valedictory of its loyalty or service. Things would not, however, work out in the manner projected by the resolutions.

The end of May found the 4th Arizona still functioning as a regiment. The Houston *Tri-Weekly Telegraph* and the *Galveston Daily News* both carried a May 29 report given by Mayor William Anders of Houston to the city's Board of Aldermen. Among the many items upon which he reported were troop movements through the city. He advised the council that, on May 21, General Magruder had advised him that the next day and for five or six days following troops would be moving through the city. Among the several regiments named to pass through Houston was Showalter's regiment. Magruder had suggested that the citizens of the city should supplement the rations of those troops passing through. Liquor was removed from the city or destroyed since "it was evident to everybody that the city would be in imminent danger of destruction if the large bodies of soldiers within her limits should become intoxicated." The mayor had appointed a committee of twelve influential citizens to make the arrangements. Mayor Anders was pleased to report that although the military had ceased to exercise authority within the city on May 23 and large numbers of troops had arrived and passed through, other than the sacking of government stores, the "mob" of soldiers was orderly and there was no damage to private property.[47]

After passing through Houston, Showalter and the regiment apparently encamped west of Houston, but the precise location is disputed. In his pension application, Private Lycurgus B. Earnest stated that the regiment disbanded at Hempstead, Texas,[48] which is about fifty miles northwest of Houston. Lt. Stephen W. Wilkinson, in his pension application, stated that they disbanded at Richmond, Texas,[49] which is located about thirty miles west of Houston. Both towns are on the Brazos River and about fifty-five miles apart. Privates S.P. Langford and M.D. Payne, as witnesses for D.D. Noel in his pension application, said the regiment disbanded at Houston.[50] Their memory is probably of a "general location" since the Houston mayor's address to the city's aldermen definitely establishes that the 4th Arizona had moved through Houston. It can be reasonably believed that its disbanding occurred somewhere west of Houston. Other than vague statements like "end of the war" or "some time after Lee's surrender," the only date found for exactly when the regiment disbanded is June 24, 1865, which is the date provided by Private John Allen Tharp, Jr., in his pension application.[51] In his pension application of 1911, Private Henry Clay Damron stated, "We were never discharged nor did we surrender—we just quit as the war closed in 1865."[52] Like many other Confederate regiments in the Trans-Mississippi Department, they just parted company with each other and headed home, into a Mexican exile, or to nearby cities. And these regiments did indeed disband without surrendering after other Confederate forces had surrendered—Generals Robert E. Lee on April 9 in Virginia, Joseph E. Johnston on April 26 in North Carolina, Richard Taylor on May 4 in Alabama, Samuel Jones on May 10 in Florida, General E. Kirby Smith on May 26 at Shreveport, and Stand Watie on June 23 in the Indian Territory. Although some members had undoubtedly left for home sooner, if June 24, 1865, as stated by Private Tharp, is the actual date on which Dan Showalter, his officers and men of the 4th Arizona Cavalry parted company for good, then it would be one of the last Confederate regiments to do so.

San Antonio, Texas, had become known as the assembly point for the now ex–Confederates seeking to travel to exile in Mexico. A fair number of the remaining members of the 4th Arizona, including Dan Showalter, headed there. Upon arrival, they sold the remaining regimental property—wagons, extra weapons, extra horses, etc.—and made a *pro rata* division of the proceeds. Then more of them headed for their homes. Some would remain in San Antonio to take the oath of allegiance, but some determined to go into exile in Mexico.[53]

When the Civil War ended, Dan Showalter was completely at "loose ends." Daniel E. Sutherland's *The Confederate Carpetbaggers* (1988) discussed and documented over fifteen reasons why many ex–Confederates fled the South for other parts after the war. Of these, several seem to have applied in Showalter's case. In his letter to Anna Forman and the regimental resolutions in May, he had exhibited very strong belligerence toward the Union and loyalty to the Confederacy. Loss of the war undoubtedly caused bitterness on his part over the result. Many of his California friends had already gone or would soon themselves become determined to go into Mexican exile. Judge David S. Terry, former Senator William McK. Gwin, Granville Oury, and Showalter's own second-in-command, F.E. Kavanaugh, were among these. There would have seemed to be little advantage in a return to California. His duel with Piercy and his later service as an officer in the Confederate Army would have ended any political influence or career there. Also, while incarcerated at Fort Yuma, he had lost his investment in the Denver Quicksilver Mining Company, and his somewhat lengthy absence from Mariposa County probably resulted in loss of any mining claims there. Mexico may have seemed to him as much an opportunity to rebuild his life and fortune as it provided an escape from conditions in his adopted, defeated nation.

Showalter may have also had some fear of imprisonment or even for his life. It had been impressed upon him in May 1862, when he took the loyalty oath at Fort Yuma to obtain his release, that if found aiding the Confederacy (which he certainly had done), there would be "just right" to hang him. It is quite possible that he was also aware of President Andrew Johnson's Proclamation of Amnesty on May 29, 1865. This proclamation exempted fourteen classes of persons from the amnesty. The seventh class included "all persons who have been or are absentees from the United States for the purpose of aiding the rebellion." The tenth exempted class consisted of "all persons who left their homes within the jurisdiction and protection of the United States and passed beyond the Federal military lines into the pretended Confederate States for the purpose of aiding the rebellion." Both of these categories would have applied to Dan Showalter. The fourteenth exemption applied to "all persons who have taken the oath of amnesty as prescribed in the President's proclamation of December 8, A.D. 1863, or an oath of allegiance to the Government of the United States since the date of said proclamation and who have not thenceforward kept and maintained the same inviolate."[54] Perhaps he thought, like Governor Allen of Louisiana, that exile was necessary to "avoid persecution, and the crown of martyrdom."[55] Although he had taken such an oath twice—in December 1861 at Camp Wright and in May 1862 at Fort Yuma—prior to the specified date, the fact that he had done so and still joined the Confederacy would no doubt have resulted in "disabilities" upon him.

Many defeated Confederates fled the South at the war's end. In the east, Secretary of State Judah Benjamin and Secretary of War John C. Breckinridge managed to escape, with difficulty, through Florida to Cuba. The lack of any significant numbers of Union forces in Texas and its proximity to Mexico, however, provided unreconciled Confederates with better opportunity to escape. The most well-known incident of former Confederates leaving Texas for Mexico immediately after the war is the case of General Joseph O. Shelby, who led into Mexico a remnant of his Confederate cavalry brigade, initially accompanied by such notables as Generals E. Kirby Smith and John B. Magruder; Governors Pendleton Murrah of Texas, Henry Watkins Allen of Louisiana, Thomas Reynolds of Missouri; former Governors Edward Clark of Texas and Thomas O. Moore of Louisiana; and others.[56]

Shelby's brigade was in East Texas when the war ended. They proceeded from there through Corsicana, Waco, and Austin to San Antonio.[57] The Union Army had occupied Brownsville on June 17, 1865.[58] This meant that any fleeing ex–Confederates would have to cross the Rio Grande into Mexico further up river using the crossing between Eagle Pass, Texas, and Piedras Negras, Mexico. Their last march through Texas took them through Castroville, Sabinal, Uvalde, and Fort Inge.[59] Shelby, with his command and accompanying officials, arrived at Eagle Pass on June 23.[60] They sunk their flags and cavalry guidons in the river, then crossed it into Mexico[61] using barges for their wagons, artillery, and equipment.[62] At that time, Piedras Negras was under the control of the Mexican Liberal Party, who were loyal to President Benito Juarez. The Juarista governor there for the Mexican States of Coahuila, Tamaulipas and Nuevo Leon was Andres S. Viesca (or Biesca).[63] General Shelby preferred to go into the service of the Juaristas, but his officers, with Colonel Benjamin F. Elliott as their spokesman, preferred the Imperialists (supporters of Emperor Maximilian) and French.[64]

It would have been too much to expect that Viesca would allow Shelby and his men to take their artillery pieces with them to the Imperialists. Additionally, the area between Piedras Negras and Monterrey had been devastated by Liberals, French, and bandits. This made it impossible for Shelby to take with him his artillery and supply train.[65] Shelby therefore sold his artillery and most of the wagons to Governor Viesca and divided the proceeds among his men. There were two routes to Monterrey from Piedras Negras. One was commanded by a Juarista force and could not handle heavy wagons. The route chosen was, consequently, the other—via Fuente, Gigedo, Lampazos, Beneventura, and Naria to Monterrey—about 135 miles distant.[66] On the way, when crossing the Salinas River, there was a battle with bandits.[67] Upon arrival at Monterrey, the ex–Confederates found the city commanded by French Colonel Pierre Jean Joseph Jennigros, who was, not surprisingly, irate that Shelby had sold his artillery to the Juaristas.[68] Relying upon the advice of former California Senator William Gwin and Texas Governor Clark, Shelby was able to smooth over the differences with Jennigros and receive permission to continue his march to Mazatlan by way of Saltillo, Parras, Gomez Palacio, and Durango.[69] Upon arrival at Parras, Shelby found several parties of former Confederates waiting there—and orders from the French commander in Mexico, Marshall of France Francois Achille Bazaine, that Shelby be turned back to the United States or else proceed without any delay to Mexico City.[70]

Among the parties of former Confederates waiting at Parras was the one which included Dan Showalter. His route had closely paralleled Malvina "Mina" Oury, wife of Granville Henderson Oury, formerly Delegate of Arizona Territory to the Confederate Congress and a colonel on Shelby's staff. He had also been a co-signer with Showalter on the February 14, 1865, proposal to General Smith to retake Arizona.[71] Others who had signed the proposal—C.C. Dodson and Fred A. Neville—were in the same "mess" as the

Ourys.[72] The group of which Showalter and the Ourys were part left San Antonio at about 4:00 p.m. on Tuesday, June 20, 1865, and camped two miles further on, at Leon. After passing through Castroville and later crossing the Rio Hondo, on June 21 they camped forty miles south of San Antonio.[73] In her diary entry for that night, Mrs. Oury mentioned that her husband took a meal which she had prepared "over to Col. Showalter, who is badly crippled by a fall from his horse and is suffering greatly."[74] (This fall had occurred sometime before Showalter had reached San Antonio according to a veteran of the regiment who had supervised the sale of regimental equipment there.[75]) The next day's journey took them through the community of D'Hanis to Seco Creek, where Mrs. Oury began sewing some woolen shirts for Showalter. About noon, another group, which included Texas Judge William Oldham and California Judge David S. Terry, caught up with them and would continue to travel and camp overnight with the Oury-Showalter group the rest of the way to Eagle Pass. That evening, they camped on the banks of Sabinal Creek.[76] June 23, they passed through Uvalde and camped two miles beyond it. They left this camp early on the 24th. After pausing to bathe in the Nueces River, they continued on to Turkey Creek, where they encamped.[77] A long day's journey on the 25th brought them to within six miles of Eagle Pass.[78]

Oury and Terry arose early on June 26, 1865, to cross the Rio Grande and arrange for crossing the river into Mexico. The rest of the combined groups rested and then moved on to Eagle Pass, where they arrived about 2:00 p.m. That evening, Oury and Terry returned with news that they had received permission to cross to Piedras Negras with one pistol and one rifle each. Extra weapons were redistributed among the groups, with at least some of the remaining excess presented to the Mexicans.[79] Since there was a long line of wagons ahead of them waiting to cross the river, all of the 27th and most of the 28th were spent at Eagle Pass. Mrs. Oury recorded that a great number of Shelby's men were in the town. To her disgust, Mexican peddlers lined the banks of the crossing and also a number of nude Mexican men employed to swim cattle across the river. The boats used to cross the river were towed upstream by naked Mexicans, who attached them to a cable by which they were pulled across. She described the river as being muddy and swift. Once across the river, the Ourys, Terry, Showalter and others stopped about two miles beyond Piedras Negras. Mrs. Oury thought the town an "abominable place." After making some purchases of foodstuffs in the town and leaving it late, they moved on past a small stream and encamped for the night.[80] Here the several parties consolidated into one, with Mr. Oury elected leader.[81]

They left their camp on June 29 and continued southwards, following a "way bill" of roads provided to Oury, in Piedras Negras, by a Mr. Jones. They had traveled over and beyond three hills when Judge Terry rode up to Oury and informed him of advice from a Mr. La Spiers, who had traveled the route three months previous, that there was a "nearer and better" route. The party backtracked to the other route. It was a hot and dry journey before they found water and camped for the night.[82] On June 30, their route took them through an irrigated area to the town of Morelos, where they purchased corn before going on another thirty miles and then camping for the night.[83] Because of some missing mules, they got a late start on Saturday, July 1. They took their noon meal and a siesta atop a mountain. About five miles further on, they found a large lake, where they filled their water barrels and watered their animals. They then retreated a mile, to where there was good grass to camp for the night. During the night, one of the mules wandered through the camp eating green corn shucks. Mr. Oury awoke and contained the noisy mule. The next morning, according to Mrs. Oury, "Col. Showalter complained that Mr. Oury kept him awake 'fussing' with the mule."[84]

The trip on July 2 was a gradual ascent over the mountains. They did not stop at midday due to a lack of water, but continued on over a little stream to the town of San Juan Sabinas, where they rested at the ranch of a Dr. Smith. They were here plagued by the begging of some Kickapoo Indians, who were camped nearby, and had to maintain a double watch that night. The next day they traveled only three miles, to an excellent camping spot Judge Terry had discovered the previous evening. They paused here a few days to wash, fish, and rest their animals. Mrs. Oury noted in her diary, on July 4, that "Col. Showalter, who can now walk a little with crutches," came to visit them that evening.[85] Dr. Smith had been absent at Saltillo,[86] but returned to his ranch that evening. Judge Terry visited him the next morning to learn about the roads ahead. Smith told him that water was scarce along the road they had expected to take. They were therefore compelled to alter their route to the road going to Parras. Showalter, who had apparently passed through the area on his way to Texas, assured the others that this route would pass through some pretty towns and countryside having abundant fruits. The change in route meant that they would have to purchase corn for their animals. That night, a mule belonging to Showalter broke into their provisions and ate a half sack of their sugar.[87]

After a breakfast of fish, they left this camp of two days at 8:00 a.m. on Monday, July 5, 1865. They stopped at eleven for their noon meal and a siesta.[88] Their route took them through grassy lands with abundant water due to recent rains in the mountains. After eighteen miles, they camped near a pond. About nine that evening, a body of Juarista soldiers entered the camp. The former Confederates gave the nearly starved Mexican soldiers some bread.[89] The next morning, they were visited by a Mexican officer seeking two deserters. They then marched ten miles, rested by a pond at noon, and then moved on until nearly dark, then camping at a small water hole that had a little grass. After traveling several miles on the 7th, they learned they had taken the wrong road about two miles back. They cut across rough country to regain the proper roadway and nooned along a clear, but alkaline, stream. They traveled that day twenty-five miles in intense heat.[90]

Monclova, the second city (1,000–1,200 inhabitants) of the Mexican State of Coahuila, was reached on July 8. They camped here next to a large corral, where they purchased corn and green stalks for their mules. In a neighboring corral were about twenty-five deserters from the Confederate Army who had joined the Juaristas, but, becoming disaffected, had been disarmed and dismounted. Mrs. Oury thought Monclova was a pretty town, but that the women were "dark, homely, slovenly and utterly devoid of taste." While at Monclova, Judge Terry and F.E. Kavanaugh, both of whom had several racehorses with them, organized races. Their night's campsite was three miles south of the town.[91] Finding a pond of water, they traveled only a short distance on the 9th before camping. A Mexican drove a steer into the camp, which was purchased by Terry's group for $15. The Mexican would not sell any more cattle, but Terry shared some of the beef with the others.[92]

Travel on July 10 was between two ranges of mountains, with views of numerous peaks. The vegetation was covered with thorns. Facing a dry camp, they retreated a short distance and camped near a tank (depression in the rocks that held water). That evening, a "pedestrian" came into the camp. He took supper with Showalter's mess. This unnamed man seems to have accompanied them thereafter.[93] July 11 was another almost waterless day. When they took their noon break, they had to use water out of holes in the road—and pay for it. That afternoon, they passed a ranch that had a large tank, but did not stop to fill their water kegs since Mexicans there told them that there was plenty of grass and water only a few miles ahead. The Mexicans had lied, and the ex–Confederates had to make a waterless camp when dark arrived. They started out early on July 12 with expectation that water would be found in only a few more miles, but the countryside was barren. At noon, they found some water, but only poor grass for the animals. They were able to buy a fat cow from a Mexican and had a good meal, which was enhanced by the fruit of a Pitahaya cactus.[94]

On Thursday the 13th, the travelers began to encounter yet another difficulty—mosquitos. Heavy rains in the mountains had resulted in nearly swamping the countryside. They left camp about six, hoping to find grass in twenty-one miles. Terry returned to a ranch and organized horseraces against Mexicans. He lost both races, and his horses were jaded and almost given out. Showalter, Oury, a Captain Sharp, and those with them did not pause, but drove on until night. They were delayed for an hour by a wagon train loaded with cotton, which blocked the crossing of a creek. When they halted, they found only a small patch of grass, which the animals were prevented from eating by the mosquitos, which covered the blades.[95] They let the mules graze until 8:00 a.m. the next morning before resuming their journey on July 14. They soon found good grass, but again mosquitos made it inedible for the mules, which were dancing about and constantly swatting at the insects with their tails. The travelers had just begun their supper at four when a small rain shower occurred. It cooled off the temperature, but brought on a myriad of mosquitos. Some tried smoking to keep the insects off. Some tied their heads in towels and handkerchiefs. Others attacked the insects with brushes. Mrs. Oury burned sugar in a frying pan, which kept them off only for a while. Only Mr. Oury and Showalter had "mosquito bars," which they used to gain sleep. Most just had to endure. A severe storm that night drove everyone beneath their wagons.[96]

Travel on July 16 was also filled with travails. They started their march at 10:00 a.m. over a rough road and having to climb a very steep hill through a gap in the mountains. Within three miles of Parras, it was discovered that they had again taken the wrong road. They backtracked and took another road. It ran out. Mr. Oury set out to find the correct route. Mexicans at a ranch refused to sell them corn, saying that the French had taken it all. Finally, after a long day of hard travel, they camped in a field full of weeds. There was no grass for the mules, nor had the group any to feed them. There was no wood for fires, and a heavy storm arrived, which lasted through most of the night.[97]

On the morning of Monday, July 17, Oury found grass two miles ahead. The camp was moved there and, later that morning, the travel-weary ex–Confederates journeyed on into Parras. Oury's ambulance (a wagon with springs) was unloaded of everything except the seats and a barrel for brandy. While others of the party rode their horses, the Ourys and Showalter rode the ambulance into town. Parras was a large and important town and full of elegantly uniformed French soldiers. Fruits and grapes, from which wine and brandy were made, were abundant. A supply of these was obtained and, while Mrs. Oury watched over them, the men scattered to have their animals shod. Oury himself went to visit the French commandant to obtain permission to continue the journey.[98] The camp was moved again—a few miles closer to Parras, where there was good water and grass and also a quantity of mesquite beans, which were good animal feed. On Tuesday, the French commander visited their camp with twenty-eight of his soldiers. Fruits and vegetables—and brandy—were purchased. Those who had lagged behind with Terry arrived on Thursday, July 27. The next morning, in the ambulance, Dan Showalter escorted Mrs. Oury into town, where she enjoyed herself shopping.[99]

A few days later, Mrs. Oury wrote in her diary: "Our party is becoming much reduced. Col. Showalter and mess, and another party have taken leave of us and propose going to Durango, thence to Mazatlan, from there the Col. will join us at Guaymas. We will miss him greatly, he is very sociable, spent most of his time with us, is a constant talker and very entertaining. He still has no use of his leg, and I learn that after starting he sold his wagon to Capt. Dave [Terry] and is going to undertake the trip mule back. The men of his mess are good men."[100] As shall be seen, Dan Showalter was to never rejoin the Ourys at Guaymas.

Among the parties of former Confederates at Parras was one of fifty-two men led by Colonel Benjamin F. Elliott,[101] which had, by agreement, separated from Shelby's force at Monterrey. The date given for their arrival in Mazatlan by one old veteran of this group is identical with the date other sources provide for Dan Showalter's arrival there. This, and the dangers of the 500-mile journey to there from Parras, very strongly indicated that Showalter and others of his "mess" traveled in company with Elliott and his men. Evidently, the French commander at Parras, Colonel Marguerite Jacques Vincent de Preuil,[102] had not yet received orders from Marshall Bazaine that the ex–Confederates were to be directed to Mexico City, and allowed them to head west. They left Parras on August 9, 1865. The journey from Parras to Durango, at the foot of the Sierra Madre Oriental mountain range, was by a well-traveled road. At Durango, it was necessary for the travelers to dispose of their wagons and excess animals and purchase burros, jennets (young donkeys) and small ponies to serve as pack animals. None of the group knew anything about packing equines, but learned quickly by practice and necessity. Their trail was an arduous one, up and down across rugged mountains. Additionally, the route was waylaid by robbers and murderers, making continual vigilance necessary.[103] And at high elevations it was very cold, even in summer—they even awoke one morning to find their blankets covered with snow.[104] Nevertheless, the 500-mile trip was completed in ten days, with Mazatlan, on the Pacific coast, reached on August 19, 1865.[105] Dan Showalter had evidently ridden ahead and had arrived a day earlier.[106] That he had arrived at Mazatlan was known in California before the month was over.[107]

When Showalter, Elliott and the others arrived at Mazatlan, it had been, since 1864, under the control of Mexican Imperialist and French forces, and would remain so until November of 1866. Some of the arrivals almost immediately took ship for San Francisco.[108] A few sailed off to South America.[109] Some decided to raise cotton in the area.[110] Among these was Elliott, who prospered in his farming, but, after about a year, returned to his home in Missouri.[111] At least one of Elliott's men, F.W. Westlake, joined the Mexican Liberal Army (Juaristas), in which he served until the defeat and execution of Emperor Maximilian. He was then honorably discharged and returned to Missouri.[112]

Dan Showalter did not continue on to Guaymas, as he had indicated to Mrs. Oury, but instead settled in Mazatlan. This may have been a decision to settle there permanently since he invested in a hotel or public house located at "Presidio of Mazatlan."[113] Although Presidio de Mazatlan is now within the city limits of the City of Mazatlan, in the 1860s it was not. It was in an area called Villa Union[114] along the Rio Presidio, about ten miles southeasterly of the city. His establishment was variously reported as a hotel[115] or as a public house (saloon).[116] It seems most probable that the business was a combination—

a saloon with lodging rooms above. Showalter was not the only owner of the establishment. Either there is disagreement or else different accounts do not name all of the partners that he had. The *Mariposa Gazette* of March 3, 1866, said that there was a partner named "Beans."[117] The *Daily Alta California* of November 19, 1865, reported that the establishment was owned by "Showalter, Greathouse and Company."[118] On February 23, 1866, the same newspaper stated that the partner was named "Beur."[119] Perhaps all of those named were partners. Beans and Beur may have been the "and Company." Greathouse was Ridgley Greathouse, himself an interesting character of the times. He had been involved, in 1863, as the registered owner of the ship *J.M. Chapman*, which Asbury Harpending and he armed and crewed at San Francisco. Their plot to operate the ship as a Confederate privateer was thwarted by San Francisco Police and the U.S. Navy.[120] The name of Showalter's establishment is also disputed. A November 1865, letter to the *Daily Alta California* referred to it as the "Ox Hide and Tail House."[121] Greathouse family accounts state that it was the similar "Ox Head and Tail."[122] A genealogy including information about Greathouse called it the "Planter's Hotel."[123] This name was also applied in a single-sentence mention of Showalter in the *Daily Reese River Reveille* of Austin, Nevada.[124]

It should perhaps be remembered that at this time Showalter was an exile in a foreign land, where a different language was spoken. Whether or not he was conversant in Spanish is unknown. Having long been a resident of California, it is possible that he had at least a working knowledge of it. He was no doubt distraught over both his lost prospects in California and the defeat of the Confederacy. It also seems very possible that he was still much troubled by the injury he had suffered in the fall from his horse prior to his journey into exile. Some or all of theses factors may have played a part in his alcohol intoxication at the time of his death.

The most complete report of an early date of the circumstances of his death appeared on Page 1 of the *Daily Alta California* of February 25, 1866. This article, "From Mazatlan—How Dan. Showalter Died," first gave news of Mazatlan—fighting in the area between Mexican Liberals and the French—and then concluded:

> The death of Showalter occurred in this wise. Showalter and a man named Beur had a hotel at the presidio of Mazatlan, within Corona's lines. A few days before his death, he got on a drunken spree and commenced smashing the furnature and fixtures, when the bar-tender remonstrated with him on his conduct, telling him that it was not treating his partner, who was absent, right to thus destroy his property. To this Showalter replied: "By G-d, I am a gentleman, Sir!" The bar-tender retorted, "You don't act like one." Whereupon Showalter drew a dirk-knife and slapped the bar-tender with it, with a view of provoking a fight. The bar-tender instantly drew a pistol and fired at Showalter, the ball taking effect in his arm below the elbow, breaking the bone, and ranging upwards wedged near the shoulder. Showalter was rendered incapable of fighting by the shot, but the bar-tender got a double-barreled gun, and but for the interference of outsiders would have given him the contents and finished him. As it was, Showalter died of lockjaw, caused by the wound.[125]

An almost identical account was published on March 10, 1866, in the *Mariposa Gazette*, which quoted the *Mazatlan Times* of March 8. This article provided some background of Showalter's life and, in regard to his death, differed from the *Alta*'s account only in the name of the partner, who it called "Beans."[126]

Curiously, neither of these accounts stated the date of the incident which led to his death. This must be calculated from the date he died. The obituary from the *Mazatlan Times* stated that he died on March 4, 1866.[127] Tetanus (the present-day term for lockjaw) has a usual incubation period of about eight days.[128] This would indicate that the brawl would have occurred on or about Saturday, February 24. Exactly who it was that shot Showalter is not definitely known. All accounts state that it was the bartender. The more complete accounts, such as that quoted preceding, all indicated that the bartender was not one of the partners. "Beans" (or "Beur"?) was indentified in most reports as a partner,[129] so can be eliminated as the slayer. In her last diary entry, written October 9, 1881, Mrs. Oury mentioned that Showalter had been killed by "young Mr. Kavanaugh."[130] The fact that Kavanaugh left Mazatlan almost immediately for Mexico City (over 600 miles distant), where he soon after died (on February 28, 1866), supports this. Did he leave Mazatlan to avoid prosecution, civil or social, for the death of Showalter? In any event, the weight of evidence is that F.E. Kavanaugh was indeed the slayer.

The mortal remains of Dan Showalter rest somewhere under the grounds of Mazatlan's Parque Gral. Angel Flores or the adjoining primary school. The park includes a large monument to General Flores' memory (Mazatleco.com.mx).

The death of Dan Showalter was "big news" in Mazatlan. There was then a newspaper, the *Mazatlan Times*, published by A.D. Jones, who boasted that it was the only English-language periodical in Mexico.[131] This weekly published an obituary—probably written by Jones himself—on March 8, 1866. It read:

> It is our painful duty this week to announce the death of Col. Dan. Showalter, which occurred in this city on Sunday, 4th inst., at half past 5 o'clock p.m. Colonel Showalter was a native of Green county Penn. He was for several years a citizen of California, and in 1860 was elected to the Assembly from Mariposa county. Soon after the adjournment of the Legislature in the spring of 1861 Showalter started for Texas to join Confederate forces. Entering the army as a private his valor and bravery brought him to notice. He participated in many a hard fought battle, was at the re-taking of Galveston, Jan. 1st, 1863, and for his gallantry on that occasion was made Lieut. Col. of the 4th Arizona regiment. Subsequently he was selected Col. of that regiment, and commanded as such when the Confederate armies were disbanded. At the close of the war, Col. Showalter came to Mexico, and reached this port on the 18th of August last. Col. Showalter was a man of commanding appearance, was possessed of the noblest and most generous impulses, and was the soul of honor. He was held in high esteem by his fellows, and in the walks of civil life his urbanity and genial disposition made him friends among all men who appreciate genuine worth. On Monday afternoon the remains of Col. Showalter was interred in the foreign burying ground near this city. His funeral was attended by the greater part of Americans in this city, who with thousands in other lands, will keep fresh and green the memory of the lamented Showalter. Col. Showalter was yet in the prime of life, being only 37 years of age.[132]

Back in those days, cemeteries were located outside of towns for reasons of public health. Mazatlan's "foreign cemetery"—also known as the Protestant cemetery—was on the eastern slope of the peninsula, with the city of Mazatlan on the western slope. It had originated after a cholera epidemic, in 1851, created the need for a burying ground for Protestants. Most foreigners who died in Mazatlan were Protestants, and it was thus natural that Dan Showalter, though probably a Catholic, be buried among other Americans. There was not official or governmental supervision over the Panteon de Protestantes. As the city grew and expanded eastward, population pressure overran the cemetery location. There were apparently few grave markers remaining since, in the early 1900s, its grounds became used for sports fields. On October 25, 1921, the German Benevolent Society, which had become its owners, donated and deeded it to the municipal government upon the stipulation that, within three years, the city erect on the site a square, park, or playground. This was done in 1924, on an 804-meters-square portion of the land. The park was named after General Angel Flores (a hero of the 1910 Mexican Revolution and Governor of the State of Sinaloa, 1920–1924[133]), who had recently died. Parque Gral. Angel Flores was not more than carelessly maintained and was overrun by pigs and donkeys for many years but is now a well-maintained, attractive park. In 1943, a portion of the area was taken to construct Escuela Primaria Public Gral. Angel Flores (Gen. Angel Flores Public Primary School).[134] It is not known whether or not there was ever in this cemetery a grave marker for Dan Showalter. Today, his mortal remains are located somewhere under the grounds of the park or of the school.

Nine

The Man Dan Showalter

There have been only two biographical articles about Dan Showalter. The first, by retired military officer and university professor Clarence C. Clendenen, was published, in 1961, in the *California Historical Society Quarterly* (Vol. 40, No. 4, Dec. 1961). He tried to evaluate Showalter as a person, but despaired, writing that the information about him was "so fragmentary and sketchy that it is difficult to evaluate him and form a picture of his personality." Nevertheless, he tried, and credited Showalter as, during his lifetime, "attaining a degree of importance as embodying and symbolizing the spirit of opposition to the Union that affected a considerable fraction of the population of the state." His violence, wrote Clendenen, "epitomized the wild spirit of the frontier." Clendenen felt that there was no question but that Showalter possessed both leadership qualities and personal courage in a high degree. He was credited with an above average education for his time, as being affable and sociable, and, in his devotion to the Confederate cause, passionate and sincere. Clendenen's conclusion was that "one can summarize only by saying that Dan Showalter, Confederate colonel from California, was a fascinating and baffling character, who probably deserved a better fate than a sordid death in a barroom in Mexico."[1] The next was a chapter by Dr. Laurence Fletcher Talbott (California Polytechnic State University) in his 1999 book, *California in the War for Southern Independence*. Talbott based his chapter principally upon Clendenen's earlier work and *Official Records of the Union and Confederate Armies in the War of the Rebellion*, adding in a mistaken reliance upon a 1960s article ("El Monte and the Confederacy") found at the El Monte History Museum. His conclusions mirrored and quoted those of Clendenen. He did, however, express an insight into the character of Showalter in the title of his chapter—"The Irrepressible Dan Showalter."[2]

Since Dr. Clendenen and Dr. Talbott wrote, greatly enhanced accessibility to sources via the internet and contacts with members of Showalter's family have provided more information than was available to the professors. This additional information and a diligent search for and beyond it permit the present authors to evaluate the life and personality of Dan Showalter in greater detail and insight.

The Family Man

There exists little information regarding Dan Showalter's relationships with members of his family, but what there is largely indicates fond feelings for his full siblings. When young (in his teens), he had journeyed with his brother John to the mines of (probably) California and returned. He admitted feeling no desire to remain at home when his father remarried, but, after setting out alone for California in 1852, he had written his sister Elizabeth's husband, Sam O'Connor, from New York City. It would seem most likely that he wrote to siblings at least occasionally while mining or serving in the legislature. He definitely wrote about the duel in 1861 to his brother William, explaining that affair. In his 1864 letter to Anna Forman, Dan, assuming that his brothers had sided with the Union, stated that he cared for no contact with them. In this same letter, though, he requested that Anna write his sister Kate, letting her know that he was well. Upon arriving on the Rio Grande in July of 1864, the large amount of trade in and out of Matamoros, Mexico, presented Dan with an opportunity to write to his relatives in the United States. For some fifty years after the Civil War, families of his sisters read and reread letters received from him during this period.[3] They remembered him fondly. Present-day, more distant relatives, as is evidenced by the enthusiasm of distant relatives contacted by the authors, are quite proud of the relationship. Whatever relationship he may have had with his father was soured when the father remarried. It cannot be known whether Dan's reaction was due to his fondness for his mother, disgust at the old man's remarrying, or both. He seems to have had little or no relationship with the half-siblings resulting from his father's remarriage—but then, they would have been considerably younger than he, and he was by then, to use terminology of the day, "his own man." He seemed to have a particular fondness for his sister Kate and, to a lesser degree, with Elizabeth and William. It cannot be said that Dan Showalter was without love and feeling for members of his family.

Why Confederate?

Given that Dan Showalter was born and raised in Pennsylvania, lived his adult life in California, and, in fact, never lived in the South, it is probably surprising to most that he chose to serve in the Confederate Army. His factional loyalty and addresses in the 1861 California legislature establish that his pro–Southern, pro-secession identity had been established prior to the Civil War. The question, then, is actually how he came to hold such positions.

Greene County, Pennsylvania—the scene of Showalter's birth and childhood—is the most southwesterly county of the state. As such, it was bordered on both the south and the west by Virginia (now West Virginia). This made it a border region with citizens from Virginia or sympathetic to Virginia ideals. In 1860, a majority of its voters cast their ballots for John C. Breckinridge, the Southern Democratic candidate for President. The attitude of the county's people was apathy toward the slavery issue and in favor of compromise with the South. Peace Democrats dominated the politics of the county throughout the Civil War and, in 1864, it was one of only twelve Pennsylvania counties that voted against the reelection of President Lincoln. During most of the period of the war, it was represented in Congress by Jesse Lazear, himself from Greene County, who opposed the administration's suspension of habeas corpus and the emancipation proclamation. In May 1864, he called for a suspension of hostilities.[4] Dan's holding pro–Southern views was not, therefore, out of context with those held by many in his home area.

Nor was he alone in his family in holding these sentiments. A grandniece, Regina

Seeley, recalled members of her family displaying a picture of Confederate President Jefferson Davis in their South Dakota home many years after the war. She also recalled that, of the immediate family, brother William was a "Confirmed Northern, Union man," but that sister Elizabeth and brother John were Confederate sympathizers. Mrs. Seeley also wrote that some of the Showalters—apparently from a Virginia branch of the family— had married into a Douglass family in Alabama and had some household slaves.[5]

With regional and family background like this, it would not have been unusual for Dan, in California, to have become associated with former Southerners. Among these were men like Thomas Laspeyre from Louisiana, Samuel H. Brooks from Tennessee, George W. Patrick from Alabama, David S. Terry from Texas, and Zachariah Montgomery from Kentucky. Another reinforcement was his residence in the southern mining district of Mariposa County, which was "so heavily populated by masters, slaves, and white Southerners that sympathy for slave holding rights ran high."[6] Committed to his views, opposition to them only impelled Dan into stronger convictions about them. Once his California political career was ruined by the duel and attacked on all sides, Dan didn't have much choice but to go South.

As a Military Commander

Dan Showalter was far from a noted commander of Confederate forces and his unit was less than distinguished in notable battles or campaigns, yet there is enough evidence to evaluate him as a commander of men during wartime. One measure of an effective commander is that he holds the respect of his subordinates. There are some references to this, which indicate the opinions of some who served under his command. Private P.H. Hill of Company G, in a letter to his wife, wrote, "I am very pleased with my officers."[7] When Captain Amzi Bradshaw of Company D resigned his commission for reasons of health on August 6, 1864, he stated, "I wish it distinctly understood that it is not in consequence of any dislike that I entertain towards my superior officers[;] on the contrary after a long and familiar acquaintance it is with many regrets that I part with them."[8] As a captain and company commander, Bradshaw had only two superior officers—Major Kavanaugh and Showalter. The return to service with the regiment by deserters and other absentees in April 1865 implies some level of confidence in Showalter by the returnees. The resolutions of loyalty by the regiment (under his leadership and guidance) made on May 19, 1865, long after the prospects of the Confederacy had become worse than desperate, very strongly imply that his men were willing to follow him even in extremis.

Related to this aspect of the successful or good commander is his concern for and care of those under his command. In her letter to her mother, Mrs. Dryden (wife of Assistant Surgeon Robert H. Dryden) indicated that Showalter also expressed concern for and rendered assistance to the dependents of his men. His arguments with Colonel Ford over horses, weapons, and other supplies for the regiment, though aggravating to his superior, are evidence that Showalter worked actively to ensure their proper supply.

Another measure of an effective commander is the performance of himself and his command in battle. In late 1863, General McCulloch expressed regret over losing the services of Showalter and his battalion in the Indian Territory, which indicates that they had performed at least creditably there. As mentioned previously, a contemporary observer of the campaign to and on the Rio Grande noted the 4th Arizona being "as good troops as we can desire to have." Colonel Ford, in his memoirs, credited Dan Showalter as having performed well during the skirmish at Las Rucias in July of 1864. There is documentation that, prior to Palmito Ranch in September 1864, Showalter provided Ford with timely and concise information regarding the enemy and Mexican intentions. During the Palmito Ranch skirmish, he and his men held out, unsupported, against greatly superior forces for two days. That Showalter and the 4th Arizona were, throughout the campaign to Brownsville, in the fore and given the most advanced position thereafter strongly implies that Colonel Ford held them in the most confidence of all of his units. The fact that Ford ordered him under arrest afterwards only upon the orders of General Drayton implies that Ford himself was not all that displeased with the performance of either Showalter or the regiment.

A good commander must also exercise control of his men. Contrary to Colonel Day's self-serving—and latter-day—reports of the regiment fleeing in confusion at Palmito Ranch, they held their position for two days. The "burst-up" of the regiment in February of 1864 occurred while the majority of the unit was under command of Captain Saunders. Dan Showalter was still absent in San Antonio, awaiting conclusion of his court martial. Indeed, this "burst-up" seems to have been made possible by the absence of so many of the regiment's officers in San Antonio as witnesses for the court martial and Major Kavanaugh's being absent sick. As seen previously, most of these men did, a few months later, return to the colors.

Dan Showalter did not neglect the administrative aspects of command either. Very soon after assuming command when Colonel Baird was detached, he provided district headquarters with reports that had not previously been supplied. As late as May 1865, he requisitioned supplies of blank forms needed for reporting purposes and solicited copies of department and district orders not available to him. There are very few records of the 4th Arizona extant. Of the eight Regimental Returns that survive (all for 1864), one is for the month preceding his assumption of command (the missing reports), three are from months in which he was in active command, and the final three are for the three months immediately after Palmito—when he had ingrained the habit of regular reporting.

Dan Showalter was neither a great commander nor a disastrous commander—he never really had much opportunity to prove himself as either. But the records that exist do seem to indicate that he was a competent and trusted subordinate commander. And as such, he fulfilled the role that was allotted to him.

Personality

There is all too little information from letters or memoirs to enable anything like a complete analysis or evaluation of Dan Showalter's personality. What little there is does seem to indicate that, by and large, he was a very personable man with the virtues and faults of the highly individualistic frontiersman.

Showalter seemingly possessed a sense of fair-play. As a California legislator, he opposed a bill by fellow Democrats to legislate the State Librarian out of office in order to depose a "Know-Nothing" office holder as he felt that the librarian, who was performing an acceptable job, should be allowed to retain his position until the end of his term. He vigorously argued that weight inspectors who had already just spent large sums for their official seals be reimbursed when a change in the law would have eliminated their jobs. He also spoke in support of payment of a man who had accepted state employment in an unauthorized position arguing that the man had taken the post in good faith and had done the job. These stands contrasted sharply with his general conservatism in the expenditure of state funds and only emphasize his concern for individuals.

He definitely had the ability to get along with men. His 1857 running-mate loaned him a horse. When Zach Montgomery's "run" for Speaker of the Assembly failed in 1861, Showalter was quickly put forward as the candidate of his faction. Later during the same legislative session—and after his participation and speaking on controversial matters—he was elected Speaker *pro tem* with votes from all four factions. In a January 1863 letter, an unknown former Californian fondly wrote, "I have known *Dan.* for a long time ... my friend."[9]

It seems that he may have had even more impact with women. His sisters passed on an incident (the pubic hair story) that indicates he was quite popular with women. Mrs. Dryden, in her 1866 letter about her experiences during the war, reflected her relief and appreciation for his actions when he encountered her near Bonham in December 1863. Mina Oury wrote several times about Showalter in her diary—always with some affection. He often supped with she and her husband, and had escorted her into Parras on a shopping trip. In her final diary entry of October 9, 1881, she recalled that "the Colonel had many noble qualities."[10] Her most extensive comments about Showalter were on July 23, 1866, when he was about to leave their party. She wrote, "We will miss him greatly, he is very sociable, spent most of his time with us, is a constant talker and very entertaining."[11] His letter to Anna Forman certainly exhibits great tenderness.

There can be no doubt that Dan Showalter could, at times, be quite intemperate in expression. His attitude and comments in support of Milton Latham for the United States Senate in 1857 have been cited. Some of his speeches in the 1861 Assembly—particularly his "arch-traitor" speech—were certainly inflammatory. While a prisoner at Camp Wright, California, in early December 1861, he raged and threatened Hugh Gorley in his effort to obtain release. Colonel John S. Ford remembered that he was "very mad" in Brownsville after being confined to the town. The circumstance of his death in Mazatlan is yet another evidence of his sometime bad temper. This aspect of his personality, however, seems to have exhibited itself only when Showalter was under stress and not dominant in his life.

Alcoholic beverages were prevalent on the American frontier. Indeed, Showalter's home county had been in the center of the 1791 "Whiskey Rebellion." Doubtless the liquor was free-flowing at both the dinner in San Francisco hosted by the two newly-elected California Senators and the George Ryer testimonial, which he attended in 1857. Many legislators in those days were known to be hard drinking men. Then, too, there was very little diversion other than drink in the mining camps. It would not have been unusual for Dan Showalter to imbibe intoxicants. But to assert that he was an alcoholic, as some present-day writers have done, is probably a gross exaggeration. The memoirs of Colonel John S. Ford clearly indicate that Showalter was probably drunken in the aftermath of (but not during) the September 1864 battle at Palmito Ranch. All contemporary press accounts of his 1866 death in Mazatlan definitely aver that he was drunk at the time. The testimony by a contemporary who knew him that most directly implies that he may have been an alcoholic was that of Mrs. Mina Oury, who wrote, in 1881, that he "fell victim of his passion for whiskey."[12] Perhaps when angry, as after Palmito, or in pain, as he probably was during the trip through Mexico and at Mazatlan, he succumbed to binge drinking.

His record in the legislature and with the 4th Arizona (except perhaps after Palmito) indicate that alcohol did not dominate his life to the extent that his performance was in any way detrimentally impacted.

So who was this man, Dan Showalter? He was a highly individualistic, sometimes emotional frontier miner and politician. At the same time, he was a capable legislator, successful miner, and competent military commander. And—importantly—more so than any other person's, his life and career illustrate more completely than any other's the secession crisis in 1861 California and its aftermath. Those of us today, like his contemporaries, regardless of opinions about him, must concede that Dan Showalter was an exceedingly interesting man and, like his one-time acquaintance Hugh Gorley, acknowledge that he was "one whose abilities warranted a better fate."[13]

Appendix A

Regina Seeley's Letter

The following fifteen-page letter was written by Dan Showalter's grandniece, Regina Seeley of Anaheim, California, on July 1, 1978, when she was aged 82, to Ed Showalter of Latrobe, Pennsylvania, and is published here for the first time with the permission of Mr. Showalter. Organization, spelling, and punctuation are as given in the original. Like Mrs. Seeley, the authors wish the actual manuscripts or copies of Dan Showalter's letters—and the book Mrs. Seeley had written—had survived.

It must be remembered that Mrs. Seeley was relating handed-down memories from her mother and aunt. Therefore, some of what she wrote does not always match up with the actual facts.

2627 E. La Palma # 126
Anaheim, Calif. 92806
July 1, 1978

My dear Ed,

Rec'd your very welcome letter yesterday. There's so much to go over that I will wait and write you a full account later. I'm already convinced that your family & mine have to be related. It just isn't possible for there to be so many coincidences. My grandmother's father was a William, her brother (one of several) was John and then there was Dan. I have much to zerox, also. Grandmother had nephews Jim & Jerome, among others. I don't dare start on it. Meantime I want to get pictures taken of Great Uncle Dan. We are all Catholics. Also Grandma Showalter O'Connor spoke of living in a "dog-trot" house given to St. Vincent's & called "Sportsmen Hall"—In 1790, I believe two Showalter brothers, John & Elihu signed deeds or something for the Benedictines. West Alexandria figured in the family—somewhere, I have much to look up.

My grandmother told my mother that originally some one of the Showalters lived in a "dog-trot" house—which I believe is composed of 2 big rooms—or houses—with a covered roof, open at 2 ends, so that riders could be protected by the roof against rain and snow. She (Elizabeth Showalter O'Connor) said the house was given to St. Vincent's Church, I presume in the late 1700's—and that it was called Sportsman's Hall. There were 2 Showalters involved—a John and Elihu. Three names were often mentioned—William, John & Elihu.

In Grandmother's obituary, which I enclose (copy) it mentions 2 brothers John of Davenport and Elihu of DeWitt (both in Iowa). Grandmother also said that her brothers, John and Dan went to Montana before 1850—As Uncle Dan went to Calif. to pan for gold & got into politics. The two brothers found a small fortune in gold, returned to Latrobe and used some of the money building a butcher shop and a brick works. Also, altho' I've forgotten details, one of the wealthier Showalters gave a house to Aunt Kate—after the tragic death of Aunt Kate's son in Oregon—More about that later. This farm was called "Rose Hill" or some such name.

Also Grandmother had a slightly different account of the duel. (Her story) Uncle Dan—my great Uncle Dan) thought it was to be a duel of honor, so he fired into the air. However Percy shot at Uncle Dan, the rifle shot grazing one ear. Upon this Uncle Dan ordered another shot, at which he shot Percy dead. The duel took place along the Sacramento in a beautiful grove of trees. After this, Uncle Dan recruited a company of 250 Confederate sympathizers & set off to join Gen. Magruder in the retaking of Galveston. Also, Grandmother read us letters from her brother Dan. He had written from some old battlefield of the Mexican War. He spoke of a bivouac along a river—of the quiet & peace at night. The letter was written on one single sheet of heavy paper—No envelope—it was folded and had her name & a Pennsylvania address—sealed with sealing wax. it had been forwarded to Iowa & reached Dakota Territory by settlers who carried mail in the early days. Late on, Aunt Mary, with whom Grandma was living, sent the letters (several) on to Aunt Kate who was, I believe some 20 years younger than Eliz. (she was oldest, I understand. Anyway when Aunt Kate visited us, I was going to the Univ. of S. Dak. at Vermilion, (from 1914–1917) & again the letters were read. I wish now I had taken notes. Also Uncle Dan was in some Northern prison, he told of prison life—his leaving—I don't remember whether he escaped or was freed. Anyway, he was supposed to have been so embittered that, upon the war's end, he refused to swear allegiance to the new government—that he crossed the line from Laredo, Texas to the Mexican side. There he lived—he would come across with other Confederate cronies for trips to the Laredo bars or saloons—he is or was very hot-heade—he got into a fight with a younger Yankee—it came to blows–& Dan, old and weak was killed. He asked to be buried in his Confederate uniform, with his sword & the stars and bars of the South. He supposed to have been buried at Laredo in a military grave yard. I never went to Laredo—I don't know whether there would be any way to find out. My Mother, later on, as I grew older said that Uncle Dan was quite fickle & had a way of jilting women. Mama said he was like old Jeb Stuart—both men were described as having "petticoat fever." There was a sort of hushed story that one of his loves asked for his picture & a lock of his red hair before he went to California & Uncle Dan obliged her about the picture—only instead of a lock of his auburn curls he is said to have a small amount of "pubic hair" tied with some blue baby ribbon. It seems that the Showalter women didn't approve of Uncle Dan's amorous affairs. The other Showalter men presumably married & lived circumspect lives.

In 1909, when I was 13, Mama & I went back to Davenport to visit Uncle John (83 years old) who was a very large old man with a mane of white hair. He was an old tyrant. They were living in Betancourt—a suburb of Davenport with Uncle (Great) Elihu was dead or they feuding—for we didn't meet him or his family. I remember we ate our doors & Uncle John ordered everyone around. We had fried chicken, sweet potatoes, hot corn bread, all kinds of salad, pickled fruit, you name it. And two young cousins of mine, had sort or mops or anyway, sticks with long strings of paper, which they had to wave over us to keep the flies away. And I don't remember Uncle John's wife's name—She was a fat old gal—just smiled and said—"Yes, dear"—smiling & fanning herself. Uncle John roared that he knew damned well (much "tching" from his wife—the [illegibl] got to her, if she wasn't shocked, she rolled her eyes around—he evidently enjoyed shocking everyone—anyway—he said if he cold get back to Montana, he would find where the vein of gold was, that he & Dan had lost track of. I believe he must have been near 100 then. Anyway—he was very old.

There were other cousins in Davenport of my mother's. there was an Uncle Will—my mother had lived with them when her father, grandfather S. S. O'Connor taught at Iowa City—also a cousin of hers—Jerome—he was some older than Mama—his sister, Aunt Mary Ann Showalter raised his 8 kids when his wife died. Mama was born in 1869—died in 1934—Grandmother, as you can see by the obituary I sent on was 76 in 1900, when she died. I remember her wlll, as we were out in South Dakota, nursing my Mother's oldest brother John, dying of cancer, We had come up to Dakota from Oklahoma, where I was born, Apr. 22, 1896.

Elizabeth Showalter O'Connor had 8 children: Charles, John,[2] Mary,[3] Sam,[4] Dan,[5] Eliza,[6] another Charles,[7] the first one died in infancy, Elihu,[8] Alice[9] (my mother), Regina[10]—for whom I was named. Charles, the second one, also died a tragic death. He was playing in a band in Redfield S. Dak when a drunken sheriff, trying to arrest a man, fired into a crown of the band boys & accidentally killed the young Charles—about 21.

Now, as I remember, Grandmother Eliz. Showalter O'Connor's father was William—but I may have been wrong. 1900 is hard to remember. My mother must have talked about it—Elizabeth, my grandmother She was the scholar of the family, having finished and academy education at some academy for a girl—I thought at St. Vincents—now, I'm not too sure. Her best friend was an O'Connor girl from someplace in Washington County—the O'Connors having come to Philadepphia, then to Pittsburg where he (the original) was a John O'Connor, married to Eliza Aston, in 1820—there were *15* children (Heavens). My grandfather Samuel (Elizabeth's husband)—he was educated at an Academy at West Alexandria & later at St. Vincent's College near Latrobe—he was the eldest & he taught school from Pennsylvania, through Iowa, Missiouri & finally So. Dak. territory where he and his 3 sons took up homesteads. Also, some of our family went to a Mount-de-Chantal (Sp?) near Wheeling, West Virginia.

This is certainly a hodge-podge of a letter. You may never be the same again! I write just as the spirit moves me. Am sorry I can't type any more.

It seemed to me that there was a large family in my grandmother Showalter's family. I do remember that she said her family brought the first cuckoo clock from Switzerland. Also, that her Mother spent the last years—many of them in a wheelchair. There was some story about the family taking another Showalter child—named Mary Ann (not the one in Iowa) and something about her racing the sheriff from Latrobe to the farm—before he (sheriff) could serve the papers to take Mary Ann away from them. One incident, I *do* remember. I was curious about her race horse—and asked her name—it was a mare—in So. Dak. we had geldings for riding. Grandmother said the mare was named Fanny Hill. I thought the name strange as our horses had such prosaic as "Old Ned,"—Bess—Gypsy—Star, etc. She then said, "Yes, she was named Fanny Hill." When I asked why she was named Fanny Hill—she answered—"Because she was *so fast*!" Everyone laughed—it wasn't until I was married & had a grown son that I read the book "Fanny Hill"—an early day British prostitute that I knew why everyone laughed—poor child, I thought they were all laughing at me & was rather hurt. I couldn't for the life of me see why "Fanny Hill" was funny.

One of my memories of my grandmother—she must have been about 76—the last year we were all together out at the homestead farm. She rode everywhere—side saddle—even 18 miles from the farm to Miller So. Dak. She had taught Old Ned to "single pace"—by crowding him on a walk—I rode on her lap—she took eggs & butter in a basket to Miller—where she exchanged it for coffee & tea. She weighed about 98 lbs.—had long auburn brainds that she wound around her head. We had a picture of Jefferson Davis in an "everlasting" frame. She had a big home—made lomm. In her girl hood she wove the household [illegible word]—for sheets & her father's white suits that he wore in the fields—as he "over saw" the works. Since her mother was paralyzed & grandmother was the eldest she was the hostess—they entertained a great deal—her father called her—among the enduring little [illegible word]—his little spit-fire, his good right arm—I know she was the one he confided all the problems—Aunt Kate said that their father (I'm sure it was William) was a Confirmed Northern, Union man, while (Grandmother) Elizabeth, John and Dan were Confederate sympathizers—also—somewhere along the line, there were Showalters married into a Douglass family in Alabama—who had a few house-hold slvaes—had come from Virginia—that, I cannot confirm. I know Mama wrote to some Aunt in Birmingham—I don't remember any name but Douglass. I do remember that I got a letter of sympathy when Mama died in 1934.

While my mother kept house for her uncle Charles O'Connor (whose wife had died) in Washington County near Claysville (? I believe) she visited Latrobe, meeting some cousins. Somewhere I had 2 pictures of beautiful young girls—2 or 3 years old—but I have travelled so many times on my way to California that I have some how managed to lose old pictures, books, etc., along the way.

Aunt Kate Showalter married a well-to-do older man, Jim Finch, who had a drygoods store—in Pittsburg, I believe. Jim drank but was wealthy. They had one son named Jim. He became an attorney & after Jim Sr's death, Aunt Kate moved to Albany to be near her son Jim, wife and twin daughters. Young Jim was trying a case—both attorneys quarreled and finally they were throwing things at each in Court. Jim, who was hot-tempered in his anger threw an ink well at his opponent, which unfortunately struck the man in the temple & killed him. Jim was tried for murder, found guilty & sentenced to be hanged. Actually it should have been man slaughter—but at that time Oregon was a very prejudiced state, against Catholics and Jim Jr., didn't stand a chance. The young Jim wouldn't allow his wife or the twin daughters come into court but Aunt Kate went every day and she walked to the scaffold with him, where he stood comforted by a priest until the trap was sprung. I remember it well, because I was going to the U. of S. D.—1914–1917—it occurred during those years. She stayed at our Hotel in Andover So. Dak—my stepfather—Frank D[illegible] & my mother were in the hotel business almost all of their married life. Was at that time that Mama & I saw again the letters from Great Uncle Dan Showalter. Apparently my Aunt Mary O'Connor Phillips had sent all the family keepsakes & letters to Aunt Kate, 20 years younger than granfmother Elizabeth. At that time—1916–1917—Aunt Kate, having used all of her money defending her son had little or no money left–& some of the Latrobe Showalters offered her a home as long as he lived. I don't remember ever hearing from her again. She was very old & very weak—a very small broken little body—but with a clear, sharp mind. At night we would hear her walking the floor—back & forth. She must have been with us for 6 or more months. We had her during the cold weather—we had steam heat & her room was warm. At that time—all of the family letters & pictures were in small round topped trunk—I wish & have wished many times that we had copied those old letters. Also, I had hoped there might be some way of locating the owners of Rose Farm—perhaps today, some of these old letters might be in some obscure trunk in some forgotten attic. Of course, it could have been destroyed long ago.

I am so sorry I can't type any more. My left arm is very crippled. When it was broken in the "donkey" episode—both bones were broken & pulled out of the socket. It was in a cast from Aug. 25 until after Thanksgiving—the one bone kept pulling out of socket & it has been quite a battle to gain re-use of it—but I crochet & knit—to strengthen it. However, I am very active—I walk 2 miles before breakfast every morning—am still driving. Work in mosaics—having made a 4" by 6' mosaic in glass Venetian tile of our Lady of Guadalupe—in an old Indian church of that name in *Zuni* N. Mex. when I taught during my 52 years of teaching. The old plaza church was build by one of Coronado's men—a priest, in 1629. It had been burned down, destroyed several times—however while I taught there in 1969–1970—they restored it—it took me 2 years to do the mosaic.

Now, I am hoping to rewrite a book I wrote some years ago—if I live that long!

[Here, Mrs. Seeley has drawn a happy face.]

Well, by now, you're probably gasping for breath, rubbing your poor eyes & wondering how in the dickens you got into this!!

Best to you and your family. I really feel somehow we will find a relationship. It may be I'll have to get a census report from Washington D. C. Or does Latrobe have a historic society? I imagine Pennsylvania might have one. I'll look it up at our [illegible]. So will write.

Thinking you for your being friendly to a profuse letter—take care—

Sincerely
Regina

Appendix B

Showalter in Fiction

Dan Showalter's strong personality, his passionate expressions of his beliefs and loyalties, and the drama of events in his life, such as the contentious 1861 California legislature, the duel with Piercy, and his capture at Minter's Ranch, would certainly furnish material for a fictionalized, "based on actual events" cinematographic presentation. Perhaps surprisingly, Dan Showalter has figured—as a minor character—in only three works of literature.

His first appearance was in *The Little Lady of Lagunitas: A Franco-Californian Romance*, published by Richard Savage in 1892. This is a narrated novel, with very little dialogue, that tells the story of a Louisiana Frenchman in California who was very high in the Knights of the Golden Circle and went east, at the beginning of the Civil War, to join the Confederacy. This protagonist, just before dying of wounds received in the Battle of Atlanta, learns that his wife, in California, has died, leaving behind a young daughter. The author was a staunch Union man. Underage, he had been discharged from the California Volunteers, but, by the efforts of his father, a Lincoln official in California, obtained an appointment to West Point in 1864. After graduation from West Point, he served as an Engineer officer on the frontier and, later, during the Spanish-American War. Although the story is about a Confederate, his novel is definitely anti–Southern. Dan Showalter is mentioned twice in the novel. He is mentioned first (on Page 79 of the Aolib online edition) as being "fresh from the deadly field of honor" and as among California exiles to the Confederacy, who had left the state "not in honor." The second reference (on Page 82) states that the novel's hero, Maxime Valois, is too well known "to be allowed to follow Showalter, Terry, and their fellows over the Colorado desert" to Texas. Since this is a work of fiction, the inaccuracy of Showalter, and Terry too, crossing the Colorado desert can be perhaps excused as literary license.[1]

It was over one hundred years later that Showalter was again mentioned in fiction. This was in *The Trail Through Mohawk*, published in 2012 by San Diego, California, television journalist and author John Culea. This is a Western novel with romantic and religious overtones, written in the style of the journal of a teacher's ancestors. The story begins in 1859 and is set in the area of Yuma, Arizona. On Page 137, the male ancestor of the teacher writes of becoming a spy for Major Edwin Rigg of the 1st California Infantry, then the commander at Fort Yuma. In this context, the November 1861 capture of the Showalter Party at Minter's Ranch is briefly explained. What little there is about this incident and Showalter is historically accurate.[2]

Finally, Western author Don Chenhall's short story "The Frog" was published by the *Rope and Wire Blog*. It is about the death of William "Frog" Edwards, a member of the Showalter Party who died in the Arizona desert, in 1862, after slaying two Union soldiers at La Paz on the Colorado River. Early in the story, Edwards tells a companion that his path had all begun at a meeting of the Knights of the Golden Circle in San Francisco during the fall of 1861. At this meeting, Dan Showalter had explained his plan to gather men and travel the Overland Trail to Texas for the purpose of joining the Confederacy. Edwards told his companion that where the money raised for this endeavor came from was secret. He then mentions the capture of the Showalter Party and having suffered the poor conditions while imprisoned at Fort Yuma. Again, literary license can be credited with the historical inaccuracies (Showalter was not near San Francisco in the fall of 1861) of this well-written and entertaining little Western story.[3]

Appendix C
Prevalent Misinformation Refuted

While the internet has made much more information available to many more individuals, it has also widely spread some information that is so erroneous as to practically be fiction. Sadly, information of this type is, once published on the web, virtually impossible to correct and has been taken as "fact" by some readers and perpetuated in other postings. This type of erroneous, even ridiculous, information can be attributed to incomplete or very poor research, the acceptance of contemporary political attacks as fact, and fantastic leaps to conclusions. Not all such errors are harmful. An example of the harmless would be the inclusion of Dan Showalter in a list of "Prominent Arizona Confederates" on the website of the Arizona Division of the Sons of Confederate Veterans (since corrected).[1] Although he was imprisoned for some months at Fort Yuma in California, across the Colorado River from Arizona, and commanded a regiment of the Arizona Brigade, which was intended for the recapture of that area from the Union, there is absolutely no indication, much less evidence, that Dan Showalter ever set foot in what was the Confederate Arizona Territory or what is now the State of Arizona. He certainly hoped to do so, though!

Unfortunately, the vast majority of such errors in relation to Dan Showalter do not reflect well upon him. One "California in the Civil War" internet encyclopedia article states that "one partisan warrior, Dan Showalter, once robbed a stagecoach of all its gold, leaving a receipt behind with the driver to keep him out of trouble with his bosses."[2] This is obviously the result of sloppy research or writing which added Showalter's name to an actual incident of the Civil War in California, which occurred in June 1864 while Showalter was in Texas. A group of Confederate partisans led by a man styling himself as Confederate Captain R. Henry Ingram did rob a stage from Placerville on its way to Sacramento and did leave a receipt claiming the proceeds for the Confederacy. This robbery has been accurately related many times,[3] and there is no explanation or justification for the "encyclopedia" article writer's error.

Similarly, an amateur book reviewer on amazon.com wrote about historian Alvin M. Josephy, Jr.'s *The Civil War in the American West*: "An accurate and detailed history of the Western Theater of the Civil War, which was largely forgotten by history. He was one of the first historians to fully understand the impact that California had on the war as he gives an accounting of the Federal raid on the Dan Showalter Ranch in San Bernardino on October 5, 1861."[4] Josephy wrote no such thing. On page 238 of this book, Josephy has five accurate lines about the November 1861 capture of the Showalter Party near Warner's Ranch in San Diego County. The reviewer got all of his "facts" wrong—it wasn't a raid, it wasn't the Dan Showalter Ranch, and it wasn't in San Bernardino. Josephy, a fine historian, and his book are as much maligned by this so-called reviewer as Showalter. Unfortunately, the review has been repeated on americancivilwar.com—a rather extensive website.

An interesting assertion is made on the "Jesse James Photo Album" website that Dan Showalter was among the traveling companions of the Rev. Robert Sallee James, the father of noted outlaws Frank and Jesse James, on an overland journey that the senior Mr. James made to California in 1850.[5] While this is possible, it seems highly unlikely. To begin with, family history has Dan making his first mining trip with his brother John (who is not mentioned in the "Jesse James Photo Album") prior to 1850, as cited previously in Chapter One. The "Jesse James Photo Album" website, in addition to Dan Showalter, lists another traveler in the party as "Merriman Little, [who] later won a seat in the California Assembly as a Douglas Democrat, siding with the South." In fact, no person named Merriman Little ever sat in the California Assembly and California's Douglas Democrats supported the Union and not Southern secession. When contacted, the website's author was unable to recollect his exact source(s) for Dan being part of the James party to California but did provide several possible sources.[6] All of these were checked by the authors but none of them had any mention of Showalter. This being said, a major problem is a matter of timing. Any overland trek to California by the Showalter brothers would have commenced at Independence, Missouri, adjacent to the James family's "territory" in Clay County, Missouri. The James odyssey is said to have taken from April 21 to August 1, 1850[7] (though some sources state it was in 1851[8]).

The fact of Dan Showalter's use of alcoholic beverages perhaps after the skirmish at Palmito Ranch in 1864 and definitely during the 1865 trip into Mexican exile and the circumstances leading to his death in 1866 have been reviewed in the preceding text. Some latter day writers have emphasized this aspect of his life—or even expanded upon it. In *Rebels in the Rockies: Confederate Irregulars in the Western Territories* (2014), one usually reliable researcher and author stated that Showalter was "noted for hard drinking" and that he "did have a habit of occasionally going on a drunk and shooting up the town. He was always apologetic later and carefully paid for the damage done."[9] Dan's fascinating life no doubt inspired inclusion of this gratuitous comment which has no real bearing upon the subject of the book. Unable to find any source for the statements, the authors of this book contacted the author requesting source information. The author graciously responded that he was unable to find such in his notes and that, at the time, he felt the information was "not important enough to be worth a footnote." He felt that perhaps the comment was an "aside" in a letter or book written by someone after the war and provided two possibilities.[10] Both possibilities were rechecked by the authors with no such statement found. Unless and until some contemporary or near contemporary source should be found, the "shoot up the town" reference must be considered as inaccurate.

Undoubtedly the greatest perpetuator of errors and misstatements about Showalter is a lengthy internet article by Serge Noirsain entitled "The Arizona Brigade: The Legion That Never Set Foot in the Desert."[11] The author is a Belgian historian and writer specializing in the American Civil War, who has published over one hundred articles and four books on the subject. His having received a 2001 award for his writing from the French Académie de Marine[12] and his use of footnotes in the mentioned article has given it some color of authority, and his work has been often quoted or cited. Unfortunately—at least in the case of the 4th Arizona and Dan Showalter—the article contains several errors of fact in addition to some unsupportable aspersions. Writing about the 4th Arizona, in one place he quotes from a letter by a Private William Carothers that the officers of the regiment "spend most of their time playing cards and betting on horse races." Noirsain's citation to Boyd Finch's *Confederate Pathway to the Pacific* is correct, but reading the cited work reveals that Private Carothers was not a member of the 4th Arizona, but of the 2nd Arizona! Noirsain wrote that, late in the war, because of "acts of violence on the civil population," the 4th was hunted down in northern Texas by other Confederate units. Documentation found and cited in this work shows this to actually have been Baird's second, Frontier Expedition unit. Regarding Showalter, Noirsain stated that he was "a corrupt, alcoholic, and irate California politician," and that he was "evil minded." Even Dan's opponents in the legislature and in the Unionist press never alleged that he was corrupt. It is impossible to prove that he was an alcoholic, although there is no question that, on one occasion, possibly two, he was drunk. "Irate" is possibly a reasonable construction from a few of his legislative addresses and the regiment's 1865 "valedictory." The use of "evil minded" of Showalter's conduct during the duel with Piercy indicates that Noirsain is completely ignorant of the prevalence and acceptance of dueling in California during Showalter's time and that most accounts identify Showalter as the aggrieved party in the duel. These and other errors and unsustainable opinions published as fact cast doubt upon the historicity of all of Noirsain's writings. It is to be hoped that he has not done such a "hatchet job" on the other three regiments of the Arizona Brigade.

Appendix D

Memorialization of Showalter

As mentioned in the text, if there ever was a grave marker for Dan Showalter in Mazatlan, Mexico, it has long since disappeared. There is a cenotaph, in the form of a Veteran's Administration marker, located on the grounds of Beauvoir, the Jefferson Davis Home and Presidential Library at Biloxi, Mississippi. This monument was placed, probably in the 1970s, by a distant Showalter relative, retired Air Force Reserve Colonel Clyde E. Noble, who was then a professor at Tulane University.[1] Colonel Noble used his kinship to Dan Showalter as his ancestor qualification for membership in the Military Order of the Stars and Bars (an organization of descendants of the Confederate officer corps).[2]

There is one historical marker that mentions Dan Showalter. This is the Texas Historical Marker for "Camp San Fernando" erected at Kingsville, Texas, in 1966. The text of the marker includes the sentence "On March 30, 1864, the Arizona companies of Lt. Col. Dan Showalter reached Camp San Fernando."[3]

There is a unique 150-ton granite monument located in Sam Hicks Memorial Park in Old Town Temecula, California, at Moreno Drive and Mercedes Street. Dedicated in 1969, it is named the "They Passed This Way Monument." The monument was the result of research by Temecula local historians Sam Hicks and Tom Hudson identifying persons notable in California or regional history who had a connection to the area. Dan Showalter's name is found on the main face of the monument, the eighth name listed and immediately following that of explorer John C. Frémont and two above that of California Governor J.G. Downey. In 1970, Hicks and Hudson authored a small book, *They Passed This Way: Biographical Sketches, Tales of Historic Temecula Valley at the Crossroads of California's Southern Immigrant Trail*, explaining the local connection of those named on the monument. It includes two paragraphs about Showalter.[4]

In the early 2000s, Los Angeles' General John Bell Hood Camp 1208 of the Sons of Confederate Veterans sought permission from the City of El Monte, California, to place a plaque in Pioneer Park on Santa Anita Avenue in that city. This memorial plaque would have commemorated the "El Monte Battalion" organized in El Monte, in 1861, by Dan Showalter and thus would have included his name. Although such a plaque would have revealed a now largely unknown aspect of El Monte's history, as revealed in the text of this work, the story of the battalion is based upon early sensationalized press reports and later assumptions based upon them. The City of El Monte declined to grant permission for the memorial plaque.[5]

There is no historical monument or plaque at or near the site of the capture of the Showalter Party near Minter's Ranch in northern San Diego County, California. This event has generally been identified as the "only" or "closest thing to" a Civil War battle in California. Recognizing this significance, a local camp of the Sons of Union Veterans of the Civil War at one time began working for a California State Historical Marker to commemorate it. Hopefully, one day, there will be a marker commemorating the Affair at Minter's Ranch and Dan Showalter's roll in it.

The most notable battle of Showalter and the 4th Arizona was their two-day fight against both Federal and Mexican Liberal forces at Palmito Ranch, Texas, in September 1864. There is a Texas historical marker at this site, but it is in commemoration of the May 1865 engagement there as "the last land engagement of the Civil War." The earlier battle is not mentioned,[6] and the greater significance of the May 1865 event makes it seem doubtful that Showalter's and the 4th's activities there ever will be.

The Drum Barracks Civil War Museum in Wilmington (part of Los Angeles), California, occupies the last remaining building of the Union Civil War barracks there. From November 2011 through August 2012, it maintained a temporary exhibit, "Dan Showalter: California's Arch Rebel." Researcher and co-curator of this exhibit was co-author Robert Arconti.[7] On November 19–20, 2011, a smaller version of this exhibit was displayed at Vail Ranch in Temecula, California, in conjunction with reenactments of the duel with Piercy and the capture of the Showalter Party at Minter's Ranch.[8]

There are apparently no sites or roadways named after Dan Showalter. Of the numerous streets, drives, places, and avenues with the name "Showalter," only

The "They Passed This Way" Monument in a downtown Temecula, California, park includes the names of fifty-six notable individual who passed through the area during frontier times. The name of Dan Showalter is found on its front side immediately beneath that of John C. Frémont and two above that of California Governor John C. Downey (photographed 2014 by Gene C. Armistead).

two seemed possibly to have been in localities where they might have been named after him. A "Showalter Court" in Rancho Cucamonga, California, near El Monte, turned out to have been named for a Jacob Schowalter family that had moved to that area in 1911.[9] A better possibility is "Showalter Road," a short, two-home road proceeding south off of Pauba Road near the Temecula Library. The City of Temecula has no records relating to its naming since the name was already in existence when the city was incorporated in 1989. The fact that Dan Showalter's name is on the "They Passed This Way" Monument argues for it, but there was also a prominent photographer by the name of Showalter resident in Temecula during the last half of the twentieth century. Still, it would be nice to think that this small road at least perpetuates his memory.

Chapter Notes

Introduction

1. *Official Records of the Union and Confederate Armies in the War of the Rebellion*, Series 1, Vol. 50, Part II, 458. Hereafter cited as *OR-A*, Series-Volume-Part (if any), page(s).
2. Jerry D. Thompson, "A Duel in the Desert: Henry Skillman and the Union Army in the Trans-Pecos," draft for "Drama in the Desert: The Hunt for Henry Skillman in the TransPecos, 1862–1864," *Password*, Vol. 37, No. 3 (1992) of El Paso Historical Society, citing reports of Capt. A.H. French on Apr. 14, 1864, and May 5, 1864, from Letters Received, Dept. of New Mexico, Records Group 393, National Archives 7 Records Administration. Courtesy Jerry D. Thompson. See also Jefferson Morgenthaler, *The River Has Never Divided Us: A Border History of La Junta de Los Rios* (Austin: University of Texas Press, 2004), 113–114.
3. *OR-A*, 1-50-II, 1078.
4. Showalter to Anna Forman, dated Feb. 7, 1864, at San Antonio, *OR-A*, 1-50-II, 1079–1080. Hereafter cited as *OR-A* Letter to A. Forman.

Chapter One

1. Wilmer L. Kerns, "Three Showalter Immigrants," n.d. but apparently 1930s, accessed via http://www.salisburtypa.com/jacobshowalter.htm, accessed June 19, 2013. Hereafter cited as Kerns. W.J. Showalter, "Showalter Family Originally Came from Switzerland," clipping dated Aug. 7, 1933, from, apparently, a Pennsylvania newspaper, from files of Dr. Susan M. Showalter Kudlik of Pittsburgh, PA.
2. "Report of the Commission to Locate Sites of the Frontier Forts of Pennsylvania," USGenWebArchives Pennsylvania, http://usgwarchives.net/pa/1pa/1picts/fontier forts/frontierforts/htm, accessed May 25, 2013.
3. Kerns.
4. Susan M. Showalter Kudlik in telephone interview with author Arconti, Apr. 28, 2013. John's middle initial is sometimes seen in family records as "M." or "A." but these are presumed to be transcription errors. Likewise, his birth date is given variously as 1796 or 1798 in family records, but that stated is most common.
5. 1810 Federal Census of the United States, Fayette County, PA.
6. Showalter family records in possession of Edward Showalter, Latrobe, PA; Robert L. Showalter, Doylestown, PA; Susan M. Showalter Kudlik, Pittsburgh, PA.
7. Showalter family records in possession of Edward Showalter, Latrobe, PA; Robert L. Showalter, Doylestown, PA; Susan M. Showalter Kudlik, Pittsburgh, PA.
8. 1860 Federal Census, Mariposa County, California, Township 1 (Hornitos P.O.), Page 46, Dwelling 529.
9. Burris E. Esplen, IV, Associate Archivist, Diocese of Pittsburg, email to author Arconti, dated June 21, 2012.
10. *OR-A*, 1-50-I, 38.
11. Clarence C. Clendenen, "Dan Showalter: California Secessionist," *California Historical Society Quarterly*, Vol. 40, No. 4 (Dec. 1961), 317–318. Hereafter cited as Clendenen.
12. Col. Clyde E. Noble (USAF Ret.), letter to author Armistead, May 22, 2013.
13. Cenotaph of Daniel Showalter, Beauvoir, the Jefferson Davis Home and Presidential Library, Biloxi, MS.
14. Samuel T. Wiley, *Biographical and Historical Cyclopedia of Westmoreland County, Pennsylvania* (Philadelphia: John M. Gresham & Co., 1890), 347–348. Hereafter cited as Wiley. Unpublished family records in possession of Robert L. Showalter, Doylestown, PA.
15. Regina Seeley, letter to Edward Showalter, July 1, 1978. Original letter in possession of Edward Showalter, Latrobe, PA. Copy courtesy Edward Showalter. Hereafter cited as Seeley letter.
16. Jerome Oetgen, *An American Abbot: Boniface Wimmer, O.S.B.* (Latrobe, PA: Archabbey Press, 1976), 71.
17. "The Monastery Letter," from *The Illustrated History of St. Vincent Archabbey, Latrobe, Pa.* (Latrobe, PA: St. Vincent Archabbey, n.d.), http://noel.men.org/MonasteryLetter.htm, accessed May 26, 2013.
18. John Boucher, *History of Westmoreland County, Pennsylvania* (New York: Lewis Publishing Co., 1906), 311–318.
19. Oetgen, 71.
20. Seeley letter.
21. Unpublished family records in possession of Robert L. Showalter, Doylestown, PA.
22. Seeley letter.
23. "Klondike at Home," *Davenport Daily Leader* (Oct. 3, 1898).
24. Wiley, 347–348. Unpublished family records in possession of Robert L. Showalter, Doylestown, PA.
25. Hugh A. Gorley, *The Loyal Californians of 1861* (a paper prepared and read before the California Commandery of the Military

Order of the Loyal Legion of the United States, Jan. 31, 1893). Hereafter cited as Gorley, *Loyal Californians*.

26. James Hadden, *A History of Uniontown* (Uniontown, PA: 1913), 483–518.

27. Clendenen, 310.

28. Seeley letter.

29. Unpublished letter, Dan Showalter to Sam O'Connor, Nov. 13, 1852, from Showalter family records, courtesy Robert L. Showalter. Hereafter cited as Letter to O'Connor.

30. Notes by Sister Anastasia Showalter in Showalter family records in possession of Susan M. Showalter, Pittsburgh, PA.

31. Daniel Cooledge Fletcher, *Reminiscences of California and the Civil War* (Ayer, MA: Press of Huntley S. Turner, 1894), 15–16. Hereafter cited as Fletcher.

32. "The Compass: New York Passenger Information," Immigrant Ships Transcribers Guild, http://immigrantships.net/newcompass/pass_arrivals_usa/usapasslist_arrivals/newyork.html, accessed July 8, 2013.

33. "User: Gatoclass/SB/SS Illinois (1851)," *Wikipedia, the Free Encyclopedia*, http:en.wikipedia.org/wiki/User:Gatoclass/SB/SS_Illinois_(1851), accessed July 8, 2013. "News of the Morning," *New York Times* (Nov. 13, 1852).

34. Fletcher, 18–19.

35. Seeley letter.

36. John Haskell Kemble, "The Gold Rush by Panama, 1848–1851," *Pacific Historical Review*, Vol. 18, No. 1, 49. Hereafter cited as Kemble.

37. Kemble, 46.

38. Kemble, 49.

39. Fletcher, 21.

40. Ulysses S. Grant, *Personal Memoirs of U.S. Grant*, Vol. 1 (New York: Charles L. Webster & Company, 1885), 194. Hereafter cited as Grant.

41. Kemble, 50.

42. Kemble, 55.

43. Kemble, 51.

44. Fletcher, 21.

45. Grant, 195.

46. Grant, 198.

47. Kemble, 51.

48. "News of the Morning," *New York Times* (Nov. 13, 1852).

49. Kemble, 52–53.

50. Fletcher, 24.

51. Mark A. Evans, San Francisco, Aug. 8, 1850, to his brother near Philadelphia, San Francisco History Center, San Francisco Public Library, cited in Lynn A. Bonfield, "When Money Was Necessary to Make Dreams Come True: The Cost of the Trip from Vermont to California via Panama," *Vermont History*, Vol. 76, No. 2 (Summer/Fall 2008), 140. Hereafter cited as Bonfield.

52. Kemble, 53.

53. Horace C. Snow, *"Dear Charlie" Letters Recording the Everyday Life of a Young 1854 Miner as Set Forth by Your Friend, Horace Snow With Suitable Gold Rush Engravings* (Agua Fria, CA: Mariposa County Historical Society, 1979), 4B. Hereafter cited as Snow.

54. Kemble, 51.

55. "Crossing the Isthmus of Panama," *Otago Witness* (New Zealand, Nov. 19, 1853), 3, http://paperspast.natlib.govt.nz/egi-bin/paperspast?a+d&d=OW18531119.2.10&1, accessed July 8, 2013.

56. Snow, 4B.

57. Fletcher, 23.

58. Kemble, 53.

59. Fletcher, 25.

60. Kemble, 56.

61. Fletcher, 26–27.

62. Fletcher, 28.

63. *OR-A*, 1–50-I, 38.

64. Louis J. Rasmussen, *San Francisco Passenger Ship Lists*, Vol. 4 (Colma, CA: San Francisco Historic Record & Genealogy Bulletin, 1964), 226–227.

65. "*Winfield Scott* Vessel History," Channel Islands National Marine Sanctuary, http://channelislands.noaa.gov/shipwreck/dbase/cinms/winfieldscott1.html, accessed July 17, 2013.

66. Bonfield, 135.

67. Kemble, 55.

68. Fletcher, 17.

69. "California, Australia, &c," *Alexandria Gazette & Virginia Advertiser* (Apr. 8, 1853), 2.

70. In all places where dollar amounts are cited in this text, http://www.measuringworth.com has been used for calculation of the 2013 purchasing power value also shown.

71. Bonfield, 135, n146.

72. Letter to O'Connor.

Chapter Two

1. 1860 Federal Census of California, Mariposa County, 670. *Mariposa Gazette* (June 1, 1861), 2.

2. "Mother Mariposa—the Formation of Merced County," Mariposa County History and Genealogy, http://www.mariposaresearch.net/mother.html, accessed July 29, 2013.

3. Newell D. Chamberlain, *The Call of Gold: True Tales on the Gold Rush to Yosemite* (Mariposa, CA: Gazette Press, 1936). 20. Hereafter cited as Chamberlain.

4. Chamberlain, 20.

5. Chamberlain, 145.

6. Chamberlain, 20.

7. Chamberlain, 149.

8. Chamberlain, 21–22.

9. Jean-Nicolas Perlot (translated by Helen Harding Bretnor, edited by Howard R. Lamar), *Gold Seeker: Adventures of a Belgian Argonaut during the Gold Rush Years* (New Haven: Yale University Press, 1985), 95.

10. Chamberlain, 23.

11. Chamberlain, 20–21.

12. "Volume III—Technical Background Report," *County of Mariposa General Plan*, http://ca-mariposacounty.civicplur.com/DocumentCenter/Home/View/2013, 11–4, accessed July 31, 2013. Hereafter cited as *Mariposa Co. General Plan*.

13. Leonard L. Richards, *The California Gold Rush and the Coming of the Civil War* (New York: Alfred A. Knopf, 2007), Kindle edition location 1392–1424.

14. James J. Rawls and Richard J. Orsi, eds., *A Golden State: Mining and Economic Development in Gold Rush California* (Berkeley: University of California Press, 1999), 63.

15. C. Hart Merriam, "Distribution and Classification of the Mewan Stock of California," *American Anthropologist*, New Series 9 (1907), 347.

16. John Muir, *My First Summer in the Sierra* (Boston: Houghton Mifflin, 1911), 17–18.

17. *Mariposa Co. General Plan*, 11–18.

18. Hubert Howe Bancroft, *History of California*, Vol. VI: 1848–1859 (San Francisco: The History Company, 1890), 377–378 fn 37.

19. Snow, vii.

20. Snow, 1.

21. Snow, 13.

22. Snow, 19, 112.

23. Snow, 53.

24. Snow, 75.

25. Snow, 11, 80.

26. Isaac in the *Sacramento Daily Transcript* (Jan. 14, 1851), 1; Jacob in the *Sacramento Daily Union* (Sept. 8, 1852); John in the *Sacramento Daily Union* (July 14, 1856). Hereafter cited as *Union*.

27. *Union* (June 7, 1858), 1.

28. San Francisco *Bulletin* (Sept. 16, 1858), 2.

29. *Union* (July 14, 1856).
30. *Mining & Scientific Press* (San Francisco, Jan. 19, 1867), 38.
31. "Calaveras Co. CA Death Index S," 34, http://calaverasgenealogy.com/uploads/Deaths_S.pdf, last updated Jan. 24, 2012, accessed Jan. 7, 2014.
32. BLM Serial No. CACAAA 114165, United States Department of the Interior, Bureau of Land Management Records, http://www.glorecords.blm.gov/results/default.aspx?search, accessed Jan. 7, 2014.
33. "Collection of Minerals from the States of California and Nevada," *Catalogue of a Cabinet of Minerals Presented for Exhibition at the Industrial Fair of the Mechanics' Institute by Capt. J.M. Aiken of Coulterville, Mariposa Co., Cal.* (San Francisco: Mining and Scientific Press Book and Job Print, 1865), 3.
34. Jill Cossley Batt, *The Last of the California Rangers* (New York: Funk & Wagnalls, 1928), 219.
35. *Daily Alta California* (San Francisco, Nov. 15, 1856), 2. Hereafter cited as *Alta*.
36. "November 4, 1856, General Election," *JoinCalifornia Election History for the State of California*. http://www.joincalifornia.com/election/1856-11-04, accessed June 24, 2013.
37. "The Legislature," *Los Angeles Star* (Jan. 3, 1857), 2. Hereafter cited as *Star*.
38. "A Short Session," *Union* (Jan. 1, 1856), 3.
39. *A Journal of the Eighth Session of the Assembly of the State of California Begun on the Fifth Day of January One Thousand Eight Hundred and Fifty-seven and Ended on the Twenty-ninth Day of April One Thousand Eight Hundred and Fifty-seven at the City of Sacramento* (Sacramento: James Allen, Printer, 1857), 9. Hereafter cited as *1857 Assembly Journal*.
40. *1857 Assembly Journal*, 10–11.
41. *1857 Assembly Journal*, 12–16.
42. "Dr. Scott, of California," *New York Times* (Oct. 16, 1861). Hereafter cited as *NY Times*.
43. *1857 Assembly Journal*, 18–20.
44. *1857 Assembly Journal*, 93.
45. *1857 Assembly Journal*, 20–69.
46. *1857 Assembly Journal*, 69–70.
47. *1857 Assembly Journal*, 72–89.
48. *1857 Assembly Journal*, 94.
49. *1857 Assembly Journal*, 96–97.
50. William F. Thompson, Jr., "M.S. Latham and the Senatorial Controversy of 1857," *California Historical Society Quarterly*, Vol. 32, No. 2 (June 1953), 145–147.

51. James O. Meara, *Broderick and Gwin, the Most Extraordinary Contest for a Seat in the Senate of the United States Ever Known: A Brief History of Early Politics in California* (San Francisco: Bacon & Co., Publishers, 1881), 170–172. Hereafter cited as Meara.
52. *1857 Assembly Journal*, 98–100.
53. Meara, 173.
54. *1857 Assembly Journal*, 101.
55. *1857 Assembly Journal*, 103.
56. Meara, 181–182.
57. *1857 Assembly Journal*, 106–107.
58. *1857 Assembly Journal*, 134.
59. *1857 Assembly Journal*, 139–140.
60. *Journal of the Eighth Session of the Senate of the State of California Begun on the Fifth Day of January, One Thousand Eight Hundred and Fifty-Seven, and Ended on the Twenty-Ninth Day of April, One Thousand Eight Hundred and Fifty-Seven, at the City of Sacramento* (Sacramento: James Allen, State Printer, 1857), 122. Hereafter cited as *1857 Senate Journal*.
61. *1857 Assembly Journal*, 141.
62. *1857 Senate Journal*, 124.
63. *Alta* (Jan. 20, 1857), 2.
64. "Views from the Capital," *Marysville Daily Herald* (Jan. 21, 1857), 2. Hereafter cited as *Daily Herald*.
65. "The Vote to Adjourn, etc.," *Union* (Jan. 21, 1857), 2.
66. "Too True," *Union* (Jan. 22, 1857), 1.
67. *1857 Assembly Journal*, 141.
68. *1857 Assembly Journal*, 158.
69. *1857 Assembly Journal*, 189–190.
70. *1857 Assembly Journal*, 222–223.
71. *1857 Assembly Journal*, 236.
72. *1857 Assembly Journal*, 240.
73. *1857 Assembly Journal*, 251–252.
74. *1857 Assembly Journal*, 305.
75. *1857 Assembly Journal*, 318–319.
76. "The State Treasurer," *Star* (Feb. 28, 1857), 2.
77. *1857 Assembly Journal*, 532.
78. *1857 Senate Journal*, 748.
79. *1857 Assembly Journal*, 320.
80. *1857 Assembly Journal*, 341.
81. *1857 Assembly Journal*, 344.
82. *1857 Assembly Journal*, 358.
83. *1857 Assembly Journal*, 497–498.
84. *1857 Assembly Journal*, 360.
85. *1857 Assembly Journal*, 366.
86. *1857 Assembly Journal*, 425.
87. *1857 Assembly Journal*, 432.

88. *1857 Assembly Journal*, 485.
89. *1857 Assembly Journal*, 458–459.
90. *1857 Assembly Journal*, 477.
91. *1857 Assembly Journal*, 488.
92. *1857 Assembly Journal*, 519.
93. *1857 Assembly Journal*, 534–537.
94. *1857 Assembly Journal*, 544–545.
95. *1857 Assembly Journal*, 558.
96. *1857 Assembly Journal*, 564–567.
97. *1857 Assembly Journal*, 569.
98. *1857 Assembly Journal*, 578–579.
99. *1857 Assembly Journal*, 650–651.
100. *1857 Assembly Journal*, 677–678.
101. *1857 Assembly Journal*, 684.
102. *1857 Assembly Journal*, 699–700.
103. *1857 Assembly Journal*, 708.
104. *1857 Assembly Journal*, 709–710.
105. *1857 Assembly Journal*, 710. "State Prison" and "What Does it Mean," *Union* (Apr. 11, 1857), 2.
106. "Legislative Proceedings," *Union* (Apr. 11, 1857), 1; "News of the Morning," *Union* (Apr. 11, 1857), 2.
107. *1857 Assembly Journal*, 714.
108. "Legislative Proceedings … Assembly…," *Union* (Apr. 11, 1857), 1.
109. "State Prison," *Union* (Apr. 11, 1857), 2.
110. "Legislative Proceedings … Assembly…," *Union* (Apr. 13, 1857), 1, 4.
111. *1857 Senate Journal*, 802.
112. *1857 Senate Journal*, 911.
113. Quis, "Letter from Sacramento," *Alta* (Apr. 11, 1857), 1.
114. "News from the Capital," *Daily Herald* (Apr. 14, 1857), 2.
115. *1857 Assembly Journal*, 716.
116. *1857 Assembly Journal*, 720.
117. *1857 Assembly Journal*, 788–790.
118. "News from the Capital," *Daily Herald* (Apr. 11, 1857), 2.
119. *1857 Assembly Journal*, 823–824.
120. *1857 Assembly Journal*, 802–803.
121. *1857 Assembly Journal*, 793–794.
122. *1857 Assembly Journal*, 819–820.
123. *1857 Assembly Journal*, 858.
124. *1857 Assembly Journal*, 872–874.
125. "Charles A. 'Charley' King," Old City Cemetery Committee, Inc. (Sacramento). http://www.oldcitycemetery.com/CharlesAKing.htm, accessed 2013.

126. "Complimentary Benefit to Mr. George Ryer," *Union* (Mar. 2, 1857), 2.
127. "Last Hour of the Session," *Union* (May 2, 1857), 1.
128. *1857 Assembly Journal*, 876–877.
129. Quis, "Letter from Sacramento," *Alta* (May 1, 1857), 2.
130. "Last Hour of the Session," *Union* (May 2, 1857), 1.
131. "News from the Capital," *Daily Herald* (Apr. 30, 1857), 2.
132. "The Late Legislature," *Star* (May 16, 1857), 2.
133. Connie Zheng, "Chinese American Heroes—Attorneys," Chinese American Heroes, http://www.chineseamericanheroes.org/history, accessed Sept. 10, 2014.
134. "Mokelumne Hill Convention," *Union* (Apr. 27, 1857), 2.
135. "The Wagon Road Movements," Part Two of Chapter III, "Early Governments in Nevada," *The Nevada Observer: Nevada's Online State News Journal* (Apr. 4, 2006), http://www.nevadaobserver.com/Reading%20Room%20Documents/Early%20Governments/, accessed June 12, 2013.
136. Sonoma *Union Democrat* (May 9, 1857), http://www.newspaperabstracts.com/link.php?id=12909, accessed June 12, 2013.
137. http://www.measuringworth.com, accessed Nov. 23, 2013.
138. Thomas Frederick Howard, *Sierra Crossing: First Roads to California* (Berkley: University of California Press, 1998), 143.
139. "Democratic County Convention," *Mariposa Democrat* (July 2, 1857), http://www.mariposaresearch.com.net/1857DEMCON.html, accessed Mar. 31, 2013.
140. "The Democratic Convention To-Day," *Union* (July 14, 1857), 2. "Democratic State Convention," *Union* (July 15, 1857), 2.
141. "The Convention—Its Labors," *Union* (July 16,1857), 2.
142. "Democratic State Convention—Second Day," *Union* (July 16, 1857), 2.
143. "A Swift Express Messenger," *Alta* (Sept. 13, 1857). 2.
144. "Election Returns," *Union* (Sept. 19, 1857), 3.
145. Paula Mitchell Marks, *Precious Dust: The Saga of the Western Gold Rushes* (Omaha: University of Nebraska Press, 1998), 159.
146. "Denver Quicksilver Mining Company" (notice), *Union* (Feb. 4, 1862), 3, and (Feb. 18, 1862), 3.
147. *Union* (Dec. 13, 1875).
148. Snow, 110.

149. Daniel Cornford, "We All Live More Like Brutes Than Humans," in James J. Rawls, Richard J. Orsi and Marlene Smith-Baranzini, eds., *A Golden State: Mining and Economic Development in Gold Rush California* (Berkeley: University of California Press, 1999), 93. Hereafter cited as Cornford.
150. Cornford, 82.
151. Cornford, 93.
152. "Democratic Lecompton Convention. First Day," *Union* (June 23, 1859), 1.
153. "Democratic Lecompton Convention. Second Day," *Union* (June 24, 1859), 1.
154. "Democratic Lecompton Convention, Third Day," *Union* (June 25, 1859), 1.
155. "Lecompton Gubernatorial Delegation," *Union* (June 16, 1859), 2.
156. Cornford, 84–87.
157. United States 1860 Federal Census of California, Mariposa County, Township No. 1, page 48.
158. Richard Winger, "What Are Ballots For?" *Libertarian Party News*, Extra Research Edition (1988), http://webarchive.org/web20110 61145955/http://www.ballot-access.org/winger/wabf.html, accessed Nov. 21, 2013.
159. "Dave Leip's Atlas of U.S. Presidential Elections—1860 Presidential General Election Data," http://uselectionatlas.org/RESULTS/date.php?year=1860&datatype=national&def=1&f=0&off, accessed Mar. 24, 2013.
160. "1860 California Election Returns by County," https://docs.google.com/document/pub?id=lo6st-iYDzAGfWghdjRs4PNoX MhaDIp4IIkGw26kTTio, accessed Mar. 24, 2013. Hereafter cited as "1860 California Election Returns by County."
161. "Mariposa Nominations," *Union* (Sept. 11, 1860), 4. *Visalia Weekly Delta* (Sept. 15, 1860), 2.
162. "United States presidential election in California, 1860," *Wikipedia, the Free Encyclopedia*, accessed Mar. 24, 2013.
163. "1860 California Election Returns by County."
164. "The Legislature Elect," *Star* (Dec. 8, 1860), 2. "The Next Legislature," *Union* (Dec. 29, 1860), 2.
165. M. David DeSoucy, *San Bernardino County Sheriff's Department* (Charleston, SC: Arcadia Publishing, 2006), 14.
166. Morris Katz (edited by Norton B. Stern), "Memoirs of Morris Katz—San Bernardino Pioneer," *Western States Jewish History*, Vol. 1, Issue 1 (Oct. 1969), 14–15, http://www/wsjhistory.org/Volume%20One.htm, accessed July 4, 2014. Hereafter cited as Katz.
167. "San Bernardino," *Star* (Nov. 17, 1860), 2.
168. Katz, 14–15.
169. "The Campaign in San Bernardino," *Star* (Sept. 1, 1860), 2.
170. Katz, 15.
171. Luther A. Ingersoll, *Ingersoll's Century Annals of San Bernardino County 1769 to 1904 ...* (Los Angeles: Luther A. Ingersoll, 1904), 344.
172. "The Next Legislature," *Union* (Nov. 23, 1860), 2.
173. "1860 California Election Returns by County."
174. Untitled article, *Mariposa Gazette* (Jan. 8, 1861), 3. Hereafter cited as *Gazette*.

Chapter Three

1. *Journal of the House of Assembly of California at the Twelfth Session of the Legislature Begun on the Seventh Day of January, 1861, and Ended on the Twentieth Day of May, 1861, at the City of Sacramento* (Sacramento: C. T. Botts, State Printer, 1861), 5–6. Hereafter cited as *1861 Assembly Journal*.
2. *1861 Assembly Journal*, 6–7.
3. *1861 Assembly Journal*, 7–10; *Union* (Jan. 8, 1861), 6–7.
4. *1861 Assembly Journal*, 10–19; *Union* (Jan. 9, 1861), 1.
5. *1861 Assembly Journal*, 19–29; *Union* (Jan. 10, 1861), 2.
6. "News of the Morning," *Union* (Jan. 11, 1861), 2.
7. *1861 Assembly Journal*, 29–42; *Union* (Jan. 11, 1861), 1.
8. *1861 Assembly Journal*, 42–47; *Union* (Jan. 12, 1861), 1.
9. *1861 Assembly Journal*, 49–50; *Union* (Jan. 14, 1861), 1.
10. *1861 Assembly Journal*, 50–51; *Union* (Jan. 14, 1861), 1.
11. *1861 Assembly Journal*, 51; *Union* (Jan. 14, 1861), 1. In reference to the Bulkhead Bill: *Union* (Apr. 10, 1860), 2; *NY Times* (May 14 and 15, 1860).
12. *1861 Assembly Journal*, 51–52; *Union* (Jan. 14, 1861), 1.
13. *Union* (Jan. 15, 1861), 1.
14. *Union* (Jan. 15, 1861), 1.
15. *1861 Assembly Journal*, 52–68; *Union* (Jan. 16, 1861), 1.
16. *1861 Assembly Journal*, 68–70; *Union* (Jan. 16, 1861), 1.
17. *1861 Assembly Journal*, 71; *Union* (Jan. 17, 1861), 1.

18. *1861 Assembly Journal*, 71–79; *Union* (Jan. 17, 1861), 1.
19. *1861 Assembly Journal*, 80.
20. *1861 Assembly Journal*, 80–88; *Union* (Jan. 18, 1861), 1.
21. *1861 Assembly Journal*, 88–89.
22. *1861 Assembly Journal*, 89–91; *Union* (Jan. 19, 1861), 1.
23. *Union* (Jan. 19, 1861), 1.
24. *1861 Assembly Journal*, 131–133.
25. *1861 Assembly Journal*, 133–135.
26. *Union* (Jan. 21, 1861), 1.
27. *Union* (Jan. 22, 1861), 4.
28. *1861 Assembly Journal*, 138–143.
29. *1861 Assembly Journal*, 144–148; *Union* (Jan. 24, 1861).
30. *The Bay of San Francisco: The Metropolis of the Pacific Coast and Its Suburban Cities, a History*, Vol. 2 (Chicago: Lewis Publishing Company, 1892), 425.
31. *1861 Assembly Journal*, 153–155; *Union* (Jan. 25, 1861), 1, 4.
32. *1861 Assembly Journal*, 156–157.
33. *1861 Assembly Journal*, 157–169.
34. *Union* (Jan. 26, 1861), 1.
35. *1861 Assembly Journal*, 172; *Union* (Jan. 26, 1861), 1.
36. *Union* (Jan. 28, 1861), 1.
37. *1861 Assembly Journal*, 173–174.
38. *1861 Assembly Journal*, 177.
39. *1861 Assembly Journal*, 182; *Union* (Jan. 31, 1861), 1.
40. *1861 Assembly Journal*, 183.
41. *Union* (Jan. 31, 1861), 1.
42. *1861 Assembly Journal*, 190–191; *Union* (Feb. 2, 1861), 1.
43. *1861 Assembly Journal*, 193–194.
44. *1861 Assembly Journal*, 194.
45. *1861 Assembly Journal*, 195–196.
46. *1861 Assembly Journal*, 197–212.
47. *Union* (Feb. 9, 1861), 1.
48. *1861 Assembly Journal*, 216–220.
49. *1861 Assembly Journal*, 223–224.
50. *1861 Assembly Journal*, 226–227.
51. *1861 Assembly Journal*, 228–231.
52. *Union* (Feb. 14, 1861), 1.
53. *1861 Assembly Journal*, 234.
54. *1861 Assembly Journal*, 235.
55. *1861 Assembly Journal*, 238.
56. *Union* (Feb. 15, 1861), 1.
57. *1861 Assembly Journal*, 241–244.
58. *1861 Assembly Journal*, 245–247.
59. *1861 Assembly Journal*, 249–250.
60. *1861 Assembly Journal*, 252.
61. *1861 Assembly Journal*, 261–262.
62. *Union* (Feb. 19, 1861), 1.
63. "Douglas and Breckinridge Compromise Meeting," *Union* (Feb. 20, 1861), 2.
64. "Democratic Fusion Meeting," *Union* (Feb. 27, 1861), 2.
65. *1861 Assembly Journal*, 273–274; *Union* (Feb. 27, 1861), 1.
66. *1861 Assembly Journal*, 275–278.
67. *1861 Assembly Journal*, 285.
68. *Union* (Mar. 1, 1861), 1.
69. *Alta* (Mar. 1, 1861), 1.
70. *Union* (Mar. 2, 1861), 1.
71. *Union* (Mar. 4, 1861), 4.
72. *Union* (Mar. 5, 1861), 1.
73. *Union* (Mar. 5, 1861), 4.
74. *Union* (Mar. 7, 1861), 4.
75. *Union* (Mar. 8, 1861), 1.
76. *Union* (Mar. 9, 1861), 1.
77. *1861 Assembly Journal*, 326–327.
78. *1861 Assembly Journal*, 327–328.
79. *1861 Assembly Journal*, 329–330.
80. *1861 Assembly Journal*, 330–331.
81. *1861 Assembly Journal*, 331.
82. *1861 Assembly Journal*, 332.
83. *Alta* (Mar. 10, 1861), 1.
84. *Union* (Mar. 11, 1861), 1.
85. *1861 Assembly Journal*, 333–336.
86. *1861 Assembly Journal*, 336–348.
87. *1861 Assembly Journal*, 348.
88. *1861 Assembly Journal*, 351–352.
89. *1861 Assembly Journal*, 353.
90. *1861 Assembly Journal*, 354.
91. *1861 Assembly Journal*, 355–369.
92. *1861 Assembly Journal*, 370.
93. "No United States Senator," *Alta* (Mar. 13, 1861), 2.
94. "A Remarkable Case of Fusion," *Union* (Mar. 13, 1861), 4.
95. *1861 Assembly Journal*, 373–385.
96. "The Horace Smith Case," *Union* (May 7, 1861), 3.
97. *Union* (Mar. 14, 1861), 1.
98. *1861 Assembly Journal*, 389–394; *Union* (Mar. 14, 1861), 1.
99. *Alta* (Mar. 25, 1861), 2.
100. *1861 Assembly Journal*, 398–404.
101. *1861 Assembly Journal*, 409–410; *Union* (Mar. 16, 1861), 8.
102. *1861 Assembly Journal*, 410–416.
103. *Alta* (Mar. 17, 1861), 1.
104. *1861 Assembly Journal*, 429–432; *Union* (Mar. 20, 1861), 1.
105. *1861 Assembly Journal*, 432–438; *Union* (Mar. 20, 1861), 1.
106. "John Nugent" (obituary), *Union* (Mar. 30, 1880), 2.
107. *Alta* (Mar. 21, 1861), 1.
108. *1861 Assembly Journal*, 438–453; *Alta* (Mar. 22, 1861), 2; *Union* (Mar. 22, 1861), 1.
109. "The Senatorial Imbroglio," *Union* (Mar. 22, 1861), 4.
110. *Alta* (Mar. 23, 1861), 1.
111. *NY Times* (Apr. 19, 1861).
112. *1861 Assembly Journal*, 457–473.
113. *1861 Assembly Journal*, 473–474.
114. *1861 Assembly Journal*, 475–487.
115. *1861 Assembly Journal*, 487–501.
116. *1861 Assembly Journal*, 502–503.
117. *1861 Assembly Journal*, 505.
118. *1861 Assembly Journal*, 505–509.
119. *1861 Assembly Journal*, 510–528.
120. *1861 Assembly Journal*, 531.
121. *1861 Assembly Journal*, 531–548.
122. *1861 Assembly Journal*, 551–560.
123. *1861 Assembly Journal*, 560–578.
124. *Alta* (May 13, 1861), 1.
125. *Alta* (Mar. 29, 1861), 1.
126. *1861 Assembly Journal*, 578.
127. *1861 Assembly Journal*, 588–589.
128. *1861 Assembly Journal*, 603; *Union* (Apr. 3, 1861), 1.
129. *1861 Assembly Journal*, 604–605; *Union* (Apr. 3, 1861), 1.
130. *1861 Assembly Journal*, 606–611; *Union* (Apr. 3, 1861), 1, 4.
131. *1861 Assembly Journal*, 614–615.
132. *1861 Assembly Journal*, 616–624.
133. *1861 Assembly Journal*, 624–634.
134. *1861 Assembly Journal*, 639.
135. *1861 Assembly Journal*, 648–650.
136. *Union* (Apr. 12, 1861), 1.
137. *Mariposa Gazette* (Apr. 16, 1861), 2.
138. *1861 Assembly Journal*, 689–691; *Union* (Apr. 13, 1861), 1.
139. *1861 Assembly Journal*, 689–690; *Union* (Apr. 13, 1861), 1.
140. *The Statutes of California Passed at the Twelfth Session of the Legislature, 1861: begun Monday the seventh day of January, and ended on Monday, the twentieth day of*

May (Sacramento: Charles T. Botts, State Printer, 1861), 148–149.
   141. *1861 Assembly Journal*, 705–707.
   142. *1861 Assembly Journal*, 709–713.
   143. *Union* (Apr. 18, 1861), 1.
   144. *1861 Assembly Journal*, 732–733.
   145. *Union* (Apr. 23, 1861), 4.
   146. *1861 Assembly Journal*, 768; *Union* (Apr. 27, 1861), 1.
   147. *1816 Assembly Journal*, 771.
   148. *Union* (Apr. 27, 1861), 1.
   149. *Union* (Apr. 27, 1861), 1.
   150. *1861 Assembly Journal*, 772.
   151. *Union* (Apr. 27, 1861), 1.
   152. *Union* (Apr. 29, 2862), 1.
   153. *1861 Assembly Journal*, 781–783.
   154. *Union* (May 1, 1861), 1; *Union* (May 2, 1861), 1.
   155. *Union* (May 1, 1861), 1; *Union* (May 2, 1861), 1.
   156. *1861 Assembly Journal*, 799–817.
   157. *Alta* (May 4, 1861), 2; *Union* (May 4, 1861), 1.
   158. *1861 Assembly Journal*, 849.
   159. *Union* (May 14, 1861), 4.
   160. *Union* (May 15, 1861), 1.
   161. *Union* (May 16, 1861), 3.
   162. *1861 Assembly Journal*, 890–891; *Union* (May 18, 1861), 2; *Union* (May 27, 1861), 2.
   163. *1861 Assembly Journal*, 914–915.
   164. *1861 Assembly Journal*, 915–917; *Union* (May 21, 1861), 1.
   165. *Union* (May 21, 1861), 1.
   166. *Union* (May 21, 1861),.
   167. *Alta* (May 25, 1861), 1.
   168. *1861 Assembly Journal*, 922; *Union* (May 21, 1861), 1.
   169. "Sine Die Adjournment," *Alta* (May 19, 1861), 1.
   170. *Mariposa Gazette* (June 4, 1861), 2.

Chapter Four

   1. "Letter from Sacramento," San Francisco *Daily Evening Bulletin* (May 22, 1861).
   2. G.V.M., "Sights and Doings in Sonoma," *Union* (June 4, 1861), 1.
   3. Roger D. McGrath, "A Violent Birth: Disorder, Crime and Law Enforcement," pp. 27–73 in John F. Burns and Richard J. Orsi, eds., *Taming the Elephant: Politics, Government and Law in Pioneer California* (Berkley: University of California Press, 2003), 39.
   4. Florence Donnelly, "Dramatic Piercy Showalter Duel at Fairfax is Recalled," *Marin Independent* (Apr. 24, 1948), 1, 11 and 16. reproduced by the Fairfax Historical Society, 2009. Hereafter cited as Donnelly.
   5. J.P. Munro-Fraser, *History of Marin County, California: Including its Geography, Geology, Topo-Graphy and Climatology* ... (San Francisco: Alley, Brown & Co., 1880), 127, hereafter cited as Munro-Fraser; *Marin County Journal* (June 1, 1861), 2. Hereafter cited as *Journal*.
   6. James H. Wilkins, "Political Factions Are Rocked by Duel That Snuffs Out Two Lives," *San Francisco News* (1929), republished in *Fairfax Historical Society Newsletter* (June 1998), 3. Hereafter cited as Wilkins.
   7. "Possibly a Duel—The Showalter and Piercy Difficulty," *San Francisco Daily Evening Bulletin* (May 24, 1861), 3. Hereafter cited as *Bulletin*.
   8. "Whitehall Rowboat," *Wikipedia, the Free Encyclopedia*, http://en.wikipedia.org/wiki/Whitehall_Rowboat, accessed Dec. 1, 2013.
   9. "The Showalter and Piercy Duel," *Union* (May 27, 1861), 2; Wikins, 4.
   10. Wilkins, 3.
   11. "Possibly a Duel," *Bulletin* (May 24, 1861), 3; "News of the Morning," *Union* (May 25, 1861), 2.
   12. *Journal* (June 1, 1861), 2; *Union* (May 25, 1861), 2.
   13. Wilkins, 4.
   14. "Proceedings of the Court had upon the Death of Justice Brosnan," in "Memorials to Nevada Supreme Court Justices," http://nsla.nevadaculture.org/dmdocuments/Memorials_Justices.pdf, accessed Dec. 1, 2013.
   15. "The Showalter and Piercy Duel," *Union* (May 27, 1861), 2; "The Showalter and Piercy Duel," *Alta* (May 26, 1861), 1; Wilkins, 4.
   16. Richard Snowden Samuels, *California*, http://www.richsamuels.com/nbcmm/snowden/, accessed Aug. 23, 2013, 10–12, 62–63, 105, 168–170, 174–175; George A. Scheele, "Snowden and Warfield Descendants in the California Gold Rush," *Snowden and Warfield Family Genealogy Website*, http://www.snowden-warfield.com/Stories/CaliforniaGoldRush.htm, accessed Dec. 4, 2013; "Charles S. Fairfax," *Wikipedia, the Free Encyclopedia*, http://en.wikipedia.org/wiki/Charles_S._Fairfax, accessed Dec. 4, 2013.
   17. "The Showalter and Piercy Duel," *Union* (May 27, 1861), 2; Wilkins, 5; Donnelly, D-2.
   18. "No. 679 Home of Lord Charles Snowden Fairfax," California Historical Landmarks—Marin, Office of Historic Preservation, California State Parks, http://ohp.parks.ca.gov/?page_id=21429, accessed Dec. 4, 2013.
   19. William Sagar, Secretary, Fairfax Historical Society letter Mar. 27, 2013 to Gene Armistead; Wilkins, 5.
   20. *Alta* (May 8, 1875), 1.
   21. *Alta* (May 26, 1861), 1.
   22. "The Piercy-Showalter Duel," *San Francisco Call* (May 26, 1861), extract published in *Marin County Journal* (June 1, 1861), 2.
   23. "Murrays Here in the 50's," *Marin Independent* (Apr. 24, 1948), 16; Donnelly, D1; *Fairfax Historical Society Newsletter* (June 1998), 7.
   24. "Murrays Here in the 50's," *Marin Independent* (Apr. 24, 1948), 16; *Fairfax Historical Society Newsletter* (June 1998), 7.
   25. Wilkins, 3.
   26. Wilkins, 5.
   27. Wilkins, 6.
   28. Donnelly, D1.
   29. *Alta* (May 26, 1861), 1; Wilkins, 5–6.
   30. "Henry Baker Letter: San Francisco, to Thomas S. Fitch: ALS, 1861 Jan. 10," California Historical Society—North Baker Research Library, http://beta.worldcat.org/archivegrid/data/122569465, accessed Dec. 3, 2013.
   31. Sonora *Union Democrat* (Jan. 12, 1861).
   32. "William Tell Coleman," *Wikipedia, the Free Encyclopedia*, http://en.wikipedia.org/wiki/William_Tell_Coleman, accessed Dec. 1, 2013.
   33. "Boards of Commissioners 1850-Present," State of California Board of Pilot Commissioners for the Bays of San Francisco, San Pablo and Suisun, http://www.bopc.ca.gov/bios.htm, accessed Dec. 3, 2013. Hereafter cited as Board of Pilot Commissioners.
   34. "It Was Not So," *Alta* (May 31, 1861), 1.
   35. "Thomas Hayes (19th century)," *Wikipedia, the Free Encyclopedia*, http://wikipedia.org/wike/Thomas_Hayes_(19th_century), accessed Dec. 1, 2013.
   36. Board of Pilot Commissioners.
   37. "Sonoma & Marin Railroad," http://localwiki.net/sonoma-valley/Sonoma_%26_Marin_Railroad, accessed Dec. 1, 2013.
   38. "San Quentin," *Sausalito News* (Mar. 22, 1889), 3; "Births-Marriages-

Deaths," San Francisco *Morning Call* (Dec. 11, 1893), 10.

39. *Stockton Daily Argus* (May 27, 1861). This is the only source that names Sorrel as a second.

40. Joan Reutinger, "Dr. Alfred Taliaferro: Marin's First Physician," Bolinas *Coastal Post* (Jan. 1997), http://www.coastalpost.com/97/1/6.htm, accessed Dec. 1, 2013.

41. Wilkins, 5.

42. Munro-Fraser, 122.

43. *History of Tulare and Kings Counties, California, with Biographical Sketches* (Los Angeles: Historic Record Company, 1913), 338–339.

44. Wilkins, 6.

45. *Alta* (May 26, 1861), 1.

46. "...-Duel-...," *Union* (May 25, 1861), 2.

47. Dan Showalter letter, May 28, 1861, at Sacramento, to brother William A. Showalter. Transcript from files of Dr. Maurice A. Showalter via Jean Showalter Bendl to Robert L. Showalter, courtesy of Robert L. Showalter. Hereafter cites as Showalter Letter to Brother.

48. *Alta* (May 26, 1861), 1.

49. *Alta* (May 26,1861), 1.

50. Wilkins, 5.

51. Showalter Letter to Brother.

52. *Alta* (May 26, 1861), 1.

53. Wilkins, 5.

54. *Alta* (May 26, 1861), 1.

55. Wilkins, 5.

56. Wilkins, 6.

57. *Alta* (May 26, 1861), 1.

58. *Alta* (May 26, 1861), 1.

59. *Alta* (May 26, 1871), 1.

60. Showalter Letter to Brother.

61. Wilkins, 6.

62. Wilkins, 6.

63. Showalter Letter to Brother; "Colonel Hayes' Interference," *Union* (May 29, 1861), 2; *Alta* (May 26, 1861), 1; Watkins, 6; "The Showalter and Piercy Duel," *Union* (May 27, 1861), 2.

64. *Alta* (May 26, 1861), 1; Wilkins, 6; "Colonel Hayes' Interference," *Union* (May 29, 1861), 2: Showalter Letter to Brother; "The Showalter and Piercy Duel," *Union* (May 27, 1861), 2; Donnelly, D9.

65. Wilkins, 6; *Alta* (May 26, 1861), 1; Donnelly, D9.

66. Donnelly, D9.

67. *Marin County Journal* (June 1, 1861), 1.

68. "Funeral of Mr. Piercy," *Marin County Journal* (June 1, 1861), 2.

69. "Lone Mountain Cemetery," San Francisco History—SF Genealogy, http://www.sfgenealogy.com/sfhistory/hemlon.htm, accessed Dec. 3, 2013; "Lone Mountain (California), Wikipedia, the Free Encyclopedia, http://en.wikipeida.org/wiki/Lone_Mountain_(California), accessed Dec. 3, 2013; "City of the Silent—Tales from Colma—Timeline," http://www.notfrisco.com/colmatales/timeline.html, accessed Dec. 3, 2013.

70. "The Showalter and Piercy Duel," *Alta* (May 26, 1861), 1.

71. "The Showalter and Piercy Duel, *Alta* (May 26, 1861), 1.

72. "Colonel Hayes' Interference," *Union* (May 29, 1861), 2.

73. "California," *NY Times* (June 26, 1861).

74. G.V.M., "Sights and Doings in Sonora," *Union* (June 4, 1861), 1.

75. "California," *NY Times* (June 26, 1861).

76. "The Showalter and Piercy Duel," *Alta* (May 25, 1861), 1.

77. "Another Victim to this Code," *Alta* (May 26, 1861), 2.

78. Article beginning "Our quiet little village," *Marin County Journal* (June 1, 1861), 2.

79. "News of the Morning," *Union* (May 27, 1861), 2.

80. "California," *NY Times* (June 26, 1861).

81. Showalter Letter to Brother.

82. Article included in note attached to "Showalter Letter to Brother." Note dated Mar. 2, 1998, and signed by Edw. D. Showalter and attributed to "the files of Dr. Maurice A. Showalter," material given to Edw. D. Showalter by cousin Jean Showalter Bendl. The final note reads, "Uncle Doc. May have had the Original letter, I recall him reading it to me years ago in his office." Courtesy Robert L. Showalter.

83. "The Showalter and Piercy Duel," *Alta* (May 26, 1861), 1.

84. Wilkins, 6.

85. Article beginning "Rumor says," *Marin County Journal* (June 1, 1861), 2.

86. Untitled and unsigned photograph caption, *Fairfax Historical Society Newsletter* (June 1998), 7.

87. "Larkspur Woman Dies Near 100th Birthday," Marin *Independent Journal* (Apr. 30, 1956), http://www.sfgenealogy.com/boards/mcbits/archive2/3178.html, accessed June 9, 2013.

88. The British Newspaper Archive, http://www.britishnewspaperarchive.co.uk/search/results?basic search, accessed Nov. 4, 2013, has results for ten English and Scottish newspapers that reported news of the duel between July 1 (London *Morning Chronicle*) and July 27 (*Newcastle Guardian & Tyne Mercury*).

89. "Trove," a digitized collection of historic newspapers from the National Library of Australia, contains articles about the duel from six different newspapers during Aug. 1861. http://trove.nla.gov.au/newspaper, accessed Nov. 2, 2013.

90. "The Showalter and Piercy Duel," *Union* (May 27, 1861), 2.

91. G.V.M., "Sights and Doings in Sonoma," *Union* (June 4, 1861), 1.

92. Showalter Letter to Brother.

93. "His Whereabouts," *Union* (May 29, 1861), 3.

94. Thomas Jefferson Gregory, *History of Yolo County, California: with Biographical Sketches...* (Los Angeles: Historic Record Company, 1913), 124–125.

95. "8th Annual Fair of the State Agricultural Society—Third Day—at the Stock Grounds," *Union* (Sept. 20, 1861), 1.

96. Donnelly, D2.

97. Cited in *San Mateo County Gazette* (June 15, 1861).

98. "Eighty-Fifth Festival of American Liberty," *Union* (July 6, 1861), 1.

99. "Affairs in California," *NY Times* (Aug. 4, 1861).

100. Untitled article, San Francisco *Bulletin* (July 5, 1861), 2.

101. "By Magnetic Telegraph, Special Dispatches to the Bulletin," San Francisco *Bulletin* (July 6, 1861).

102. "Affairs in California," *NY Times* (Aug. 4 1861).

103. "8th Annual Fair of the State Agricultural Society, 3rd Day, at the Stock Grounds," *The Grizzly Bear*, Vol. 9, No. 5 (Sept. 1911), 4.

104. "Silver Palace Restaurant, Good Food with a History," Railtown 1897 State Historic Park, http://www.railtown1897.com/doc.asp?ID=103, accessed Mar. 3, 2013.

105. "California and the Civil War: The Biderman Flag," The California Military Museum, California State Military Department, http://www.militarymuseum.org/BidermanFlag.html, accessed Mar. 7, 2013.

106. Winfield J. Davis, *History of Political Conventions in California, 1849–1892* (Sacramento: California State Library, 1893), 180–181.

107. "Nevada Territorial Legislature," *Union* (Oct. 9, 1861), 2.

108. (Myron Angel), *Reproduction of Thompson and West's History of Nevada with Illustrations*

and Biographical Sketches of Its Prominent Men and Pioneers (Berkley: Howell-North, 1958. Originally, Oakland: Thompson & West, 1881), 266–267.

109. *OR-A*, 1-50-I, 41.

110. "The Bryants of Bridgeport," *Mono County Historical Society 2012 Newsletter*, 2.

111. "A Report in Tulare" citing the Visalia *Delta* (Sept. 26, 1861), *Union* (Oct. 1, 1861), 5; "Hope It Is True," *Marin County Journal* (Oct. 5, 1861), 1.

112. Untitled article, *Mariposa Gazette* (Nov. 19, 1861), 2.

113. "30 Years Ago," *Union* (Oct. 3, 1891), 5.

114. "News of the Morning," *Union* (Oct. 3, 1861), 2.

115. L. Burr Belden, "John Brown," in Leroy R. Hafen's *The Mountain Men and the Fur Trade of the Far West*, Vol. 7 (Glendale, CA: Arthur H. Clark, 1969), 54. footnote gives as source the Gene Caley reminiscences, San Bernardino County Pioneer Society Records. Hereafter cited as Caley per Belden.

116. L. Burr Belden, "San Bernardino Sesquicentennial 1810–May 20th–1960," *San Bernardino Sun-Telegram* (May 20, 1960), S-7. Hereafter cited as Belden.

117. Caley per Belden, 54.

118. Belden, S-7.

119. John Brown, Jr., *History of San Bernardino and Riverside Counties*, Vol. 1 (Chicago: Lewis Publishing Co. for the Western Historical Association, 1922), 50.

120. Belden, S-7.

Chapter Five

1. Richard H. Orton, *Records of California Men in the War of the Rebellion, 1861 to 1867* (Sacramento: J.D. Young, Supt. State Printing, 1890), 6. Hereafter cited as Orton.

2. Letter of Hancock to Mackall dated May 7, 1861, at Los Angeles, *OR-A*, 1-50-I, 479–480.

3. Percival J. Cooney, "Southern California in Civil War Days," *Annual Publications of the Historical Society of Southern California*, Vol. 13 (Los Angeles: McBride Printing Col, 1924), 59.

4. "El Monte and the Confederacy," *The Landmark: Bulletin of the El Monte Historical Society*, Vol. 1, No. 2 (Sept. 1961), 2. Hereafter cited as "El Monte and the Confederacy."

5. "El Monte and the Confederacy," 1.

6. Orton, 18.

7. Edna Howard Fowler, Historian-General, "Historical Department," *The United Daughters of the Confederacy Magazine*, Vol. 13, No. 9 (Sept. 1950), 11.

8. John Crippen, Jr., "The Golden Knights of Dan Showalter," *Westways* (Nov. 1959), 8.

9. Richard Savage, *The Little Lady of the Lagunitas: A Franco-Californian Romance*, http://www.aolib.com/reader_6011.htm, copyright 2009–2011, accessed Apr. 23, 2014.

10. Letter from "Dan. Showalter" to "Brig. Gen. Wright" dated Feb. 27, 1862, at Fort Yuma located in "Documents chiefly for the history of Arizona collected by Capt. G.C. Smith for H.H. Bancroft," Microfilm roll BANC MSS C-E-64, Folder 9, in Miscellaneous Historical Papers 1844–1876, courtesy Bancroft Library, University of California, Berkeley. Hereafter cited as Showalter Letter in Bancroft Collection.

11. "El Monte and the Confederacy," 4.

12. "El Monte and the Confederacy," 4–5.

13. Martin Hardwick Hall, *The Confederate Army of New Mexico* (Austin: Presidial Press, 978), 13. Hereafter cited as Hall.

14. Hall, 29.

15. Hall, 31.

16. Hall, 19.

17. "El Monte and the Confederacy," 4.

18. "Letter from the South," *Union* (Dec. 7, 1861), 1.

19. Gene Armistead, "California's Confederate Militia: The Los Angeles Mounted Rifles," *California State Military Museum*, http://www.militarymuseum.org/LosAngelesMountedRifles2.htr.

20. Report of Turner to Ketchum dated Oct. 5, 1861, *OR-A*, 1-50-I, 28–30. Hereafter cited as Turner Report.

21. Report of Baylor, Texas Mounted Rifles, dated Nov. 2, 1862, at Dona Ana, cited in Orton, 15.

22. Orton, 25.

23. Herbert M. Hart, *Pioneer Forts of the Far West* (Seattle: Superior Publishing Co., 1967), 171; Duane Preimsberger, "Rebs & Yankees in Temecula Area: Camp Wright's Role During Civil War Told," *Temecula Valley Historical Society Newsletter*, Vol. 10, No. 6 (June 2010), 2.

24. *OR-A*, 1-50-I, 698.

25. Hugh A. Gorley, "*The Loyal Californians of 1861*," War Paper No. 12, Commandery of the State of California, Military Order of the Loyal Legion of the United States (1893), 7. Hereafter cited as "Loyal Californians." These units are also named in the Report of Rigg to Carleton, Dec. 4, 1861, *OR-A*, 1-50-I, 33–35.

26. *OR-A*, 1-50-I, 698.

27. "Loyal Californians," 7–8.

28. Turner Report, 28–30.

29. Report of Wellman to Rigg, Nov. 22, 1861, *OR-A*, 1-50-I, 42–42.

30. "Loyal Californians," 8.

31. Letter of T. Wilson at to Sumner, *OR-A*, 1-50-I, 35. There was no date on the letter but it was captured with a letter of E. M. Morgan dated Nov. 27, 1861.

32. Turner Report, 28–30.

33. Emily Gerstbacher, "Temecula History: A Chronology 1797–1993," http://oldtemecula.com/history/history1/htm, accessed July 6, 2013.

34. Turner Report, 28–30.

35. Letter of Benbrook to Frank, Nov. 26, 1861, at Temecula, *OR-A*, 1-50-I, 40. Hereafter cited as Benbrook Letter.

36. Letter of Roberts to Brother, Nov. 26, 1861, at Temecula, *OR-A*, 1-50-I, 41–42. Hereafter cited as Roberts Letter.

37. Letter of Showalter to Coulter dated Nov. 26, 1861, at Temecula, *OR-A*, 1-50-I, 41.

38. Letter of "Dan S." to Crenshaw, dated Nov. 26, 1861, at Temecula, *OR-A*, 1-50-I, 41.

39. Letter of Showalter to Allison and Powell, undated, at Temecula, *OR-A*, 1-50-I, 40–41. Hereafter cited as Letter of Showalter to Allison and Powell.

40. Letter "On the Way" to Brooks, dated Nov. 26, 1861, at Temecula, *OR-A*, 1-50-I, 41.

41. Letter of Benbrook to Friend Frank, dated Nov. 26, 1861, at Temecula, *OR-A*, 1-50-I, 40.

42. Statement of Levi Rogers to Maj. E.A. Rigg, *OR-A*, 1-50-I, 38.

43. Statement of Crowell to Rigg, *OR-A*, 1-50-I, 38. Hereafter cited as Crowell statement.

44. Roberts letter.

45. Statement of Showalter to Rigg, *OR-A*, 1-50-I, 38.

46. Crowell statement.

47. Letter of Wilson to Sumner, misdated Dec. 30, 1861, at Temecula, *OR-A*, 1-50-I, 35.

48. Letter of Morgan to Cable, dated Nov. 27, 1861, at Temecula, *OR-A*, 1-50-I, 35.

49. Report of Rigg to Carleton, dated Dec. 4, 1861, at Camp Wright,

OR-A, 1–50-I, 33–35. Hereafter cited as Rigg Report.
50. Rigg Report, 33–35.
51. "Loyal Californians," 8.
52. Report of Wellman to Rigg, dated Nov. 30, 1861, OR-A, 1–50-I, 43–44. Hereafter cited as Wellman 1st Report.
53. "Loyal Californians," 9.
54. Rigg Report, 33–35.
55. "John S. Minter," http://our amazingancestors.us/minter_John/john-s-minter.html, accessed Mar. 1, 2013.
56. Wellman 1st Report, 43–44.
57. Wellman 1st Report, 43–44.
58. Wellman 1st Report, 43–44.
59. Letter of Rigg to Carlton, dated Nov. 29, 1861, at Camp Wright, OR-A, 2–2, 163–164.
60. Letter of Drum to Camp at or near Oak Grove, dated Dec. 9, 1861, at San Francisco, OR-A, 1–50-I, 752.
61. "Loyal Californians," 10.
62. "The Particulars of the Arrest of Showalter and Party," *Alta* (Dec. 14, 1861), 1.
63. Untitled article, *Mariposa Gazette* (Dec. 24, 1861), 2.
64. Letter of Fergusson to West, dated Feb. 13, 1863, at Mesilla, AS, OR-A, 1–15, 682–683.
65. Statement of T.A. Wilson, Inclosure {sic} No. 2 of Rigg Report, 36.
66. Statements of la Cruz, Jan. 30, 1862, and Dickey, Jan. 31, 1862, at Fort Yuma to Rigg, OR-A, 1–50-I, 838–840.
67. Letter of Letter of Showalter to Allison and Powell, 40–41.
68. "Loyal Californians," 10–11.
69. Rigg Report, 33–35, with Inclosures (Statements), 36–39.
70. Cited in *Mariposa Gazette* (Dec. 24, 1861), 2.
71. Rigg Report, 33–35.
72. OR-A, 1–50-I, 50, 39–40.
73. Rigg Report, 33–35.
74. Report of Wellman, to Rigg, dated Dec. 3, 1861, at Camp Wright (Wellman's 2nd Report), OR-A, 1–50-I, 44–45.
75. Letter of Morgan to Wild, dated Nov. 30, 1861, at Temecula, OR-A, 1–50-I, 40.
76. Rigg Report, OR-A, 1–50-I, 33–35.
77. "Loyal Californians," 12.
78. "Loyal Californians," 12.
79. Hugh A. Gorley (edited by Belle Gorley), "Incidents of the March," *Selections from the Numerous Letters and Patriotic Speeches of My Husband* (San Francisco: Bonnard & Daly, 1876), 68. Hereafter cited as "Incidents of the March."

80. "Loyal Californians," 13.
81. Letter of Drum to Carleton dated Dec. 10, 1861, at San Francisco, OR-A, 1–50-I, 578.
82. Order of Carleton to Eyre dated Dec. 13, 1861, at Los Angeles, OR-A, 1–50-I, 762.
83. Bert M. Fireman, "How Far Westward the Civil War?" *The 1963 All Posse-Corral Brand Book of the Denver Posse of the Westerners* (Morrison, CO: Buffalo Bill Press, 1965), 168. Hereafter cited as Fireman.
84. Letter of Carleton to Eyre, dated Nov. 4, 1861, at Los Angeles, OR-A, 1–50-I, 700–701.
85. *Alta* (Dec. 11, 1861), 1.
86. "Fort Lafayette," *Wikipedia, the Free Encyclopedia*, http://en.wikipedia.org/wiki/Fort_Lafayette, accessed July 21, 2013.
87. *Mariposa Gazette* (Dec. 17, 1861), 4.
88. "Affairs at Camp Latham," San Francisco *Evening Bulletin* (Dec. 27, 1861), 3.
89. Letter of Fritz to Eyre dated Dec. 10, 1861, at near San Bernardino, OR-A, 1–50-I, 761.
90. Letter of Eyre to Fritz, dated Dec. 11, 1861, at Camp Carleton, OR-A, 1–50-I, 761.
91. Letter of Fritz to Fergusson, dated Dec. 11, 1861, at Camp Carleton, OR-A, 1–50-I, 759–760.
92. "Military Matters," *San Francisco Bulletin* (Dec. 16, 1861).
93. "Later from the South," *Union* (Dec. 7, 1861), 1.
94. "Fort Yuma," *Alta* (Dec. 14, 1861), 1.
95. "Military Movements, etc.," *Alta* (Dec. 30, 1861), 1.
96. "Col. Carleton's Command," *Alta* (Dec. 12, 1861), 2.
97. Letter of Carleton to Eyre dated Dec. 13, 1861, at Los Angeles, OR-A, 1–50-I, 762.
98. Civis, "San Bernardino Correspondence," *Star* (Jan. 18, 1862), 2.
99. Letter of Cutler to Fergusson, dated Feb. 18, 1862, at Los Angeles, OR-A, 1–50-I, 875.
100. Selden, "First Letters From the South," *Alta* (Mar. 15, 1862), 1.
101. Compiled Service Record of Chauncey R. Wellman.
102. Letter of Carleton to Drum dated Feb. 26, 1862, at Los Angeles, OR-A, 1–50-I, 894.
103. "Loyal Californians," 14.
104. "Incidents of the March," 64–68.
105. Frank Love, *Hell's Outpost: A History of Old Fort Yuma* (Yuma, AZ: Yuma Crossing, 1992), 1. Hereafter cited as Love.

106. Love, 3.
107. Love, 1.
108. Steve Lech, *Pioneers of Riverside County: The Spanish, Mexican and Early American Periods* (Charleston, SC: The History Press, 2012), 86.
109. Love, 2.
110. Civis, "San Bernardino Correspondence," *Star* (Jan. 18, 1862), 2.
111. OR-A, 1–50-I, 852, 853, 856, 874, 893, 927, 981.
112. Regimental Return, 1st California Cavalry, dated Mar. 1, 1862, cited in CSR of Chauncey R. Wellman.
113. "Fort Yuma," *California Farmer & Journal of Useful Sciences* (Jan. 3, 1862), 10.
114. Letter of Carleton to Rigg, dated Feb. 12, 1862, at Los Angeles, OR-A, 1–50-I, 861.
115. "Well Set to Work," *Union* (Feb. 4, 1862), 2.
116. "State Summary," *California Farmer & Journal of Useful Sciences* (Feb. 7, 1862), 5.
117. "J.M. Van Dyke," *Mariposa Gazette* (May 6, 1862), 2.
118. Civis, "Correspondence," *Los Angeles Stat* (May 17, 1862), 2.
119. Letter of Cutler to Rigg dated Feb. 12, 1862, at Los Angeles, OR-A, 1–50-I, 922.
120. "Escape and Re-capture," *Alta* (Mar. 25, 1862), 1.
121. Letter of Cutler to Rigg, dated Mar. 15, 1862, at Los Angeles, OR-A, 1–50-I, 931.
122. Order dated Dec. 23, 1861, at Camp Latham, OR-A, 1–50-I, 782.
123. OR-A, 1–50-I, 838, 852–853, 856.
124. OR-A, 1–50-I-893.
125. OR-A, 1–50-I, 927.
126. Letter of Carleton to Rigg, dated Dec. 21, 1861, at Los Angeles, OR-A, 1–50-I, 781.
127. Letter of Wright to Thomas dated Dec. 28, 1861, at San Francisco, OR-A, 1–50-I, 788.
128. Letter of Seward to Stanton, dated Jan. 29, 1862, at Washington, OR-A, 1–50-I, 827–828.
129. Letter of Carleton to Rigg, dated Feb. 12, 1862, at Los Angeles, OR-A, 1–50-I, 861–861.
130. Letter of Carleton to Fergusson, dated Feb. 20, 1862, at Los Angeles, OR-A, 1–50-I, 883–884.
131. Letter of Drum to Lee dated Sept. 12, 1862, at San Francisco, OR-A, 1–50-II, 116.
132. "A Good Notice for Lord Lyons," *Union* (Dec. 20, 1861), 2.
133. "Letter from Los Angeles," *Alta* (Feb. 17, 1862), 1.

134. "How Happened he Here?" *Alta* (Mar. 3, 1862), 2. Copied by *Union* (Mar. 5, 1862), 3, and *Mariposa Gazette* (Mar. 11, 1862), 2.
135. Showalter Letter in Bancroft Collection.
136. Carl P. Schlicke, *General George Wright: Guardian of the Pacific Coast* (Norman: University of Oklahoma Press, 1988), 232.
137. Theodore Henry Hittell, *History of California*, Vol. IV (San Francisco: N. J. Stone & Co., 1897), 326: also *The Union Army: A History of Military Affairs in the Loyal States 1861-65*, Vol. IV (Madison, WI: Federal Publishing Co., 1908), 399.
138. Frank Love, "Confederate Sympathizer Imprisoned Here," *Yuma Sun* (Aug. 25, 2004), http://www.yumasun.com/articles/showalter-1034-confederate-arizona.html, accessed July 22, 2013.
139. George H. Pettis, *The California Column* (Historical Society of New Mexico No. 11) (Santa Fe: Historical Society of New Mexico, 1908), 7.
140. John J. Earle, "The Sentiment of the People of California With Respect to the Civil War," *Annual Report of the American Historical Association for the Year 1907*, Vol. 1 (Washington, D.C.: Government Printing Office, 1908), 132.
141. Letter of Wright to Thomas dated Apr. 30, 1862, at San Francisco, *OR-A*, 1-50-I, 1041.
142. Letter of Carleton to Rigg, dated Apr. 3, 1862, at Los Angeles, *OR-A*, 1-50-I, 980-981.
143. "Release of the Showalter Party," *Union* (May 28, 1862), 4.
144. George Hand & Neil B. Carmony—ed., *The Civil War in Apacheland: Sergeant George Hand's Diary: California, Arizona, West Texas, New Mexico, 1861-1864* (Silver City, NM: High-Lonesome Books, 1996), 33.
145. Civis, Untitled correspondence, *Star* (May 3, 1862), 2.
146. "Release of the Showalter Party," *Union* (May 28, 1862), 4.
147. Civis, "Correspondence," *Star* (May 17, 1862), 2.
148. Juvenal, "Hornitos Correspondence," *Mariposa Gazette* (May 27, 1862), 2.
149. "The New Mines," *Union* (June 30, 1862), 4.
150. Letter of Ehrenberg dated Nov. 6, 1862, at La Paz, NMT, *OR-A*, 1-50-II, 247-248.
151. "Murdered by a Secessionist," *Union* (June 4, 1862), 2. Hereafter cited as "Murdered by a Secessionist."
152. Fireman, 167.
153. Fireman, 166.
154. "Murdered by a Secessionist."
155. Fireman, 166-167.
156. "Murdered by a Secessionist."
157. Fireman, 167. Complete names of the Privates from "Murdered by a Secessionist."
158. "Murdered by a Secessionist."
159. Fireman, 167.
160. Orton, 653.
161. Fireman, 170.
162. "Letter from Camp Latham," *Union* (Sept. 19, 1862), 4.
163. "Our Letter from the Southern Counties," *Alta* (Aug. 16, 1862), 2.
164. "From California," *Philadelphia Press* (Feb. 5, 1863), 2; "From San Francisco," *NY Times* (Feb. 5, 1863); "From California," Washington *Daily National Republican* (Feb. 26, 1863), 1.
165. Munro-Fraser, 682-683; and Doris Widger, "Shattuck Page," http://widgewood,wordpress.com/shattuck-page/, accessed Dec. 11, 2013.
166. "Unlinked Shattucks Initiated by Charles Henry Shattuck III," *Robert Kline's Genealogy Page*, http://we.rootsweb.ancestry.com/cgi-bin/igm.cgi?op=GET&db=rckline-u-shattu&id=15213, updated May 17, 2012, accessed Nov. 8, 2013.
167. "Dan Showalter," *Union* (Nov. 22, 1862), 2.
168. Report of Fergusson to West dated Feb. 13, 1863, at Mesilla, *OR-A*, 1-15, 682-683.
169. Cornelius C. Smith, "Some Unpublished History of the Southwest," *Arizona Historical Review*, Vol. 4, No. 4 (Jan. 1932), 47.
170. "In Texas," San Francisco *Evening Bulletin* (Mar. 11, 1863), 1.

Chapter Six

1. Letter of Showalter to Anna Forman in *OR-A*.
2. Confederate Compiled Service Record of George L. Patrick, National Archives and Records Administration. Hereafter cited as NARA.
3. *Mariposa Gazette* (May 6, 1862), 2.
4. Form 86 Military Service Records—Research Ticket, NARA, research date Mar. 14, 2013.
5. *OR-A*, Letter of Showalter to Anna Forman.
6. "Secesh for Texas," San Francisco *Evening Bulletin* (Mar. 11, 1863), 1.
7. "In Texas," *Alta* (Mar. 13, 1863), 1.
8. "Incidents," Houston *Tri-Weekly Telegraph*, Jan. 7, 1863, 4.
9. Fuller accounts of the Battle of Galveston can be found in: *OR-A*, 1-15, 199-226; *Official Records of the Union and Confederate Navies in the War of the Rebellion* (hereafter cited as *OR-N*), 1-19, 437-44; J. Thomas Scharf, *History of the Confederate States Navy from Its Organization to the Surrender of Its Last Vessel* (New York: Gramercy Books, 1996; originally published 1887), 505-513; and Edward T. Cotham, Jr., *Battle on the Bay: The Civil War Struggle for Galveston* (Austin: University of Texas Press, 1998), 108-126.
10. O.M. Roberts, "Chapter 10," *Confederate Military History*, Vol. 11 (Atlanta: Confederate Publishing Co., 1911).
11. Mrs. M. Looscan article in *Houston Post* (May 23, 1895), cited in Roberts. Hereafter cited as Looscan.
12. Looscan.
13. Kosciuszko Dewitt Keith information provided for *Burke's Texas Almanac and Immigrant's Handbook for 1883, with Which is Incorporated Hanford's Texas State Register* (Houston: J. Burke, 1883), 67. Hereafter cited as Keith.
14. William Wiess, "First Federal Defeat at Sabine Pass," *Confederate Veteran*, Vol. 20, No. 3 (Mar. 1912), 108. Hereafter cited as Wiess.
15. William T. Block, Jr., "The Memoirs of Captain Koscuiszko D. Keith," *Texas Gulf Historical and Biographical Record*, Vol. X (Nov. 1974), 41-64.
16. Francis Richard Lubbock, *Six Decades in Texas or Memoirs of Francis Richard Lubbock, Governor of Texas in War-Time, 1861-1863* (Austin: Ben C. Jones & Co., Printers, 1900), 458. Hereafter cited as Lubbock.
17. Philip Robert Caudill, *Moss Bluff Rebel: A Texas Pioneer in the Civil War* (College Station: Texas A&M University Press, 2009), 29.
18. Edward T. Cotham, Jr., *Sabine Pass: The Confederacy's Thermopylae* (Austin: University of Texas Press, 2004), 46. Hereafter cited as Cotham, *Sabine Pass*.
19. Report of Watkins dated Jan. 23, 1863, aboard steamer Bell, *OR-N*, 1-19, 566.
20. Detailed report of Watkins,

dated Jan. 23, 1863, aboard "Flagship" *OR-N*, 1-19, 564.

21. Order of Bell to Dillingham dated Jan. 18, 1863, aboard Steam Sloop, *OR-N*, 1-19, 538-539.

22. Letter of H. Bell to Farragut, dated Jan. 18, 1863, *OR-N*, 1-19, 538.

23. Report of Sherfy dated Apr. 12, 1864, at Champaign, IL, *OR-N*, 1-19, 559.

24. William T. Block, Jr., ed., "The Diary of 1st Sergeant H. N. Connor," http://www.wtblock.com/wtblockjr/diaryof.htm, accessed June 9, 2013.

25. Keith.

26. Wiess, 108.

27. William T. Block, Jr., "From Cotton Bales to Black Gold: A History of the Pioneer Wiess Families of Southeastern Texas," *Texas Gulf Historical and Biographical Record*, Vol. 8, No. 1 (Nov. 1973), 40-61; http://www.wtblock.com/wtblockjr/cotton_bales_gold.htm, accessed Dec. 15, 2013.

28. Letter of John A. Drummond, Opelousas, LA, May 15, 1903, Elbridge Gerry Littlejohn Collection, Galveston and Texas History Center of the Rosenberg Library, Galveston, cited in Cotham, *Sabine Pass*, 51, 219 fn 22.

29. Wiess, 108.

30. Supplemental report of Watkins dated Mar. 14, 1863, at Houston, TX, *OR-N*, 1-19, 568.

31. This summary of the Battle Off Sabine Pass was compiled from several more detailed sources: Report of Sherfy dated Apr. 12, 1864, at Champaign, IL, *OR-N*, 1-19, 558-562; Detailed report of Watkins, dated Jan. 23, 1863, aboard steamer Bell, *OR-N*, 1-19, 564-566; Supplemental report of Watkins, dated Mar. 14, 1863, at Houston, TX, *OR-N*, 1-19, 567-570; Cotham, *Sabine Pass*, 47-56; Keith; Wiess; Looscan; Lubbock, 458-461; Zack Sabel, "Further of the Naval Battle," Houston *Tri-Weekly Telegraph* (Jan. 26, 1863), 1; untitled article, Houston *Tri-Weekly Telegraph* (Feb. 2, 1863), 2.

32. Detailed report of Watkins dated Jan. 23, 1863, aboard steamer Bell, *OR-N*, 1-19, 566.

33. "Where Dan Showalter Is," *Star* (Mar. 21, 1863), 2.

34. "The Victory Off Sabine!" Houston *Tri-Weekly Telegraph* (Jan. 26, 1863), 1.

35. Untitled article, Houston *Tri-Weekly Telegraph* (Feb. 2, 1863), 2.

36. *OR-A*, 1-50-I, 1108.

37. Special Orders No. 81, HQ, Dept. of Texas, New Mexico & Arizona, dated Feb. 21, 1863, at Houston, *OR-A*, 1-50-II, 332-333.

38. Theophilus Noel, *A Campaign from Santa Fe to the Mississippi: Being a History of the Old Sibley Brigade from Its Organization to the Present Time; Its Campaigns in New Mexico, Arizona, Texas, Louisiana and Arkansas in the Years 1861-2-3-4* (Santa Fe: Stagecoach Press, 1961), 181.

39. Letter of Baylor to Magruder, dated Jan. 29, 1863 at San Antonio, *OR-A*, 1-50-II, 298.

40. Special Orders No. 81, *OR-A*, 1-50-II, 333.

41. Roster of Commissioned Officers of the Arizona Brigade dated Mar. 1, 1863, at Columbus, TX, per Compiled Service Record of Dan Showalter, NARA.

42. Regimental Rosters of Mar., June, and Sept. 1864, Showalter CSR.

43. Letter of Magruder to Cooper, dated June 8, 1862, at Houston, *OR-A*, 1-26-II, 57.

44. *OR-A*, 1-26-II, 73.

45. General Order No. 79, Oct. 12, 1864.

46. Letter of Beldon to Magruder, dated Apr. 5, 1863, at Alexandria, LA, *OR-A*, 1-24-II, 814.

47. "Muster Roll, Mariposa Battalion," *Mariposa County, California, Genealogy & Historical Research Home Page*, http://www.mariposaresearch.net/batallion.htm, accessed Dec. 21, 2013.

48. George W. Tyler, "Bell County Rangers and Confederate Soldiers," *Belton Journal* (Jan. 31, 1918), http://files.usgwarchives.net/tx/bell/military/civilwar/rangers.txt, accessed Dec. 22, 2013.

49. Letter of Magruder to Smith, dated June 26, 1863, at Houston, *OR-A*, 1-26-II, 85.

50. Letter of Lt. Col. D. Showalter to Capt. E.P. Tanner, dated June 3, 1863, at San Antonio, TX, in Showalter CSR.

51. Letter of Major. A.G. Dickinson dated June 22, 1863, at San Antonio to Capt. A. P. Turner. NARA.

52. Letter of Baird to Turner dated Apr. 30, 1863, at San Antonio, *OR-A*, 1-15, 1064.

53. Letter of Baird to Turner dated May 5, 1863, at San Antonio, *OR-A*, 1-15, 1075-1076.

54. Letter of Showalter to Capt. E.P. Turner dated July 11, 1863 at Houston, TX, in Showalter CSR.

55. Untitled article, Columbus, GA, *Daily Enquirer* (Oct. 21, 1863).

56. Cindy Jones, "Fourth Texas Cavalry, Arizona Brigade," *Handbook of Texas Online*, http://www.tshaonline.org/handbook/online/articles/qkfl7, accessed Mar. 11, 2013. Published by Texas State Historical Association.

57. J.L. Bryan, "Bradshaw, Amzi," *Handbook of Texas Online*, http://www.tshaonline.org/handbook/online/articles/fbryy, accessed Dec. 28, 2013. Published by Texas State Historical Association.

58. J.A. Tharp "Soldier's Application for Pension" filed Jan. 21, 1910, from Texas State Library and Archives Commission, Austin, TX.

59. Patricia Adkins-Rochette, *Bourland in North Texas and Indian Territory During the Civil War: Fort Cobb, Fort Arbuckle & the Wichita Mountains* (La Vergne, TN: Lightning Source, Inc., 2004) cited by the author in her "LeKaester's Company E," http://www.bourlandcivilwar.com/LeKoester.htm, accessed Dec. 28, 2013.

60. Letter of Dickinson to Turner dated Oct. 12, 1863, at San Antonio, *OR-A*, 1-53-Supplement, 899.

61. Letter of Baird to Capt. [Turner] dated Oct. 10, 1863, at Austin, CSR of Spruce M. Baird.

62. Report of Steele dated Feb. 15, 1864, at Austin, TX, *OR-A*, 1-22-I, 28.

63. Letter of Bankhead to Boggs dated May 29, 1863 at Houston, *OR-A*, 1-26-II, 20-21.

64. Special Orders No. 145 dated May 30, 1863, at Houston, TX, *OR-A*, 1-26-II, 26.

65. "Krumbhaar's Texas Battery," *Handbook of Texas Online*, http://www.tshaonline.org/handbook/online/articles/qkk01, accessed Dec. 30, 2013. Published by the Texas State Historical Association.

66. David Paul Smith, *Frontier Defense in the Civil War: Texas' Rangers and Rebels* (College Station: Texas A&M University Press, 1992), 68. Hereafter cited as Smith.

67. Baird letter dated July 27, 1863, at San Antonio, in CSR of Col. S.M. Baird.

68. Smith, 66.

69. Letter of Steele to Bankhead dated July 11, 1863, at Fort Smith, *OR-A*, 1-22-II, 921-922.

70. Letter of Bankhead to headquarters in Houston, dated July 11, 1863, at Bonham, *OR-A*, 1-22-II, 922-923.

71. Letter of Magruder to Boggs, dated Aug. 11, 1863, at near Millican, TX, *OR-A*, 1-22-II, 963-964.

72. Smith, 68.

73. *OR-A*, 1-53-Supplement, 887–890.
74. Mark K. Christ, *Civil War Arkansas, 1863: The Battle for a State* (Norman: University of Oklahoma Press, 2010), 216. Hereafter cited as Christ.
75. Letter of Bankhead dated Aug. 20, 1863, at Camp Bankhead, *OR-A*, 122-II, 972–973.
76. Letter of Bankhead dated Aug. 23, 1863, at Camp Bankhead, *OR-A*, 122-II, 977–988.
77. Letter of Bankhead dated Aug. 27, 1863, at Camp Bankhead, *OR-A*, 122-II, 981.
78. Letter of Steele to Cabell dated Aug. 30, 1863, at Camp on Middle Boggy with attached memorandum *OR-A*, 122-II, 984–985.
79. *OR-A*, 1-22-II, 987.
80. Letter of Steele to District Headquarters in Little Rock dated Sept. 11, 1863, from Camp on the Middle Boggy, *OR-A*, 1-22-II, 1012; Christ, 220.
81. Letter of Carrington, to Gen. Magruder dated Aug. 30, 1863, at Houston, *OR-A*, 1-22-II, 985; Letter to Bankhead dated Sept. 1, 1863, at Houston, *OR-A*, 1-26-II, 197.
82. Smith, 71–72.
83. Letter of Steele to District Headquarters dated Sept. 11, 1863, *OR-A*, 1-22-II, 1012–1013.
84. Letter of Crosby of Bankhead, dated Sept. 13, 1863, at Camp Watie, *OR-A*, 1-22-II, 1014–1015.
85. Letter of Steele to Cabell dated Sept. 15, 1863, at Camp Watie, *OR-A*, 1-22-II, 1015–1016.
86. Letter of Bankhead dated Sept. 15, 1863, *OR-A*, 1-22-II, 1016.
87. Compiled Service Record of Pvt. John W. Hill.
88. Letter of Crosby to Bankhead dated Sept. 18, 1863, at Camp Watie, *OR-A*, 1-22-II, 1020.
89. Letter of Crosby to Bankhead dated Sept. 19, 1863, at Camp Watie, *OR-A*, 1-22-II, 1022–1023.
90. Letter of Yancey, McCulloch, dated Sept. 22, 1863, at Sabine Pass, *OR-A*, 1-22-II, 1024.
91. Letter of Crosby to Cooper dated Sept. 23, 1863, at Camp Watie, *OR-A*, 1-22-II, 1025–1036.
92. Letter of Steele to Dept. Headquarters dated Oct. 24, 1863, at Camp Brazil, *OR-A*, 1-22-II, 1048.
93. Letter of Gallagher to Bankhead, dated Sept. 18, 1863, at Arkadelphia, *OR-A*, 1-22-II, 1026–1027.
94. Letter of Smith to Holmes, dated Oct. 2, 1863, at Shreveport, *OR-A*, 1-22-II, 1030.
95. Letter of Steele to McCulloch dated Oct. 13, 1863, at Camp Sabine, *OR-A*, 1-22-II, 1044.
96. "Troops in Arkansas and the Indian Terrigory about November 10, 1863," *OR-A*, 1-22-II, 1066–1067.
97. Letter of Duval to Gano, dated Nov. 30, 1863, at Doaksville, IT, *OR-A*, 1-22-I, 1083–1084.
98. Letter of Wm. Steele to Gano dated Dec. 2, 1863, at Doaksville, IT, *OR-A*, 1-22-II, 1085.
99. Special Orders No. 214, Headquarters, Trans-Mississippi Dept., dated Dec. 11, 1863, at Shreveport, LA, *OR-A*, 1-22-II, 1094.
100. Smith, 77.
101. Smith, 73.
102. Smith, 82.
103. Smith, 83–84.
104. Letter of Rose Ellen Ritchie Dryden to her mother, dated Nov. 23, 1865, at San Antonio, typescript copy at University Library Special Collections, University of Texas Arlington, Arlington, TX, 4. Hereafter cited as Dryden.
105. Emma Baker, "Brown, John Henry," *Handbook of Texas Online*, http://www.tsha.online.org/handbook/online/articles/fbr94, accessed Dec. 31, 2013.
106. John Henry Brown, *Indian Wars and Pioneers of Texas* (St. Louis: L. E. Daniel, Publisher, 1880), 117–118. His account within this source was republished as "Raid Into Cook County, December 1863" in *Frontier Times*, Vol. 17, No. 12 (Sept. 1940), 459–463. Brown also mentions Showalter, including an abbreviated version of the pursuit in his *History of Texas, From 1685 to 1892*, Vol. 2 (St. Louis: L.E. Daniel, Publisher, 1892), 419, 421, 439.
107. B., "From Bonham. Indian Raid," Houston *Tri-Weekly Telegraph*, Dec. 31, 1863, 2.
108. Dryden, 4.
109. Letter of Turner to Baird, dated Dec. 15, 1863, at McNeel's, TX, *OR-A*, 1-26-II, 509.
110. Dryden, 4–6.
111. General Orders, No. 217, Headquarters, Dist. of Tex., N. Mex., and Ariz., dated Dec. 15, 1863, at McNeel's, Brazoria Co., Texas, *OR-A*, 1-26-II, 509–510.

Chapter Seven

1. Confidential letter of Turner to Ford dated Dec. 22, 1863, at McNeel's, TX, *OR-A*, 1-26-II, 525–526.
2. Letter of Magruder to Murrah dated Dec. 20, 1863, at McNeel's, *OR-A*, 1-26-I, 516.
3. William John Hughes, *"Rip" Ford, Texan: The Public Life and Service of John Salmon Ford, 1836-1883* (Dissertation in History for Degree of Doctor of Philosophy, Texas Technological College, 1958), 298n. repositories.tdl.org/ttu-ir/bitstream/handle/.../31295015061848.pdf?, accessed Mar. 28, 2013. This dissertation was the basis for Hughes' book *Rebellious Ranger: Rip Ford and the Old Southwest* (Norman: University of Oklahoma Press, 1964). Hereafter cited as Hughes.
4. Letter of Ford to Turner dated Jan. 6, 1864, at San Antonio, *OR-A*, 1-53, 923.
5. Letter of Ford to Turner dated Dec. 29, 1863, at San Antonio, *OR-A*, 1-26-II, 560–561.
6. Letter of Ford to Turner dated Jan. 6, 1864, at San Antonio, *OR-A*, 1-53, 922.
7. Letter of Baird to Ford dated Jan. 18, 1864, at San Antonio, Spruce M. Baird Papers, 1864, Pearce Civil War Collection, Navarro College, Corsicana, Texas.
8. Letter of McCullouch to Turner dated Jan. 6, 1864, at Bonham, *OR-A*, 1-53, 924.
9. *OR-A*, Letter to A. Forman.
10. A. Russell Buchanan, *David S. Terry of California, Dueling Judge* (San Marino, CA: The Huntington Library, 1956), 131–132, 139.
11. *OR-A*, Letter to A. Forman.
12. "Letter from Dan. Showalter," *Sonoma County Democrat* (Sonoma, CA, July 23, 1864), 1.
13. Letter of Ford to Turner dated Jan. 22, 1864, at San Antonio, *OR-A*, 1-53, 953.
14. Letter of Ford to Turner, dated Feb. 5, 1864, at San Antonio, *OR-A*, 1-34-II, 946.
15. Letter of Ford to Baird dated Feb. 5, 1864, at San Antonio, *OR-A*, 1-34-II, 947.
16. John S. Ford Papers TCM 94.1.0837, Texas Confederate Museum Collection, Haley Memorial Library and History Center, Midland, TX. Hereafter cited as Ford Papers.
17. Letter of Ford to Heermann dated Feb. 21, 1864, at San Antonio, *OR-A*, 1-34-II, 980.
18. Clarence Wharton, "Spruce McCoy Baird," *New Mexico Historical Review*, Vo. 27, No. 4 (Oct. 1952), 307. Hereafter cited as Wharton.
19. Abstract from return of the District of Texas, New Mexico, and Arizona for the month of Apr. 1864, *OR-A*, 1-34-III, 800.
20. Organization of the Army of

the Trans-Mississippi Department, Sept. 30, 1864, *OR-A*, 1-41-III, 966-969.

21. Organization of the Army of the Trans-Mississippi Department, Dec. 31, 1864, *OR-A*, 1-41-IV, 1141-1144.

22. Letter of Magruder to Boggs dated June 6, 1864, at Houston, *OR-A*, 1-34-IV, 650-651.

23. Wharton, 307.

24. Wharton, 308.

25. Letter of Ford to Turner dated Feb. 26, 1864, at San Antonio, *OR-A*, 1-34-II, 992.

26. Letter of Ford to Turner dated Feb. 28, 2864, at San Antonio, *OR-A*, 1-34-II, 1004-1005.

27. Letter of Ford to Turner dated Mar. 9, 1864, at San Antonio, *OR-A*, 1-34-II, 1033; Ford Papers, TCM94.1.0838.

28. Ford Papers, TCM94.1.0839.

29. Special Requisition and Cover Letter of Showalter, Showalter CSR.

30. Letter of Showalter to Maj. W.A. Alston, dated Mar. 25, 1864, at Helena, TX.

31. Letter of Ford to Turner dated Mar. 22, 1864, at Banquete, *OR-A*, 1-34-II, 1069.

32. Jerry D. Thompson, "Benavides, Santos," *Handbook of Texas Online*, http://www.tshaonline.org/handbook/online/articles/fbe47, accessed Jan. 10, 2014.

33. Benavides to Ford dated Mar. 21, 1864, at Laredo, *OR-A*, 1-34-I, 648-649.

34. Dickinson to Slaughter dated Mar. 24, 1864, at San Antonio, *OR-A*, 1-34-II, 1081-1082.

35. Ford to Turner dated Mar. 31, 1864, at Camp Patterson, *OR-A*, 1-34-II, 1106-1107.

36. Ford to Turner dated Apr. 9, 1864, at Camp Patterson, *OR-A*, 1-34-III, 754.

37. O.M. Roberts, "Texas," in *Confederate Military History: A Library of Confederate States History, Written by Distinguished Men of the South*, Vol. 11, edited by Clement Evans (Honolulu: University Press of the Pacific, 2004), 125. Originally published 1899. Hereafter cited as Roberts.

38. Ford to Turner dated Apr. 17, 1864, at Laredo, *OR-A*, 1-34-III, 775-776.

39. Ford Papers, TCM94.1.0840.

40. Ford Papers, TCM94.1.0841

41. James M. Beverly, *A History of the Ninety-First Regiment, Illinois Volunteer Infantry, 1862-1865* (White Hall, IL: Pearce Printing Co., 1913), 11.

42. Ford Papers, TCM94.1.0842.

43. "Record of Events," Regimental Return, June 1864.

44. Ford to Slaughter dated June 20, 1864, at Young's Ranch, *OR-A*, 1-34-IV, 684-685.

45. Ford report dated July 2, 1864, at Ringgold Barracks, *OR-A*, 1-34-I, 1054-1055.

46. Report of Herron dated June 26, 1864, at Brownsville, *OR-A*, 1-34-I, 1053-1054.

47. Ford report dated July 2, 1864, at Ringgold Barracks, *OR-A*, 1-34-I, 1055-1056.

48. Ford report dated July 2, 1864, at Ringgold Barracks, *OR-A*, 1-34-I, 1056.

49. Paragraph IV, Special Order No. 178, *OR-A*, 1-34-IV, 695.

50. Herron to Dwight dated June 26, 1864, at Brownsville, *OR-A*, 1-34-IV, 559-560.

51. Ford to Slaughter dated July 2, 1864, at Ringgold Barracks, *OR-A*, 1-41-II, 989.

52. Ford to Slaughter dated July 3, 1864, at Ringgold Barracks, *OR-A*, 1-41-II, 990.

53. Ford to Slaughter dated July 7, 1864, at Ringgold Barracks, *OR-A*, 1-41-II, 994-996.

54. Ford to Slaughter dated July 9, 1864, at Ringgold Barracks, *OR-A*, 1-41-II, 1001.

55. John Salmon Ford, *Memoirs of John Salmon Ford*, Vol. IV (typed transcript copy from Dolph Briscoe Center for American History, University of Texas, Austin, TX), 1099. Hereafter cited as Ford *Memoirs*.

56. Ford *Memoirs*, 1090.

57. Ford *Memoirs*, 1099.

58. Ford *Memoirs*, 1100.

59. Ford *Memoirs*, 1100-1101.

60. Ford *Memoirs*, 1101.

61. Beverly, 30.

62. Ford *Memoirs*, 1102.

63. Carlos, untitled article dated July 29, 2864, at Carricitos Rancho, Houston *Daily Telegraph* (Aug. 16, 1864). "Carlos" was a frequent correspondent to Texas newspapers during Ford's expedition and from Brownsville.

64. Ford *Memoirs*, 1103.

65. Letter of Maj. Gen. N.J.T. Dana to U.S. Vice Consul M.M. Kimmey dated Jan. 8, 1864, at Matagorda Bay, TX, *OR-A*, 1-34-II, 44-45.

66. Letter of Herron to Dwight dated June 15, 1864, at Brownsville, *OR-A*, 1-34-IV, 386; Letter of Canby to Halleck dated July 22, 1864, at New Orleans, *OR-A*, 1-41-II, 325-326; Letter of Christensen to Banks dated July 5, 1864, at New Orleans, *OR-A*, 1-41-II, 46.

67. Beverly, 12.

68. Report of Captain James W. Fry dated Aug. 4, 1864, at Fort Brown, *OR-A*, 1-41-I, 185-186.

69. Ford *Memoirs*, 1103.

70. Report of Captain James W. Fry dated Aug. 4, 1864, at Fort Brown, *OR-A*, 1-41-I, 186.

71. Frederick H. Dyer, *A Compendium of the War of the Rebellion*, Vol. 1 (Dayton: National Historical Society & Press of Morningside Bookshop, 1979), 881. Hereafter cited as Dyer.

72. Ford *Memoirs*, 1107.

73. Ford *Memoirs*, 1105.

74. Frank Cushman Pierce, *A Brief History of the Lower Rio Grande Valley* (Menasha, WI: Collegiate Press George Benter Publishing Co., 1917), 48.

75. Ford *Memoirs*, 1103.

76. Ford *Memoirs*, 1108.

77. Multiple letters by Ford and Showalter in both *OR-A* and Ford Papers.

78. Beverly, 26-27.

79. Beverly, 5, 11, 27, 43.

80. Seely letter.

81. Beverly, 27, 31.

82. J. Irvine Dungan, *History of the 19th Regiment Iowa Volunteer Infantry* (Davenport: Luse & Griggs, 1865), 117.

83. Term used in multiple letters by both Ford and Showalter found in both *OR-A* and the Ford Papers.

84. Ford *Memoirs*, 1109; *OR-A*, 1-41-II, 1069-1070.

85. Ford *Memoirs*, 1108.

86. Letter of Showalter to Ford dated Aug. 10, 1864, at "Palmetto Ranch."

87. Dyer, 881.

88. Letter of Giddings to Showalter dated Aug. 10, 1864, at "near San Martin."

89. Dudley G. Wooten, *A Comprehensive History of Texas, 1685-1897*, Vol. II (Dallas: William G. Scarff, 1898), 553. Hereafter cited as Wooten.

90. *OR-A*, 1-41-II, 1069.

91. Ford *Memoirs*, 1159.

92. Ford Papers, TCM94.1.1006.

93. For the preceding three paragraphs: Ford *Memoirs*, 1108, 1117; Richard B. McCaslin, *Fighting Stock: John S. "Rip" Ford of Texas* (Fort Worth: Texas Christian University Press, 2011), 178. Hereafter cited as McCaslin; Letter of Ford to Lt. W. Kearny dated Aug. 26, 1864, at Fort Brown, *OR-A*, 1-41-II, 910; Letter of Ford to Capt. J.E. Dwyer dated Sept. 3, 1864, at Fort Brown, *OR-A*,

1-41-II, 909; Report of Capt. James H. Fry dated Aug. 8, 1864, at Fort Brown.

94. Comision Pesquisidora de la Frontera del Norte, *Reports of the Committee of Investigation Sent in 1873 by the Mexican Government to the Frontier of Texas* (New York: Baker & Godwin, Publishers, 1875), 151. Hereafter cited as Comision Pesquisidora.

95. Jerry Thompson, "Cortina, Juan Nepomuceno," *Handbook of Texas Online*, http://www.tshaonline.org/handbook/online/articles/fco73, accessed Aug. 14, 2013.

96. Letter of Ford to Dwyer dated Sept. 3, 1864, at Fort Brown, OR-A, 1-41-III, 909.

97. Comision Pesquisidora, 189.

98. Correspondence of the *New York Herald*, June 26, 1864, from City of Mexico, provided to Secretary of State Seward by Mexican Ambassador Matias Romero, July 16, 1864, and reproduced as part of Executive Document No. 73, "Message of the President of the United States of March 20, 1866," *Executive Documents Printed by Order of the House of Representatives During the First Session of The Thirty-Ninth Congress, 1865-'66* (Washington, D.C.: Government Printing Office, 1866), 33. Hereafter cited as Exec. Doc. 73.

99. Letter of Cortina to Mexican Minister of War dated Apr. 24, 1864, at China, Exec. Doc. 73, 323.

100. Exec. Doc. 73, 197.

101. McCaslin, 185.

102. Ford *Memoirs*, 1113.

103. Ford *Memoirs*, 1109.

104. Ford *Memoirs*, 1110.

105. Ford *Memoirs*, 1112.

106. Ford *Memoirs*, 1123-1125.

107. Letter of Ford to Dwyer dated Aug. 29, 1864, at Brownsville, OR-A, 1-41-II, 1088-1089.

108. James Clements Monday and Frances Brannen Vick, *Petra's Legacy: The South Texas Ranching Empire Of Vela and Mifflin Kennedy* (College Station: Texas A&M University Press, 2007), 126.

109. McCaslin, 186.

110. The name is rendered in various forms in contemporary reports. The authors have chosen to use the spelling "Echazarrete" in all cases without [ ] or further footnote as it seems to be the most common.

111. Joint written statement of Colonels Canales, Cerda & Hidalgo & Major Puente to Colonel Ford afterwards at Brownsville, Ford *Memoirs*, 1146-1151.

112. Letter of Ford to Dwyer dated Sept. 3, 1864, at Fort Brown, OR-A, 1-41-III, 909.

113. Letter of Ford to Veron dated Aug. 24, 1864, at Brownsville, OR-A, 1-41-III, 910.

114. Letter of Veron to Ford dated Aug. 25, 1864, at Bagdad, OR-A, 1-41-II, 1089.

115. Letter of Ford to Kearny dated Aug. 26, 1864, at Fort Brown, OR-A, 1-41-III, 910.

116. Pierce, 50.

117. Letter of Day to Commander of the French Forces dated Sept. 8, 1864, at Brazos Santiago, OR-Armies, 1-41-III, 100-101.

118. Letter of Ford to Showalter, dated Aug. 31, 1864, at Fort Brown, Ford Papers, TCM94.1.0843.

119. Ford *Memoirs*, 1125.

120. Letter of Showalter to Ford, dated Sept. 5, 1864, at Camp Palmetto, Ford Papers, TCM94.1.0844.

121. Letter of Showalter to Ford dated Sept. 5, 1864, at Camp Palmetto, Ford Papers, TCN94.1.0845.

122. Letter of Seward to Canby dated Sept. 30, 1864, at Washington, OR-A, 1-41-III, 497-498.

123. Comision Pesquidora, 151.

124. "Reported Defeat of Mejia by Gen. Cortinas," *New York Times* (Sept. 9, 1864).

125. "General News; From the Rio Grande. Details of the Demonstration by Cortinas," *New York Times* (Sept. 20, 1864), 1.

126. "Exciting News from the Rio Grande...," *NY Times* (Sept. 20, 1864), 1.

127. "Later from New-Orleans:...," *NY Times* (Sept. 20, 1864).

128. Beverly, 51.

129. "Affairs on the Rio Grande," Washington *Daily National Intelligencer* (Sept. 20, 1864), 1.

130. "The Capture of Brownsville by Cortinas," *New York Tribune* (Sept. 20, 1864), 4.

131. "From Brownsville: The Movement of Cortinaz Is Confirmed," *Oswego Palladium* (Sept. 20, 1864).

132. In "News of the Morning," *SDU* (Sept. 20, 1864), 2.

133. "Further Intelligence: The Affair at Brownsville," *SDU* (Sept. 20, 1864), 2.

134. "From the Rio Grande," *Richmond Whig and Public Advertiser* (Oct. 1, 1864), 1.

135. "The Latest News from the Rio Grande," *New York Herald* (Sept. 27, 1864), 1.

136. "Important from the Rio Grande," *New York Herald* (Sept. 27, 1864), 1.

137. "Ninety-first Infantry," *Report of the Adjutant General of the State of Illinois for the Years 1861-1866*, Vol. 5, 334-336.

138. Beverly, 12.

139. Hubert Howe Bancroft, *History of the North Mexican States and Texas*, Vol. II (Vol. XVI of *The Works of Hubert Howe Bancroft*) (San Francisco: History Company, Publishers, 1889), 468.

140. Ford *Memoirs*, 1159-1160.

141. Ford *Memoirs*, 1156-1157.

142. James W. Daddysman, *The Matamoros Trade: Confederate Commerce, Diplomacy, and Intrigue* (Newark: University of Delaware Press, 1984).

143. T.R. Fehrenbach, *Lone Star: A History of Texas and the Texans* (New York: DaCapo Press, 2000; originally published 1968), 387.

144. Hughes, 314.

145. Hughes, 319-320.

146. McCaslin, 181.

147. Milo Kennedy, Anthony K. Knopp & Antonio Zavalita, *Further Studies in Rio Grande Valley History* (Brownsville: University of Texas at Brownsville & Texas Southmost College, 2006), 143.

148. Norman Rozeff, "The Story of Union Forces in South Texas During the Civil War" (Harlingen Historical Preservation Society, revised Jan. 2011). Hereafter cited as Rozeff. http://www.cameroncountyhistoricalcommission.org/StoryOfUnionForces.htm, accessed May 18, 2013.

149. Stephen A. Townsend, *The Yankee Invasion of Texas* (College Station: Texas A&M University Press, 2006), 110.

150. See Pierce, 49.

151. See Jerry D. Thompson, *Vaqueros in Blue and Gray* (Buffalo Gap, TX: State House Press, 2000; originally published 1977), 118; and Jerry D. Thompson and Lawrence T. Jones, *Civil War and Revolution on the Rio Grande Frontier* (College Station: Texas A&M University Press, 2004), 82.

152. Wooten, 553.

153. Report of Day dated Sept. 8, 1864, at Brazos Santiago, OR-A, 1-41-I, 749.

154. Ford *Memoirs*, 1127.

155. Ford Papers TCM94.1.0846.

156. Wooten, 553.

157. Ford *Memoirs*, 1127-1128.

158. Ford *Memoirs*, 1128.

159. Ranger, "The Battles of San Martin and Palmetto Ranch, Fought Sept. 9th, 1864," Austin *Weekly State Gazette* (Oct. 19, 1864), 1. Hereafter cited as Ranger.

160. Ranger.
161. Ford *Memoirs*, 1128.
162. Ford Papers, TCM94.1.0534.
163. Ford Papers, TCM94.1.535
164. Letter of Ford to Veron dated Sept. 6, 1864, at Brownsville, *OR-A*, 1-41-III, 912.
165. Ford *Memoirs*, 1131.
166. Letter of Day to Drake dated Sept. 8, 1864, at Brazos Santiago, *OR-A*, 1-41-III, 99-100.
167. Letter of Pierce to Herron dated Sept. 8, 1864, at Matamoros, *OR-A*, 1-41-III, 101.
168. Letter of Day to Drake dated Sept. 14, 1864, at Brazos Santiago, *OR-A*, 1-41-III, 184.
169. Letter of Ford to Commanding Officer, U.S. Forces, dated Sept. 12, 1864, at Fort Brown, *OR-A*, 1-41-III, 947.
170. Letter of Day to Ford dated Sept. 13, 1864, at Brazos Santiago, *OR-A*, 1-41-III, 947.
171. Carlos, "Brownsville," Houston *Daily Telegraph* (Sept. 30, 1864), 2.
172. Pierce, 50-51.
173. Letter of Day to Drake dated Oct. 9, 1864, at Brazos Santiago, *OR-A*, 1-41-III, 721-722.
174. Letter of Canby to Banks dated Sept. 15, 1861, at New Orleans, *OR-A*, 1-41-III, 197-198.
175. Letter of Drayton dated Sept. 15, 1864, at Brownsville, *OR-A*, 1-41-III, 931.
176. Letter of Root to Dwyer dated Sept. 14, 1861, at Brownsville, *OR-A*, 1-41-III, 956.
177. Letter of Drayton dated Sept. 15, 1864, at Brownsville, *OR-A*, 1-41-III, 931.
178. Rozeff, 55.
179. "Record of Events," Regimental Return, Sept. 1864. NARA.
180. John Salmon Ford (edited by with Stephen B. Oates), *Rip Ford's Texas* (Austin: University of Texas Press, 1991 but originally published 1963), 371. Hereafter cited as *Rip Ford's Texas*.
181. Ford *Memoirs*, 1127.
182. "Record of Events," Regimental Return, Sept. 1864, NARA.
183. Ranger, lines 22-23.
184. Ranger.
185. Ford *Memoirs*, 1127-1128.
186. *Rip Ford's Texas*, 371.
187. Nacion, "Letter from the Rio Grande," Houston *Tri-Weekly Telegraph* (Nov. 4, 1864), 2.
188. Regimental Returns for Sept., Oct., 7 Nov. 1864, per abstracts in Compiled Service Record of Major F.E. Kavanaugh, NARA.

189. Compiled Service Records of Major F.E. Kavanaugh, NARA.
190. Ford Papers.
191. Ford *Memoirs*, 1134.
192. Report of Lt. Col. Giddings included in Ford *Memoirs*, 1134-1138.
193. "The French at Matamoras," *Dallas Herald* (Oct. 15, 1864), 2.
194. Carlos, untitled letter, Houston *Daily Telegraph* (Oct. 26, 1864), 2.
195. Letter of Gen. Pile to Maj. Drake dated Dec. 5, 1864, at Brazos Santiago, *OR-A*, 1-41-IV, 767-768.
196. Letter of Col. Jones to Lt. Col. Drake dated Feb. 28, 1865, at Brazos Santiago, *OR-A*, 1-48-I, 1005.
197. *Rip Ford's Texas*, 371.
198. Ford *Memoirs*, 1158-1159.
199. Douglas Southall Freeman, *Lee's Lieutenants: A Study in Command, Volume Two: Cedar Mountain to Chancellorsville* (New York: Charles Scribner's Sons, 1971; originally published 1943), 325-326.
200. McCaslin, 184.
201. *Rip Ford's Texas*, xxvii.
202. Carlos, untitled letter, Houston *Daily Telegraph* (Oct. 26, 1864), 2.
203. Annotated on Regimental Return for Nov. 1864, Compiled Service Records of F.S. Fritter, A. King and H. Krowell, NARA.
204. Austin *State Gazette* (Nov. 2, 1864).
205. Nacion, "Letter from the Rio Grande," Houston *Tri-Weekly Telegraph* (Nov. 4, 1864), 2.
206. Carlos, untitled letter, Houston *Daily Telegraph* (Aug. 16, 1864), 2.
207. Carlos, untitled letters, Houston *Daily Telegraph* (Sept. 21, 1864, and Sept. 28, 1864).
208. Confederate, "Letter from Brownsville," Houston *Tri-Weekly Telegraph*, Apr. 28, 1865, 3.
209. Ford *Memoirs*, 1159.
210. Compiled Service Records of Capt. T. A. Wilson, NARA.
211. Ford *Memoirs*, 1159.

Chapter Eight

1. Regimental Returns for Sept., Oct., and Nov. 1864, cited in Compiled Service Record of F.E. Kavanaugh, NARA.
2. "Dr. T. [sic] E. Kavanaugh" (obituary), Santa Fe *New Mexican* (May 25, 1866).
3. Hampton Sides, *Blood and Thunder: The Epic Story of Kit Carson and the Conquest of the American West* (New York: Anchor Books, 2007), 326-338.
4. Hall, 375.
5. Compiled Service Record of F.E. Kavanaugh, NARA.
6. Regimental Return, Oct. 1864, NARA.
7. Regimental Returns, Nov. and Dec. 1864, NARA.
8. Regimental Return, Dec. 1864, NARA.
9. Ford Papers, TCM94.1.0862.
10. Ford Papers, TCM94.1.0864.
11. Ford Papers, TCM94.1.0274 and TCM94.1.0609.
12. Letter of Thomas H. O'Callaghan dated Mar. 1, 1865, at San Patricio to Gen. J.G. Walker, National Archives "Confederate Papers Relating to Citizens of Business Firms, 1861-65," microfilm roll M346.
13. Citation from the Goliad *Messenger* in the Shreveport (LA) *Semi-Weekly News*, Apr. 1, 1865, 2.
14. Sioux, "Editor Telegraph," Houston *Tri-Weekly Telegraph*, Jan. 27, 1865, 2.
15. Houston *Tri-Weekly Telegraph*, Mar. 8, 1865, 4.
16. William Gouverneur Morris, *Address Delivered Before the Society of California Volunteers at Its First Annual Celebration, San Francisco, April 25th, 1866* (San Francisco: Commercial Steam Printing House: Francis, Valentine & Co., 1866), 22.
17. *OR-A*, 1-50-II, 332-333.
18. Letter of Headquarters Trans-Mississippi Department to Maj. Gen. J.B. Magruder dated Apr. 5, 1863, at Alexandria, LA, *OR-A*, 1-22-II, 814.
19. Letter Turner to Gen. S. Cooper dated June 8, 1863, at Houston, *OR-A*, 1-26-II, 57-58.
20. *OR-A*, 1-48-II, 648-649, 681, 700-701, 703-705, 721. Also *OR-A*, 4-3, 76, 961, 1035-1036.
21. *OR-A*, 1-50-II, 1078.
22. "Guarding Against Trouble," *Union*, Sept. 10, 1864, 2.
23. *OR-A*, 1-48-II, 1104.
24. *OR-A*, 4-4. Also *OR-A*, 4-3, 76, 961, 1035-1036., 960-962.
25. *OR-A*, 1-53-Supplement, 1044-1046.
26. James F. Morgan, "Confederate Governor John Robert Baylor: Father of Arizona Territory," *Confederate Veteran*, Vol. XXXIII, No. 3 (May 1985), 31.
27. Untitled article, Houston *Tri-Weekly Telegraph*, Mar. 8, 1865, 4.
28. *OR-A*, 1-53-Supplement, 1046-1047.
29. "Items of Interest," Houston

Tri-Weekly Telegraph, Mar. 17, 1865, 2.

30. Letter of W.S. Rather to Lt. Duggan dated Mar. 29, 1865, at near Brownsville, Ford Papers, TCN94.1.1203.

31. Letter of Capt. T.D. Sanders to Capt. Turner dated Apr. 8, 1865, at near Richmond, Texas, and included in the Compiled Service Record of Capt. T.D. Sanders.

32. Wm. T. Robinson letter dated Apr. 15, 1865, at Houston to Mr. Murry, Bredett Corydon Murray Papers (MS1047), Arizona Historical Society, Tucson. Untitled articles, Houston Tri-Weekly Telegraph, Apr. 28, 1865, 2, 4.

33. Special Orders (not numbered) of Brig. Gen. Slaughter dated Apr. 1, 1865, at Banquette, Texas, Ford Papers, TCM94.1.0600. "Military Execution at Brownsville," New York Daily Tribune, May 13, 1865, 8.

34. Untitled article, Houston Tri-Weekly Telegraph, May 10, 1865, 2, 4.

35. Untitled article, Houston Tri-Weekly Telegraph, May 16, 1865, 2. Dallas Herald, May 18, 1865, 1.

36. Showalter letters of May 2 and May 3, 1865, from camp near Richmond, Texas, CSR.

37. Jerry Coffee, "Re: trying to find info on CSA Texas Officer," The Texas in the Civil War Message Board—Archive, Nov. 26, 2005.

38. Notice (advertisement), Austin, Texas, Weekly State Gazette, Aug. 10, 1864, 2 and Aug. 17, 1864, 2.

39. Galveston Daily News, May 20, 1895, 6.

40. Cibolero, "Headquarters Sims' Regiment T. M. V.," Houston Tri-Weekly Telegraph, Mar. 27, 1865, 1.

41. Notice (advertisement), Houston Tri-Weekly Telegraph, Nov. 14, 18, 28, 30, 1865.

42. Affidavit in file of J.D. McKissick, Con. Papers.

43. Letter of Asst. Adj. Gen. Thos. M. Jack to Maj. Gen. J.B. Magruder, dated Apr. 14, 1865, at Houston, OR-A, 1-48-II, 1279.

44. W, "Campaign from Hempstead to Red River, the "success. Fare of the Country—Agricultural Interests, etc.," Houston Tri-Weekly Telegraph, May 24, 1865, 1.

45. Showalter letters dated May 2 and May 3, 1865, at near Richmond, Texas, Showalter CSR.

46. Untitled article, Houston Tri-Weekly Telegraph, May 19, 1865, 1.

47. "City Council," Houston Tri-Weekly Telegraph, May 31, 1865, 1 and Galveston Daily News, June 1, 1865, 1.

48. Texas Soldier's Application for Pension No. 22929 of Lycurgus B. Earnest.

49. Texas Soldier's Application for Pension No. 38048 of Stephen W. Wilkinson.

50. Texas Soldier's Application for Pension No. 19735 of D.D. Noel.

51. Texas Soldier's Application for Pension No. 17973 of J.A. Tharp.

52. Texas Soldier's Application for Pension No. 19766 of Henry Clay Damron.

53. Tennessee Soldier's Application for Pension No. 11164 of Jas. T. M'Cutchen.

54. Proclamation 134—Granting Amnesty to Participants in the Rebellion, with Certain Exceptions, President Andrew Johnson, May 29, 1865.

55. Sarah A. Dorsey, Recollections of Henry Watkins Allen: Brigadier-general Confederate States Army, Ex-Governor of Louisiana (New York: Doolady, 1866), 299. Hereafter cited as Dorsey.

56. Dorsey, 326.

57. "Shelby Expedition," Handbook of Texas Online, http://www.tshaonline.org/handbook/online/articles/qms01, accessed Aug. 16, 2013. Hereafter cited as "Shelby Expedition."

58. Dorsey, 326.

59. Edwin Adams Davis, Fallen Guidon: The Saga of Confederate General Jo Shelby's March to Mexico (College Station: Texas A & M University Press, 1995), 55. Hereafter cited as E.A. Davis.

60. Dorsey, 327.

61. "Shelby Expedition."

62. Dorsey, 327.

63. E.A. Davis, 65. Andrew F. Rolle, The Lost Cause: The Confederate Exodus to Mexico (Norman: University of Oklahoma Press, 1965), 57.

64. John Newman Edwards, Shelby's Expedition to Mexico: An Unwritten Leaf of the War (Fayetteville: University of Arkansas Press, 2002; originally published, 1872), 33. Hereafter cited as Edwards.

65. Edwards, 34.

66. E.A. Davis, 74.

67. E.A. Davis, 83–88.

68. E.A. Davis, 98.

69. E.A. Davis, 107–109.

70. E.A. Davis, 114–115.

71. Cornelius Cole Smith, "Some Unpublished History of the Southwest," Arizona Historical Review, Vol. 4, No. 1 (Apr. 1931), 32–33. Hereafter cited as Smith, v4n1.

72. Smith, v4n1, 33, 53.

73. Smith, v4n1, 53.

74. Smith, v4n1, 54.

75. Tennessee Soldier's Application for Pension No. 11164 of Jas. T. M'Cutchen.

76. Smith, v4n1, 53–54.

77. Smith, v4n1, 54–55.

78. Smith, v4n1, 56–57.

79. Smith, v4n1, 57.

80. Smith, v4n1, 58–59.

81. Smith, v4n1, 60.

82. Smith, v4n1, 60–61.

83. Smith, v4n1, 61–62.

84. Smith, v4n1, 62.

85. Smith, v4n1, 63.

86. Smith, v4n1, 63.

87. Cornelius Cole Smith, "Some Unpublished History of the Southwest," Arizona Historical Review, Vol. 4, No. 4 (Jan. 1932), 46. Hereafter cited as Smith, v4n4.

88. Smith, v4n4, 46.

89. Smith, v4n4, 47.

90. Smith, v4n4, 48–49.

91. Smith, v4n4, 49–50.

92. Smith, v4n4, 51.

93. Smith, v4n4, 51.

94. Smith v4n4, 52.

95. Smith, v4n4, 53.

96. Smith, v4n4, 54–55.

97. Smith, v4n4, 56.

98. Smith, v4n4, 57.

99. Cornelius Cole Smith, "Some Unpublished History of the Southwest," Arizona Historical Review, Vol. 5, No. 1 (Apr. 1932), 62. Hereafter cited as Smith, v5n1.

100. Smith, v5n1, 65.

101. Sam Box, "End of the War—Exiles in Mexico," Confederate Veteran, Vol. XI, No. 3 (Mar. 1903), 123. Hereafter cited as Box.

102. Anthony Archer, General Jo Shelby's March (New York: Random House, 2010), 122.

103. Box.

104. Photocopy of handwritten memoir of Thomas W. Westlake, 139, Watson-Westlake Papers, folder 11, State Historical Society of Missouri, Columbia.

105. Box.

106. "Death of Col. Showalter," Mariposa Free Press (Mar. 10, 1866) citing Mazatlan Times (Mar. 8, 1866).

107. "Arrival of Ex-Rebels in Mazatlan," Austin (NV) Daily Reese River Reveille (Aug. 30, 1865), 2.

108. Box.

109. F.W. Westlake, "Confederate Who Served in Mexican Army," Confederate Veteran, Vol. XVI, No. 8 (Aug. 1908), 382. Hereafter cited as Westlake.

110. Box.
111. Deryl P. Sellmeyer, *Jo Shelby's Iron Brigade* (Gretna, LA: Pelican Publishing Co., 2007), 291.
112. Westlake.
113. "Death of Showalter," San Francisco *Golden Era* (Mar. 11, 1866), 8. "How Showalter Was Killed," *SDU* (Feb. 26, 1866), 5. "Perished by the Sword," *Mariposa Gazette* (Mar. 3, 1866), 2.
114. "From Texas," *DAC* (Nov. 19, 1865), 1.
115. "How Showalter Was Killed." "Perished by the Sword," Chris H. Bailey, *The Stulls of Millsborough: A Genealogical History of John Stull "the Miller" Pioneer of Western Maryland*, Vol. 1 (MD: Chris H. Bailey, 2000). Hereafter cited as Bailey.
116. "Death of Showalter."
117. "Perished by the Sword."
118. "From Texas."
119. "Further from Mazatlan—How Dan Showalter Died," *Alta* (Feb. 25, 1866), 1.
120. For details of this affair and Greathouse's part in it see Asbury Harpending, *The Great Diamond Hoax and Other Stiring Incidents in the Life of Asbury Harpending* (San Francisco: James H. Barry Co., 1913), 73-89.
121. "From Texas."
122. Marisue Potts email to Gene C. Armistead, Mar. 20, 2013. Hereafter cited as Potts.
123. Bailey.
124. "Confederates in Mexico," Austin (NV) *Daily Reese River Reveille* (Nov. 21, 1865), 2.
125. "From Mazatlan—How Dan. Showalter Died," *DAC* Feb. 28, 1866), 1.
126. "Perished by the Sword."
127. "Death of Col. Showalter," *Mariposa Free Press* (Mar. 10, 1866).
128. "Tetanus," *Wikipedia, the Free Encyclopedia*, accessed Sept. 23, 2013.
129. "Perished by the Sword."
130. Smith, v5n1, 62.
131. Mazatlan," *Wikipedia, the Free Encyclopedia*, accessed Sept. 24, 2013.
132. "Death of Col. Showalter," *Mariposa Free Press* (Mar. 10, 1866).
133. "Angel Flores," *De Wikipedia, la encyclopedia libre*, accessed Sept. 24, 2013, and translated by Gene C. Armistead.
134. Enrique Vega Ayala, "Los pantoncs pcrdidos dc Mazatlan," noroeste.com, dated Feb. 11, 2011, accessed Sept. 23, 2013, translated by Gene C. Armistead.

Chapter Nine

1. Clendenen, 324.
2. Laurence Fletcher Talbott, *California in the War for Southern Independence* (Los Angeles: Hale & Co., 1996), 85-103.
3. Seeley letter.
4. Eric Fonner, "Anti-war Sentiment in Greene County, Pennsylvania," *Pennsylvania in the Civil War*, http://pennsylvaniainthecivilwar.blogspot.com/2008/03/investigation-into-anti-war-sentiment_21.htm, Mar. 21, 2008, accessed Dec. 12, 2013.
5. Seeley letter.
6. Stacey L. Smith, "Remaking Slavery in a Free State: Masters and Slaves in Gold Rush California," *Pacific Historical Review*, Vol. 80, No. 1 (Feb. 2011), 41.
7. Letter of P.H. Hill to Mrs. P.H. Hill dated Jan. 10, 1865, at Camp Hood, Cameron County, TX, in the P.H. Hill Collection, Texas Heritage Museum, Hill College, Hillsboro, TX.
8. Letter of Amzi Bradshaw to Showalter dated Aug. 6, 1864, at Brownsville, TX, included in the CSR of Amzi Bradshaw.
9. Junius, "The Naval Fight off Sabine," Houston *Tri-Weekly Telegraph* (Feb. 3, 1863), 2.
10. Smith, v5n1, 62.
11. Smith, v5n1, 65.
12. Smith, v5n1, 62.
13. Gorley, *Loyal Californians*, 14.

Appendix B

1. Richard Henry Savage, *The Little Lady of the Lagunitas: A Franco-Californian Romance*, http://www.aolib.com/reader_6011.htm, copyright 2009-2011, accessed Apr. 23, 2014. "Richard Henry Savage," *Wikipedia, the Free Encyclopedia*, http://en.wikipedia.org/wiki/, accessed May 10, 2014.
2. Note, Synopsis and Story Line provided by John Culea to Gene C. Armistead, postmarked Sept. 18, 2009. The novel was published in 2012 by Amazon Digital Services.
3. Don Chenhall, "The Frog," *Rope and Wire: A Western Lifestyle Online Community*, http://www.ropeandwire.com/FullStories/The_Frog.html, accessed June 15, 2014.

Appendix C

1. "Prominent Arizona Confederates," Arizona Division, Sons of Confederate Veterans, http://home.earthlink.net/_csscv/arizodivisionsonsofconfederateveterans/id5.html, accessed May 17, 2014.
2. "Encyclopedia California in the Civil War," *NationMaster*, http://www.nationmaster.com/encyclopedia/California-in-the-Civil-War, accessed Mar. 13, 2013.
3. Among the sources telling the story of this stagecoach robbery are Eugene B. Block, *Great Stagecoach Robberies of the West* (Garden City, NY: Doubleday & Company, 1962), 116-125; Alvin M. Josephy, Jr., *The Civil War in the American West* (New York: Alfred A. Knopf, 1991), 238; and Talbott, 183-193.
4. Parker J. Bena, "An Accurate and Detailed History of the War's Western Theater" (book review of *The Civil War in the American West* by Alvin M. Josephy), Oct. 14, 2007, http://www.amazon.com/review, accessed May 17, 2014.
5. Ron J. Pastore, "Robert S. James: Minister, Husband, Father," *Jesse James Photo Album*, http://jessejamesphotoalbum.com/robert-sallee-james/, accessed Mar. 19, 2015.
6. Ron J. Pastore, Email to Gene C. Armistead, dated Mar. 29, 2015.
7. Carlynn Trout, "Robert Sallee James (1818-1850)," *Historic Missourians*, http://shs.umsystem.edu/historicmissourians/name/j/james/index.html, accessed Mar. 29, 2015; Mike Graves, "Rev. Robert Sallee James," *Find a Grave*, http://www.findagrave.com/cgi-bin/fg.cgi?page=gr&Grid=127676458, accessed Mar. 29, 2015; "Robert S. James," *Wikipedia, the Free Encyclopedia*, http:en.wikipedia.org/wiki/Robert_S_James, accessed Mar. 19, 2015.
8. Debbie Quinn Pastore, "The James Family," *Genealogy Trails History Group*, http://genealogytrails.com/kin/jesse-james.html, accessed Mar. 29, 2015
9. Walter Earl Pittman, *Rebels in the Rockies: Confederate Irregulars in the Western Territories* (Jefferson, NC: McFarland, 2014). Showalter briefly discussed pp. 204-205.
10. Email dated Aug. 21, 2014, from Walter Earl Pittman to Gene C. Armistead.
11. Serge Noirsain, "The Arizona Brigade: The Legion That Never Set Foot in the Desert," Confederate Historical Society of Belgium, http://www.chabpbelgium.com, accessed Apr. 26, 2013.
12. http://www.noirsain.net/, accessed May 21, 2014.

Appendix D

1. Handwritten note from Clyde E. Noble to Gene C. Armistead, dated May 22, 2013, and postmarked at Athens, GA.
2. Ben H. Willingham and Jeffrey L. Sizemore, *Military Order of the Stars and Bars: 75 Years of Heritage* (White House, TN: Military Order of the Stars and Bars, 2013), 212. Email from Toni Turk, Commander General, Military Order of the Stars and Bars, to Gene C. Armistead, May 9, 2013.
3. "Kleberg County Historical Markers," Travel South Texas, http://www.fortours.com/pages/hmkleberg.asp, accessed Jan. 17, 2014.
4. "They Passed This Way/Temecula Valley Museum," Temecula Valley Museum, Temecula, CA, http://www.temeculavalleymuseum.org/page_id=224, accessed Mar. 5, 2013.
5. Rowland King, "Confederate Cavalry in El Monte: A Plaque to Honor Them," *The Vidette, California Division, Sons of Confederate Veterans*, Issue 10 (Nov. 13, 2002), 3–4. Cindy Arora, "El Monte Turns Down Confederate Veterans," *San Gabriel Valley Tribune*, Oct. 21, 2002, http://www.freerepublic.com/focus/f-news/773439/posts, accessed Jan. 30, 2013.
6. "Battle of Palmito Ranch Texas Historical Marker," accessed June 8, 20144, http://www.stxmaps.com/go/texas-historical-marker-battle-of-palmito-ranch.httml.
7. Robert Arconti, "Dan Showalter: California's Arch Rebel—Credit Where Credits Due," Aug. 5, 2012, http://caarchrebel.blogspot.com/2012/08/credit-where-credits-due.html.
8. "Temecula: Local Role in Civil War to Be Marked," *San Diego Union-Tribune* (Nov. 12, 2011), http://www.utsandiego.com/news/2011/nov/12/Temecula-local-role-in-civil-war, accessed Nov. 2, 2013
9. Email from Mayuko Nakajima, Assistant Planner, City of Rancho Cucamonga, to Gene C. Armistead, Aug. 16, 2013.

Bibliography

Offical Records and Publications

CALIFORNIA

Board of Pilot Commissioners. "Boards of Commissioners 1850–Present, State of California Board of Pilot Commissioners for the Bays of San Francisco, San Pablo and Suisun." http://www.bopc.ca.gov/bios.htm. Accessed Dec. 3, 2013.

California Military Museum, California State Military Department. "California and the Civil War: The Biderman Flag." http://www.militarymuseum.org/Biderman Flaghtm. Accessed Mar. 7, 2013.

Mariposa County. *County of Mariposa General Plan*. Mariposa, CA: Mariposa County Board of Supervisors, 2006. Chapter 11, Cultural and Historic Resources, of Volume III, Technical Background Report. http://mariposacounty.org/index. Accessed July 31, 2013.

Orton, Richard H., Brig. Gen. & Adjutant-General of California. *Records of California Men in the War of the Rebellion, 1861 to 1867*. Sacramento: J.D. Young, Supt. State Printing, 1890.

State Assembly. *A Journal of the Eighth Session of the Assembly of the State of California Begun on the Fifth Day of January One Thousand Eight Hundred and Fifty-seven and Ended on the Twenty-ninth Day of April, One Thousand Eight Hundred and Fifty-seven at the City of Sacramento*. Sacramento: James Allen, State Printer, 1857.

State Assembly. *Journal of the House of Assembly of California at the Twelfth Session of the Legislature Begun on the Seventh Day of January, 1861, and Ended on the Twentieth Day of May, 1861, at the City of Sacramento*. Sacramento: C.T. Botts, State Printer, 1861.

State Parks, Office of Historic Preservation. http://ohp.parks.ca.gov/ListedResources. Accessed Feb. 6, 2013. Links to information on California State Historic Markers: No. 311—Warner's Ranch, San Diego County, No. 482—Camp Wright, San Diego County, No. 502—Oak Grove Stage Station, San Diego County, No. 679—Home of Lord Charles Snowden Fairfax.

State Senate. *Journal of the Senate of the State of California at the Twelfth Session of the Legislature of the State of California*. Sacramento: C.T. Botts, State Printer, 1861.

The Statutes of California Passed at the Twelfth Session of the Legislature, 1861: Begun Monday the seventh day of January, and ended on Monday, the twentieth day of May. Sacramento: Charles T. Botts, State Printer, 1861.

ILLINOIS

"91st Infantry." *Report of the Adjutant General of the State of Illinois for the Years 1861–1866*, Vol. 5 (1900–1902). http://www.illinoiscivilwar.org/cw91-agr.html. Accessed May 18, 2013. Unit that opposed 4th Arizona at Palmito Ranch in Sept. 1864, 334–336.

MEXICO

Comision Pesquisidora de la Frontera del Norte, Mexican Congress. *Reports of the Committee of Investigation Sent in 1873 by the Mexican Government to the Frontier of Texas*. New York: Baker & Godwin, Printers, 1875. Pages iii–iv, 151–152, 189 on Cortina activities in Matamoros and Brownsville area during 1864.

OKLAHOMA

Application file nos. 751 of J.D. Henderson, 1628 of William F.M. Strong, 2262 of Henry W. Wilson, and 2642 of Joseph Smith Skaggs. Confederate Soldier's Pension Applications, Oklahoma State Library, Oklahoma City.

PENNSYLVANIA

Richards, H.M. *Report of the Commission to Locate the Site of the Frontier Forts of Pennsylvania*, Vol. 1—*Indian Forts of the Blue Mountains*. Clarence M. Busch, State Printer of Pennsylvania, 1896.

TENNESSEE

Confederate Soldier's Pension Applications, Tennessee State Library and Archives, Nashville. Application file no. 11164 of James Thomas M'Cutchen.

TEXAS

Confederate Soldier's Pension Applications, Texas State Library and Archives Commission, Austin. 23 soldiers' and 19 widows' application files relating to the 4th Arizona Cavalry.

United States

Bureau of Land Management, Department of the Interior. *General Land Office Records.* http://www.glorecords.blm.gov/results/default.aspx?searchCriteria=type=patent/st=CA. Accessed Jan. 7, 2014. Can be searched by state and name.

Bureau of the Census. *1810 Federal Census, Pennsylvania.* National Archives Microfilm Publication M252, Roll 162.

Bureau of the Census. *1860 Federal Census, Mariposa County, California.* Township No. 1, 42.

Channel Islands National Marine Sanctuary. "*Winfield Scott* Vessel History." http://channelislands.noaa.gov/shipwreck/dbase/cinms/winfieldscott1.html. Accessed July 17, 2013.

House of Representatives. *Executive Documents Printed by Order of the House of Representatives During the Second Session of the Thirty-Eighth Congress, 1864-'65.* Washington, D.C.: Government Printing Office, 1865. Includes State Department June 1864 correspondence relating to Brownsville and Matamoros.

House of Representatives. *Executive Documents Printed by Order of the House of Representatives During the First Session of the Thirty-Ninth Congress, 1865-'66.* Washington, D.C.: Government Printing Office, 1866.

House of Representatives. *First Session of the Forty-Fourth Congress; Executive Documents Printed by Order of the House of Representatives, 1875-76,* Vol. 1. Washington, D.C.: Government Printing Office, 1876. Secretary of the Interior's report on the Denver Quicksilver Mining Co. in which Showalter held shares on 333.

National Archives and Records Administration. *Compiled Service Records of Confederate Soldiers Who Served in Organizations from the State of Texas* (Record Group 109). Baird's Cavalry (Fourth Regiment, Arizona Brigade; Showalter's Regiment), M323, rolls 180 and 181.

Navy Department. *Official Records of the Union and Confederate Navies in the War of the Rebellion,* 2 series of 30 volumes. Washington, D.C.: 1894-1922. Series 1, Vol. 19 (1905).

President of the United States. *Proclamation 134—Granting Amnesty to Participants in the Rebellion, with Certain Exceptions.* President Andrew Johnson. May 29, 1865.

War Department. *Atlas to Accompany the Official Records of the Union and Confederate Armies.* Washington, D.C., 1895.

War Department. *Official Records of the Union and Confederate Armies in the War of the Rebellion,* 4 series of 70 volumes in 128 parts. Washington, D.C.: 1880-1901. Series I, Vol. 15 (1886), Vol. 22, Part 2 (1888), Vol. 26, Part 2 (1889), Vol. 34, Parts 1-2 (1897), Vol. 53, and Supplement (1898). Series 2, Vol. 2 (1897), Series 4, Vol. 3 (1900).

Manuscript and Photograph Collections

Arizona Historical Society, Tucson. Bredett Corydon Murray Papers (MS1047). Letter of William T. Robinson dated April 15, 1865, to Bredett Corydon Murray.

Bancroft Library, University of California Berkeley, Berkeley. Miscellaneous Historical Papers 1844-1876, Folder 9 (Microfilm roll BANC MSS C-E-64). Feb. 27, 1862, letter of Showalter to Gen. George Wright.

Dolph Briscoe Center for American History, University of Texas at Austin, Austin. John Salmon "Rip" Ford Papers Memoirs, Volume VI (1864). Typescript, miscellaneous papers, 1864.

Ellis County Museum, Waxahachie, TX. Photograph, "Confederate Recruiting Squad with New Enlistees," March-April 1864, identified as Stoke's Company, 4th Cavalry Regiment, Arizona Brigade.

McCain Library and Archives, University of Southern Mississippi, Hattiesburg. M16, Jackson (Alexander Melvome) Papers. Item No. 12 is a Carte-de-viste of Finis Ewing Kavanaugh.

Pearce Museum, Navarro College, Corsicana, TX. Civil War Collection, Spruce Baird Papers—1864 (Accession No. 2002.342). Letter of Spruce M. Baird dated Jan. 18, 1864.

Rosenberg Library Special Collections, Galveston and Texas History Center, Galveston. Elbridge Gerry Littlejohn Collection. Letter of John A. Drummond dated May 15, 1903.

Showalter, Edward D., papers, files of Dr. Maurice A. Showalter, Latrobe, PA. Given to holder by Jean Showalter Bendl. Notes, letters and newspaper clippings relating to the Showalter family.

Showalter, Robert L., papers, Mr. Robert L. Showalter, Latrobe, PA. Notes, letters and newspaper clippings relating to the Showalter family.

State Historical Society of Missouri, Columbia. Photocopy of handwritten memoir of Thomas W. Westlake, Watson-Westlake Papers, Collection C0186. Pages 133-140 in folders 10 and 11 are Westlake's account of his trip from Austin, TX, to Mazatlan, Mexico.

Texas Heritage Museum at Hill College, Hillsborough. P.H. Hill File. Letter of P.H. Hill dated 1865 to wife.

UT Arlington Library Special Collections, University of Texas Arlington. TX Historical Manuscripts Collection. Rose Ellen Ritchie Dryden letter dated Nov. 23, 1865, to her mother.

Correspondence

Coffee, Jerry. "Re: trying to find info on CSA Texas Officer," *The Texas in the Civil War Message Board,* Nov. 26, 2005.

Culea, John, San Diego. Handwritten note accompanied by synopsis and story line for his novel *The Trail to Mohawk* to Gene C. Armistead, Sept. 18, 2009.

Esplen, Burris E., IV, Associate Archivist, Diocese of Pittsburgh, Pittsburgh. Email to Robert D. Arconti, June 21, 2012.

Kudlik, Dr. John J. (Showalter relative), Pittsburgh. Email to Gene C. Armistead, Oct. 9, 2014.

Kudlik, Susan M. Showalter (Showalter relative), Pittsburgh. Telephonic interview with Robert D. Arconti, Apr. 28, 2013.

Nakajima, Mayuko (Assistant Planner, City of Rancho Cucamonga, CA). Email to Gene C. Armistead, Aug. 16, 2013.

Noble, Clyde E. (Showalter relative), Athens, GA. Handwritten note to Gene C. Armistead, May 22, 2013.

Pastore, Ron J. Email to Gene C. Armistead, Mar. 29, 2015.

Pittman, Walter Earl. Email to Gene C. Armistead, Aug. 21, 2014.

Potts, Marisue (West Texas Historical Association), Matador, TX. Email to Gene C. Armistead, Mar. 20, 2013.
Sagar, William (Secretary, Fairfax Historical Society), Fairfax, CA. Letters to Gene C. Armistead, Mar. 27, 2013, and Apr. 6, 2013.
Turk, Tom (Commander General, Military Order of the Stars and Bars). Email to Gene C. Armistead, May 9, 2013. Provided an address for a distant Showalter relative.

Newspapers, Historic

Digital newspaper archival programs make numerous old and historical newspapers from the past available. Particularly useful in research for this study were the California Digital Newspaper Collection of the Center for Bibliographical Studies and Research at the University of California, Riverside (http://www.cdnc.ucr.edu/cgi-bin/cnc) and the Texas Digital Newspaper Program of the University of North Texas Libraries (http://www.tdnp.unt.edu/explore/collections/TDNA/). Articles from the *New York Times*, one of the premier newspapers during the Civil War, can be searched at http://www.nytimes.com/ref/membercenter/nytarchive.html (the New York Times Article Archive). Two newspapers were found in the Nevada Digital Collection of the University of Nevada, Las Vegas, accessible via the Cooperative Libraries Automated Network. Additional newspapers can be found at Chronicling America: Historic American Newspapers (http://chroniclingamerica.loc.gov/) of the National Digital Newspaper Program at the Library of Congress. The National Library of Australia at Canberra's "Trove" (http://trove.nla.gov.au/ndp/) has an easily searchable database of digitized newspapers. The British Newspaper Archive (http://www.britishnewspaperarchive.co.uk/search/results?...) has a similar database but charges to access issues. Articles from contemporary newspapers are included under "Articles" in the Bibliography. Issues of the following historical newspapers, for the years indicated, contained articles mentioning or pertaining to Showalter's activities.

Alexandria (VA) *Gazette & Virginia Advertiser*—1853
Austin (NV) *Daily Reese River Reveille*—1865
Austin (TX) *Weekly State Gazette*—1864
Bellville (TX) *Countryman*—1865
Burnley *Advertiser* (Lancashire, England)—1861
Charleston (SC) *Mercury*—1863
Clarksville (TX) *Standard*—1863, 1865
Columbus (GA) *Daily Enquirer*—1863
Dallas (TX) *Herald*—1865
Davenport (IA) *Daily Leader*—1898
Ebensburg (PA) *Democrat & Sentinel*—1866
The Empire (Sydney, New South Wales, Australia)—1861
Hampshire *Advertiser* (Hampshire, England)—1861
Houston (TX) *Daily Telegraph/Tri-Weekly Telegraph/Weekly Telegraph*—1863–1866
Inverness *Courier* (Inverness-shire, Scotland)—1861
Launceson Examiner (Launceston, Tasmania, Australia)—1861
Leeds *Times* (West Yorkshire, England)—1861
Leicester *Chronicle* (Leicestershire, England)—1861
Los Angeles (CA) *Star*—1857, 1860, 1862–1863
Maitland Mercury & Hunter River General Advertiser (Maitland, New South Wales, Australia)—1861
Manchester *Times* (Manchester, England)—1861
Mariposa (CA) *Democrat*—1857
Mariposa (CA) *Free Press*—1866
Mariposa (CA) *Gazette*—1861–1862, 1866
Marysville (CA) *Daily Herald*—1857
The Mercury (Hobart, Tasmania, Australia)—1861
Morning Chronicle (London, England)—1861
New York (NY) *Daily Tribune*—1865
New York (NY) *Herald*—1863
New York (NY) *Times*—1852, 1860–1864
Newcastle Chronicle and Hunter River District News (Newcastle, New South Wales, Australia)—1861
Newcastle Guardian & Tyne Mercury (Wear, England)—1861
Oswego (NY) *Palladium*—1864
Otago Witness (Otago, New Zealand)—1853
Paisley Herald & Renfrewshire Advertiser (Renfrewshire, Scotland)—1861
Perth Gazette and Independent Journal of Politics and News (Perth, Western Australia, Australia)—1861
Philadelphia (PA) *Inquirer*—1863
Philadelphia (PA) *Press*—1862–1863
Redwood City (CA) *San Mateo County Gazette*—1861
Richmond (VA) *Whig and Public Advertiser*—1864
Sacramento (CA) *Daily Record-Journal*—1891
Sacramento (CA) *Daily Transcript*—1851
Sacramento (CA) *Daily Union*—1857, 1859–1866, 1875, 1891
Sacramento (CA) *Sunday Union*—1889
San Francisco (CA) *Bulletin*—1858
San Francisco (CA) *California Farmer and Journal of Useful Sciences*—1862
San Francisco (CA) *Call/Evening Call*—1893, 1900
San Francisco (CA) *Daily Alta California*—1856, 1857, 1860–1863, 1865–1866, 1875
San Francisco (CA) *Daily Evening Bulletin/Evening Bulletin*—1861, 1863, 1865
San Francisco (CA) *The Golden Era*—1866
San Francisco (CA) *Mining & Scientific Press*—1867
San Mateo County (CA) *Gazette*—1861
San Rafael (CA) *Marin County Journal*—1861
Santa Fe (NM) *New Mexican*—1866
Sausalito (CA) *News*—1889
Shreveport (LA) *Semi-Weekly News*—1865
Sonoma (CA) *Sonoma County Democrat*—1864
Sonoma (CA) *Union Democrat*—1857
Stockton (CA) *Daily Argus*—1861
Sydney Morning Herald (Sydney, New South Wales, Australia)—1861
Visalia (CA) *Weekly Delta*—1860–1861
Washington (D.C.) *Daily National Intelligencer*—1864
Washington (D.C.) *Daily National Republican*—1863
Washington (PA) *Reporter*—1863
Western Times (Devon, England)—1861
Zanesville (OH) *Daily Zanesville Courier*—1861

Articles

Ainsworth, Ed. "Ballots and Bullets." *Los Angeles Times Sunday Magazine* (Aug. 28, 1938). About the duel.
Arconti, Robert D. "Dan Showalter: California's Arch Rebel." http://caarchrebel.blogspot.com. This blogspot includes 21 postings between July 31, 2012, and Oct. 6, 2014. Material found in the postings is incorporated into this book. Perhaps new information or commentary will be posted on this blog after publication of this book.
Arizona Division, Sons of Confederate Veterans. "Prominent Arizona Confederates." http://home.earthlink.

net/_csscv/arizodivisionsofconfederateveterans/id5.html. Accessed May 17, 2014.
Armistead, Gene C. "California's Confederate Militia: The Los Angeles Mounted Rifles." http://www.militarymuseum.org/LosAngelesMountedRifles2.htm. This *California State Military Museum* article includes information on a group that preceded Showalter's attempted route to Texas.
Baker, Emma. "Brown, John Henry." *Handbook of Texas Online*. http://www.tsha.online.org/handbook/online/articles/frb94. Accessed Dec. 31, 2013.
Bakken, Gordon Morris. "The Courts, the Legal Profession, and the Development of Law in Early California." Chapter 3 of *Taming the Elephant: Politics, Government and Law in Pioneer California*. Berkeley: University of California Press, 2003. On importance and prevalence of dueling in 1850s California, 39.
Barnhart, Don. "Warriors of the Lone Star—the Mexico Connection." *Warriors of the Lone Star Newsletter and Reflections on Texas Military History, the Old West, and Native Americans*. http://warrirosofthelonestar.bolgspot.com/2012/04/mexico-connection.html. Posted Apr. 29, 2012. Accessed May 17, 2013. Civil War activity along the Rio Grande.
"Battle of Palmito Ranch Texas Historical Marker." http://www.stxmaps.com/go/texas-historical-marker-battle-of-palmito-ranch.html. Accessed June 8, 2014.
Beck, Derrell. "Mesa Grande Chronicles First White Settler at Mesa Grande." *Ramona* (CA) *Home Journal* (July 1, 2010). http://www.ramonajournal.com/.
Belden, L. Burr. "San Bernardino Sesquicentennial 1810–May 20th–1960." San Bernardino *Sun-Telegram* (May 20, 1960).
Bena, Parker J. "An Accurate and Detailed History of the War's Western Theater" (book review of *The Civil War in the American West* by Alvin M. Josephy). http://www.amazon.com/Civil-American-West-Alvin-Josephy/dp/0679740031. Review written Oct. 14, 2007. Accessed May 17, 2014. The reviewed book is excellent—but the review itself is highly inaccurate.
Blackstock, Joe. "Assemblyman Remembered for Losing State's Last Political Duel." Ontario (CA) *Inland Valley Daily Bulletin* (Sept. 10, 2013). http://www.sbsun.com/government-and-politics/20130910/assemblyman-remembered-for-. Accessed Nov. 2, 2013.
Block, William Theodore, Jr. "Capt. K.D. Keith: Confederate Hero and Sabine Pass Pioneer." *Port Arthur News* (Jan. 2, 1974). http://www.wtblock.com/wtblockjr/captain1.htm. Accessed Aug. 13, 2013. Battle off Sabine Pass.
_____. "Civil War Comes to Jefferson County, Texas: The Road to Gettysburg, 1861–1863." *Blue & Gray Magazine*, Vol. IV, No. 1 (Sept. 1986). Information on Battle off Sabine Pass is included, 10–18.
_____. "The Cottonclad Gunboat 'Uncle Ben': Cotton-Carrying Workhorse of the Sabine." Reprint, *Beaumont Enterprise* (Oct. 24, 1974). One of the gunboats at Battle off Sabine Pass.
_____. "The Diary of 1st Sergeant H.N. Connor." http://www.wtblock.com/wtblockjr/diaryof/htm. Accessed Aug. 13, 2013. Sgt. Connor was a participant in Battle off Sabine Pass.
_____. "11th Battalion, Texas Volunteers, Confederate States Army." *East Texas Historical Journal*, Vol. XXX, No. 1 (1992). http://www.wtblock.com/wtblockjr/Spaight.htm. Accessed Aug. 13, 2013. Unit participated in Battle off Sabine Pass, 44–57.
_____. "From Cotton Bales to Black Gold: A History of the Pioneer Wiess Families of Southeastern Texas." *Texas Gulf Historical and Biographical Record*, Vol. 8, No. 1 (Nov. 1973). http://www.wtblock.com/wtblockjr/cotton_bales_gold.htm. Accessed Dec. 15, 2013.
_____. "The Memoirs of Captain Koscuiszko D. Keith." *Texas Gulf Historical and Biographical Record*, Vol. X (Nov. 1974). Information on naval battle off Sabine Pass, 41–64.
_____. "Requiem for a Confederate Gunboat: The CSS Josiah H. Bell." http://www.wtblock.com/wtblockjr/josiah_h_bell.htm. Accessed Aug. 13, 2013. Boat involved in Battle off Sabine Pass.
_____. "Sabine Pass in the Civil War." *East Texas Historical Journal*, Vol. IX, No. 2 (Oct. 1971). Information on Battle off Sabine Pass included, 129–136.
_____. "Sgt. H.N. Connor: A Sabine Saddle Soldier's Civil War Exploits." *Beaumont Sunday Enterprise-Journal* (Aug. 22, 1976). Connor participated in Battle off Sabine Pass.
Bonfield, Lynn A. "When Money Was Necessary to Make Dreams Come True: The Cost of the Trip from Vermont to California via Panama." *Vermont History*, Vol. 76, No. 2 (Summer/Fall 2008), 130–148.
Box, Sam. "End of the War—Exiles in Mexico." *Confederate Veteran*, Vol. XI, No. 3 (March 1903). Box with Elliott's group to Mazatlan, 121–123.
Brigandi, Phil. "The Southern Emigrant Trail." *The Branding Iron*, No. 256 (Fall 2009). Los Angeles Westerners Corral. Capture of Showalter party, 11.
Brown, John Henry. "Raid Into Cook County, December 1863." *Frontier Times*, Vol. 17, No. 12 (Sept. 1940), 459–463. Showalter's Dec. 1863 pursuit of Indians, 463.
Bryan, J. L. "Bradshaw, Amzi." *Handbook of Texas Online*. http://www.tshaonline.org/handbook/online/articles/fbyrr. Accessed Dec. 2, 2013.
"The Bryants of Bridgeport." *Mono County Historical Society 2012 Newsletter* (2012). Aurora, Nevada, 2.
"Calaveras Co. CA Death Index S." http://calaverasgenealogy.com. Last updated Jan. 24, 2012. Accessed Jan. 7, 2014.
"California and the Civil War: The Biderman Flag." *California State Military Museum*. http://www.militarymuseum.org/BidermanFlag.html. Accessed Mar. 7, 2013.
"California Bound." *SF Genealogy*. http://www.sfgenealogy.com/californiabound/cb135.htm. Accessed Jun. 10, 2013. Ship "SS Illinois," 5.
California Historical Society—North Baker Research Library. "Henry Baker letter: San Francisco, to Thomas S. Fitch: ALS, 1861, Jan. 10." http://beta.worldcat.org/archivegrid/data/122569465. Accessed 2013.
"The California Rangers as Told by Capt. W. J. Howard." *Washington Post* (Apr. 28, 1907), reprint from *San Francisco Chronicle* (date?), transcribed by E. Feroben for Mariposa County Family Chronicles. http://www.mariposaresearch.net/. Accessed Mar. 6, 2013.
"Channel Islands National Marine Sanctuary *Winfield Scott* Vessel History." http://channelislands.noaa.gov/shipwreck/dbase/cinms/winfieldscott1.html. Accessed Nov. 8, 2013. The ship upon which Showalter reached San Francisco.
"Charles A. 'Charley' King." *Old City Cemetery Committee, Inc. of Sacramento, CA*. http://www.oldcitycemetery.com/CharlesAKing.htm. Accessed Jun. 30, 2013.
Chenhall, Don. "The Frog." *Rope and Wire: A Western Lifestyle Online Community*. http://www.ropeandwire.com/FullStories/The_Frog.html. Accessed June

15, 2014. This is a Western fiction short story about William Edwards who was a member of the Showalter Party.

"City of the Silent—Tales from Colma—Timeline." http://www.notfrisco.com/colmatales/timeline.html. Accessed Dec. 2, 2013.

Clendenen, Clarence C. "Dan Showalter: California Secessionist." *California Historical Society Quarterly*, Vol. 30, No. 4 (Civil War Commemorative Issue, Dec. 1961), 309–325.

Cooney, Percival J. "Southern California in Civil War Days." *Annual Publications of the Historical Society of Southern California*, Vol. 13, 54–68.

Cox, Mike. "Bagdad." *Texas Escapes*. http://www.texas escapes.com/MikeCoxTexasTales/Bagdad-Mexico. htm. Posted Apr. 3, 2007. Accessed May 17, 2013.

Crippen, John, Jr. "The Golden Knights of Dan Showalter." *Westways* (Nov. 1959), 8–9. No sources cited, contrived dialogues, speculative assumptions.

"Dave Leip's Atlas of U. S. Presidential Elections—1860 General Election Data." http://uselectionatlas.org/ RESULTS/date.php?year=1860&datatype=national &def=&. Accessed Mar. 24, 2013.

Delaney, Robert W. "Matamoros, Port for Texas during the Civil War." *Southwestern Historical Quarterly*, Vol. 58 (April 1955), 473–487. Summarizes trade through Matamoros during the war.

Donnelly, Florence. "Dramatic Piercy Showalter Duel at Fairfax is Recalled." San Rafael (CA) *Marin Independent* (Apr. 24, 1948).

Earle, John Jewett. "The Sentiment of the People of California With Respect to the Civil War." *Annual Report of the American Historical Association for the Year 1907*. Washington, D.C.: Government Printing Office, 1908, 125–135.

"1860 California Election Returns by County." http:// docs.google.com/document/pur?id=106st-iYDzAGf QfhdjRs4PNoXMhsiP4iiKgW26K. Accessed Mar. 24, 2013.

"8th Annual Fair of the State Agricultural Society, 3rd Day, at the Stock Grounds." *The Grizzly Bear*, Vol. 9, No. 5 (Sept. 1911).

"El Monte and the Confederacy." *The Landmark: Bulletin of the El Monte Historical Society*, Vol. 1, No. 2 (Sept. 1961). El Monte Battalion & Showalter, 1–5.

"El Monte and the Confederacy, Part Two." *The Landmark: Bulletin of the El Monte Historical Society*, Vol. 1, No. 3 (Dec. 1961). El Monte Battalion & Showalter, 1–3.

"El Monte Turns Down Confederate Veteran." West Covina (CA) *San Gabriel Valley Tribune* (Oct. 19, 2002).

Ellerbe, Rose L. "History of Temescal Valley." *Annual Publications, Historical Society of Southern California*, Vol. XI (1920), 12–20. Distances Los Angeles to Fort Yuma via intermediate locations, 12.

Ely, Glen Sample. "Gone from Texas and Trading with the Enemy: New Perspective on Civil War West Texas." *The Southwestern Historical Quarterly*, Vol. 110, No. 4 (April 2007). Henry Skillman, 444–445.

"Fairfax History—Page One." http://www.marindirect. com/fxhistory/history.html. Accessed Dec. 4, 2013. Charles Snowden Fairfax role in the duel.

Fireman, Bert M. "How Far Westward the Civil War?" *The 1963 All Posse Corral Brand Book of the Denver Posse of the Westerners*. Morrison, CO: Buffalo Bill Press, 1964, 163–170. Showalter party and La Paz Incident, 166–170.

Flanigan, Kathleen. "The Ranch House at Warner's." *The Journal of San Diego History, San Diego Historical Society Quarterly*, Vol. 42, No. 4 (Fall 1996).

Foner, Eric. "Anti-War Sentiment in Greene County, Pennsylvania." *Pennsylvania in the Civil War*. http:// pensylvaniainthecivilwar.blogspot.com/2008/03/ investigation-into-anti-war-sentiment_21.htm. Updated Mar. 21, 2008. Accessed Dec. 12, 2013.

"Fort Lafayette." *Wikipedia, the free encyclopedia*. http:// en.wikipedia.org/wiki/Fort Lafayette. Accessed July 21, 2013.

Fowler, Edna Howard. "History Department." *United Daughters of the Confederacy Magazine*, Vol. 13, No. 9 (Sept. 1950). Showalter as of Knights of the Golden Circle, 11.

Gerstbacher. "Temecula History: A Chronology 1797–1993." http://oldtemecula.com/history/history1/htm. Accessed 2013.

"Ghost Town USA's Guide to Ghost Towns, Mining Camps, and Other Formerly Inhabited Places in Mariposa County, California, Locations beginning with H." http://freepages.history.rootsweb.ancestry. com/_gtusa/ca/mrp-co/h.htm. Accessed June 7, 2013.

Givens, Murphy. "Confederates, at War's End, Flee to Mexico." Corpus Christi (TX) *Caller-Times* (Dec. 14, 2011).

Gowdy, Cathy. "Larkspur Woman Dies Near 100th Birthday." *Marin Independent Journal* (Apr. 30, 1956), 1, 4. http://www.sfgenealogy.com/boards/mcobits/ archive2/3178.html. Accessed June 9, 2013.

Graves, Mike. "Rev. Robert Sallee James." *Find a Grave*. http://www.findagrave.com/cgi-bin/fg.cgi?page= 127676458. Accessed Mar. 29, 2015.

Harley, R. Bruce. "Father of San Bernardino Valley: Senator William A. Conn." *Odyssey* (Quarterly of City of San Bernardino Historical & Pioneer Society), Vol. 11, No. 4 (Oct.–Nov.–Dec. 1989). Piercy's 1860 election victory over Conn, 53–54.

Hart, Herbert M. "Historic California Posts: Camp Wright." *California State Military Museum*. http:// www.militarymuseum.org/CpWright.html. Accessed July 6, 2013.

Hiltner, Nita. "San Bernardino County: A Look Back." Riverside (CA) *Press-Enterprise* (Oct. 22, 2011). http:// www.pe.com. Accessed Mar. 5, 2013. On Piercy's 1860 election.

"History of Sheriff's Department." *San Bernardino County Sheriff-Coroner Department*. http:www.co. san-bernardino.ca.us/sheriff/History.asp. Accessed Mar. 5, 2013. Some information about Piercy.

Hogan, Terry. "Backtracking: Bagdad and the American Civil War." http://www.thezephyr.com/backtrack/ bagdad.htm. Accessed May 17, 2013.

Immigrant Ships Transcribers Guild. "The Compass: New York Passenger Information." http://immigrant ships.net/newcompass/pass_arrivals_usa/usapass list_arrivals/newyork.ht ml. Accessed July 8, 2013.

"John S. Minter." http://ouramazingancestors.us/minter_ John/john-s-minter.html. Accessed Mar. 1, 2013. Biography of owner of Minter's Ranch.

Jones, Cindy. "Fourth Texas Cavalry, Arizona Brigade." *Handbook of Texas Online*. http://www.tshaonline. org/handbook/online/articles/qkfl7. Accessed Mar. 11, 2013.

Jones, Thomas R. "Important Happenings in California Fifty Years Ago." *The Grizzly Bear: A Monthly Magazine Devoted to All California*, Vol. IX, No. 1 (May 1911). Duel, 3.

Katz, Morris, and edited by Norton B. Stern. "Memoirs of Morris Katz—San Bernardino Pioneer." *Western States Jewish History*, Vol. 1, Issue 1 (Oct. 1969). Information about Piercy's election to the Assembly in 1860.

Keller, Keith. "The Intriguing Case of California Confederates." SouthernHeritage411www. http://www.southernheritage411.com. Accessed Jun. 25, 2013. Showalter mentioned as California legislator and duelist who went to the Confederacy, 2.

Kemble, John Haskell. "The Gold Rush by Panama." *Pacific Historical Review*, Vol. 18, No. 1, Rushing for Gold (Feb. 1949), 45–56.

Kerns, Wilmer L. "Three Showalter immigrants." http://www/salisburypa.com/jacobshowalter.html. Accessed June 19, 2013.

King, Rowland. "California Confederates." *The Vidette* (Newsletter of California Division of Sons of Confederate Veterans), Issue 18 (May 26, 2003). El Monte Battalion and Showalter, 7–8.

_____. "California Volunteers, El Monte Battalion, Confederate States Army." *The Vidette*, Issue 28 (Mar. 20, 2004). El Monte Battalion, 1–2.

_____. "Confederate Cavalry in El Monte." *The Vidette*, Issue 10 (Nov. 13, 2002). El Monte Battalion, 3–4.

Konrei. "November 29, 1861—California Secessionists Surrender." *Once a Civil War*. http://konreicivilwar.blogspot.com/2013/06/november-29-1861-california.html. Posted June 11, 2013. Accessed March 19, 2015.

"Krumbhaar's Texas Battery." *Handbook of Texas Online*. http://www.tshaonline.org/handbook/online/articles/qkk01. Accessed Dec. 30, 2012.

"Larkspur Woman Dies Near 100th Birthday." *Marin County Independent Journal* (Apr. 30, 1956). On "Marin County Obit—Board—Murray," http://sfgenealogy.com/boards/mcobitsl.html. Posted Aug. 4, 2006 by Cathy Gowdy. Accessed Apr. 24, 2013. Ellen Murray witnessed approach and aftermath of duel.

"Last Meeting." *Texas Research Ramblers Genealogical Society Newsletter*, Vol. XVIII, No. 5 (May 15, 2008). Steamboat at Battle off Sabine Pass, 1–3.

"Lone Mountain (California)." *Wikipedia, the Free Encyclopedia*. http://en.wikipedia.org/wiki/Lone_Mountain_(California). Accessed Dec. 3, 2013.

"Lone Mountain Cemetery." San Francisco History—SF Genealogy. http://sfgenealogy.com/sfhistory/hemon.htm. Accessed Dec. 3, 2013.

"Lord Fairfax' Manor." *Marin Independent Journal* website. http://extras.marinig.com/special/landmarks/landmarks13.html. Accessed Mar. 23, 2013.

Love, Frank. "Civil War Immediately Affected Fort Yuma." *Yuma* (AZ) *Sun* (Jan. 27, 2007)

_____. "Confederate Sympathizer Imprisoned Here." *Yuma* (AZ) *Sun* (Aug. 25, 2002).

_____. "Southern Sympathizer Was a General in Nickname Only." *Yuma* (CA) *Sun* (Dec. 15, 2005).

Masterson, Rosemary. "The Machado-Silvas Family." *The Journal of San Diego History, San Diego Historical Society Quarterly*, Vol. 15, No. 1 (Winter 1969). Information on John Minter family.

"Mazatlan." *Wikipedia, the Free Encyclopedia*. http://en.wikipedia.org/wiki/Mazatlan. Accessed Sept. 24, 2013.

Merriam, C. Hart. "Distribution and Classification of the Mewan Stock of California." *American Anthropologist*, New Series 9 (1947). Indian name of Horseshoe Bend, 346.

"The Monastery Letter." From *Illustrated History of St. Vincent Archabbey, Latrobe, Pa*. Latrobe, PA: St. Vincent Archabbey, n.d. http://noel.men.org/Monastery Letter.htm. Accessed May 26, 2013.

Morgan, James F. "Confederate Governor John Robert Baylor: Father of Arizona Territory." *Confederate Veteran*, Vol. XXXIII, No. 3 (May 1985), 28–32. Information on Capt. Kennedy's 1st California Battalion Cavalry, CSA, 31.

"Mother Mariposa—the Formation of Merced County." *Mariposa County History and Genealogy*. http://www.mariposaresearch.net/mother.html. Accessed July 29, 2013.

"Muster Roll, Mariposa Battalion." *Mariposa County, California, Genealogy & Historical Research Home Page*. http://mariposaresearch.net/battalion.htm. Accessed Dec. 21, 2013.

Noirsain, Serge. "The Arizona Brigade: The Legion That Never Set Foot in the Desert." *Confederate Historical Society of Belgium*. http://www.chabpbelgium.com. Accessed Apr. 26, 2013.

"November 4, 1856, General Election." *JoinCalifornia Election History for the State of California*. http://www.joincalifornia.com/election/1856-11-04. Accessed June 24, 2013.

Osment, Noel. "Showalter's March to Mexico Took Detour." San Diego (CA) *UT-San Diego* (Sept. 16, 2009). http://www.utsandiego.com/news.

Pastore, Debbie Quinn. "The James Family." *Genealogy Trails History Group*. http://genealogytrails.com/kin/jesse-james.html. Accessed Mar. 29, 2015.

Pastore, Ron J. "Robert S. James: Minister, Husband, Father." *Jesse James Photo Album*. http://jessejamesphotoalbum.com/robert-sallee-james/. Accessed Mar. 19, 2015.

Pate, J. Neil. "Unlikely Hero, Ridgeley Greathouse, Buried in Pauper's Grave." *Azie* (TX) *News* (Aug. 15, 2012). http://www.azienews.net/news.asp?Story-20188. Accessed Mar. 19, 2013.

Pearson, Timothy. "Westerners: Virginia Native Charlie Fairfax and His Two Dueling Friends Make Their Mark in the History of California." *Wild West* (Aug. 2006), 60, 62.

Perkins, Robert, and William Burns, III. "Unsung Heroes: A History of the Fourth Cavalry Regiment, Arizona Brigade." *The Guidon, the Newsletter of the Colonel Sherrod Hunter Camp 1525 Sons of Confederate Veterans*, Vol. XIX, No. 8 (May 2011), Vol. XIX, No. 9 (June 2011).

"Piercy vs Showalter." *Marin History Museum*. http://marinhistorymuseum.blogspot.com. Posted Jan. 3, 2013. Accessed Mar. 6, 2013.

"Preface." *American Jewish Historical Quarterly*, No. 7 (1899). Information on U.S. Major David Fergusson who reported Showalter in Chihuahua, v–vi.

Preimsberger, Duane. "Camp Wright's Role During Civil War Told." *Temecula Valley Historical Society Newsletter*, Vol. 10, Issue 6 (June 2010). Duel, Showalter party, 1–3.

"Proceedings of the Court Had upon the Death of Justice Brosnan" in "Memorials to Nevada Supreme Court Justices." http://nsla.nevadaculture.org/dm documents/Memorials.pdf." Accessed Dec. 1, 2013.

Railtown 1897 State Historic Park. "Silver Palace Restaurant, Good Food with a History." http://www.railtown 1897.com/doc.asp?ID=103. Accessed Mar. 3, 2013.

Rentiger, Joan. "Dr. Alfred Taliaferro: Marin's First Physician." Bolinas (CA) *Coastal Post* (Jan. 7, 1997). http://coastalpost.com/97/1/6.htm. Accessed Mar. 29, 2013.

"Robert S. James." *Wikipedia, the Free Encyclopedia.* http://en.wikipedia.org/wiki/Robert_S_James. Accessed Mar. 29, 2015.

Rogers, Rob. "After 150 Years, Marin Remains True to Its Roots." San Rafael (CA) *Marin Independent Journal* (Mar. 23, 2011). http://www.maringij.com/150/ci_17665891. Accessed Mar. 5, 2013.

Rosch, Harriet, and Donna Jackson. "The Compass, New York Passenger Information, New York Daily Times Published Passenger Lists." *Immigrant Ships Transcribers Guild.* http://immigrantships.net/newcompass/pass_arrivals_usa/usapasslist_arrivals/newyork.html. Accessed Nov. 8, 2013.

Rozeff, Norman. "The Story of Union Forces in South Texas During the Civil War." Harlingen Historical Preservation Society, Harlingen, TX. http://www.cchc.us/Articles/StoryofUnionForces.pdf, updated Jan. 2011. Accessed May 18, 2013. Information on Sept. 1864 Battle at Palmito Ranch, 55–56 of 82.

"Silver Palace Restaurant." *Railtown 1897 State Historic Park Visitor Information.* http://www.railtown1897.com. Accessed Mar. 7, 2013. Two pages about Biderman flag.

Smith, Cornelius Cole. "Some Unpublished History of the Southwest." *Arizona Historical Review*, Vol. 4, No. 1 (April 1931), 32–33. Vol. 4, No. 3 (Oct. 1931), 50–63. Vol. 4, No. 4 (Jan. 1932), 46–67. Vol. 5, No. 1 (Apr. 1931), 62–64. Covers the journey into exile from San Antonio to Parras from diary of Mrs. Mina Oury.

Smith, Joe. "Tales of the Sierra: An Affair of Honor Between Legislators." *Modesto Bee & News Herald* (Apr. 3, 1963), 9.

Smith, Stacey L. "Remaking Slavery in a Free State: Masters and Slaves in Gold Rush California." *Pacific Historical Review*, Vol. 80, No. 1 (Feb. 2011), 28–63. An excellent review that does much to explain the why of support for the Confederacy in California.

"Sonoma & Marin Railroad." http://localwiki.net/sonoma-valley/Sonoma%26_Marin_Railroad. Accessed Dec. 1, 2013.

Spaulding, Imogene. "The Attitude of California to the Civil War." *Annual Publication of the Historical Society of Southern California*, Vol. 9, Nos. 1, 2 (1912, 1913). Footnote on 117 mentions Showalter party.

Stern, Norton B. "Memoirs of Marcus Katz—San Bernardino Pioneer." *Western States Jewish History*, Vol. 1, No. 1 (Oct. 1969). Katz' commentary on 1860 Piercy election over Conn, 15–16.

"Temecula: Local Role in Civil War to Be Marked." *San Diego Union-Tribune* (Nov. 12, 2011). http://www.utsandiego.com/news/2011/nov/12/Temecula-local-role-in-civil-war. Accessed Nov. 2, 1013.

Temecula Valley Museum. "They Passed This Way/Temecula Valley Museum." http://www.temeculavalleymuseum.org/page_id=224. Accessed Mar. 5, 2013.

"Tetanus." *Wikipedia, the Free Encyclopedia.* http://en.wikipedia.org/wiki/Tetanus. Accessed Sept. 23, 2013.

"This Month in Texas History." *Texas Research Ramblers Genealogical Society Newsletter*, Vol. XVIII, No. 5 (May 15, 2008). Amzi Bradshaw recruitment of a company for Showalter's Regiment, 8.

Thompson, Jerry D. "Cortina, Juan Nepomuceno." *Handbook of Texas Online.* http://www.tshaonline.org/handbook/online/articles/fco73. Accessed Aug. 14, 2013.

_____. "A Duel in the Desert: Henry Skillman in the TransPecos, 1862–1864." Draft for article published as "Drama in the Desert: The Hunt for Henry Skillman in the Trans Pecos, 1862–1864." *Password*, Vol. 37, No. 3 (1992) of El Paso Historical Society. Courtesy Dr. Jerry D. Thompson.

Thompson, William F., Jr. "M. S. Latham and the Senatorial Controversy of 1857." *California Historical Society Quarterly*, Vol. 32, No. 2 (June 1953), 145–159. Showalter's role in the election, 147–148, 158.

Travel South Texas. "Kleberg County Historical Markers." http://www.fortours.com/pages//hmkleberg.asp. Accessed Jan. 17, 2014.

Trout, Carlynn. "Robert Sallee James (1818–1850)." *Historic Missourians.* http://shs.umsystem.edu/historicmissourians/name/j/james/index.html. Accessed Mar. 29, 2015.

Tyler, George W. "Bell County Rangers and Confederate Soldiers." *Belton Journal* (Jan. 31, 1918). http://files.usgwarchives.net/tx/bell/military/civilwar/ramgers.txt. Accessed Dec. 22, 2013.

"Unlinked Shattucks Initiated by Charles Henry Shattuck III." *Robert Kline's Genealogy Page.* http://we.rootsweb.ancestry.com/cgi-bin/igm.cgi?op=GET&db=rckline-u-shattuck&id-15213. Updated May 17, 2012. Accessed Nov. 8, 2013.

"United States Presidential Election in California, 1860." *Wikipedia, the free Encyclopedia.* http://en.wikipedia.org/wiki/United_States_presidential_election_in_California, 1860. Accessed May 24, 2013.

Untitled photograph caption. *Fairfax Historical Society Newsletter.* June 1998. A witness to the Showalter-Piercy duel is pictured, 7.

"User: Gatoclass/SB/SS Illinois (1851)." *Wikipedia, the Free Encyclopedia.* http://en.wikipedia.org/wiki/User:Gatoclass/SB/SS_Illinois_(1851). Accessed July 8, 2013.

Vega Ayala, Enrique (translated by Gene C. Armistead). "Los panteones perdidos de Mazatlan." *Noroeste* (Nov. 2, 2011). http://www.noreste.com.mx/publicaciones.phd?id=730818. Accessed Mar. 18, 2013. Explains what happened to the Mazatlan cemetery in which Showalter was buried.

"Versatility Was Proud Boast of Area Civil War Outfit." *Port Arthur News* (Oct. 11, 1970). Unit took part in Battle off Sabine Pass.

Virden, Bill. "The Affair at Minter's Ranch." *The Journal of San Diego History, San Diego Historical Society Quarterly*, Vol. 7, No. 1 (April 1961), 23–25.

"The Wagon Road Movements," Part Two of Chapter III, "Early Governments in Nevada." *The Nevada Observer: Nevada's Online State News Journal* (Apr. 4, 2006). http://www.nevadaobserver.com/Reading%20Room%20Documents/Early%20Governments. Accessed June 12, 2013.

Watford, W. H. "The Far-Western Wing of the Rebellion." *California Historical Society Quarterly*, Vol. XXXIV (1955), 125–148. Showalter party, 136.

Watterson-Hemphill, Vera M. "Descendants of John Watterson." http://familytreemaker.genealogy.com/users/w/a/t. Accessed Apr. 7, 2013. Showalter's family.

Westbrook, Ray. "Ridgley Greathouse Might Have Been the South's Hope in Civil War." Lubbock (TX) *Avalanche-Journal* (Jan. 24, 2011). http://www.lubockonline.com/columnists/2011-01-24/Ridgley-greathouse-might-have-been-souths-hope-civil-war. Accessed Mar. 19, 2013.

Westlake, F.W. "Confederate Who Served in Mexican Army." *Confederate Veteran*, Vol. 16, No. 8 (Aug. 1908), 332. Author in Mazatlan same time as Showalter.

Wharton, Clarence. "Spruce McCoy Baird." *New Mexico Historical Review*, Vol. 27, No. 4 (Oct. 1932).

Wiess, William. "First Federal Defeat at Sabine Pass." *Confederate Veteran*, Vol. 20, No. 3 (Mar. 1912). Article by a veteran of the battle off Sabine Pass, 108.

Wilkins, James H. "Political Factions are Rocked by Duel that Snuffs Out Two Lives." *San Francisco (CA) News* (1929) reprinted in *Fairfax Historical Society Newsletter* (June 1998), 2–7.

Williams, James. E. "A Revised List of Texas Confederate Regiments, Battalions, Field Officers, and Local Designations." http://jameswilliams.tripod.com/tex confederat.htm. Copyright 2007. Last updated Mar. 30, 2013. Accessed Apr. 6, 2013. Identifies locations of military camps where the 4th Arizona served.

"Waynesburg College, Waynesburg, Greene County, Pennsylvania." *Periodicals in the Historical Library and Archives of the Cumberland Presbyterian Church and the Cumberland Presbyterian Church in America.* (Showalter attended when it was Madison College.) http://www.cumberland.org/hfcpc/schools. Accessed Mar. 6, 2013.

"Whitehall Rowboat." *Wikipedia, the Free Encyclopedia*, http://en.wikipedia.org/wiki/Whitehall_Rowboat. Accessed Dec. 4, 2013.

"Who Owns the West? Patented Public Land in Sonoma County." http:www.ewg.org/mining/patents/index.php?since=1872id. Accessed Mar. 22, 2013. Contains information on the Denver Quicksilver Mining Co. in which Showalter held shares.

Widger, Doris. "Shattuck Page." http://widgewood.word press.com/shattuck-page. Accessed Dec. 11, 2013.

"William Tell Coleman." *Wikipedia, the Free Encyclopedia.* http://em/wolo[edoa/prg/wiki/William_Tell_Coleman. Accessed Dec. 1, 2013.

Winger, Richard. "What Are Ballots For?" *Libertarian Party News*, Extra Research Edition, 1988.

Zitny, John D. "Crimes Among the Notables." *Bulletin of the San Bernardino County Bar Association* (Jan. 2014), 1–2. Piercy's 1860 election and the duel.

Books

Adkins-Rochette, Patricia. *Bourland in North Texas and Indian Territory During the Civil War....* La Vergne, TN: Lightning Source, 2004. Showalter, 169, 183.

Allardice, Bruce S. *Confederate Colonels: A Biographical Register.* Columbia: University of Missouri Press, 2008. S.M. Baird, 49; B.F. Elliott, 139.

(Angel, Myron). *Reproduction of Thompson and West's History of Nevada with Illustrations and Biographical Sketches of its Prominent Men and Pioneers.* Berkley, CA: Howell-North, 1958. Originally published 1881. Showalter in Esmeralda, 266–267.

Archer, Anthony. *General Jo Shelby's March.* New York: Random House, 2010. B.F. Elliott in Mexico, 117, 122, 142.

Bailey, Chris S. *The Stulls of Millsborough: A Genealogical History of John Stull "the Miller" Pioneer of Western Maryland*, Vol. 1. Chris H. Bailey, 2000.

Bancroft, Hubert Howe. *The Works of Hubert Howe Bancroft, Vol. XVI, History of the North Mexican States and Texas, Vol. II.* San Francisco: History Company, 1889. The skirmish at Palmito Ranch, 468.

_____. *The Works of Hubert Howe Bancroft, Vol. XXIII, History of California, Vol. VI: 1848–1859.* San Francisco: History Company, 1890, 377–378, footnote 9.

_____. *The Works of Hubert Howe Bancroft, Vol. XXIV, History of California, Vol. VII (1860–1890).* San Francisco: History Company, 1890. Showalter at Fort Yuma, 289–290.

_____. *The Works of Hubert Howe Bancroft, Vol. XXXV, California Inter Pocula.* San Francisco, 1888. Duel, 76.

Batt, Jill Cossley. *The Last of the California Rangers.* New York: Funk & Wagnalls, 1928. 1857 legislative campaign, 219.

The Bay of San Francisco, the Metropolis of the Pacific Coast, Its Suburban Cities: A History, Vol. II. Chicago: Lewis Publishing Co., 1892. Broderick Resolutions of 1859, 425.

Beattie, George William, and Helen Pruitt. *Heritage of the Valley: San Bernardino's First Century.* Oakland: Biobooks, 1951. Showalter Party, 382–383.

Belden, L. Burr. *San Bernardino Sesquicentennial 1819-May 20th, 1960.* San Bernardino: San Bernardino Sun-Telegram, 1960. Piercy 1860 election and Showalter at San Bernardino, S-7.

Beverly, James M. *A History of the Ninety-First Regiment Illinois Volunteer Infantry 1862–1865.* White Hall, IL: Pierce Printing Co., 1913. Foe of 4th Arizona Cavalry at Palmito.

Black, Esther Boulton. *Rancho Cucamonga and Dona Merced.* San Bernardino: San Bernardino County Museum Association, 1975. Duel, 59.

Block, Eugene B. *Great Stagecoach Robberies of the West.* Garden City, NY: Doubleday, 1962.

Block, William Theodore. *A History of Jefferson County Texas, from Wilderness to Reconstruction.* Beaumont: Lamar University, 1976. Battle off Sabine Pass, 106.

Boucher, John. *History of Westmoreland County, Pennsylvania.* New York: Lewis Publishing Co., 1906. Showalter's home area and family, 311–318.

Bricken, Gordon. *The Civil War Legacy in Santa Ana.* Santa Ana: Santa Ana Historical Society, 2002. El Monte and Showalter Party, 7.

Brown, John, Jr., and James Boyd. *History of San Bernardino and Riverside Counties, Vol. I.* Chicago: Lewis Publishing Company, 1922. Duel, Piercy 1860 election, 148–149.

Brown, John Henry. *History of Texas, from 1785 to 1892, Vol. 2.* St. Louis: L.E. Daniel, Publishers, 1892. Showalter in north Texas, 419, 421, 439.

_____. *Indian Wars and Pioneers of Texas.* St. Louis: L.E. Daniel, Publishers, 1880. 1863 Indian pursuit, 115–118.

Buchanan, A. Russell. *David S. Terry of California: Dueling Judge.* San Marino: Huntington Library, 1950. Showalter, 129–130, 135, 139.

Burchfield, Christopher. *Choose Your Weapon: The Duel in California, 1847 to 1861.* Oroville, CA: I&L Publishing, 2002. 233–238. Chap. 48 summarizes the duel but has error as to the time as well as some assumptions about Showalter.

Burke's Texas Almanac and Immigrant's Handbook for 1883, with Which Is Incorporated Hanford's Texas State Register. Houston: J. Burke, 1883. Battle off Sabine Pass, 65–68.

Burns, John F., and Richard J. Orsi, eds. *Taming the Elephant: Politics, Government and Law in Pioneer California.* Berkeley: University of California Press, 2003. See Roger D. McGrath, "A Violent Birth: Disorder, Crime and Law Enforcement," 27–73.

Catalogue of a Cabinet of Minerals Presented for Exhibition at the Industrial Fair of the Mechanics' Institute by Capt. J.M. Aiken of Coulterville, Mariposa Co., Cal.

San Francisco: Mining and Scientific Press Book and Job Print, 1865. Showalter Mine, 3.

Caudill, Philip Robert. *Moss Bluff Rebel: Texas Pioneer in the Civil War.* College Station: Texas A&M University Press, 2009. Battle off Sabine Pass, 29.

Chamberlain, Newell D. *The Call of Gold: True Tales on the Gold Road to Yosemite.* Lafayette, CA: Great West Books, 2002. Originally published 1936. Mining in Mariposa County.

Chiaquist, Craig. *Deep California: Images and Ironies of Cross and Sword on El Camino Real.* Bloomington, IN: Universe, 2008. Duel, 607.

Christ, Mark K. *Civil War Arkansas, 1863: The Battle for a State.* Norman: University of Oklahoma Press, 2010.

Christenson, Lynne Newell, and Ellen L. Sweet. *Images of America: Ranchos of San Diego County.* Charleston, SC: Arcadia Publishing, 2008. For people and places related to Minter's Ranch.

Cornford, Daniel. "We All Live More Like Brutes Than Humans." In James J. Rawls, Richard J. Orsi, and Marlene Smith-Baranzini, eds., *A Golden State: Mining and Economic Development in Gold Rush California.* Berkeley: University of California Press, 1999. This chapter on 78–104 provides much good information regarding conditions among miners.

Cossley-Batt, Jill L. *The Last of the California Rangers.* New York: Funk & Wagnalls, 1928. Showalter's 1858 Assembly campaign, 219.

Cotham, Edward T., Jr. *Battle on the Bay: The Civil War Struggle for Galveston.* Austin: University of Texas Press, 1998. Battle of Galveston, 105–139.

_____. *Sabine Pass: The Confederate Thermopylae.* Austin: University of Texas Press, 2004. Battle off Sabine Pass, 46–58.

Cragen, Dorothy Clora. *The Boys in the Sky-Blue Pants: The Men and Events at Camp Independence and Forts of Eastern California, Nevada and Utah, 1862–1877.* Fresno: Pioneer Publishing Company, 1975. Ferris Forman, 10. Showalter Party, 18–19. Letter to Anna Forman, 79–80.

Culea, John. *The Trail through Mohawk.* John Culea, 2012 (Kindle). Minter's Ranch mentioned, 145.

Daddysman, James W. *The Matamoros Trade: Confederate Commerce, Diplomacy and Intrigue.* Newark: University of Delaware Press, 1984. Showalter at Palmito Ranch, 179–181.

Davis, Edwin Adams. *Fallen Guidon: The Saga of Confederate Jo Shelby's March to Mexico.* College Station: Texas A&M University Press, 1995. March to Parras, 28–118.

Davis, Winfield J. *History of Political Conventions in California, 1849–1892.* Sacramento: California State Library, 1893. Showalter briefly, 180–181, 203, 653.

DeSoucy, M. David. *San Bernardino County Sheriff's Department.* Charleston, SC: Arcadia Publishing, 2002. Piercy resignation, 14.

Dorsey, Sarah Ann Ellis. *Recollections of Henry Watkins Allen: Brigadier-general Confederate States Army, Ex-Governor of Louisiana.* New York: M. Doolady, 1866. Reasons for exile, 299–300. Shelby expedition early dates, 325–326.

Dungan, J. Irvine. *History of the 19th Regiment Iowa Volunteer Infantry.* Davenport: Luse & Griggs, 1865.

Dyer, Frederick H. *A Compendium of the War of the Rebellion Compiled and Arranged from Official Records of the Federal and Confederate Armies, Reports of the Adjutant Generals of the Several States, the Army Registers and Other Reliable Documents and Sources, Vol. I.* Des Moines: Dyer Publishing Co., 1908. Minter's Ranch, 655, 689–690, 1000, 1002.

Edwards, John Newman. *Shelby's Expedition to Mexico: An Unwritten Leaf of the War.* Norman: University of Oklahoma Press, 2002. Originally published 1872. Shelby's adjutant gives useful information on march to Paras, Mexico.

Eldredge, Zoeth Skinner. *History of California, Vol. 4.* New York: Century History Co., 1915. Duel, 124. Minter Ranch, 204.

Ferenbach, T.R.. *Lone Star: A History of Texas and Texans from Pre History to the Present; the People, Politics, and Events That Have Shaped Texas.* New York: Da Capo Press, 2000. Originally published 1968. Battle at Palmito Ranch, 383–387.

Fetzer, Leland. *San Diego County Place Names, A to Z.* San Diego: Sunbelt Publications, 2005. Minter Ranch mentioned on Camp Wright, 156.

Finch, L. Boyd. *Confederate Pathway to the Pacific: Major Sherrod Hunter and Arizona Territory, C.S.A.* Tucson: Arizona Historical Society, 1996. Showalter, 99–100, 147–148, 203–204, 207–210, 215, 218, 220–222, 224, 227, 243–244.

Fletcher, Daniel Cooledge. *Reminiscences of California and the Civil War.* Ayer, MA: Press of Huntley S. Turner, 1894. Routes to California during the Gold Rush, 15–29.

Fonner, D. Kent. *All Quiet on the Border: The Civil War Era in Greene County, Pennsylvania.* Create Space Independent Publishing Platform, 2012. Showalter, 33, 66, 72, 122.

Ford, John Salmon, edited by Stephen B. Oates. *Rip Ford's Texas.* Austin: University of Texas Press, 1991. Originally published 1963. Showalter in Rio Grande Expedition, 346, 358–360, 362–363, 365–366, 368–376, 389.

Freeman, Douglas Southall. *Lee's Lieutenants: A Study in Command, Vol. Two: Cedar Mountain to Chancellorsville.* New York: Charles Scribner's Sons, 1971. Originally published 1943. On Drayton's removal from Army of Northern Virginia, 325–326.

Frazier, Donald Shaw. *Blood & Tears: Confederate Empire in the Southwest.* College Station: Texas A&M University Press, 1995. Showalter Party, 103. Plan to invade Calif. from Texas, 295.

Gorley, Hugh Alexander. *The Loyal Californians of 1861: A Paper Prepared and Read Before California Commandery of the Military Order of the Loyal Legion of the United States, January 31, 1893.* Hugh A. Gorley, 1893. Showalter party at Camp Wright, 7–14.

Gorley, Hugh Alexander, and Belle Hamilton Gorley. *Selections from the Numerous Letters and Patriotic Speeches of My Husband (1876).* Belle Hamilton Gorley, 1876. Journey to Fort Yuma by a portion of Showalter Party, 64–69.

Grant, Ulysses S. *Personal Memoirs of U.S. Grant, Vol. 1.* New York: Charles L. Webster & Company, 1885. Grant writes about his 1852 journey across the isthmus of Panama, 194–199.

Gregory, Thomas Jefferson. *History of Yolo County, California: with Biographical Sketches....* Los Angeles: Historic Record Company, 1913. A Showalter 1861 associate, 124–125.

Hadden, James. *A History of Uniontown.* Uniontown, PA: New Werner Co., 1913. Information on Showalter's home area and family, 483–518.

Hafen, Leroy R. *The Mountain Men and the Fur Trade of the Far West, Vol. 7.* Glendale, CA: Arthur H. Clark,

1969. Section "John Brown" by L. Burr Belden on 54 relates to Piercy.

Hall, Martin Hardwick. *The Confederate Army of New Mexico*. Austin: Presidial Press, 1978. For information on F.E. Kavanaugh and G.L. Patrick.

Hand, George, edited by Neil B. Carmony. *The Civil War in Apacheland: Sergeant George Hand's Diary: California, Arizona, West Texas, New Mexico, 1861–1864*. Silver City, NM: High-Lonesome Books, 1996. Release of Showalter Pary from Fort Yuma, 33.

Harpending, Asbury. *The Great Diamond Hoax: And Other Stiring Incidents in the Life of Asbury Harpending*. San Francisco: James H. Barry Co., 1913. Information relating to Ridgeley Greathouse, Showalter partner in Mazatlan hotel, 73–89.

Hart, Herbert M. *Pioneer Forts of the Far West*. Seattle: Superior Publishing Co., 1967. Fort Yuma, 171.

Higginson, Thomas Wentworth. *Army Life in a Black Regiment*. Boston: Fields, Osgood & Co., 1870. Palmito Ranch, 24.

History of Tulare and Kings Counties, California, with Biographical Sketches. Los Angeles: Historic Record Company, 1913. A duel witness, 338–339.

Hittell, Theodore Henry. *History of California, Vol. IV*. San Francisco: N.J. Stone & Co., 1897. Showalter Party, 325–326.

Hoover, Mildred Brooke, Hero Eugene Rensch, Ethel Grace Rensch, and William N. Abeloe. *Historic Spots in California*. Stanford: Stanford University Press, 2002. Originally published 1932. Duel, 187.

Howard, Thomas Frederick. *Sierra Crossing: First Roads to California*. Berkeley: University of California Press, 1998. Information relative to wagon roads, 143.

Howell, Kenneth W. *Seventh Star of the Confederacy: Texas During the Civil War*. Denton: University of North Texas Press, 2009. Battle off Sabine Pass, 134–136, 147.

Hudson, Tim. *Three Paths Along a River: The Heritage of the Valley of the San Luis Rey*. Desert Southwest Publications, 1964. Capture of Showalter Party, 150–152.

Hudson, Tim, and Sam Hicks. *They Passed This Way: Biographical Sketches, Tales of Historical Temecula Valley at the Crossroads of California's Southern Immigrant Trail*. Temecula: Laguna House, 1970. Showalter and Party, 4.

Hughes, William John. *Rebellious Ranger: Rip Ford and the Old Southwest*. Norman: University of Oklahoma Press, 1964. Showalter on the Rio Grande, 220–227, 293.

Hunt, Aurora. *The Army of the Pacific: Its Operations in California, Texas, Arizona, New Mexico, Utah, Nevada, Oregon, Washington, Plains Region, Mexico, Etc., 1860–1866*. Mechanicsburg, PA: Stackpole Books, 1951. Showalter Party, 72–66. La Paz Incident, 341.

Hunt, Jeffrey William. *The Last Battle of the Civil War: Palmetto Ranch*. Austin: University of Texas Press, 2002. Two paragraphs on Sept. 1864 battle, 24.

An Illustrated History of Southern California, Embracing the Counties of San Diego, San Bernardino, Los Angeles, and Orange, and the Peninsula of Lower California from the Earliest Period of Occupancy to the Present Time; .... Chicago: Lewis Publishing Co., 1890. Information about Piercy, 420–421.

An Illustrated History of Southern California, Embracing the Counties of San Diego, San Bernardino, Los Angeles, and Orange, and the Peninsula of Lower California from the Earliest Period of Occupancy to the Present Time: .... Chicago: Lewis Publishing Co., 1892. Duel, 420.

Ingersoll, Luther A. *Ingersoll's Century Annals of San Bernardino County 1769 to 1904 ....* Los Angeles: Luther A. Ingersoll, 1904. Piercy's 1860 election, 154. Showalter Party, 344–345.

Irby, James A. *Back Door at Bagdad: The Civil War on the Rio Grande*. El Paso: Texas Western Press of the University of Texas El Paso, 1977. At Brownsville, 21, 48.

Jordan, John W., and James Hadden. *Genealogical and Personal History of Fayette and Greene Counties Pennsylvania, Vol. II*. New York: Lewis Historical Publishing Co., 1912. On Hugh A. Gorley, 404.

Josephy, Alvin M., Jr. *The Civil War in the American West*. New York: Vintage, 1991. Duel, 236. Showalter party, 238.

Kennedy, Elijah Robinson. *The Contest for California in 1861: How Colonel E.D. Baker Saved the Pacific States to the Union*. Boston: Houghton Mifflin, 1912. El Monte and the Bear Flag, 211. Showalter Party, 250–251.

Kennedy, Milo, and Anthony Keith Kopp. *Boom and Bust: The Historical Cycles of Matamoros and Brownsville*. Fort Worth: Eadkin Press, 1991. Battle at Palmito, 136.

Kennedy, Milo, Anthony Keith Kopp, and Antonio Zavalita. *Further Studies in Rio Grande Valley History*. Brownsville: University of Texas at Brownsville & Texas Southmost College, 2006. Battle at Palmito, 143.

Kibby, Leo P. *California, the Civil War, and the Indian Problem*. Los Angeles: Journal of the West/Lorrin L. Morrison & Carloll Spear Morrison, Publishers, 1967. Showalter party, 22.

Lause, Mark A. *A Secret History of the Civil War*. Champaign: University of Illinois Press, 2011. Showalter presumed with Knights of the Golden Circle, 115, 121–122, footnotes 49–190.

Lech, Steve. *Pioneers of Riverside County: The Spanish, Mexican and Early American Periods*. Charleston, SC: History Press, 2012. Showalter party, 86.

Love, Frank. *Hell's Outpost: A History of Old Fort Yuma*. Yuma: Yuma Crossing, 1992. Civil War period including Showalter's stay, 47–54.

Lubbock, Francis Richard. *Six Decades in Texas: or, Memoirs of Francis Richard Lubbock, Governor of Texas in War-Time, 1861–1863*. Austin: Ben C. Jones, Printers, 1900. Battle off Sabine Pass, 458–460.

Marks, Paula Mitchell. *Precious Dust: The Saga of the Western Gold Rushes*. Lincoln: University of Nebraska Press, 1998. Use of quicksilver in gold mining, 159.

Masich, Andrew E. *The Civil War in Arizona: The Story of the California Volunteers, 1861–1865*. Norman: University of Oklahoma Press, 2006. Showalter party, 160.

McCaslin, Richard B. *Fighting Stock: John S. "Rip" Ford of Texas*. Fort Worth: Texas Christian University Press, 2011. Final chapter covers period on Rio Grande.

McGarth, Roger D. "A Violent Birth: Disorder, Crime and Law Enforcement." In *Taming the Elephant: Politics, Government and Law in Pioneer California*, John F. Burns and Richard J. Orsi, eds. Berkeley: University of California Press, 2003, 27–73. A superb but concise summary of the prevalence and importance of dueling in 1850s California, 39.

Meara, James O. *Broderick and Gwin, the Most Extraordinary Contest for a Seat in the Senate of the United*

States Ever Known: A Brief History of Early Politics in California. San Francisco: Bacon & Co., Publishers, 1881. Showalter's roll, 170–172.

Monday, James Clements, and Frances Brannen Vick. *Petra's Legacy: The South Texas Ranching Empire of Vela and Mifflin Kennedy*. College Station: Texas A&M University Press, 2007.

Moore, Fred H., and Ella Mae Moore, eds. *Lone Star Blue and Gray: Essays on Texas in the Civil War (Texas History Reprint Series No. 17)*. Austin: Texas State Historical Association, 1995. Showalter taking Brownsville, 327.

Morganthaler, Jefferson. *The River Has Never Divided Us: A Border History of La Junta de Los Rios*. Austin: University of Texas Press, 2004. Information on the death of Captain Henry Skillman, 113–114.

Morris, William Gouverneur. *Address Delivered Before the Society of California/Volunteers at its First Annual Celebration, San Francisco*. San Francisco: The Society, 1866. Showalter in plots against California and his recent death, 22.

Muir, John. *My First Summer in the Sierra*. Boston: Houghton Mifflin, 1911. Horseshoe Bend in Mariposa County described and pictured, 17–19.

Munro-Fraser, J.P. *History of Maring County, California: Including Its Geography, Geology, Topography and Climatology....* San Francisco: Alley, Brown & Co., 1880. Duel, 127–129.

Noel, Theophilus. *A Campaign from Santa Fe to the Mississippi: Being a History of the Old Sibley Brigade from Its Organization to the Present Time: Its Campaigns in New Mexico, Arizona, Texas, Louisiana and Arkansas in the Years 1861-2-3-4*. Santa Fe: Stagecoach Press, 1961.

Oetgen, Jerome. *An American Abbott: Boniface Wimmer, O.S.B.* Latrobe, PA: Archabbey Press, 1976. Sportsman's Hall of Showalter Family, 71.

O'Flaherty, Daniel. *General Jo Shelby, Undefeated Rebel*. Chapel Hill: University of North Carolina Press, 1954. Date that Col. Elliott separates from Shelby, footnote on page 417.

O'Meara, James. *Broderick and Gwin: The Most Extraordinary Contest for a Seat in the Senate of the United States Ever Known: A Brief History of Early Politics in California*. San Francisco: Bacon & Co., Publishers, 1881. Showalter's role in the election, 145, 159–161, 170–173, 180–182.

Perlot, Jean-Nicholas, edited Howard R. Lamar, and translated by Helen Harding Bretnor. *Gold Seeker: Adventures of a Belgian Argonaut During the Gold Rush Years*. New Haven: Yale University Press, 1985.

Pettis, George H. *Historical Society of New Mexico No. 11: The California Column*. Santa Fe: New Mexico Printing Co., 1908. Showalter Party, 6–8.

Pierce, Frank Cushman. *A Brief History of the Lower Rio Grande Valley*. Menasha, WI: Collegiate Press—George W. Banta Publishing Co., 1917. Activities on the Rio Grande June–Sept. 1864, 48–51.

Pittman, Walter Earl. *Rebels in the Rockies: Confederate Irregulars in the Western Territories*. Jefferson, NC: McFarland, 2014. 204–206, 216–218.

Pourade, Richard P. *The History of San Diego: The Silver Dons, 1833–1865*. San Diego: Union-Tribune Publishing Co., 1963. Showalter party, 247–248.

Rasmussen, Louis J. *San Francisco Passenger Ship Lists*, Vol. 4. Colma: San Francisco Historic Record & Genealogy Bulletin, 1964.

Rawls, James J., Richard J. Orsi, and Marlene Smith-Baranzini, eds. *A Golden State: Mining and Economic Development in Gold Rush California*. Berkeley: University of California Press, 1999. Section by Cornford, Daniel, "We all live more like brutes than humans," 63, is particularly useful.

Richards, Leonard L. *The California Gold Rush and the Coming of the Civil War*. New York: Alfred A. Knopf, 2007. Kindle edition location 1392–1424.

Roberts, O.M. *Confederate Military History: A Library of Confederate States Military History, in Twelve Volumes, Written by Distinguished Men of the South, and Edited by Gen. Clement A. Evans of Georgia, Vol. 11: Texas, Florida*. Atlanta: Confederate Publishing Co., 1911. Battle off Sabine Pass, 97–102.

Rolle, Andrew F. *The Lost Cause: The Confederate Exodus to Mexico*. Norman, OK: University of Oklahoma Press, 1965. Col. Elliott's trip to Mazatlan, p 77.

Roske, Ralph J. *Everyman's Eden: A History of California*. New York: Macmillan, 1968. This excellent general history of California comments about Showalter 308–309 in a very reasonable manner.

Sagar, William, and Brian Sagar. *Images of America: Fairfax*. Charleston, SC: Arcadia Publishing Co., 2005. Duel, 20.

Samuels, Richard Snowden. *California*. http://www.richsamuels.com/nbcmm/snowden/. Published 2012. Accessed Dec. 4, 2013. Duel, 175–176.

Savage, Richard Henry. *The Little Lady of Lagunitas: A Franco-Californian Romance*. http://www.aolib.com/reader_6011.htm accessed May 16, 2014. Originally published 1882. Mentions Showalter crossed the desert, 146.

Scharf, J. Thomas. *History of the Confederate States Navy from Its Organization to the Surrender of Its Last Vessel*. New York: Gramercy Books, 1996. Originally published 1887. Battles of Galveston and off Sabine Pass, 505–513.

Schlicke, Carl P. *General George Wright: Guardian of the Pacific Coast*. Norman: University of Oklahoma Press, 1988. Showalter party, 232.

Sellmeyer, Daryl P. *Jo Shelby's Iron Brigade*. Gretna, LA: Pelican Publishing, 2007. Col. Elliott's trip to Mazatlan, 289–291.

Sides, Hampton. *Blood and Thunder: The Epic Story of Kit Carson and the Conquest of the American West*. New York: Anchor Books, 2007. F.E. Kavanaugh, 326, 334, 338.

Smith, Cornelius Cole. *William Sanders Oury: Historymaker of the Southwest*. Tucson: University of Arizona Press, 1967. Mrs. Oury account of journey to Parras, 154–155.

Smith, David Paul. *Frontier Defense in the Civil War: Texas' Rangers and Rebels*. College Station: Texas A&M University Press, 1992.

Snow, Horace C. *"Dear Charlie" Letters Recording the Everyday Life of a Young 1854 Miner as Set Forth by Your Friend, Horace Snow with Suitable Gold Rush Engravings*. Fresno: Pioneer Publishing Co., 1979. Snow's account of trip across Panama and Life and Mining in Mariposa County near contemporary with Showalter.

Spencer, John D. *The American Civil War in the Indian Territory*. Oxford: Osprey, 2008. On arms furnished Showalter's battalion, 43–44.

Sutherland, Daniel E. *The Confederate Carpetbaggers*. Baton Rouge: Louisiana State University Press, 1988. Reasons and motivations of Southerners who went into exile, 9–30.

Sutton, John Richard. *Civil Government in California*. New York: American Book Co., 1923. Impeachment of State Treasurer Henry Bates in 1857, 320.

Sweet, Ellen L., and Lynne Newell. *Historic Stage Routes of San Diego County*. Charleston, SC: Arcadia Publishing, 2011. Showalter party, 93.

Talbott, Laurence Fletcher. *California in the War for Southern Independence*. Los Angeles: Hale & Co., 1996. Chapter about Showalter, 85–104.

Thompson, Jerry D. *Cortina: Defending the Mexican Name in Texas*. College Station: Texas A&M University Press, 2007. Ford lack of objectivity in regard to Cortina, 8–9.

_____. *Juan Cortina and the Texas-Mexico Frontier 1859–1877*. El Paso: Texas Western Press of the University of Texas El Paso, 1994. Ford-Cortina relationship, 3.

_____. *Tejano Tiger: Jose de los Santos Benavides and the Texas-Mexico Borderlands, 1823–1891*. Fort Worth: TCU Press, 2017. Operations along the Rio Grande, 174, 185, 188–189, 197.

_____. *Vaqueros in Blue and Gray*. Austin: Presidial Press, 1977. Showalter working with S. Benavides, 114, 118.

Thompson, Jerry D., and Lawrence T. Jones. *Civil War and Revolution on the Rio Grande Frontier*. College Station: Texas A&M University Press, 2004. Showalter after Las Rucias skirmish, 82.

Tinkman, George Henry. *California Men and Events, Time 1769–1890*. Stockton, CA: Record Publishing Co., 1915. Senate election in legislature in 1861, 203. Duel, Fort Yuma, death at Mazatlan, 206–207.

Titchenal, Oliver Ray. *The Titchenal Saga: 350 Years of Faith and Hope and Family Life in America: The Genealogy and History of Thirteen Generations of the Tichenor and Titchenal Families Coupled with American and Local History*. North Ridgeville, OH, 1995. www.titchenal.com. Chap. XVI, "Life in Hornitos, During the Civil War," 229–243.

Townsend, Stephen A. *The Yankee Invasion of Texas*. College Station: Texas A&M University Press, 2006. Palmito Ranch, 110.

Trafzer, Clifford E. *The Kit Carson Campaign: The Last Great Navajo War*. Norman: University of Oklahoma Press, 1982. F.E. Kavanaugh, 69.

Tuthill, Franklin. *The History of California*. San Francisco: H.H. Bancroft & Co., 1866. Duel, 569–570.

The Union Army: A History of Military Affairs in the Loyal States 1861–65—Records of the Regiments in the Union Army—Cyclopedia of Battles—Memoirs of Commanders and Soldiers, Vol. IV. Madison, WI: Federal Publishing Co., 1908. Mentioned 399.

Van Dor, Paul E. *History of Fresno County, California, With Biographical Sketches*. Los Angeles: Historic Record Co., 1918. Showalter party, 147.

Wiley, Samuel T. *Biographical and Historical Cyclopedia of Westmoreland County, Pennsylvania*. Philadelphia: John M. Gresham & Co., 1890. Showalters, 347–348.

Wilkerson, David. *The 47th Indiana Infantry: A Civil War History*. Jefferson, NC: McFarland, 2012. Activities in Brownsville area, 292–293.

Williams, Wolcott Bigelow. *Past and Present of Eaton County, Michigan, Historically: Together with Biographical Sketches*. Lansing, MI: Michigan Historical Publications Association, 1906. Biography of Chauncey R. Wellman, 633–634.

Willingham, Ben H., and Jeffrey L. Sizemore. *Military Order of the Stars and Bars: 75 Years of Heritage*. White House, TN: Military Order of the Stars and Bars, 2013. Showalter as a qualifying ancestor, 212.

Wooten, Dudley G. *A Comprehensive History of Texas, 1685–1897, Vol. II*. Dallas: William G. Scarff, 1898. Ford's operations on the Rio Grande, 553–555.

Wright, Arthur A. *The Civil War in the Southwest*. Big Mountain Press, 1964. Showalter party, 47, 77.

Yeary, Mamie. *Reminiscences of the Boys in Gray 1861–1865*. Dallas: Smith & Lamar, 1912. One veteran (F. B. Norris) of the 4th Arizona, 570.

Index

Acapulco, Mexico 12–13
Adams, Ames 39
Agua Caliente, CA 93
Agua Fria, CA 16–17
Ah Fong 33
Ah Young 33
Aiken, Eugene 116
Albuquerque, NM 87–88
Alcatraz 99
Alderete, Pablo B. 121
Alexandria Gazette & Virginia Advertiser 13
Allegheny Mountains 9
Allen, Henry Watkins 167–168
Alleyton, TX 157
Allison, — 90, 103
Alston, — 132
Alturas County, CA 58
Amador County, CA 42, 50, 96
American Party 30
Amyx, Fleming 45, 54, 63, 66–67
Anaheim, CA 183
Anders, William 166
Anderson, James M. 20, 36–37, 40–43, 57
Angel Mountain, CA 92
Anti-Lecompton Democrats 31, 41
Apache Indians 116
Arconti, Robert D. 194
Arizona, District of 1, 109
"The Arizona Birgade: The Legion That Never Set Foot in the Desert" 191–192
Arizona Historical Review 107
Ark, steamer 138–138
Arkadelphia, AR 125
Arkansas River Valley 121
Armistead, Gene C. 96, 149, 194

Army Units, Confederate:
 1st Arizona Cavalry 116, 121–122
 1st California Cavalry Battalion 162
 1st Texas Heavy Artillery 113, 115
 2nd Arizona Cavalry 117
 2nd Louisiana Infantry 113
 2nd Texas Cavalry 114
 2nd Texas Mounted Rifles 110
 3rd Arizona Cavalry 117, 162
 4th Arizona Cavalry 107, 109, 117–166, 174, 178–179, 191–192
 4th Arizona-Texas *see* 4th Arizona Cavalry
 4th Texas Cavalry *see* 4th Arizona Cavalry
 4th Texas-Arizona *see* 4th Arizona Cavalry
 7th Texas Cavalry 111
 11th Texas Battalion 113–114
 13th Texas Cavalry 122, 164
 17th Texas Field Battery 121–122, 125
 19th Texas Cavalry 120
 31st Texas Cavalry 157
 33rd Texas Cavalry 137, 142, 147
 35th Texas Cavalry 164
 Advance Force 137–157
 Arizona Brigade 116–117
 Army of New Mexico *see* Sibley's Brigade
 Army of Northern Virginia 110
 Baird's Cavalry *see* 4th Arizona Cavalry
 Boggy Depot, IT 123–124
 Border Regiment 122–123
 Camp Baird, TX 131
 Camp Bankhead, IT 123
 Camp Hood, TX 157
 Camp Mariposa, TX 120
 Camp McCulloch, TX 164
 Camp Patterson, TX
 Camp Sabine, IT 125
 Camp Slaughter, TX 164
 Camp/Fort Washita, IT 125
 Camp Watie, IT 124
 Camp Wilson, TX 157
 Cater's Battalion 136
 Cavalry of the West *see* Expeditionary Force
 Darden's Texas Regiment 127, 130
 El Monte Battalion 87–88, 193
 Expeditionary Force CSA 129–156
 Frontier Regiment Texas State Troops 122–123, 130
 Krumbhaar's Battery *see* 17th Texas Field Battery
 Light Horse of the Plains 131, 164–165
 Post of San Antonio, TX 120–121, 132
 Richardson's Texas Regiment 127, 130
 Shelby's Brigade 168
 Shell-Bank Battery 116
 Showalter's Cavalry *see* 4th Arizona Cavalry
 Sibley's Brigade 111, 116, 157
 Spaight's Battalion *see* 11th Texas Battalion
 Terry's Texas Rangers 164

Army Units, Mexican:
 Exploradores del Bravo Battalion 149, 152
 Faithful of Tamaulipas Battalion 141

Army Units, Union:
 1st California Cavalry 1, 95, 99–101, 103
 1st California Infantry 89, 94, 106
 1st Missouri Light Artillery 137, 141, 147
 1st Texas Cavalry 132–134, 136–138, 147
 2nd California Cavalry 105
 4th California Infantry 107–108

4th United States Infantry 11, 90
5th California Infantry 106
18th New York Cavalry 137–138
19th Iowa Infantry 137–138
52nd Massachusetts Infantry 111–112
81st Colored Infantry 137–138
91st Illinois Infantry 137, 142–144, 147, 149, 152
Army of the Frontier 121
Camp Carleton, CA 100–101
Camp Drum, CA 101
Camp Wright, CA 89, 91–94, 97–101, 106, 167, 180

Arroyo Colorado, TX 133–134, 159
Aspinwall, William Henry 10
Aspinwall, Panama 10–11
Aston, Eliza *see* O'Connor, Eliza Aston
Aurora, NV 83–84
Austin, NV 173
Austin, TX 130, 164, 168
Austin *Weekly State Gazette* 148, 155
Australia 81
Automobile Club of Southern California 87
Avery, J.M. 61
Aylette, W.D. 24, 58

Baechtel, Martin 44
Bagdad, Mexico 140–141, 143, 150
Baine, A.C. 30
Baird, Don E. 117
Baird, Spruce McCoy 117–121, 126–132, 160, 164, 179
Baker, — 90
Baker, Edward D. 46–47
Baker, Henry 75
Bald Hill, CA 74
Baldwin, — 36
Bancroft, Hubert Howe 104, 145
Bancroft Library 104
Bankhead, Smith P. 120–125
Banks, J.A. 63–64
Banks, Nathaniel P. 128, 136, 151
Banquete, TX 132, 135, 157
Barnett, Ysabel 194
Barrett, James 99, 101
Bates, Henry 23
Battle of New Orleans (1815) 21
Baylor, George R. 117
Baylor, John Robert 88, 100, 112, 116–117, 160–161
Bayo del Rio, Mexico 143
Bazaine, Francois Achille 168, 172
Beans, — 173
Bear Flag 86

Bear Valley, CA 35
Beatty, Elwood T. 20–21, 24–25, 29
Beauregard, P.G.T. 111
Beauvoir, MS 6
Bedford County, VA 96
Bee, — 127, 164
Behn, Ferdinand 107
Bell, Henry H. 112, 114
Bell, John 33–34
Bell County, TX 118
Belle (steamer) 143
Benavides, Refugio 134, 137–138, 149, 153
Benavides, Santos 128, 132, 134
Benbrook, Charles M. 90–91, 96, 106–107
Benecia, CA 108
Beneventura, Mexico 168
Benjamin, Judah 167
Bennett, C.E. 99–100
Bergman, J. 194
Berkeley, CA 104
Beur, — 173
Beverly, James M. 137
Biderman, J.W. "Jack" 82–83
Biderman Flag *see* Gillis-Biderman Flag
Biesca, Andres S. *see* Viesca, Andres S.
Big Bear, CA *see* Holcomb Valley, CA
Bishop, TX 132
Blair, A.W. 40, 45, 54, 57, 67
Blunt, James G. 121–123
Boca del Rio, TX 142
Boggs, William R. 131
Bonham, TX 121–126, 130, 164, 180
Bonwill, C.E.H. 144
Bourland, James G. 122–123
Bowie, George W. 1, 54, 106
Bradshaw, Amzi 120, 127, 178
Brazil Creetk, IT 125
Brazoria County, TX 126
Brazos River 164, 166
Brazos Santiago, TX (island) 136–137, 141–144, 147–148, 154, 157, 159
Breckinridge, John C. 33–34, 48–49, 167, 177
Breckinridge Democrats 34, 36–37, 39, 41, 50, 52, 55–57, 61, 65–66
Brecks *see* Breckinridge Democrats
Brent, Joseph Lancaster 20, 31, 57
Bridgewater, MA 12
Brierly, Wake 75, 77–78
Briggs, H.W. 39–40, 45, 52
Broderick, David C. 21–22, 28, 44–46, 75
Brooks, Preston 63

Brooks, Samuel 91
Brosnan, Cornelius M. 72–73, 76
Brotherhood 5
Brown, — 164
Brown, John Henry 126
Brownsville, TX 109, 128–129, 132–137, 139–145, 148–149, 152–156, 158–159, 168, 179
Bruner, W.H. 75
Buchanan, James 19, 73
Buell, W.M. 40–41, 46
Buena Vista, CA 94, 102
Bullhead City, AZ 107
buncombe 53–54
bunk *see* buncombe
Burch, John C. 28, 32
Burke, E. 64
Burkholder, Anne 6
Burnell, Ransom 42–44, 48, 58–59, 61–64, 68–69
Burney, Robert J. 163
Burns, A. 82
Burns, Bill 16
Burns Creek, CA 30
Burrita, Mexico 142
Butte County, CA 41–42, 47
Butterfield Overland Mail 88; *see also* Southern Emigrant Trail
Byrne, Edward 75

Cabell, William L. 123–124
Cabell's Arkansas Brigade 123
Cable, Hezekiah 89, 91
Cahuilla Indians 89
Cairo, IL 143
Cajon Pass, CA 85
Calaveras County, CA 18, 20, 30, 41, 43–44, 47, 49, 52, 68, 75, 81, 84
California Column 105
California Gold Rush 7; route to 8–12
California Historical Society Quarterly 176
"California in the Civil War" 190
California in the War for Southern Independence 176
California Rangers 19
California State Assembly 19–29, 36–70
California State Capitol 38
California State Capitol Museum 83
California State Insane Asylum 24
California State Library 38
California State Senate 19–20, 41, 44–45, 48, 50–51, 54–58, 64, 66, 68, 76
California State Supreme Court 73

Index

Calloway, — 66
Calvary Presbyterian Church 20
Camargo, TX 139
Cameron County, TX 159
Campbell, Alex 46–47, 55–56, 59, 63–64
Canadian River 121, 123
Canales, — 141
Canby, E.R.S. 136, 142, 151
Cape Girardeau, MO, Battle of 120
Cape Horn 9
Carillo, Ramon 89
Carleton, James H. 2, 89, 94, 97, 99–100, 102–105, 161
Carlos 151, 156
Carothers, William 192
Carpenter, — 126
Carricitos ranch, TX 133, 135–136
Carrington, W.H.D. 133, 148–150, 153
Carrizo Creek, CA 91, 94, 99, 102–103
Carroll County, TN 96
Carson City, NV 83
Carson Valley, NV 30, 56
Cass County, GA 96
Casserly, — 57
Castro, Estevan 23
Castroville, TX 168–169
Cater, Tom 134
Catholic Church 7, 139, 186
Catlin, — 22
Cementon, PA 5
Cerda, Julian 141
Cerda, Mariano G. 141
Chagres, Panama 10
Chagres River 9
Chamberlain, — 130
Chandler, T.J. 67, 75
Channel Islands National Marine Sanctuary 13
Channel Islands National Park 13
Chapalac, M. Cota 194
Charbonneau, J.E. 194
Chenhall 188–189
Cherry, John W. 37, 41, 44
Chickasaw Indians 126
Chihuahua, Mexico 1, 95, 108–109, 120
Childs, William 41, 43, 47, 63
Chino Hills, CA 90
Chivalry *see* Breckinridge Democrats
Choctaw County, MS 96
Choctaw Nation, IT 123
Chriswell, Calvin M. 103, 106
Chum, F.N. 91, 96, 103
Cibolo, TX 162
The Civil War in the American West amateur review 190

"Civis" 101, 106
Clark, — 60
Clark, Curtis 82
Clark, Edward 168
Clark, Harvey 111
Clark, Robert C. 25–27
Clarke, Fletcher S. 143–144
Clarksville, TX 138
Clay County, MO 96
Claysville, PA 6
Cleghorn Canyon, CA 85
Clendenen, Clarence C. 6, 8, 176
Cobb's Ranch, TX 138
Cockrel, S.B. 134
Cocopah 107
Coffin, Abel 114
Cohn, B. 107
Coleman, William Tell 43, 61, 75
Colma, CA 78
Colon, Panama *see* Aspinwall, Panama
Colorado River 97, 100, 102–103, 107
Colorado Steam Navigation Co. 107
Colorado Territory 31
Columbus, TX 117, 141
Colusa County, CA 41
Comanche Indians 121, 126, 145
Compromise of 1850 19
"Confederate" 156
The Confederate Carpetbaggers 167
Confederate Cotton Bureau 135
Confederate Military History 113
Confederate Pathway to the Pacific 192
Confederate States of America, recognition of 68
Conn, William A. 34–35
Conness, John 34, 36–37, 39–42, 45–49, 51, 53, 56, 58, 61–66, 68
Connor, H.N. 114
Constitutional Union Party 33
Continental (steamer) 143
Contra Costa Steam Navigation Co. 75
Conway, — 121
Cook, Devin 83
Cooke, Philip S. G. 194
Cooke County, TX 126, 164
Cooper, Douglas H. 121, 124–125
Cooper, Samuel 160
Coopwood, Bethel 162
Corona, — 173
Corpus Christi, TX 130, 132, 158
Corsicana, TX 168
Cortina, Jose Maria 140

Cortina, Juan Nepomuceno 133, 135, 139–146, 148–153, 155
Cortina Wars 139
Cotitlo, TX 133
Cotton, — 131
Cottonwood Springs, TX 1
Coulter, — 90
Councilman, C.W. 64
Covarrubias, Jose Maria 22
Creanor, — 54
Creel, Reuben W. 1
Crenshaw, G.H. 84, 90
Crippen, John, Jr. 87
Crittenden, John J. 48, 52
Crittenden Compromise *see* secession crisis debates
Crocker, Charles 40–42, 44, 46, 52–53, 64
Crosby, J.F. 124
Crowell, Henry 91, 96–97, 106–107, 109, 118, 155
Cruces, Panama 11, 13
Cubero, NM 157
Culea, John 188
Curtis, N. Greene 37, 53, 59, 68
Cutler, Ben C. 101, 103
Cypress Lawn Memorial Park 78

Daily Alta Califonia 22, 27, 53, 55–59, 69, 74–76, 78–79, 94, 99–100, 108, 160, 173
Daily Evening Bulletin 71
Daily Reese River Reveille 173
Dallas, TX 164
Damron, Henry Clay 166
Darg, — 161
da Saphien, Candelaria 16
David Copperfield (Charles Dickens) 13
Davidson, M.O. 161
Davis, Jefferson 20, 54, 66, 103, 111, 116, 160–161, 178
Day, Henry Martyn 137, 141–142, 144, 146–147, 149–151, 179
Dead Man's Hollow, TX 136
Degolyer Library 158
Delaware River 9
Del Norte County, CA 40, 46
Democratic Party 19, 21
Denver, Arthur St. Clair 31
Denver, James W. 31, 54–55, 57
Denver, CO 31
Denver Quicksilver Mining Co. 31, 161
De Preuil, Marguerite Jacques Vincent 172
Devil's Backbone hills 123
Devine, Thomas Jefferson 139
De Wolf, Henry 139
D'Hanis, TX 169
Dickey, Haywood H. 88, 95, 103, 106

Dickinson, A.G. 120–121, 132
Dillingham, John 114–115
Doaksville, IT 125
Dodson, C.C. 168
Dona Ana, NM 89, 110
Donley, Anna Marie *see* Donley, Mary Ann
Donley, Mary Ann 6, 8, 185
Doub, Valentine E. 72, 76
Dougherty, J. 39–41, 46, 48–49, 61
Douglas, David 109
Douglas, Stephen A. 33–34, 47–48
Douglas Democrats 34, 36–37, 39, 41, 43, 50, 55–56, 61
Douglass family 178, 186
Dowling, Dick 114
Downey, John G. 31–32, 40, 49, 69, 193–194
Drayton, Thomas E. 134–135, 139, 150–152, 154–155
Drum, Richard C. 94, 99
Drum Barracks Civil War Museum 101, 194
Drummond, John A. 115
Dryden, Robert H. 126, 129, 178
Dryden, Rose Ellen 126–127, 178, 180
Dryke's Ranch, CA 94
dueling 71–80
Dunn, — 133
Durango, Durango, Mexico 168, 172
Durst, D.P. 41
Duval, B.G. 125

Eagle Lake, TX 118
Eagle Pass, TX 109, 120, 128–130, 168–169
Earnest, Lycurgus B. 166
Ebonal Ranch, TX 135
Echazarrete, Miguel 141, 149, 151–153
Eden's, IT 124
Edgerton, Henry 61
Edinburg, TX 133–136
Edwards, William "Frog" 96, 103, 106–108, 189
Edwin Forrest Theatre 28
Ehrenberg, Herman 107
1860 Presidential Election 33–34
El Dorado County, CA 31, 34, 39, 43, 60–61, 68
El Monte, CA 85–90, 99, 102, 109, 193, 195
El Monte Historical Society Museum 87, 176
El Paso, TX 1, 88
El Paso County, TX 1, 162
El Paso del Norte, Mexico 139
Elliott, Benjamin F. 168, 172
Elliott, John D. 164

Ellis County, TX 120, 127, 129
Ellis County Museum 129
Elm Creek, TX 126
Elmore settlement, TX 126
Ensenada, Baja Cfa, Mexico 108
Erie County, PA 96
Esmeralda County, CA *see* Mono County, CA
Esmeralda County, NV 84
Esmeralda Star 83
Esquela Primaria Publico Gral. Angel Flores 174–175
Estell, James M. 25–27
Estephana Ranch, TX 136
Eureka County, CA 25
Evans, George S. 50
Evans, Mark A. 12
Exchequer Dam, CA 16
Eyre, Edward E. 99–100

Fairfax, Charles Snowden 32, 73–75, 77, 80
Fairfax, CA 73
Fairfax Historical Society 73
Fairfield, SC 96
Falls County, TX 164
"Fanny Hill" 185–186
Fargo, Frank F. 34, 36–37, 39–44, 46–47, 53–55, 58, 61–62, 64–65
Farragut, David G. 114
Fayette County, PA 6
Fayette County, TX 162
Fergusson, David 95, 100–101, 104, 109
Fighting Stock: John S. "Rip" Ford of Texas 155
Fillmore, Millard 19
Finch, Boyd 192
Finch, Jim, Jr. 186
Finch, Jim, Sr. 186
Finch, Kate Showalter *see* Showalter, Katherine
Finlay, Thomas 30
Fisher, J.J. 133, 136
Flanders, — 61
Fletcher, Daniel Coolidge 10–13
Flores, Angel 174–175
Flynn, Martin 75
Folsom Prison 63
Ford, Charles 47
Ford, John Salmon "Rip" 117, 128–143, 145–158, 178–180
Forman, Anna 2, 110, 122, 130, 154, 177, 180
Forman, Ferris 59, 108
Fort Belknap, TX 164
Fort Bliss, TX 1, 88
Fort Brown, TX 129, 136, 147, 153, 157
Fort Fauntleroy 157
Fort Gibson, IT 121–122
Fort Inge, TX 168
Fort Lafayette, NY 99–100

Fort Lancaster, TX 129
Fort Leaton, TX 109
Fort Merrill, TX 130
Fort Mojave, AZ 107
Fort Scott, KS 122
Fort Smith, AR 121–124
Fort Sumter, SC 49, 63
Fort Worth, TX 164
Fort Yuma, CA 2, 87, 89–91, 95, 98–107, 120, 167
Fowler, Charles 113–115
Frank Leslie's Illustrated Newspaper 144
Frémont, John C. 19, 92, 193–194
French 128, 139–141, 143–145, 148, 154
French, Albert H. 1
Fresno County, CA 34, 37, 59
Friedberger, Arnold 18
Friedberger & Showalter 18
Frink, R.B. 72–73, 76
Fritter, F.S. 155
Fritz, Emil 99–100
"Frog" 188–189
Fuente, Mexico 168

Gainesvlle, TX 126, 164
Gainor, Thomas 107–108
Gallagher, Michael 7
Gallagher, P.A. 75
Galveston, Battle of 110–112, 118
Galveston, TX 3, 111–113
Galveston Daily News 166
Galveston Island 111
Gano, Richard M. 125
Garwood, Z.L. 68
Geftareus, "Dutchman" 91–92
Genoa, NC 30
German Benevolent Society 175
Giddings, George Henry 128, 136–138, 146–150, 152–154, 156
Giddings' Battalion CSA 136–138, 147, 153, 163
Gifford, Giles 32
Gigedo, Mexico 168
Gila City, AZ 110
Gila River 106
Gilbert, Frank D. 90, 103, 106
Gilchrist & Co. 18
Gillett, M.Y. 75
Gillis, James P. 82–83
Gillis-Biderman Flag 82–83
Glaucus 78, 81–82
Gold Hill, NV 161
Gold Hill News 161
Goliad, TX 157–158
Gomez Palacio, Mexico 168
Gonzalez' Ferry, Sonora, Mexico 90
Gordon, N.M. 62
Gorgona, Panama 11–12

Gorley, Hugh A. 92, 94, 96, 98–99, 101, 180
Grant, Ulysses S. 11
Grass Valley, CA 15
Graves, William 25
Gray, Mike 50
Greathouse, Ridgley 173
Greene, Henry A. 91, 98
Greene County, PA 6, 8, 96, 174, 177
Greenwade, — 103
Greenwood, CA 68
Gregory, Andrew J. 33–34, 60–61, 63–64, 75
Griffith, Humphrey 81
Guadalupe Ricer 130
Guaymas, Sonora, Mexico 108–109, 172
Gulf of California 108
Gulf of Mexico 113, 137, 139
Gurley, Edward J. 122
G.V.M. 71–72, 78–79, 81
Gwin, William McKindry 21–22, 28, 54, 167, 168

Hale, James A. 107
Hall, Gavin D. 20
Hall, Warren 194
Hamilton, William 92, 96, 101, 106
Hammond, R.P. 59
Hammond, William 75, 77–78, 81
Hancock, Winfield Scott 86
Hand, George 106
Haralson, John H. 72–73
Harby, — 111
Hardeman, William P. 116, 121–122
Hare, Isaac 27
Hargrave, Jospeh P. 96–97
Harpendong, Asbury 173
Harris, P.H. 41, 44, 47–48, 52, 67
Harrisburg, TX 162
Harrison, — 20
Harrison, J.B. 63
Hastings, Lansford W. 160
Haun, D.H. 46, 50–51, 63–64, 67
Hayes, Thomas 75–77
Hayne, — 76
Heacock, — 54
Healdsburg, CA 71, 81
Hebert, Paul O. 111
Heerman, Theodore 131
Helena, TX 130–131
Hempstead, TX 166
Heriot, — 113–114, 116
Hermosillo, Sonora, Mexico 109
Herron, Francis J. 133–134, 136–137, 150
Hicks, Sam 193

Hidalgo, Mariano G. 141
Higley, Horace A. 30
Hill, John W. 124
Hill, P.H. 178
Hill, Samuel 39
Hils, Andrew 149
Hoge, J.P. 54
Holcomb Valley, CA 85–86
Holman, D.B. 43
Holmes, Theophilius 111, 125
Honey Springs, IT 121–123
Hooper, Thomas 100
Hooten, W.J. 43
Hornitos, CA 15–17, 32, 58, 107
Horrell, T.M. 50
Horseshoe Bend, CA 15–17, 28, 30, 35, 58, 79, 81
Housman, John H. 54, 56
Houston, TX 111, 115–116, 118, 121, 131–132, 157–158, 163–164, 166
Houston *Tri-Weekly Telegraph* 112, 116, 155, 163, 164–166
Howard, William James 19, 27, 30
Hudson, Tom 193
Hume, John 27
Hunter, Sherrod 161–162

Illinois Bend, TX 125
Imperial Desert 101
Indian Gulch, CA 16
Indian Nation 3
Indian Territory (IT) 121–122, 124–125
Indian Wells, CA 101
Ingrahm, R. Henry 190
Irwin, Richard 22, 25, 27
Ivey, — 119

Jackson, — 162
Jackson, Helen H. 194
Jackson, MS 96
James, Robert Sallee 191
Jeagers *see* Yeagers Ferry, Colorado River
Jefferson Davis Home 6, 193
Jennigros, Pierre Jean Joseph 168
"Jesse James Photo Album" website 191
J.M. Chapman 173
Johnson, Andrew 167
Johnson, J. Neely 20, 28
Johnson, Samuel 3
Johnson, William 114
Johnston, Albert Sidney 88
Johnston, Joseph E. 111, 166
Jones, — 169
Jones, A.D. 174
Jones, R.B. 154
Jones, Samuel 166
Josephy, Alvin M. Jr. 190

Journal of the California House of Assembly of 1861 62
Juarez, Benito 139–140, 168
Juarez, Mexico *see* El Paso del Norte, Mexico

Kansas-Nebraska Act 19
Katz, Morris 34
Kavanaugh, Finis Ewing 153, 157, 167, 170, 174, 178–179
Keith, Kosciusko Dewitt 114, 116
Kelley, Sarah 9
Kelly, — 19
Kelly, John 75
Kendall, Thomas 24
Kennedy, H. 162
Kennedy, Mifflin 141
Kibbe, William C. 28, 66
Kickapoo Indians 170
King, A. 96, 118, 155
Kingston, Jamaica 9
Kiowa Indians 121
Klamath County, CA 40, 46
Knights of the Golden Circle 86–87, 90, 188–189
Know-Nothing Party 19, 30, 32
Krumbhaar, William B. 121–122
Kudlik, John D. 100
Kungle, C.H. 51, 53, 68
Kurtz, D.B. 46

La Cruz, Marto 95
La Feria, TX *see* Tio Cano, TX
La Paz, AZ 107
La Pueblo de los Indios, CA 94
La Puerta, CA 94
La Spiers, — 169
LaGrange Patriot 162
Lagunitas Mountains 72
Lake County, CA 58
Lake McClure, CA 16
Lamon, — 19
Lampazoz, Mexico 168
Lancaster, PA 9
Langford, S.P. 166
Laredo, TX 129, 132, 145, 155, 184
Larkspur, CA 80
Las Cruces, NM 95
Las Rucias ranch, TX, Skirmish at 133–134, 156, 159, 179
Laspeyre, Thomas 34, 39, 42, 44–46, 48, 55–56, 58, 60–61, 67, 69, 72, 75, 77, 84
Latham, Milton S. 21–22, 31–32, 66, 180
Latrobe, PA 7, 10, 13, 80, 183, 185–187
Lauderdale, J.D. 102
Laughlin, NV 107
Lawrence, James 96, 106
Lawrence T. Jones III Collection 158

Lazear, Jesse 177
Le Havre, France 10
Lea, Edward 112
Lecompton Democratic Convention 1859 31–32
Lee, Robert E. 110, 155, 163, 166
Lehigh River 5
LeKoester, Henry 120
Leon, TX 169
Lexington, KY 96
Library of Congress 144
Limon, — 60
Lincoln, Abraham 20, 33–34, 40, 46, 63, 66, 105, 177
Lippincott, B.S. 44, 52, 56, 59, 68
The Little Lady of the Lagunitas: A Franco-Californian Romance 87, 188
Little Rock, AR 124
London, England 81
London *Morning Chronicle* 81
London Times 104
Lone Mountain Cemetery 78
Los Angeles, CA 16, 84, 86, 91, 98–100, 102, 105–106, 108
Los Angeles, TX 132
Los Angeles County, CA 15, 31, 40, 45, 96
Los Angeles Mounted Rifles 88
Los Angeles News 88
Los Angeles Star 28, 100, 103, 106
Los Ojuelos, TX 132
Louis de Planque & Co. Photographic Studio 158
Louisville, KY 96
Lovejoy's Hotel 8
Lubbock, Francis R. 111, 113
Lubbock, Henry 111

Machado family 92
Maddon, — 150
Madison, — 161
Madison College 7–8, 98
Magdalena, Sonora, Mexico 160
Magee, John 90, 194
Magoffin, James Wiley 162
Magruder, John Bankhead 110–113, 117–119, 121–122, 124, 126–129, 131, 134, 160, 163, 164, 166, 168, 184
Magruder, Lloyd 37, 44, 47, 50, 52, 54, 59, 61, 64, 67
Malvern Hill, Battle of 110
Marin County, CA 26, 62, 72, 80–81, 96
Marin County Journal 80, 84
Marin Weekly Journal 79
Mariposa, CA 30
Mariposa Battalion 118
Mariposa County, CA 6, 15–19, 30–32, 59–60, 81, 84, 103, 167, 174

Mariposa Democrat 30
Mariposa Gazette 35, 61, 69, 79, 81, 84, 95, 99, 103, 110, 173
Marysville, CA 73
Marysville Daily Herald 22, 27, 29
Mascliff Galley 5
Masons 16
Matamoros, Mexico 128, 139–141, 143–145, 154, 158–159, 177
Mathewson, R.C. 59
Maximilian of Austria 128, 139
Maxwell's Creek, CA 16
Mazatlan, Mexico 109, 130, 162–163, 168, 172–175, 180, 193
Mazatlan Times 173–174
McCaslin, Richard B. 155
McCulloch, Henry E. 123–126, 164, 178
McDathe's Ranch, CA 72
McDougall, John A. 54–59
McDowell, Irwin 2, 161
McGrath, Roger D. 71
McKibben, J.C. 59, 61
McKissick, J.D. 164
McKune, John M. 26–27
McLaughlin, M.A. 105
McNeel's, TX 126
McRae Ranch, CA 74, 76
Mejia, Tomas 140, 143
Memphis *Appeal* 110
Mendocino County, CA 44
Mennonites 5, 7
Merced County, CA 30, 43, 59, 96
Merced River 15–17
Merritt, Samuel A. 30, 32
Mesa Grande, CA 92
Mesilla, NM 95
Methodist Protestant Church 8
Mewan Indians *see* Miwok Indians
Mexico City, Mexico 168, 172, 174
Middle Anacapa Island 13
Middle Boggy River 123
Military Order of the Loyal Legion of the United States (MOLLUS) 94, 98, 101
Military Order of the Stars and Bars (MOSB) 193
Miller, Hugh 97
Miller, N.C. 39, 44–45, 52, 54
Mining & Scientific Press 18
Minor, Hugh C 105–106
Minter, John S. 92
Mintern, J.C. 43
Minter's Ranch, CA 89, 92, 95, 109, 118, 155, 188, 193–194
Minturn, Charles 75
Mississippi River 121
Miwok Indians 17
Mokelumne Hill, CA 30

Monclova, Coahuila, Mexico 170
Mono County, CA 60, 67, 84, 96–97
Monson, A.C. 20
Montague County, TX 126
Montana 7, 185
Monterey County, CA 40, 54, 57
Monterrey, Mexico 168, 172
Montgomery, Zachariah 34, 37, 39–41, 44, 46, 51–53, 63–64, 68–69, 180
Montre, — 84, 90
Moore, James 75
Moore, John 25
Moore, Thomas O. 168
Morelos, Mexico 169
Moreno, Jose Matias 95
Morgan, Edward M. 90–91, 97–98, 101, 106
Morgan, J.H. 46
Morgan, T.A. 106
Morrison, Murray 40–41, 44, 50
Mt. Tamalpais, CA 74, 76
Mowry, Sylvester 101–102
Muir, John 16–17
Munday, Patrick 39–42, 45–46, 61, 67
Murietta, Joaquin 16, 19
Murphy, — 76
Murphy's, CA 84
Murrah, Pendleton 128–129, 168
Murray, B.C. 162
Murray, Charles 97
Murray, Ellen 74, 80
Murray, John 73–74, 80
Murray, Rose 74
Murray, William 74
Murrieta, Juan 194
Murry, — 163
My First Summer in the Sierra 16–17

"Nacion" 155–156
Napa County, CA 61
Napa Creek, CA 61–62
Napa Reporter 62
Napoleon III of France 139
Naria, Mexico 168
National Archives and Records Administration 119
Navajo Indians 157

Naval Units, Confederate:
Alabama 116
Bayou City 111–112
John F. Carr 111
Josiah H. Bell 113–116
Lady Gwin 111
Magruder Fleet, 2nd Squadron 113–114

Neptune 111–112
Uncle Ben 113–114
Naval Units, Union:
 Clifton 112
 Clinton 143
 Harriet Lane 111–112
 Hatteras 116
 Morning Light 114–116
 Owasco 112
 Rachel Seaman 114
 Tennessee 116
 Velocity 114–115
 West Gulf Blockading Squadron 112
 Westfield 112

Navarro, — 120
Neches River 113
Neuces River 130
Nevada 15, 59, 72, 76, 83
Nevada City, CA 15
Nevada County, CA 39, 45, 61, 64
Neville, Fred A. 168
New Mexico 1, 117
New Mexico, Department of 2
New Orleans, LA 134, 136, 143, 144
New Orleans, 1815 Battle of 37
New Orleans Picayune 144
New Orleans *True Delta* 143
New River 102
New York, NY 8–10, 13, 99
New York Herald 145, 159
New York Quarantine Dept. 10
New York Times 58, 78, 81–82, 143
New York Tribune 144
Newell, Samuel T. 55
Noble, Clyde E. 193
Noel, D.D. 166
Noirsan, Serge 191–192
Nolan, Matt 114
Northampton County, PA 5
Noyes, E.J. 147–150
Nueces River 169
Nugent, John 54–55, 57, 60

Oak Grove, CA 89, 93–94, 97, 102
O'Brein, Thomas 39, 44–45, 67
O'Brien, Mike 75
O'Bryan 114
O'Callaghan, Thomas H. 158
Ocampo, Francisco 92, 93
O'Connor, Alice 185
O'Connor, Charles (1st) 185
O'Connor, Charles (2nd) 185–186
O'Connor, Dan 185
O'Connor, Elihu 185
O'Connor, Eliza 185
O'Connor, Eliza Aston 185

O'Connor, Elizabeth *see* Showalter, Elizabeth
O'Connor, John (other) 185
O'Connor, John (son) 185
O'Connor, Mary 185–186
O'Connor, Regina 185
O'Connor, Sam 185
O'Connor, Sam S. 8–9, 177, 185
Oddfellows 16
Odlum, Frederick H. 113–114
Official Records of the Union and Confederate Armies in the War of the Rebellion 2, 87, 93, 99, 107, 146, 176
Official Records of the Union and Confederate Navies in the War of the Rebellion 114
Ojinaga, Mexico *see* Presidio del Norte, Mexico
Oldham, William 169
O'Neill, James D. 24
Ophir, CA 16
Orange Grove Hotel 13
Oregon 81
Oury, Granville Henderson 167–172
Oury, Malvina "Mina" 168–172, 174, 180
Owenville, TX 164
Owings, Lewis S. 162
Ox Hide and Tail Inn 173

Pacific Mail 12
Pala, CA 92
Palmito Ranch, TX 138, 142, 144, 146–153, 155–157, 159, 179, 193
Palo Alto battlefield, TX 153
Panama City, Panama 9, 11–13
Panama Railroad 10, 13
Panteon de Protestantes 175
Parque Gral. Angel Flores 174–175
Parras, Durango, Mexico 109, 168, 170–172, 180
Paso del Gigante, TX 133
Patrick, Annie 3
Patrick, George L. 3, 110
Patrick, George W. 34, 37, 40, 44, 47, 61–62, 64, 67, 110
Patrick, H.C. 30, 32
Patrick, Miss 3
Payne, M.D. 166
Pecos River 120, 129–130
Pennie, James C. 75–76
Pennsylvania Railroad 8
Pensacola, FL 114
Perlot, Jean-Nicolas 16
Perquimans County, NC 96
Perryville, Choctaw Nation, IT 122–123
Perth, Australia 81
Perth Gazette & Independent Journal of Politics 81

Petaluma 72
Peter Palmquist Cased Photographs Collection, Yale University 17
Peyri, Antonio 194
Pfalz area, Germany 5
Phelps, T.G. 54–57
Philadelphia, PA 5, 9
Phillips, Joseph 117
Phillips, Mary O'Connor *see* O'Connor, Mary
Pico, Pio 57
Piedras Negras, Mexico 168–169
Pierce, Frank Cushman 147
Pierce, Leonard, Jr. 146, 150
Piercy, Charles W. 2, 34–35, 37–38, 40–41, 47, 50, 52, 57, 62, 67–69, 71–82, 98, 101, 103, 111, 118, 161, 184
Pile, William A. 154
Pilot Knob, CA 95, 101
Pishon, Nathaniel J. 103
Pittsburgh, PA 8
Placer County, CA 39, 45, 96
Placerville, CA 190
Plan of Tacubaya 139
Planter's Hotel 173
Plumas County, CA 41
Point Isabel, TX 137–138, 148–150, 159
Port Orange, TX 113
Potter settlement, TX 126
Powell, — 90, 103
Powell, Joseph 39, 48, 51, 54, 63
Prairie Lea, TX 131
Presidio, TX 1, 109
Presidio del Norte, Mexico 1, 109
Price, Sterling 125
Pride of the Bay 80
Puente, Jose A. 141
Pujol, Mercedes 194
Pyron, C.L. 162

Quartzburgh, CA 15–16

Ramirena's Ranch, TX 135
Rancho Como se Llama, TX 133
Rancho Cucamonga, CA 195
Rancho Santa Ysabel, CA *see* Santa Ysabel, CA
Randolph, George W. 116
Ranger 148–149, 152
Rather, William S. 118, 126, 162–163
Rebels in the Rockies: Confederate Irregulars in the Western Territories 191
Reche Canyon, CA 85
Red River 121–122, 124, 126, 164
Red River Campaign 130, 136
Reno, NV 30

Renshaw, William B. 112
Republican Party 19, 32, 55–56
Resaca de la Palma, TX 143
Reynolds, Thomas 168
Rhodes, Frank 82
Richmond, TX 163, 166
Richmond Whig and Public Advertiser 144
Riddle's, IT 124
Rigg, Edwin A. 6, 89–98, 103–105
Ringgold Barracks, TX 133
Rio Bravo *see* Rio Grande
Rio Colorado 134
Rio Concho 109
Rio Grande 1–2, 89, 105, 109, 116, 128, 132–147, 150–152, 154–155, 157–159, 162, 168
Rio Grande City, TX 132–133, 139
Rio Hondo 87, 169
Rio Presidio 172
Riordan, Edward H. 153, 157
Ritchie, — 91, 97
Rix, Chastina Walbridge 13
Robee, H.M. 75
Roberts, J.A. 161
Roberts, Samuel A. 123
Roberts, T.L. 90–91, 96, 106
Robinson, William T. 163
Robinson, W.N. 137
Rockingham County, VA 6
Rogers, Levi 91, 96, 106
Rogers, Simon A. 96, 106
Rope and Wire Blog 188–189
Ross, William 36, 39, 46–47, 48, 51, 64
Ryer, George 28, 180

Sabinal Creek, TX 168–169
Sabine Lake 113–114
Sabine Pass, Naval Battle off 110–116, 118
Sabine Pass, TX-LA 3, 112–113, 115–116, 124
Sabine River 113
Sackett's Wells, CA 101
Sacramento, CA 3, 28, 31, 59, 71–72, 81–83, 108
Sacramento County, CA 32, 37–40, 51, 96
Sacramento Daily Bee 66
Sacramento Daily Union 19, 22, 26, 30, 38–39, 55, 58, 61, 67–68, 78, 81, 83–84, 102, 104, 107, 144, 160
Sacramento River 23–24
Sacred Heart Parish 6
St. Gall, Switzerland 5
St. George Hotel 66, 81
St. James Parish 6
St. Vincent Archabbey 7
St. Vincent Parish 7, 183, 185
Salinas River 168

Salt Lake, TX 133
Saltillo, Mexico 168, 170
Sampson, Joseph M. 96, 106
Samuels, John R. 103, 106
San Andreas, CA 18
San Andreas Protestant Cemetery 18
San Andreas Register 18
San Anselmo, CA 73
San Anselmo Creek 74
San Antonio, TX 1, 3, 109–110, 117–118, 120, 126, 128–134, 155–156, 160, 162–163, 167–169
San Bernardino, CA 85–88, 90, 95–97, 99, 102–104
San Bernardino County, CA 33–35, 37
San Bernardino Patriot 94–95, 97
San Bernardino *Southern News* 86
San Bruno, CA 57
San Diego, CA 13 28, 89–90, 95, 108
San Diego County, CA 46, 97
San Elizario, TX 1
San Felipe Valley, CA 93, 102
San Fernando River 132
San Francisco, CA 9, 13–16, 19–20, 27, 33–34, 37, 40, 46, 49, 54, 56–60, 62–63, 72, 75, 78, 80–82, 94, 98–99, 104, 108, 162, 172, 173
San Francisco Bulkhead Bill 40
San Francisco *Bulletin* 82, 100
San Francisco *Call* 66, 74
San Francisco *Evening Bulletin* 99, 110
San Francisco *Herald* 57
San Francisco *Morning Call* 81
San Francisco *Times* 75
San Gabriel Mountains 85
San Gabriel River Valley, CA 85, 87
San Joaquin County, CA 32, 34, 39, 59
San Joaquin River Valley 15, 84
San Jose, CA 24
San Jose Valley, CA *see* San Luis Rey River, CA
San Luis Obispo County, CA 33
San Luis Rey, CA 97
San Luis Rey River, CA 91–93
San Marcos River 130
San Mateo County, CA 57
San Patricio County, TX 130, 158, 163
San Pedro, CA 101–102, 106
San Quentin, Baja Cfa, Mexico 108–109
San Quentin, CA 51
San Quentin Prison 75–76

San Quintuc, Mexico *see* San Quentin, Baja Cfa, Mexico
San Rafael, CA 72–73, 75, 78, 80
Sanders, E.J. 82
Sanders, T.D. 163
Sands, William 96, 106–107
Sandy Hook, NJ 9
Santa Barbara County, CA 22, 33
Santa Clara County, CA 39, 45–46
Santa Cruz County, CA 40, 47
Santa Fe, NM 87–88
Santa Fe County, TX (NM) 117
Santa Fe Trail 130–131
Santa Margarits, TX 158
Santa Rosa, TX 133
Santa Ysabel, CA 89, 91–93
Santiago, Juan 194
Saunders, — 156, 179
Sausalito, CA 72
Savage, Richard 188
Schauwalder family 5
Schell, Frank 72, 75
Scobey, J.W. 50
Scotland 81
Scott, Charles L. 32
Scott, — 84, 90
Scott, J.B. 61
Scott, William Anderson 20
Scott, Winfield 50
secession crisis debates 47–53, 62, 65–67
Seco Creek, TX 169
Seddon, James A. 161
Seeley, Regina 8, 177–178, 183–187
Sepulveda, Jose 94
Se-saw-che, CA 17
Sevier, W.C. 165
Seward, William H. 104, 142
Sharp, — 171
Shasta County, CA 36, 41, 45, 47, 52
Shattuck, David Olcott 108
Shattuck, John S. 109
Shatweck, — *see* Shattuck, David Olcott
Shelby, Joseph O. 168
Sheperd, William W. 20, 27
Sherfy, J.W. 115
Short, Jacob 75
Showalter, Anne *see* Burkholder, Anne
Showalter, Chris 18
Showalter, Christian 5–6, 18–19
Showalter, Daniel 6
Showalter, Ed 183
Showalter, Elihu 184
Showalter, Elihu Thomas 6–7, 183
Showalter, Elizabeth 6, 8, 137, 177–178, 183–186

Showalter, Fannie 6
Showalter, Isaac 17
Showalter, Jacob 5–6, 17
Showalter, John (original immigrant) 5
Showalter, John (unknown relationship) 18
Showalter, John (of Iowa) 184
Showalter, John A., Jr. (brother) 6–7, 10, 177–178, 183–184, 186
Showalter, John Watterson (father) 6–7, 9, 177
Showalter, Joseph 6
Showalter, Katherine "Kate" 3, 177, 183–184, 186–187
Showalter, Mary Ann *see* Donley, Mary Ann
Showalter, Nancy 6
Showalter, Robert L. 9
Showalter, Sarah *see* Kelley, Sarah
Showalter, Susannah *see* Watterson, Susannah
Showalter, Ulrich 5–6
Showalter, William Aloysius 6–7, 79–80, 177–178, 183, 185–186
Showalter Court 195
Showalter Party 87–108
Showalter Road 195
Showalter's Mine, CA 18
Shreveport *Semi-Weekly News* 158
Sibley, Henry Hopkins 87–88, 111, 157
Siegfried, John 5
Sierra County, CA 39, 47, 59
Sierra Madre 109
Sierra National Forest 15
Sierra Nevada Mountains 16–17, 30
Simpson County, KY 96
Sims, Milton W. 164
Sinaloa State, Mexico 175
Siskiyou County, CA 44, 47, 76
Skillman, Henry 1–2
Slaughter, James E. 117, 132–133, 140, 157
Smiley, Thomas L. 21
Smith, — 170
Smith, E. Kirby 111, 118, 125, 131, 160, 163, 166, 168
Smith, E.J. 33
Smith, Horace 55
Smith, Leon 111–112
Smith, Orson K. 19, 34, 37, 40, 49, 59, 62, 64, 68
Smith, Samuel B. 72, 75, 77
Smith, Whitman B. 92
Snead, Thomas 73
Snow, Horace 12, 17–18
Solano County, CA 20
Sonoma County, CA 31, 36, 43, 46, 71, 81, 108

Sonoma County Democrat 130
Sonora, CA 30, 75, 81
Sonora, Mexico 90–91
Sonora Democrat 110
Sonora *Union-Democrat* 30
Sons of Confederate Veterans (SCV) 190, 193
Sons of Union Veterans of the Civil War (SUVCW) 192–193
Sorrell, F. 44, 47, 52, 59, 61, 63, 67, 76
South, Shirley Ann Wellman 89
Southern Emmigrant Trail 90, 125
Spaight, Ashley W. 113
Spencer, John 1
Sportsman's Hall 7, 183
SS *Illinois* 9–10
SS *Winfield Scott* 13
Standifer, Jeff 162
Stanford, Leland 82–83
Stanislaus County, CA 42, 44, 76
Stanislaus National Forest 15
Stanton, Edwin M. 104
Stearns, Abel 45
Steele, — 135
Steele, Frederick 136
Steele, William 121–126
Stevenson, Andrew M. 20
Stockton, CA 15–16, 30, 92, 96, 162
Stuart, "Jeb" 8, 184
Sumner, Charles 63, 91–92, 96, 106, 109
Sumner, E.V. 86, 89
Sutherland, Daniel E. 167
Sutter County, CA 33–34, 37
Swoup, — 161
Sydney, Australia 81
Sydney Morning Herald 12, 81
Sydney *The Empire* 81

Talbott, Laurence Fletcher 176
Taliaferro, Alfred 76, 78
Tamaulipas State, Mexico 135, 139–140
Tampacuas, TX 133
Tasmania 81
Tatman, John H. 30–31
Taylor, — 43
Taylor, Edward G. 92
Taylor, G.B. 78–79
Taylor, Richard 142, 147
Taylor, Richard (general) 166
Tehachapi Mountains 85
Tehama County, CA 41
Tejon Pass, CA 84
Temecula, CA 89–92, 95, 97, 102, 104–105, 193–195
Temescal Valley, CA 35, 90, 103
Temple, — 134

Terry, Cornelia Runnels 2, 130
Terry, David S. 28, 75, 84, 99, 130, 161, 167, 169–172
tetnas 173–174
Tharp, John Allen, Jr. 166
They Passed This Way: Biographical Sketches, Tales of Historic Temecula Valley at the Crossroads of California's Southern Immigrant Trail 193
They Passed This Way Monument 193–194
Thomas, E.P. 119
Thompson, Jerry D. 147
Tibbett, Jonathan 86, 97
Tilden, W.P. 41–42, 45, 54, 58–59
Tilton, S.S. 40, 44
Tio Cano, TX 133
Towson, AR 124
Tozer, Charles W. 76
The Trail Through Mohawk 188
Trinity County, CA 43
Trinity River 111
Tucson, AZ 160, 162
Tulare County, CA 15, 19, 32, 34, 37, 59, 76
Tuolumne County, CA 3, 34, 37, 45, 61, 75, 110
Tuolumne River 23
Turkey Creek, TX 169
Turner, Edmund P. 122, 126, 160, 165
Turner, Thomas E. 89–90
Turner, William 96, 106
Tuttle, E.B. 107
Tuttle, Edward 102
Tyler, U.U. 95

Union Hotel 104
Union Resolutions *see* secession crisis debates
Union Tunnel Company 18
Uniontown, PA 7–8
United Daughters of the Confederacy Magazine 87
Unity Township, PA 7
Ures, Sonora, Mexico 109
Utah Territory 15, 30
Uvalde, TX 168–169

Van Dyke, J.M. 103
Veron, A. 141, 150
Vestal, DeWitt, C. 92, 94
Vicksburg, MS 121
Viesca, Andres S. 168
Virginia City, NV 83, 162
Visalia, CA 84–85, 107
Visalia Delta 84
Visalia Post 84

Waco, TX 164, 168
Wainwright, Jonathan M. 112

Waldron, AR 123–125
Waldron, D.V. 42, 44
Walker, French 54
Walker, John G. 158, 162
Waller, Edwin 164
Walters, E. 43
Ward, J.W. 30–31
Ward, R.H. 96, 106
Warner, Jonathan T. 89
Warner's Ranch, CA 88–89, 91, 95, 102
Warren County, TN 96
Washington, CA 81
Washington County, AR 96
Washington *Daily National Intelligencer* 144
Washington Flat, CA 17
Washington Monument 58
Washoe, NV 40
Watie, Stand 166
Watkins, H.P. 72, 76–77
Watkins, Joseph S. 25
Watkins, Oscar M. 113–116
Watson, John H. 40
Watson, T.K. 78
Watterson, Susannah 5–6
Waxahachie, TX 127, 129
Waynesburg, PA 8
Weir, A.R. 111–112

Weller, John B. 21, 30–31, 54–55, 57
Wellman, Chauncey R. 89, 92–95, 97–98, 101–102
Wentworth, C.L. 107
West, James R. 1
West, Joseph R. 98, 100, 109
West Alexandria, PA 6
Westlake, F.W. 172
Westmoreland County, PA 7, 80
Westways 87
Whig Party 19
Whipple, Stephan 20
White, John 36, 41, 45, 47, 52, 68
Whiteley Township, PA 6
White's Ranch TX 136, 138, 143, 147, 159
Whitesides, N.E. 54
Whitman, George W. 23
Wild, — 97
Wilkins, James H. 74–75
Wilkinson, Stephen W. 166
Wilks, — 94
Willey, O.F. 63
Williamson, C.V. 76
Williamson, D.J. 48, 76
Wilmington, CA 101, 194

Wilson, — 88
Wilson, Theodore A. 91, 95–96, 106–107, 109, 118, 126, 156, 163
Wimmer, Boniface 7
Wood, — 71–72
Wood, Aaron 41–43, 46, 48, 57, 63, 68
Wood, W.C. 36, 42, 45, 57
Woods, Oliver 106
Woods, T.W. 96
Woods, William 96, 106
The Works of Hubert Howe Bancroft 146
Wright, George 89, 94, 103–105
Wright, Thomas 47

Yeagers Ferry, Colorado River 97
Yolo County, CA 36, 45, 57, 81
Yorktown, Civil War Siege of 110
Yosemite National Park 15
Young's Ranch, TX 133
Yuba County, CA 37, 46–47, 51, 63, 73, 75–76
Yuma, AZ 88
Yuma Indians 101

www.ingramcontent.com/pod-product-compliance
Ingram Content Group UK Ltd.
Pitfield, Milton Keynes, MK11 3LW, UK
UKHW050533150426
5217IPUK00026B/1922